Gulf Military Forces in an Era of Asymmetric Wars

Gulf Military Forces in an Era of Asymmetric Wars

Volume 2

Anthony H. Cordesman
Khalid R. Al-Rodhan

Published in cooperation with the Center for Strategic and International Studies,
Washington, D.C.

Praeger Security International
Westport, Connecticut · London

Library of Congress Cataloging-in-Publication Data

Cordesman, Anthony H.
    Gulf military forces in an era of asymmetric wars / Anthony H. Cordesman and Khalid R. Al-Rodhan.
        p. cm.
    Includes bibliographical references.
    ISBN 0–275–99250–0 (set : alk. paper) — ISBN 0–275–99399–X (vol 1 : alk. paper) — ISBN 0–275–99400–7 (vol 2 : alk. paper)
    1. Middle East—Armed Forces. 2. Asymmetric warfare—Middle East. 3. National security—Persian Gulf States. 4. Persian Gulf States—Military relations. 5. Armed Forces. 6. Balance of power. 7. Military readiness. I. Al-Rodhan, Khalid R. II. Center for Strategic and International Studies (Washington, D.C.) III. Title.
UA832.C67028   2007
355'.0330536—dc22   2006031049

British Library Cataloguing in Publication Data is available.

Library of Congress Catalog Card Number: 2006031049
ISBN: 0–275–99250–0 (set)
          0–275–99399–X (vol. 1)
          0–275–99400–7 (vol. 2)

First published in 2007

Praeger Security International, 88 Post Road West, Westport, CT 06881
An imprint of Greenwood Publishing Group, Inc.
www.praeger.com

Printed in the United States of America

The paper used in this book complies with the Permanent Paper Standard issued by the National Information Standards Organization (Z39.48–1984).

10 9 8 7 6 5 4 3 2 1

Contents

Figures

Acknowledgments

We are grateful to so many people who have contributed in so many ways to this book. We want to thank many regional, U.S., and European officials, who cannot be mentioned by name, for offering their time, comments, suggestions, and data to earlier versions of this book. We are also grateful to so many research assistants who have contributed to the drafting and research of this book, including William D. Sullivan, Paul S. Frederiksen, Nikos Tsafos, and William Elliott.

The analysis in this book relied heavily on the work of many governmental and nongovernmental agencies, particularly the International Institute for Strategic Studies, Jane's, the Federation of American Scientists (FAS), GlobalSecurity.org, the Energy Information Administration (EIA), the U.S. Department of State, the U.S. Department of Defense, and many other defense and energy agencies. In addition, the analysis relied heavily on the work of many regional, military, and security experts. The analysis of the Saudi internal security forces drew heavily on the work by Dr. Cordesman and Nawaf Obaid's work on the Saudi National Security in late 2005.

Iran

Iran plays a critical strategic role in the Gulf. It is the region's most populous country with 68.7 million people. It is the one Gulf country that is not Arab, and it has a unique Persian character. It has its own Shi'ite Islamist fundamentalism at a time when Sunni neo-Salafi fundamentalism is seeking control of the Gulf and the Arab world. Its opposition to Israel and its ties to Iraq, Syria, and Lebanon give it broad importance both inside and outside the Gulf.

Its strategic geography not only dominates the northern Gulf but also the shipping lines both inside and outside the Strait of Hormuz. As Map 8.1 shows, Iran's territory extends from the Caspian Sea to the Gulf. It is the second largest country in the Gulf, and one of the largest in the Middle East, with an estimated area of 1.648 million square kilometers. It has land borders with Afghanistan (936 kilometers), Armenia (35 kilometers), Azerbaijan-proper (432 kilometers), Azerbaijan-Naxcivan enclave (179 kilometers), Iraq (1,458 kilometers), Pakistan (909 kilometers), Turkey (499 kilometers), and Turkmenistan (992 kilometers).[1]

Iran's importance as a strategic player in the Gulf is compounded by the importance of its energy resources. Iran is estimated to hold 11.1 percent of the world oil reserves (132.0 billion barrels of oil) and 15.3 percent of the world's natural gas reserves (970.8 trillion cubic feet).[2] In addition, it is strategically located near the Strait of Hormuz where most of the Gulf oil passes through every day. Iran's conventional and asymmetric military capabilities near the Strait of Hormuz make Iran all the more important to global energy security.

IRAN'S CHANGING ROLE IN REGIONAL SECURITY

Iran has always been a key player in regional security and has long been a destabilizing one. The Revolution that deposed the Shah in 1979 brought radical clerical leaders like Ayatollah Khomeini to power. It was followed by the seizure of American

Source: CIA, "Iran," 2002, available at http://www.lib.utexas.edu/maps/middle_east_and_asia/iran_pol01.jpg

Map 8.1 Iran

diplomats as hostages, and Iranian efforts to export its "Islamic Revolution" to other Gulf States like Bahrain and to the Islamic world. Since that time, the United States and several European nations have consistently accused Iran of supporting terrorism. This usually took the shape of supporting proxy groups such as Hezbollah, Hamas, and Islamic Jihad. In addition, neighboring states such as Saudi Arabia and Bahrain have accused Iran of supporting local Shi'ite groups that carried out attacks against Saudi and Bahraini targets, including the 1996 Al-Khobar bombing and several attacks during the 1970s.

Several issues have given Iran added strategic visibility. Iran is the region's leading Shi'ite state at a time of growing sectarian tension. While Iran's relations with its neighboring states improved during President Mohammad Khatami's presidency in the 1990s, they are increasingly uncertain. Iran continues to have at least one major active territorial dispute with its neighbors.

The most serious is control of the three islands: the Greater Tunbs, the Lesser Tunbs, and Abu Musa. Since the withdrawal of Britain from the Gulf in the 1970s, the United Arab Emirates and Iran have argued over the ownership of the islands, and the Gulf Cooperation Council (GCC) has supported the UAE position. The GCC countries have avoided confrontation, but Iran again refused the UAE offer of arbitration by the International Court of Justice in September 2006, and the risk of a future clash or conflict remains. In addition, Iran and Qatar have claimed ownership of the North field (where most of Qatar's gas reserves are), and the issue has never been fully resolved.

Iran has said it has abandoned its goal of spreading its Shi'ite power to the southern Gulf States, but this is now being quietly questioned by many strategic and defense planners in the Gulf. The election of Mahmud Ahmadinejad as Iran's President on August 3, 2005, made a radical populist Iran's leading civil leader. His loyalty to hard-line views, his rhetoric about the return of the hidden Imam, as well as Iran's aggressive meddling in Iraq's internal affairs and aid to Shi'ite militias in gaining more power have raised growing concerns among Iran's Sunni neighbors. Leaders in Saudi Arabia, Egypt, and Jordan have accused Iran of wanting to create a "Shi'ite crescent" that includes Iran, Iraq, Lebanon, and Syria.

Iran's power and influence have also been increased by several external developments. Two of Iran's main enemies, the Taliban regime and Saddam Hussein, have been toppled by the United States since the terrorist attacks on the United States on September 11, 2001. Iran no longer faces a threat from either neighbor and may acquire an ally in Iraq, where a Shi'ite majority has come to power. Hezbollah's success in fighting Israel in the summer of 2006 has been credited in part to Iranian investment, advisory efforts, and arms transfers. This has enhanced the credibility of Iran's ability to use nonstate actors and asymmetric warfare. The same has been true of Iran's support of Shi'ite militias in Iraq, and support of Palestinian rejectionist movements like Hamas and the Palestinian Islamic Jihad.

At the same time the same invasions that toppled these two regimes have led to a major U.S. military presence in both states and a much larger U.S. air and naval presence in the Gulf. This has increased U.S. and Iranian tension and Iran's pressure on its neighbors. Iran has long used the U.S. presence in the region as a reason to condemn countries such as Kuwait and Saudi Arabia for their close alliance with the United States. In 2006, there were more than 130,000 U.S. troops in the countries on two of Iran's borders. In addition, the U.S. traditional presence in the Gulf, especially in Bahrain, Kuwait, and Qatar, has not changed.

The most destabilizing issue affecting Iran's role in regional security is proliferation. Iran's nuclear program has been under growing scrutiny by the International Atomic Energy Agency (IAEA), the EU-3 (France, Germany, and the United Kingdom), the United States, and most of Iran's neighboring states. So has the fact that it is developing a family of long-range missiles like the Shahab-3. There is increasing concern that Iran is seeking long-range nuclear strike capabilities that would be a destabilizing force in the region. The election of Mahmoud Ahmadinejad to the presidency of Iran compounded these concerns on August 3, 2005. His statements about the Holocaust and his rhetoric about the end of times have made Iran's nuclear program an existential threat to Israel and most of Iran's "one city" states.

The other side of the story is that Iran has been more conservative in modernizing its conventional military forces. Iran has never rebuilt the level of conventional forces it had before its defeat in its war with Iraq in 1988. Iran's conventional military readiness, effectiveness, and capabilities have declined since the end of the Iran-Iraq War, and Iran has not been able to find a meaningful way to restore its conventional edge in the region. As is discussed in detail, Iran was able to order only $2.3 billion worth of new arms agreements during 1997–2004. Saudi Arabia ordered $10.5 billion, Kuwait $3.1 billion, and the United Arab Emirates ordered $12.0 billion. Even a small nation like Oman spent $2.5 billion. This inability to modernize its conventional forces is seen by many experts as one of the reasons for Iran's "nuclear ambitions" and its focus on building its asymmetric capabilities.

MILITARY SPENDING AND ARMS IMPORTS

Iran has faced major problems in modernizing and financing its military forces ever since the Revolution in 1979. The United States and other Western powers ceased to sell Iran both weapons and parts and munitions for its existing weapons shortly after the Revolution. Iran built up major supplies of Chinese, Russian, and other Eastern bloc weapons during the Iran-Iraq War, but its defeat in that war in 1988 resulted in the loss of some 40 to 50 percent of its land order of battle.

It has faced serious financial problems in funding its force modernization, compounded by the systematic mismanagement of its economy. These problems have been eased in recent years by major increases in its oil revenues. Iran's oil export revenues rose from $11.2 billion in 1998, in constant 2005 U.S. dollars, to an estimated $49.2 billion in 2006.[3] Even so, the Central Intelligence Agency (CIA) estimates Iran's government revenues in 2005 were only $48.82 billion vs. expenditures of $60.4 billion.[4]

Iran has, however, used its rising oil revenues to finance higher military spending. According to the International Institute for Strategic Studies (IISS), Iran's military budget has been steadily increasing over the past few years, rising from $2.3 billion in 2000, to $3.36 billion in 2003, and to $6.2 billion in 2006, which represents a 170-percent increase in Iran's military budget since 2000.[5]

This has not, however, yet led to a major increase in Iran's arms imports. Figure 8.1 shows the trend in new Iranian arms deliveries by supplier from 1993 to 2004. There has been a steady contraction in new arms deliveries from $2.6 billion during 1993–1996, to $1.9 billion during 1997–2000, and to $0.5 billion during 2001–2004.

Russia and China, Iran's two major suppliers, have experienced sharp declines in their exports to Iran. For example, Russia's arms exports to Iran declined from $1.3 billion during 1993–1996 to $0.1 billion during 2001–2004, while China's

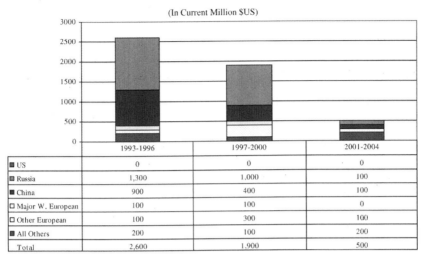

	1993-1996	1997-2000	2001-2004
US	0	0	0
Russia	1,300	1,000	100
China	900	400	100
Major W. European	100	100	0
Other European	100	300	100
All Others	200	100	200
Total	2,600	1,900	500

Source: Richard F. Grimmett, *Conventional Arms Transfers To Developing Nations, 1997-2004*, CRS, August 29, 2005; and Richard F. Grimmett, *Conventional Arms Transfers To Developing Nations, 1993-2000*, CRS, August 16, 2001.

Figure 8.1 Iran's Arms Deliveries by Supplier, 1993–2004

arms deliveries to Iran declined from $0.9 billion during 1993–1996 to $0.1 billion during 2001–2004.

Iran's new arms agreements have had a more mixed trend. As shown in Figure 8.2, the combined value of new agreements over arms purchases increased from $1.2 billion between 1993 and 1996, to $1.5 billion between 1997 and 2000, and then

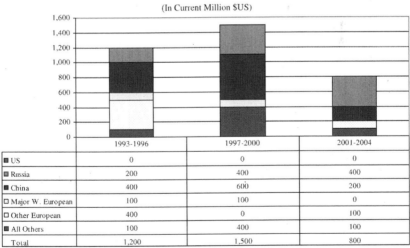

	1993-1996	1997-2000	2001-2004
US	0	0	0
Russia	200	400	400
China	400	600	200
Major W. European	100	100	0
Other European	400	0	100
All Others	100	400	100
Total	1,200	1,500	800

Source: Richard F. Grimmett, *Conventional Arms Transfers To Developing Nations, 1997-2004*, CRS, August 29, 2005; and Richard F. Grimmett, *Conventional Arms Transfers To Developing Nations, 1993-2000*, CRS, August 16, 2001.

Figure 8.2 Iran's New Arms Agreements by Supplier, 1993–2004

decreased to $0.8 billion between 2001 and 2004. Russia's share in the total value of arms imports rose from $0.2 billion between 1993 and 1996 to $0.4 billion between 1997 and 2000, and then remained the same at $0.4 billion between 1997 and 2004.

China's new arms agreements with Iran increased from $0.4 billion during 1993–1996 to $0.60 billion during 1997–2000, and then dropped to $0.20 billion during 2001–2004. Western European countries had no new arms agreements during 2001–2004, and the amount coming from "All Others" decreased from $400 million during 1997–2000 to $100 million during 2001–2004.

As is discussed later, these expenditures have led to some carefully focused purchases that have increased Iran's military capabilities in several important areas. They have not, however, been large enough to offset the steady aging of most of Iran's military inventory, its inability to obtain parts and upgrades for much of its Western-supplied equipment, and anything close to parity with the level of weapons and technology in U.S., British, and many other Gulf forces. Iran has tried to compensate by creating its own military industries, but such efforts have as yet had only limited impact.

MILITARY MANPOWER

Iran maintained active armed forces with some 545,000 men in 2006, although some 220,000 of this total are 18-month conscripts who receive limited training and have marginal military effectiveness. It also has an army reserve of some 350,000 men, although these reserves receive negligible training and Iran lacks the equipment, supplies, and leadership cadres to make effective use of such reserves without months of reorganization and training.

Iran's military manpower problems are shaped by a number of factors. Iran divided its armed forces into regular and revolutionary components following the Revolution in 1979, creating a split between the regular forces that existed under the Shah and the Revolutionary Guards installed during the rule of the Ayatollah Khomeini. This split has been reinforced by a highly compartmented or "stovepiped" military forces force, which have only made limited progress in joint warfare.

Military training is often subject to political problems, and many large-scale exercises do more to "posture" to Iran's neighbors than create effective forces. The combat-trained military personnel Iran developed during the Iran-Iraq War have virtually all left service. Iran is now a largely conscript force with limited military training and little combat experience. The deep divisions between "moderates" and "hard-liners" in Iran's government have inevitably politicized the armed forces, which remain under the command of the supreme religious leader, the Ayatollah Khomeini.

THE IRANIAN ARMY

The Iranian Army is large compared to other countries in the Gulf region. It has some 350,000 men (220,000 conscripts), organized into four corps, with four armored divisions, six infantry divisions, six artillery groups, two commando divisions, an airborne division, aviation groups, and other smaller independent formations. These latter units include independent armored, infantry, and commando brigades. See Figure 8.3.

In practice, each Iranian division has a somewhat different organization. For example, only one Iranian division (the 92nd) is well enough equipped to be considered a true armored division and two of the armored divisions are notably larger than the others. Two of the infantry divisions (28th and 84th) are more heavily mechanized than the others.[6] The lighter and smaller formations in the regular army include the 23rd Special Forces Division, which was formed in 1993–1994, and the 55th paratroop division. According to one source, the 23rd Special Forces Division has 5,000 full-time regulars and is one of the most professional units in the Iranian Army.

The airborne division and the Special Forces are trained at a facility in Shiraz.[7] The regular army also has a number of independent brigades and groups. These include some small armored units, one infantry brigade, one airborne and two to three Special Forces brigades, coastal defense units, a growing number of air defense groups, five artillery brigades/regiments, four to six army aviation units, and a growing number of logistic and supply formations. The land forces have six major garrisons and 13 major casernes. There is a military academy at Tehran, and a signal-training center in Shiraz.[8]

Iranian Tank Strength

Iran has steadily rebuilt its armored strength since the Iran-Iraq War, although its forces are still significantly smaller than under the Shah. It had some 1,613 main battle tanks in 2006, and the number has risen steadily in recent years. Iran had a total of 1,145 in 2000, 1,565 in 2003, and 1,613 in 2006. The IISS estimates that Iran's inventory of main battle tanks now includes some 168 M-47/M-48s and 150 M-60A1s, 100 Chieftain Mark 3/5s, 540 T-54/T-55s/Type-59s, 75 T-62s, 480 T-72/T-72Ss, and 100 Zulfiqars. Its T-72 strength has increased from its level in the 1990s to it current strength of 480. (Other estimates indicate that Iran may have as many as 300 Type 59s and/or 150–250 Type-69IIs.)

Only 480–580 of Iran's main battle tanks can be described as "modern" by common standards. Iran has some 865 other armored fighting vehicles, 550–640 armored personnel carriers (APCs), 2,010 towed artillery weapons, 310 self-propelled artillery weapons, more than 870 multiple rocket launchers, some 1,700 air defense guns and large numbers of light antiaircraft (AA) missiles, large numbers of antitank weapons and guided missiles, and some 50 attack helicopters. This is a large inventory of major weapons, although many are worn and obsolete.

Only part of Iran's tank inventory is operational. It is uncertain how many of Iran's Chieftains and M-47/M-48s are operational, since the total number of Chieftains includes the remainder of 187 improved FV4030/1 versions of the Mark 5 Chieftain that were delivered to the country before the fall of the Shah. Smaller problems seem

Figure 8.3 Iranian Army's Force Structure Trends, 1990–2006

	1990	2000	2005	2006
Manpower	305,000	350,000	350,000	350,000
Active	305,000	350,000	350,000	350,000
Conscripts	250,000	220,000	220,000	220,000
Combat Units	**52**	**26–28**	**26–28**	**28–29**
Army Headquarters	3	4	4	4
Armored Division	0	4	4	4
Mechanized Division	4	0	0	0
Infantry Division	6	6	6	6
Airborne Division	1	1	1	1
Special Operations Division	1	1	1	1
Commando Division	0	1	2	2
Armored Brigade	Some	0	0	0
Mechanized Brigade	Some	1	1	0
Artillery Battalion	0	4–5	4–5	4–5
Artillery Battalion	0	4–5	4–5	6
Mechanized Battalion	28	0	0	0
Main Battle Tanks	500	1,345	1,613	1,613+*
T-54	Some	400	540	540
T-59	Some	0	0	0
T-62	Some	75	75	75+
T-72	Some	480	480	480
Chieftain Mk 3/5	Some	140	100	100
M-47/-48	Some	150	168	168
M-60A1	Some	100	150	150
Zulfiqar	0	0	100	100
Light Tanks	30	80	80+	80+
Scorpion	30	80	80	80
Towsan	0	0	Some	Some
Reconnaissance	130	35	35	35
EE-9 Cascavel	130	35	35	35
Armored Infantry Fighting Vehicles	100+	440	610	610
BMP-1	100+	300	210	210

BMP-2	0	140	400	400
Armored Personnel Carriers	500	550	640	640
BTR-50/-60	Some	300	300	300
M-113	Some	250	200	200
Boragh	0	0	140	140
TOWED	Some	2,170	2,010	2,010
105 mm: M-101A1	339+	130	130	130
105 mm: Oto Melara	36	0	0	0
122 mm: D-30	0	600	540	540
122 mm: PRC type-54	0	100	100	100
130 mm: M-46/Type-59	125	1,100	985	985
152 mm: D-20	0	30	30	30
155 mm: WAC-21	0	20	15	15
155 mm: M-71	50	0	0	0
155 mm: M-114	0	70	70	70
155 mm: FH-77B	18	0	0	0
155 mm: GHN-45	130	100	120	120
203 mm: M-115	30	20	20	20
Self-Propelled	140	290	310+	310+
122 mm: 2S1	0	60	60	60
122 mm: Thunder 1	0	0	Some	Some
155 mm: M-109	100	60	180	180
155 mm: Thunder 2	0	0	Some	Some
170 mm: M-1978	0	10	10	10
175 mm: M-107	30	30	30	30
203 mm: M-110	10	30	30	30
Multiple Rocket Launchers	Some	764+	876+	876+
107 mm: PRC Type-63	Some	600	700	700
107 mm: Haseb	0	0	Some	Some
107 mm: Fadjr 1	0	0	Some	SOME
122 mm: Hadid/Arash/Noor	0	50	50	50
122 mm: BM-21	65	100	100	100
122 mm: BM-11	Some	5	7	7
240 mm: M-1985	0	9	9	9
240 mm: Fadjr 3	0	0	10	10

333 mm: Fadjr 5	0	0	Some	Some
Mortars	3,000+	6,500	5,000	5,000
60 mm:	0	Some	Some	Some
81 mm:	Some	Some	Some	Some
82 mm:	0	Some	Some	Some
107 mm: 4.2in M-30	Some	Some	Some	Some
120 mm: M-65	3,000	Some	Some	Some
Surface-to-Surface Missiles	Some	Some	Some	42+
Scud-B/-C Launchers, est. 300 MSLS	Some	10	12–18	12–18
Shahab-3	Some	Some	Some	Some
CSS-8	0	25	30	30
Oghab	Some	Some	Some	Some
Shaheen 1/-2	Some	Some	Some	Some
Nazeat	Some	Some	Some	Some
Surface-to-Air Missiles	Some	Some	Some	Some
SA-7	Some	Some	Some	0
SA-14	Some	Some	Some	0
SA-16	Some	Some	Some	0
HQ-7	Some	Some	Some	Some
Antitank Guided Weapons	Some	Some	75	75
ENTAC	Some	0	0	0
SS-11/-12	Some	0	0	0
Dragon	Some	0	0	0
AT-3 Sagger	0	0	Some	Some
AT-4 Spigot	0	Some	Some	Some
AT-5 Spandrel	0	0	Some	Some
Saeqhe	0	0	Some	Some
Toophan	0	0	Some	Some
Rocket Launchers	0	Some	Some	Some
73 mm: RPG-7	0	Some	Some	Some
Recoilless Launchers	Some	Some	Some	Some
57 mm	Some	0	0	0
75 mm: M-20	Some	Some	Some	Some
82 mm: B-10	0	Some	Some	Some

106 mm: M-40	Some	Some	200	200
107 mm: B-11	0	Some	Some	Some
Air Defense Guns	1,500	1,700	1,700	1,700
14.5 mm: ZPU-2/-4	Some	Some	Some	Some
23 mm: ZU-23 Towed	Some	Some	Some	Some
23 mm: ZSU-23-4 SP	Some	Some	Some	Some
35 mm	Some	Some	Some	Some
37 mm: M-1939	Some	Some	Some	Some
37 mm: PRC Type-55	Some	Some	Some	Some
57 mm: ZSU-57-2-Sp	Some	Some	Some	Some
57 mm: S-60	Some	Some	Some	Some
Surface-to-Air Missiles	230	Some	Some	Some
I-Hawk	30	0	0	0
RBS-70	200	Some	Some	Some
SA-7/-14/-16	Some	Some	Some	Some
HQ-7	0	Some	Some	Some
Unmanned Aerial Vehicle (UAV)	0	Some	Some	Some
Mohajer II/III/IV	0	Some	Some	Some
Aircraft	49+	77	36	17
Cessna 185	40+	50	10	10
F-27	2	19	2	2
Falcon 20	2	8	20	1
Turbo Commander 690	5	0	4	4
Helicopters	410	556	223	223
AH-1J Attack	100	100	50	50
CH-47C Heavy Transport	10	40	20	20
Bell 214A/C	250	165	50	50
Bell 204	0	30	0	0
AB-205A	35	40	68	68
AB-206	15	90	10	10
AB-12	0	12	0	0
Mi-8/-17	0	0	25	25
Hughes 300C	0	5	0	0
RH-53D	0	9	0	0

SH-53D	0	10	0	0
SA-319	0	10	0	0
UH-1H	0	45	0	0

* "+" indicates the numbers listed may be slightly less than the actual units or weapons in stock.
Source: IISS, *Military Balance,* various editions, including 1989–1990, 1999–2000, 2004–2005, and
  2005–2006.

to exist throughout the rest of the force, and some experts estimate that Iran's sustainable *operational* tank strength may be fewer than 1,000 tanks. Furthermore, Iran's Chieftains and M-60s are at least 16–20 years old, and the T-72 and Zulfiqar are Iran's only tanks with advanced fire-control systems, sights, and armor-piercing ammunition.

Iran's T-72Ss are export versions of the Soviet T-72B. Some have been built under license in Iran and are armed with a 125-mm 2A46M smoothbore gun. They have a relatively modern IA40-1 fire-control system and computer, a laser range finder, and a night and day image intensifying sighting system. The T-72S is powered by an 840-horsepower V-84MS diesel engine, has upgraded suspension and mine protection capabilities, and a combat weight of 44.5 tons. Russian sources indicate that Iran has ordered 1,000 T-72s from Russia.

As mentioned earlier, Iran has developed a main battle tank called the Zulfiqar, with a 125-mm smoothbore gun and welded steel turret of Iranian design. According to one report, the Zulfiqar is powered by a V-46-6-12 V-12 diesel engine with 780 horsepower and uses a SPAT 1200 automatic transmission. This engine is used in the Soviet T-72, but the tank transmission design seems to be closer to that of the U.S. M-60. The Zulfiqar seems to have a relatively modern fire-control system, and Iran may have improved its T-72s with a similar upgrade. The Zulfiqar's combat weight is reported to be 36 tons, and its maximum speed supposedly reaches 65 kilometers per hour at a power-to-weight ratio of 21.7 horsepower per ton. The tank is equipped has a 7.62-mm coaxial and a 12.7-mm roof-mounted machine gun. It uses the modern Slovenia Fontana EFCS-3 computerized fire-control system to provide a fully stabilized fire on the move capability. It may have a roof-mounted laser-warning device, and it could use the same reactive armor system discussed earlier. Roughly 100 Zulifqars are thought to be in service.

Iran has extended the service life of some of its T-54s, T-55s, and T-59s by improving their armor and fire-control systems, and by arming them with an Iranian-made M-68 rifled 105-mm gun similar to the one used in the M-60A1. Reportedly, the Armament Industries Division of the Iranian Defense Industries Organization produces this gun. The Revolutionary Guard is reported to have a special variant of the T-54 called the Safir-74. Iran has developed explosive reactive armor add-ons for its tanks, although the effectiveness of such armor remains unclear.

Some of Iran's 168 M-47/M-48s include an upgraded version of the M-47M. The American firm of Bowen-McLaughlin York, which also built a vehicle manufacturing plant in Iran, upgraded these tanks between 1970 and 1972. The M-47s have many of the components of the M-60A1, including the diesel engine, automatic transmission, suspension, gun control system, and fire components. The upgrade resulted in an extended operating range of the M-47 from 130 to 600 kilometers, as compared to 130 kilometers before, and increased storage space to hold 79 rounds by eliminating the bow mounted machine gun thereby reducing the crew to four. An estimated 150 conversions have been delivered to Iran.

In spite of its tank imports and production since the Iran-Iraq War, Iran's total operational main battle tank holdings are sufficient only to fully equip five to seven of its divisions by Western standards. Iran can sustain only about half the number of its main battle tanks for any period of extended maneuver warfare. At present, however, Iran's tanks are dispersed in relatively small lots among all of its regular army and some of its Islamic Revolutionary Guard Corps (IRGC) combat units—all of the IRGC units generally have only small tank force cadres, and it is unclear to what extent these forces will be armored in the future. The 92nd Armored Division is the only Iranian division that has enough tanks to realistically be considered an armored division, even by regional comparisons.

Other Iranian Armor

Iran seems to have possessed about 1,000–1,360 armored infantry fighting vehicles (AIFVs) and armored personnel carriers (APCs) in its operational inventory in 2006, although counts are contradictory, and it is difficult to estimate what parts of Iran's holdings are fully operational and/or sustainable for any length of time in combat. The IISS, for example, estimates an inventory of 690 light tanks and armored infantry fighting vehicles and 640 APCs. Virtually all estimates indicate, however, that Iran has only about half of the equipment it would need to fully mechanize its forces at its disposal.[9]

Iran appears to have retained 70–80 British-supplied Scorpions out of the 250 it received before the fall of the Shah. These light tanks are tracked weapon systems equipped with 76-mm guns. However, the Scorpion is more than 20 years old, and as few as 30 may be fully operational. Iran has developed a new light tank called the Towsan ("Wild Horse" or "Fury") with a 90-mm gun, some of which may already be in service.

As far as other armored fighting vehicles are concerned, Iran had some 210 BMP-1s and 400 BMP-2 equivalents in service. The BMPs are Soviet-designed systems, but have serious ergonomic and weapons-suite problems. They are hard to fight from, hard to exit, and too slow to keep pace with modern tanks. They also lack thermal vision systems and modern long-range fire-control systems, and their main weapons are difficult to operate in combat even from static positions. Further, Iran has at least 35 EE-9 Cascavel armored reconnaissance vehicles, and one estimate indicates an inventory of 100. The Cascavel is an acceptable design for Third World combat, although it lacks modern sensors and weapons.

Iran's Army had some 200 M-113s and other Western APCs, and a mix of BTR-40s, BTR-50s, and BTR-60s, numbering 300 in total. Iran is producing an armored fighting vehicle called the Boragh (Boraq) and a lighter APC called the Cobra or BMT-2, of which some 140 are in service. The Boragh seems to be a copy of a Chinese version of the BMP-1. It is fully tracked and amphibious and has a combat weight of 13 tons. It can carry 8–12 people, plus 2 crew members. Reports differ as to its armament—perhaps reflecting different variants. Initial reports indicate that it has a turret armed with a 73-mm smoothbore gun and antitank guided missile (ATGM) launcher. It may, however, lack the commander's position that exists in the BMP-1, and it may be armed with a 12.7-mm machine gun. Iran has developed an armor package designed to fit over the hull of the Boragh to provide protection against 30-mm armor-piercing ammunition.[10] Variants with 120-mm mortars, one-man turrets with Iranian-made Toophan ATGMs, and AT-4 ATGMs and others with 73-mm BMP-2 turret guns also seem to be deployed.

The Cobra or BMT-2 is a low-profile, wheeled troop carrier, which can hold seven personnel. Some of its versions may have twin 23-mm AA guns.

Iran had an unknown number of British Chieftain bridge laying tanks and a wide range of specialized armored vehicles as well as some heavy equipment transporters. Iran is steadily improving its ability to support armored operations in the field and to provide recovery and field repair capability. However, its exercises reveal that these capabilities still remain limited relative to those of U.S. forces as they lack recovery and field repair capability in combination with poor interoperability. Most likely, these problems will seriously limit the cohesion, speed, and sustainability of Iranian armored operations.

Iran's armored warfare doctrine seems to be borrowed from U.S., British, and Russian sources without achieving any coherent concept of operations. Even so, Iran's armored doctrine is improving more quickly than its organization and exercise performance. Iran's armored forces are very poorly structured, and the country's equipment pool is dissipated between far too many regular and IRGC units. As mentioned before, Iran has only one armored division—the 92nd Armored Division—with enough tanks and other armor to be considered a true armored unit.

Iranian Antiarmor Weapons

Iran had large holdings of antitank guided weapons and has been manufacturing copies of Soviet systems, while buying missiles from China, Russia, and the Ukraine. It has approximately 50–75 Tube-Launched Optically Tracked Wire-Guided Missiles (TOW) and 20–30 Dragon antitank guided missile launchers that were originally supplied by the United States, although the operational status of such systems is uncertain.

It has Soviet and Asian versions of the AT-2, the AT-3, and the AT-5. Iran seems to have at least 100–200 AT-4 (9K111) launchers, but it is impossible to make an accurate estimate because Iran is producing its own copies of the AT-3. Iran also has some 750 RPG-7V, RPG-11, and 3.5″ rocket launchers, roughly 150 M-18

57-mm, 200 M-20 75-mm and B-10 82-mm, and 200 M-40 106-mm and B-11 107-mm recoilless guns.

Iran produces various antitank weapons. These include an improved version of the man-portable RPG-7 antitank rocket with an 80-mm tandem HEAT warhead instead of the standard 30-mm design, the NAFEZ antitank rocket, and a copy of the Soviet SPG-9 73-mm recoilless antitank gun.

Iran also makes a copy of the Russian AT-3 9M14M (Sagger or Ra'ad) antitank guided missile. This system is a crew-operable system with a guidance system that can be linked to a launcher holding up to four missiles. It has a maximum range of 3,000 meters, a minimum range of 500 meters, and a flight speed of 120 meters per second. Iran is also seeking more advanced technology from Russia. The United States maintains that a Russian company sold Iran Krasnopol artillery shells while the company denies any connection with Iran.[11] Prospective sanctions are likely to deter arms manufacturers from filling the many needs of the Iranian military.

The Iranian copy of the AT-3 is made by the Shahid Shah Abaday Industrial Group in Tehran, and it seems to be an early version that lacks semiautomatic guidance. Hence, the operator must sight the target, rather than use a joystick, to guide the missile to the target by using the light from the missile. The Iranian version of the AT-3 also seems to have a maximum armored penetration capability of 500 millimeters, which is not enough to penetrate the forward armor of the latest Western and Russian main battle tanks. Russia has, however, refitted most of its systems to the semiautomatic line of sight guidance and warheads capable of penetrating 800 millimeters. Iran may have or be acquiring such capability, and it would significantly improve the lethality of its antiarmor forces.

Iran also makes an improved copy of the TOW missile, which it has reverse engineered from the missiles it received from the United States.

Iranian Artillery Strength

Iran had some 3,200 operational medium and heavy artillery weapons and multiple rocket launchers, and some 5,000 mortars. Its towed artillery consisted largely of Soviet designs. Self-propelled artillery included 60 2S1122-mm howitzers, and some Iranian copies. There were some 180 aging M-109 155-mm weapon systems of which Iran is seeking to produce its own weapons as part of the "Thunder" series. It had some 70 aging 170-mm, 165-mm, and 203-mm weapon systems. Iran also had large numbers of multiple rocket launchers, including some 700 107-mm weapons, 150–200 122-mm weapons, 20-odd 240-mm weapons, and some 333-mm weapons. It manufactures its own multiple rocket launchers, including the long-range Fajr series.

This total is very high compared to the artillery strength of most regional powers, and it reflects Iran's continuing effort to build up artillery strength that began during the Iran-Iraq War. Iran had to use artillery as a substitute for armor and airpower during much of the Iran-Iraq War and generally used relatively static fire. However, Iran's reliance on towed artillery and slow-moving multiple rocket launchers limits

Iran's combined arms maneuver capabilities, and Iran has failed to develop effective night and beyond-visual-range targeting capability.

Some 2,100 of Iran's weapons were towed tube artillery weapons, vs. 310 self-propelled tube weapons, and 700–900 were vehicle-mounted or towed multiple rocket launchers. Iran's holdings of self-propelled weapons still appeared to include a substantial number of U.S.–supplied systems, including 25–30 M-110 203-mm howitzers, 20–30 M-107 175-mm guns, and 130–150 M-109 155-mm howitzers. These weapons were worn, have not been modernized in over 15 years, and lack modern fire-control systems and artillery radars. Many also lacked sustainability, and a considerable number may not be operational.

Iran understands that it has less than a quarter of the self-propelled artillery it needs to properly support its present force structure and that maneuverable artillery is critical to success in dealing with Iraqi and other maneuver forces. It is attempting to compensate for the resulting lack of modern artillery and artillery mobility by replacing its U.S.–made self-propelled weapons with other self-propelled systems. Iran has purchased 60–80 Soviet 2S1 122-mm self-propelled howitzers, and it has developed an indigenous version called Raad (Thunder 1/Thunder 2). The Thunder 1 is a 122-mm weapon similar to Russian designs. The Thunder 2 is a "rapid fire" 155-mm self-propelled weapon. Both systems are now in deployment.

Iran had some 5,000 mortars. These include 107-mm and 120-mm heavy mortars and 800–900 81-mm and 82-mm mortars. The Iranian Army has at least several hundred of its heavy mortars mounted on armored vehicles.

The 700–900 multiple rocket launchers in Iran's inventory were evidence of its tactical emphasis on massed, static firepower. It is difficult to estimate Iran's inventory, but its holdings include roughly 10 M-1989 240-mm multiple rocket launchers, 500–700 Chinese Type 63 and Iranian Haseb and Fadjir-1 107-mm multiple rocket launchers, and 100+ Soviet BM-21 and Soviet BM-11 122-mm launchers, as well as some Fadjir-5 333-mm weapon systems.

Iran has produced its own multiple rocket launchers. These include some 50 122-mm, 40-round Hadid rocket launcher systems. In addition, Iran produces variants of Chinese and Russian 122-mm rockets called the Arash and Noor. Iran has transferred large numbers of its shorter-range rockets to Hezbollah in Lebanon.[12] It supplied most of the extended range versions of the Kaytushas that Hezbollah used in the fighting against Israel in 2006.

The Iranian state television announced the production of the DM-3b seeker for the Noor. The DM-3b is an active radar sensor that is used in the final stages of flight to acquire and home in on ship targets. A joint program between Iran's Aerospace Industries Organization and the China Aerospace Science and Industry Corporation developed the Noor.[13] The Falaq 1 and 2 series are examples of vehicle-mounted unguided rocket systems in the Iranian arsenal. The Falaq 1 fires a 240-mm rocket with 50 kilograms of explosives and can reach a target up to ten kilometers away. The Falaq 2 is slightly larger, carries ten more kilograms of explosives, and flies almost a full kilometer farther.[14]

Iran's land forces operate a number of Iranian-made long-range unguided rockets, including the Shahin 1 and 2, Oghab, and Nazeat. They also include some ten large 240-mm artillery rockets with a range of up to 40–43 kilometers called the Fadjr 3. Some of these systems played a major role in triggering Israel's war against Hezbollah in Lebanon in 2006, and the key longer-range systems seem to include the following:[15]

- The Shahin 1 (sometimes called the Fadjr 4) is a trailer-launched 333-mm caliber unguided artillery rocket. Two rockets are normally mounted on each trailer, and they have a solid propelled rocket motor, a maximum range of 75 kilometers and a 175-kilogram conventional or chemical warhead. The Shahin evidently can be equipped with three types of warheads: a 180-kilogram high-explosive warhead, a warhead using high-explosive submunitions, and a warhead that uses chemical weapons. There is a truck-mounted version, called the Fajr 5, with a rack of four rockets. A larger Shanin 2, with a range of 20 kilometers, is also deployed.

- The Fadjr 3 is a truck-mounted system with a 12-round launcher for 240-mm rockets. It has a maximum range of 43 kilometers and a 45-kilogram payload in its warhead.

- The Fadjr 5 is a truck-mounted 333-mm caliber unguided artillery rocket with a solid propelled rocket motor, a maximum range of 75 kilometers, and a 175-kilogram conventional or chemical warhead. It carries four rockets, and they can evidently be equipped with three types of warheads: a kilogram high-explosive warhead, a warhead using high-explosive submunitions, and a warhead that uses chemical weapons.

- The Oghab is a 320-mm caliber unguided artillery rocket that is spin stabilized in flight, has a maximum range of 34 kilometers, and has a 70-kilogram high explosives (HE) fragmentation warhead—although chemical warheads may be available. While it may have a chemical warhead, it has an operational circular error probable (CEP) that has proven to be in excess of 500 meters at maximum range. Further, Iran has no ability to target accurately the Oghab or any other long-range missile against mobile or point targets at long ranges, other than a limited ability to use remotely piloted vehicles (RPVs).

- The Nazeat is a Transporter-Erector-Launcher (TEL) launched system with conventional and possibly chemical and biological warheads. The full details of this system remain unclear, but it seems to be based on Chinese technology and uses a solid fuel rocket, with a simple inertial guidance system. Nazeat units are equipped with communications vans, meteorological vans, and a global positioning system (GPS) for surveying the launch site. Some reports indicate there are two variants of the Nazeat solid-fueled rocket system—a 355.6-mm caliber rocket with a 105-kilogram range and a 150-kilogram warhead, and a 450-mm caliber rocket with a reported range of 130–150 kilometers and a 250-kilogram warhead. Both systems have maximum closing velocities of Mach 4–5, but both also appear to suffer from poor reliability and accuracy. Other reports indicate all Nazeats are 335.6 mm and there are four versions of progressively larger size, with ranges from 80 to 120 kilometers. It is claimed to have a CEP within 5 percent of its range.

- The Zelzal 2 is a 610-mm long-range rocket, with a warhead with a 600-kilogram payload and a maximum range of up to 210 kilometers. A single rocket is mounted on a launcher on a truck. It is unguided, but is spin stabilized and is claimed to have a CEP within 5 percent of its range.
- The Fateh A-110 is a developmental system believed to be similar to the Chinese CSS-8, which is a surface-to-surface system derived from the Russian SA-2 surface-to-air missile.

Iran has made limited progress in deploying artillery fire-control and battle management systems, counterbattery radar capability, and long-range target acquisition capability, but its capability is improving steadily and it makes increasing use of RPVs to support its self-propelled weapons. Iran has actively sought more modern fire-control and targeting systems since the mid-1980s, and the equipment it supplied to Hezbollah forces in Lebanon—while not the state of the art in Iran—showed Iran has made growing progress in developing effective planning, fire-control, targeting, and damage assessment systems.

Iranian Army Air Defense Systems

Iranian land forces had a total of some 1,700 antiaircraft guns, including 14.5-mm ZPU-2/-4s, 23-mm ZSU-23-4s and ZU-23s, 35-mm M-1939s, 37-mm Type 55s, and 57-mm ZSU-57-2s. Iran also had 100–180 Bofors L/70 40-mm guns, and moderate numbers of Skyguard 35-mm twin antiaircraft guns (many of which may not be operational). Its largest holdings consisted of unguided ZU-23-2s (which it can manufacture) and M-1939s.

It is unclear how many of these systems are really operational as air defense weapons and most would have to be used to provide very short-range "curtain fire" defense of small point targets. They would not be effective against a modern aircraft using an air-to-ground missile or laser-guided weapon. The only notable exception is the ZSU-23-4 radar-guided antiaircraft gun. Iran has 50–100 fully operational ZSU-23-4s. The weapon is short ranged and is vulnerable to electronic countermeasures, but is far more lethal than Iran's unguided guns.

Iran had large numbers of SA-7 (Strela 2M) and SA-14 (Strela) man-portable surface-to-air missiles, and some more modern SA-16s and HN-5/HQ-5s as well as Misaq man-portable surface-to-air missiles. It may also have some SA-18s. It had some U.S.–made Stinger man-portable surface-to-air missiles it bought from Afghan rebels, but these may no longer be operational or may have been used for reverse-engineering purposes.

Iran also has some RBS-70 low-level surface-to-air missiles. Iran seems to be producing some version of the SA-7, perhaps with Chinese assistance. It is not clear whether Iran can do this in any large number. Iran's land-based air defense forces are also acquiring growing numbers of Chinese FM-80s, a Chinese variant of the French-designed Crotale. Some reports indicate that it has some SA-8s, but these may be token transfers obtained for reverse-engineering purposes.

Iranian Army Aviation

Iran pioneered its use of army aviation and attack helicopters during the time of the Shah, but built up its holdings of helicopters far more quickly than it expanded its training and maintenance capability. As a result, it had an ineffective and unsustainable force at the time the Shah fell. Its inability since that time to obtain adequate spare parts to help in modernizing the aircraft has long made Iranian operational helicopter holdings uncertain.

The Iranian Army seems to retain 50 AH-1J Sea Cobra attack helicopters, 20 CH-47Cs, 50 Bell-214A/Cs, 68 AB-205As, 10 AB-206s, and 25 Mi-8/Mi-17 transport and utility helicopters. There are also reports that Iran signed orders for 4 Mi-17s in 1999 and 30 Mi-8s in 2001.

These Western-supplied transport and support helicopters have low operational readiness, and they have little sustained sortie capability. They are, however, regularly used in Iranian military exercises.

Iran is also seeking to create a significant RPV force that borrows in many ways from Israeli technical developments and doctrine. It has produced some such RPVs, such as the Mohajer series—and several exercise reports refer to their use. It has sold some of these systems to Hezbollah, but insufficient data are available to assess this aspect of Iranian capabilities.

Iranian Army's Command, Control, Communications, Computers, and Intelligence (C^{4}I)

Iranian Army communications have improved, as have Iranian battle management and communications exercises. They are now capable of better coordination between branches, the density of communications equipment has improved, and the functional lines of communication and command now place more emphasis on maneuver, quick reaction, and combined arms. Iran has also improved its electronic intelligence (ELINT), communications intelligence (COMINT), jamming, and countermeasure capability, and it has been aided by Syria since the two countries signed a new defense cooperation agreement on November 14, 2005, and ratified in January 2006.[16] However, Iranian battle management and communications capabilities seem to remain relatively limited.

Iran's holdings still consist largely of aging VHF radio with some HF and UHF capability. This equipment cannot handle high traffic densities, and secure communications are poor. Iran still relies heavily on analog data handling and manually switched telephone systems. It is, however, acquiring a steadily growing number of Chinese and Western encryption systems and some digital voice, fax, and telex encryption capabilities.

Other Aspects of Iranian Army Capability

Iran's Army has improved its organization, doctrine, training, and equipment for land force operations. Iran still, however, is a slow-moving force with limited armored maneuver capability and artillery forces better suited for static defense and the use of mass fire than the efficient use of rapidly switched and well-targeted fire. Sustainability is limited, as is field recovery and repair capability. Overall manpower quality is mediocre because of a lack of adequate realistic training and a heavy reliance on conscripts.

The army has some capability for power projection and armored maneuver warfare, but does not train seriously for long-range maneuver and does little training for amphibious warfare or deployment by sea. Its logistics, maintenance, and sustainment systems are largely defensive and designed to support Iranian forces in defending Iran out of local bases. It does not practice difficult amphibious operations, particularly "across the beach" operations. It could, however, deploy into Kuwait and cross the border into Iraq. It can also move at least brigade-sized mechanized units across the Gulf by amphibious ship and ferry if it does not meet significant naval and air opposition to any such movement. It lacks the air strength and naval air and missile defense capabilities to be able to defend such an operation.

THE ISLAMIC REVOLUTIONARY GUARDS CORPS (PASDARAN)

The IRGC has contributed some 125,000 men to Iran's forces in recent years and has substantial capabilities for asymmetric warfare and covert operations. The IRGC operates most of Iran's surface-to-surface missiles and is believed to have custody over potentially deployed nuclear weapons, most or all other chemical, biological, radiological, and nuclear (CBRN) weapons, and to operate Iran's nuclear-armed missile forces if they are deployed.

IRGC Land Forces

The IRGC has small elements equipped with armor and has the equivalent of conventional army units, and some units are trained for covert missions and asymmetric warfare, but most if its forces are lightly equipped infantry trained and equipped for internal security missions. These forces are reported to have between 120,000 and 130,000 men, but such totals are uncertain. They also include conscripts recruited from the same pool as regular army conscripts, and training and retention levels are low. The IRGC land forces do, however, control the Basij (Mobilization of the Oppressed) and other paramilitary forces if they are mobilized for war.

Some sources, like the IISS, report a force structure with 20 "divisions," but most units seem to be battalion-sized elements. The total manpower pool of the IRGC could support only about five to six light infantry divisions. There is supposed to be one airborne brigade.

The IRGC often claims to conduct very large exercises, sometimes with 100,000 men or more. The exact size of such exercises is unclear, but they are generally a small fraction of IRGC claims. With the exception of small elite elements, training is very limited and largely suitable for internal security purposes. Most forces would require substantial refresher training to act in any mission other that static infantry defense.

The IRGC remains the center of Iran's hard-line security forces, but has become steadily more bureaucratic and less effective as a conventional fighting force since the end of the Iran-Iraq War in 1988. Corruption and careerism are growing problems, and the IRGC's role in the defense industry has led to financial abuses. At this point in time, it is the elite elements of the IRGC that give it real meaning beyond serving the regime's need to control its population.

The IRGC Air Force

The air force of the IRGC is believed to operate Iran's three Shahab-3 intermediate range ballistic missiles (IRBM) units (whose true operational status remains uncertain) and may have had custody of its chemical weapons and any biological weapons. While the actual operational status of the Shahab-3 remains uncertain, Iran's supreme leader, Ayatollah Ali Khamenei, announced in 2003 that Shahab-3 missiles had been delivered to the IRGC. In addition, six Shahab-3s were displayed in Tehran during a military parade in September 2003.[17]

It is not clear what combat formations exist within the IRGC, but the IRGC may operate Iran's ten EMB-312 Tucanos.[18] It seems to operate many of Iran's 45 PC-7 training aircraft, as well as some Pakistani-made trainers at a training school near Mushshak, but this school may be run by the regular air force. It has also claimed to manufacture gliders for use in unconventional warfare. These are unsuitable delivery platforms, but could carry a small number of weapons.[19]

The IRGC Naval Forces

The IRGC also has a naval branch with some 20,000 men, including marine units of some 5,000 men. Other sources show this force subordinated to the regular naval forces. Such a force could deliver small nuclear weapons or other CBRN weapons into ports and oil and desalination facilities and could be felt in operational areas in the Gulf and the Gulf of Oman.

The naval branch has bases in the Gulf, many near key shipping channels and some near the Strait of Hormuz. These include facilities at Al-Farsiyah, Halul (an oil platform), Sirri, Abu Musa, Bandaer-e Abbas, Khorramshahr, and Larak. It also controls Iran's coastal defense forces, including naval guns and an HY-3 Seersucker land-based antiship missile unit deployed in five to seven sites along the Gulf coast.

Its forces can carry out extensive raids against Gulf shipping, carry out regular amphibious exercises with the land branch of the IRGC against objectives like the islands in the Gulf, and could conduct raids against Saudi Arabia or other countries on the southern Gulf coast. They give Iran a major capability for asymmetric warfare. The Guards also seem to work closely with Iranian intelligence and appear to be represented unofficially in some embassies, Iranian businesses and purchasing offices, and other foreign fronts.

The IRGC naval forces have at least 40 light patrol boats, 10 Houdong guided missile patrol boats armed with C-802 antiship missiles, and a battery of

HY-2 Seersucker land-based antiship missiles. Some of these systems could be modified to carry a small CBRN weapon, but hardly are optimal delivery platforms because of their limited-range payload and sensor/guidance platforms unsuited for the mission.

Proxy and Covert CBRN Operations

The IRGC has a complex structure that includes both political and military units. It has separate organizational elements for its land, naval, and air units, which include both military and paramilitary units. The Basij and the tribal units of the Pasdaran are subordinated to its land unit command, although the commander of the Basij often seems to report directly to the Commander-in-Chief and Minister of the Pasdaran and through him to the Leader of the Islamic Revolution.

The IRGC has close ties to the foreign operations branch of the Iranian Ministry of Intelligence and Security (MOIS), particularly through the IRGC's Qods force. The Ministry of Intelligence and Security was established in 1983 and has an extensive network of offices in Iranian embassies. It is often difficult to separate the activities of the IRGC, the Vezarat-e Ettela' at va Aminat-e Keshvar (VEVAK), and the Foreign Ministry, and many seem to be integrated operations managed by a ministerial committee called the "Special Operations Council" that includes the Leader of the Islamic Revolution, President, Minister of Intelligence and Security, and other members of the Supreme Council for National Defense.[20]

Other elements of the IRGC can support proxy or covert use of CBRN weapons. They run some training camps inside Iran for outside "volunteers." Some IRGC still seem to be deployed in Lebanon and actively involved in training and arming Hezbollah, other anti-Israeli groups, and other elements.[21] The IRGC has been responsible for major arms shipments to Hezbollah, including large numbers of AT-3 antitank guided missiles, long-range rockets, and some Iranian-made Mohajer UAVs.[22]

Some reports indicate Iran has exported thousands of 122-mm rockets and Fajr 4 and Fajr 5 long-range rockets, including the ARASH with a range of 21–29 kilometers. These reports give the Fajr 5 a range of 75 kilometers with a payload of 200 kilograms. Iran seems to have sent such arms to Hezbollah and some various Palestinian movements, including some shiploads of arms to the Palestinian Authority.[23]

The Quds (Qods) Forces

The IRGC has a large intelligence operation and unconventional warfare component. Roughly 5,000 of the men in the IRGC are assigned to the unconventional warfare mission. The IRGC has the equivalent of one Special Forces division, plus additional smaller formations, and these forces are given special priority in terms of training and equipment. In addition, the IRGC has a special Quds force that plays a major role in giving Iran the ability to conduct unconventional warfare overseas using various foreign movements as proxies.[24] These forces have supported nonstate actors like Hezbollah in Lebanon, Hamas and the Palestinian Islamic Jihad in the Gaza Strip and the West Bank, and the Shi'ite militias in Iraq.

The budget for the Quds forces is a classified budget directly controlled by Khamenei and is not reflected in the Iranian general budget. It operates primarily outside Iran's borders, although it has bases inside and outside of Iran. The Quds troops are divided into specific groups or "corps" for each country or area in which they operate. There are Directorates for Iraq; Lebanon, Palestine, and Jordan; Afghanistan, Pakistan, and India; Turkey and the Arabian Peninsula; Asian countries of the former Soviet Union; Western Nations (Europe and North America); and North Africa (Egypt, Tunisia, Algeria, Sudan, and Morocco).

The Quds has offices or "sections" in many Iranian embassies, which are closed to most embassy staff. It is not clear whether these are integrated with Iranian intelligence operations or that the ambassador in each embassy has control of, or a detailed knowledge of, operations by the Quds staff. However, there are indications that most operations are coordinated between the IRGC and offices within the Iranian Foreign Ministry and MOIS. There are separate operational organizations in Lebanon, Turkey, Pakistan, and several North African countries. There are also indications that such elements may have participated in the bombings of the Israeli Embassy in Argentina in 1992 and the Jewish Community Center in Buenos Aires in 1994—although Iran has strongly denied this.[25]

The Quds force seems to control many of Iran's training camps for unconventional warfare, extremists, and terrorists in Iran and countries like the Sudan and Lebanon. It has at least four major training facilities in Iran. The Quds forces have a main training center at Imam Ali University that is based in the Sa'dabad Palace in northern Tehran. Troops are trained to carry out military and terrorist operations and are indoctrinated in ideology. There are other training camps in the Qom, Tabriz, and Mashhad governates and in Lebanon and the Sudan. These include the Al Nasr camp for training Iraqi Shi'ites and Iraqi and Turkish Kurds in northwest Iran and a camp near Mashhad for training Afghan and Tajik revolutionaries. The Quds seems to help operate the Manzariyah training center near Qom, which recruits foreign students in the religious seminary and which seems to have trained some Bahraini extremists. Some foreigners are reported to have received training in demolition and sabotage at an IRGC facility near Isfahan, in airport infiltration at a facility near Mashad and Shiraz, and in underwater warfare at an IRGC facility at Bandar Abbas.[26]

Role in Iran's Industries

The IRGC plays a major role in Iran's military industries. Its lead role in Iran's efforts to acquire surface-to-surface missiles and weapons of mass destruction gives it growing experience with advanced military technology. As a result, the IRGC is believed to be the branch of Iran's forces that plays the largest role in Iran's military industries.[27] It also operates all of Iran's Scuds, controls most of its chemical and biological weapons, and provides the military leadership for missile production and the production of all weapons of mass destruction.

The Basij and Other Paramilitary Forces

The rest of Iran's paramilitary and internal security forces seem to have relatively little capability in such missions. The Basij is a popular reserve force of about 90,000 men with an active and reserve strength of up to 300,000 and a mobilization capacity of nearly 1,000,000 men. It is controlled by the IRGC and consists largely of youths, men who have completed military service, and the elderly.

Iran also has 45,000–60,000 men in the Ministry of Interior serving as police and border guards, with light utility vehicles, light patrol aircraft (Cessna 185/310s and AB-205s and AB-206s), 90 coastal patrol craft, and 40 harbor patrol craft.

THE IRANIAN AIR FORCE

The Iranian Air Force still is numerically strong, but most of its equipment is aging, worn, and has limited mission capability. It had some 52,000 men: 37,000 in the air force in 2006, and 15,000 in the air defense force, which operates Iran's land-based air defenses. It had over 300 combat aircraft in its inventory (the IISS estimates 281). See Figure 8.4.

Many of these aircraft are either not operational or cannot be sustained in extended air combat. This includes 50–60 percent of Iran's U.S.– and French-supplied aircraft and some 20–30 percent of its Russian- and Chinese-supplied aircraft. It has nine fighter-ground attack squadrons with 162–186 aircraft; seven fighter squadrons, with 70–74 aircraft, a reconnaissance unit with 4–8 aircraft, and a number of transport aircraft, helicopters, and special purpose aircraft. It operates most of Iraq's land-based air defenses, including some 150 I-Hawks, 45 HQ-21s, 10 SA-5s, 30 Rapiers, 15 Tigercats, and additional forces equipped with light surface-to-air missiles.

The Iranian Air Force is headquartered in Tehran with training, administration, and logistics branches, as well as a major central Air Defense Operations Center. It has a political directorate and a small naval coordination staff. It has three major regional headquarters: Northern Zone (Badl Sar), Central Zone (Hamaden), and Southern Zone (Bushehr).

Each regional zone seems to control a major air defense sector with subordinate air bases and facilities. The key air defense subzones and related bases in the Northern Zone are at Badl Sar, Mashhad, and Shahabad Kord. The subzones and bases in the Central Zone are at Hamadan and Dezful, and the subzones and bases in the Southern Zone are at Bushehr, Bandar Abbas, and Jask. Iran has large combat air bases at Mehrabad, Tabriz, Hamadan, Dezful, Bushehr, Shiraz, Isfahan, and Bandar Abbas. It has smaller bases at least at 11 other locations. Shiraz provides interceptor training and is the main base for transport aircraft.

Figure 8.4 Iranian Air Force's Force Structure Trends, 1990–2006

	1990	2000	2005	2006
Manpower	**35,000**	**50,000**	**52,000**	**52,000**
Active	35,000	50,000	52,000	52,000
Conscripts	0	0	0	0
Fighter	**15**	**114**	**74**	**74**
F-7	0	24	24	24
F-14	15	60	25	25
MiG-29	0	30	25	25
Fighter Ground Attack	**104**	**140**	**186**	**186+***
F-4D/E	35	50	65	65+
F-5E/F	45	60	60	60+
Ch J-6	24	0	0	0
Su-24	0	30	30	30
Su-25K	0	0	7	7
Mirage F1-E	0	0	24	24
Maritime Reconnaissance	**2**	**5**	**3**	**5**
P-3F	2	0	0	0
P-3MP	0	0	3	5
C-130H-MP	0	5	0	0
Reconnaissance	**8**	**15**	**6**	**6+**
F-5	5	0	0	0
RF-4E	3	15	6	6+
Transport	**59**	**63**	**64+**	**65+**
Boeing 707	14	3	3	3
Boeing 747F	9	7	5	5
Boeing 727	0	1	1	1
C-130E/H	20	18	18	17
F-27	9	15	10	10
Commander 690	3	3	3	3
Falcon	3	4	1	1
PC-6B	0	10	10	10
Y-7	0	2	2	9
Y-12(II)	0	0	9	3
Jetstar	0	0	2	2

Il-76	0	0	Some	1+
Utility	**0**	**0**	**0**	**12**
TB-21	0	0	0	8
TB-200	0	0	0	4
Helicopters	**55 (0 armed)**	**53 (0 armed)**	**34 (0 armed)**	**34+**
AB-206	2	2	2	2
Bell 214C	39	39	30	30
CH-47	10	5	2	2+
S-61A	2	0	0	0
Shabaviz 2-75	0	0	0	Some
Shabaviz2061	0	0	0	Some
Training	**84**	**132**	**151**	**119**
F-33A/V	26	26	20	?[†]
T-33	7	7	7	7
PC-7	46	40	40	40
EMB-312	5–6	15	15	?
MiG-29B	0	5	0	?
FT-7	0	5	15	?
F-5B	0	20	20	?
TB-21	0	8	8	?
TB-200	0	4	4	?
MFI-17 Mushshaq	0	0	22	?
Surface-to-Air Missiles	**105**	**190+**	**220+**	**2,500+**
I-Hawk	0	100	150	2,400
Rapier	30	30	30	30
Tigercat	25	15	15	15
SA-2/HQ-2J	50	45	15	45
SA-5	0	0	10	10
SA-7	0	Some	Some	Some
FM-80 (Crotale)	0	Some	Some	Some
Air-to-Air Missiles	**Some**	**Some**	**Some**	**Some**
AIM-7 Sparrow	Some	Some	Some	Some
AIM-9 Sidewinder	Some	Some	Some	Some
AIM-54 Phoenix	Some	Some	Some	Some

AA-8	0	Some	Some	Some
AA-10	0	Some	Some	Some
AA-11	0	Some	Some	Some
PL-2A	0	0	some	0
PL-7	0	Some	Some	0
Air-to-Surface Missiles	**Some**	**Some**	**Some**	**Some**
AS-10	0	Some	Some	Some
AS-11	0	Some	Some	Some
AS-12	Some	0	0	0
AS-14	0	Some	Some	Some
C-801	0	0	Some	Some
AGM-65A	0	Some	3,000	Some
AGM-84 Harpoon	Some	0	0	0
Air Defense Guns	**0**	**0**	**Some**	**Some**
23 mm	0	0	Some	Some
ZSU-23	0	0	Some	Some
37 mm	0	0	Some	Some
Oerlikon	0	0	Some	Some

* "+" indicates the numbers listed may be slightly less than the actual units or weapons in stock.

† All "?" refer to weapons that Iran is believed to possess, though the exact numbers in its possession are unknown.

Source: IISS, *Military Balance,* various editions, including 1989–1990, 1999–2000, 2004–2005, and 2005–2006.

Iranian Air Strength

As is the case with most aspects of Iranian military forces, estimates of Iran's exact air strength differ by source. The IISS estimates the air force has 14 main combat squadrons. These include nine fighter ground-attack squadrons, four with 55–65 U.S.–supplied F-4D/Es, four with 55–65 F-5E/Fs, and one with 27–30 Soviet-supplied Su-24s. Iran has 7 Su-25Ks and 24 Mirage F-1 Iraqi aircraft it seized during the Gulf War, and some may be operational. Some reports indicate that Iran has ordered an unknown number of TU-22M-3 "Backfire C" long-range strategic bombers from either Russia or the Ukraine.[28] While such discussions do seem to have taken place, no purchases or deliveries can be confirmed.

Iran had five air defense squadrons, two with 20–25 F-5Bs and 60 U.S.–supplied F-14s, two with 25–30 Russian/Iraqi-supplied MiG-29s, and one with 25–35 Chinese supplied F-7Ms.[29] The Iranian Air Force had a small reconnaissance squadron with 3–8 RF-4Es. It has 1 RC-130, and other intelligence/reconnaissance aircraft, together with large numbers of transports and helicopters.

Most Iranian squadrons can perform both air defense and attack missions, regardless of their principal mission—although this is not true of Iran's F-14 (air defense) and Su-24 (strike/attack) units. Iran's F-14s were, however, designed as dual-capable aircraft, and it has not been able to use its Phoenix air-to-air missiles since the early 1980s. Iran has claimed that it is modernizing its F-14s by equipping them with Improved Hawk (I-Hawk) missiles adapted to the air-to-air role, but it is far from clear that this is the case or that such adaptations can have more than limited effectiveness. In practice, this means that Iran might well use the F-14s in nuclear strike missions. They are capable of long-range, high payload missions and would require minimal adaptation to carry and release a nuclear weapon.[30]

As a result, Iran has a large number of attack and air defense aircraft that could carry a small- to medium-sized nuclear weapon long distances, particularly since such strikes are likely to be low-altitude one-way missions. (These were the mission profiles in both NATO and Warsaw Pact theater nuclear strike plans.) Several might conceivably be modified as drones or the equivalent of "cruise missiles" using autopilots, on-board computers, and an add-on GPS.

Iran has moderate airlift capabilities for a regional power. The Iranian Air Force's air transport assets included 3 B-707 and 1 B-747 tanker transports and 5 transport squadrons with 4 B-747Fs, 1 B-727, 18C-130E/Hs, 3 Commander 690s, 10 F-27s, 1 Falcon 20A, and 2 Jetstars. Iran will have 14 Xian Y-7 transports by 2006.[31] Its helicopter strength includes 2 AB-206As, 27–30 Bell 214Cs, and 2 CH-47s, and 30 Mi-17 and Iranian-made Shabaviz 206-1 and 2-75 transport helicopters.

The IRGC also has some air elements. It is not clear what combat formations exist within the IRGC, but the IRGC may operate Iran's 10 EMB-312s.[32] It seems to operate many of Iran's 45 PC-7 trainers, as well as some Pakistani-made trainers at a training school near Mushhak, but this school may be run by the regular air force. It has also claimed to manufacture gliders for use in unconventional warfare. The IRGC has not recently expanded its air combat capabilities.[33]

Iranian Aircraft Development

Iran has made more ambitious claims about aircraft production that it cannot yet back up. Russian firms and the Iranian government tried to reach an agreement over license production of the MiG-29, but repeated attempts have failed. Likely due to the difficulty the regime has had in procuring new aircraft, Iran has been developing three new attack aircraft. The indigenous design and specifics of one of the fighters in development, the Shafagh, were unveiled at the Iran Airshow in 2002. Engineers hope to have a prototype by 2008, though it is unclear what the production numbers will be and what the real-world timetable for deployment may be.[34]

Little is known about the other two fighters in development, the Saeghe and the Azarakhsh, other than they have been reportedly derived from the F-5F. Claims have been made that the Azarakhsh is in low-rate production and has had operational weapons tests. There are also some indications that Iran is experimenting with composites in the Azarakhsh and is seeking to give it a locally modified beyond-visual-range radar for air-to-air combat.[35]

In practice, Iran is making light turboprop aircraft and a light utility helicopter. It is making enough progress so that it will probably be able to produce a jet trainer and heavier helicopters, but it is unclear how effective it can be in producing modern combat aircraft.[36]

Iran also has some indigenous capability to produce combat aircraft and drones.

Iranian Air Force Readiness and Effectiveness

In spite of Iran's efforts, readiness and force quality remain major issues. The Iranian Air Force still has many qualitative weaknesses, and it is far from clear that its current rate of modernization can offset the aging of its Western-supplied aircraft and the qualitative improvements in U.S. and southern Gulf forces. The air force also faces serious problems in terms of sustainability, command and control, and training. Iran has a pilot quality problem. Many of its U.S.–trained pilots were purged at some point during the Revolution. Its other U.S.–trained pilots and ground-crew technicians are aging to the point where many should soon retire from service, and they have not had advanced air-to-air combat and air attack training for more than 15 years.

Iran has only token numbers of advanced strike aircraft, and these consist of export versions of the SU-24 and dual-capable MiG-29s that do not compete with modern U.S. aircraft or the most modern aircraft in southern Gulf forces. Exercises like the Holy Prophet and the Force of Zolfaghar that Iran held in 2006 show that it is slowly improving its capability for joint land-air and air-sea operations. Iranian exercises and statements provide strong indications that Iran would like to develop an advanced air defense system, the ability to operate effectively in long-range maritime patrol and attack missions, effective joint warfare capabilities, and strike/attack forces with the ability to penetrate deep into Iraq, the southern Gulf States, and other neighboring powers.

Iran's exercises, military literature, and procurement efforts also make it clear that its air planners understand the value of airborne early warning and C^4I systems, the value of airborne intelligence and electronic warfare platforms, the value of RPVs, and the value of airborne refueling. As is the case with its army, the Iranian Air Force and land-based air defense forces have also benefited by Iran's cooperation with Syria and Syrian transfers of Russian methods, tactics, and technology in areas like SIGINT, ELINT, COMINT, and command and control.[37] Iran has even sought to create its own satellite program.[38] Israel and other sources claim that Iran has several joint SIGINT bases in Syria and that Iran and Syria established a joint intelligence center with Hezbollah during the Israeli-Hezbollah conflict in the summer of 2006.

Further, the air force's efforts at sheltering and dispersal indicate that it understands the vulnerability of modern air facilities and the standoff attack capabilities of advanced air forces like those of the United States.

The Iranian Air Force must also deal with the fact that its primary challenge now consists of the U.S., British, and Saudi air forces. They are high-technology air forces that operate the airborne warning and control system, have some of the most advanced electronic warfare and targeting systems in the world, and have full refueling capability. They use sophisticated, computer-aided aggressor training and have all of the range and training facilities for beyond-visual-range combat and standoff attacks with air-to-surface munitions. Iran has no airborne control system, although it may be able to use the radars on its F-14s to support other aircraft from the rear. Its overall C^4I system is a totally inadequate mix of different sensors, communications, and data processing systems. It has limited electronic warfare capabilities by U.S. standards, although it may be seeking to acquire two Beriev A-50 Mainstay Airborne Early Warning (AEW) aircraft, and has converted some aircraft to provide a limited ELINT/SIGINT capability.

Iran's air defense aircraft consist of a maximum operational strength of two squadrons of 25 export versions of the MiG-29A and two squadrons of 25–30 F-14As. The export version of the MiG-29A has significant avionics limitations and vulnerability to countermeasures, and it is not clear Iran has any operation Phoenix air-to-air missiles for its F-14As or has successfully modified its I-Hawk missiles for air-to-air combat. The AWG-9 radar on the F-14 has significant long-distance sensor capability in a permissive environment, but is a U.S.–made system in a nearly 30-year-old configuration that is now vulnerable to countermeasures.

Iran might risk using its fighters and AEW aircraft against an Israeli strike. It seems doubtful that Israel could support a long-range attack unit with the air defense and electronic assets necessary to provide anything like the air defense and air defense suppression assets that would support a U.S. strike. A U.S. strike could almost certainly destroy any Iranian effort to use fighters, however, and destroy enough Iranian surface-to-air missile defenses to create a secure corridor for penetrating into Iran and against key Iranian installations. The United States could then maintain such a corridor indefinitely with restrikes.

While Iran practices realistic individual intercept training, it fails to practice effective unit or force-wide tactics and has shown only a limited capability to fly large numbers of sorties with its U.S.–supplied aircraft on even a surge basis. It has limited refueling capabilities—although it has four B-707 tanker/transports and may have converted other transports. The Iranian Air Force lacks advanced training facilities and has only limited capability to conduct realistic training for beyond-visual-range combat and standoff attacks with air-to-surface munitions. Ground-crew training and proficiency generally seem mediocre—although the layout of Iranian air bases, aircraft storage and parking, the deployment of equipment for maintenance cycles, and the other physical signs of air unit activity are generally better organized than those of most Middle Eastern air forces.

Iranian Land-Based Air Defense

If one looks at Iran's overall air defense capability, Iran has "quantity," but its air defenses have limited "quality." Iran seems to have assigned about 12,000–15,000 men in its air force to land-based air defense functions, including at least 8,000 regulars and 4,000 IRGC personnel. It is not possible to distinguish clearly between the major air defense weapons holdings of the regular air force and of the IRGC, but the air force appeared to operate most major surface-to-air missile (SAM) systems.

Total holdings seem to include 30 Improved Hawk fire units (12 battalions/150+ launchers), 45–55 SA-2 and HQ-2J/23 (CSA-1) launchers (Chinese-made equivalents of the SA-2), and possibly 25 SA-6 launchers. The air force also had three Soviet-made long-range SA-5 units with a total of 10–15 launchers—enough for six sites. Iran has developed and deployed its own domestically manufactured SAM dubbed the Shahab Thaqeb. The SAM requires a four-wheeled trailer for deployment and closely resembles the R440 SAM.[39]

Iran's holdings of lighter air defense weapons include 5 Rapier squadrons with 30 Rapier fire units, 5–10 Chinese FM-80 launchers, 10–15 Tigercat fire units, and a few RBS-70s. Iran also holds large numbers of man-portable SA-7s, HN-5s, and SA-14s, plus about 2,000 antiaircraft guns—including some Vulcans and 50–60 radar-guided and self-propelled ZSU-23-4 weapons.[40] It is not clear which of these lighter air defense weapons were operated by the army, the IRGC, or the air force. The IRGC clearly had larger numbers of man-portable surface-to-air launchers, including some Stingers that it had obtained from Afghanistan. It almost certainly had a number of other light air defense guns as well.

In addition to its fighter defenses, Iran has assigned some 12,000–15,000 men in its air force to land-based air defense functions, including at least 8,000 regulars and 4,000 IRGC personnel. It is not possible to distinguish clearly between the major air defense weapons holdings of the regular air force and IRGC, but the air force appeared to operate most major surface-to-air missile systems.

There are no authoritative data on how Iran now deploys its land-based air defenses, but Iran seems to have deployed its new SA-5s to cover its major ports, oil facilities, and Tehran. It seems to have concentrated its Improved Hawks and Soviet- and Chinese-made SA-2s around Tehran, Isfahan, Shiraz, Bandar Abbas, Kharg Island, Bushehr, Bandar Khomeini, Ahwaz, Dezful, Kermanshah, Hamadan, and Tabriz.

Although Iran has made some progress in improving and updating its weapons, sensors, and electronic warfare capability—and has learned much from Iraq's efforts to defeat U.S. enforcement of the "no-fly zones" during 1992–2003, its current defenses are outdated and poorly integrated. All of its major systems are based on technology that is now more than 35 years old, and all are vulnerable to U.S. use of active and passive countermeasures. Iran is trying to reduce this vulnerability by improving its C^4I systems, jamming, tactics, and radars, but faces major limitations on what it can do without major new transfers of modern, advanced weapons and technology from a source like Russia.

Iran's air defense forces are too widely spaced to provide more than limited air defense for key bases and facilities, and many lack the missile launcher strength to be fully effective. This is particularly true of Iran's SA-5 (S-200) sites, which provide long-range, medium-to-high altitude coverage of key coastal installations. These units seem to have been upgraded to the S-200VE "Vega-E" by Belorussian specialists.[41] However, too few launchers are scattered over too wide an area to prevent relatively rapid suppression.

Iran also lacks the low-altitude radar coverage, overall radar net, command and control assets, sensors, resistance to sophisticated jamming and electronic countermeasures, and systems integration capability necessary to create an effective air defense net. Its land-based air defenses must operate largely in the point defense mode. Iran lacks the battle management systems, and its data links are not fast and effective enough to allow it to take maximum advantage of the overlapping coverage of some of its missile systems—a problem further complicated by the problems in trying to net different systems supplied by Britain, China, Russia, and the United States. Iran's missiles and sensors are most effective at high-to-medium altitudes against aircraft with limited penetrating and jamming capability.

Iran also lacks the low-altitude radar coverage, overall radar net, command and control assets, sensors, resistance to sophisticated jamming and electronic countermeasures, and systems integration capability necessary to create an effective air defense net.

This situation may, however, change in the future, and improvements in Iran's land-based air defenses could be a factor in the timing of any U.S. or Israeli strikes. Iran purchased 20 Russian 9K331 Tor-M-1 (SA-15 Gauntlet) self-propelled surface-to-air missiles in December 2005.[42] Global Security indicates that this is a modern short-range missile that has the capability to simultaneously attack two targets using a relatively high powered and jam-resistant radar, and it has "electronic beam control and vertically launched missiles able to maintain high speed and manoeuvrability inside an entire engagement envelope; the high degree of automation of combat operation provided by the electronic equipment suite." It is said to be capable of detecting targets at a distance of 25 kilometers and attack them at a maximum distance of 12 kilometers. For what it is worth, Russian sources claim that Tor is much more efficient than similar systems like France's Crotale and Britain's Rapier.

The basic combat formation is a firing battery consisting of four TLARs and the Rangir battery command post. The TLAR carries eight ready missiles stored in two containers holding four missiles each. It is claimed to have an effective range of 1,500 to 12,000 meters against targets flying at altitudes between 10 and 6,000 meters. The maximum maneuvering load factor limit on the weapon is said to be 30 "Gs".[43] It should be noted that Russian manufacturer claims are no less exaggerated than those of European and U.S. manufacturers.

Delivery dates ranging from 2006–2009 have been reported, but the Tor is too range limited to have a major impact on U.S. stealth attack capability, although its real-world performance against cruise missiles still has yet to be determined. It might have more point defense lethality against regular Israeli and U.S. strike fighters like the F-15 and the F-16 using precision-guided bombs, but would be lethal against such aircraft with standoff air-to-surface missiles only if it could be deployed in the flight path in ways which were not detected before the attack profile was determined.

Iran also announced in February 2006 (along with several other weapons and military exercise announcements that seemed timed to try to deter U.S. or Israeli military action) that it was mass producing a new man-portable, low-altitude, short-range air defense missile called the Mithaq-2.[44] It was said to be electronic warfare and IR-flare resistant, and it seemed to be based on the Chinese QW-1 Vanguard. If it is the QW-1, it is an IR-homing missile introduced in the mid-1990s. It may, however, be a variant of the QW-2 with an improved IR seeker. China claims it has an effective range of 500–5,000 meters at target altitudes of 30–4,000 meters. The maximum maneuvering load factor limit on the weapon is said to be 30 Gs. In spite of Iranian claims, it does not seem superior to the Russian SA-14s already in Iranian inventory and is too short-ranged to have more than a minimal deterrent effect.[45]

Some reports indicate that Iran is seeking more modern Soviet SA-300 missiles and to use Russian systems to modernize its entire air defense system. If Iran could acquire, deploy, and bring such systems to a high degree of readiness, they would substantially improve Iranian capabilities. A report in *Jane's* claims that Iran is building surface-to-air missile defense zones around its nuclear facilities that will use a single battery of S-300PMU (SA-10) missiles to defend the Bushehr reactor and will deploy the S-300V (SA-12b) to provide wide area defense coverage of other targets which it will mix with the TOR-M1 to provide low-altitude point defense.

This is a logical Iranian approach to improving its defenses, and Iran has sought to purchase the S-300 in the past. It seems to have advanced electronic warfare capabilities, sensors, computer systems, and software. The SA-10 is reported to be able to intercept aircraft at a maximum slant range of 32,000 to 43,200 meters, and a maximum effective defense perimeter of 150 kilometers (90 miles). The minimum effective interception altitude is claimed to be 10 meters. One variant of the missile is reported to have some BMD capability and be able to engage ballistic missile targets at ranges of up to 40 kilometers (25 miles). Each battery is said to have a load of 32 missile rounds on its launchers, a battery deployment time as low as five minutes, and the ability to fire three missiles per second. A standard battery consists of an 83M6E2 command post (CP), up to six 90Zh6E2 air defense missile complexes, 48N6E2 air defense missiles, and technical support facilities.[46]

If Iran were to get the SV-300 (SA-12a and SA-12b), it would get a system with far more advanced sensors, electronic warfare capabilities, and significant point defense capabilities against ballistic missiles. A Russian S-300V brigade has the following components: 9M82 SA-12b Giant missiles (2 per launcher) and TELAR, 9M83 SA-12a Gladiator missiles (4 per launcher) and TELAR, Giant and Gladiator launcher/loader vehicles, 9S15 Bill Board Surveillance Radar system, 9S19 High Screen Sector Radar system, 9S32 Grill Pan Guidance Radar system, and 9S457 Command Station. The SA-12a is a dual-role antimissile and antiaircraft missile with a maximum range between 75 and 90 kilometers. The SA-12b GIANT missile is configured as an ATBM role with a longer maximum range of between 100 and 200 kilometers. Each unit can detect up to 200 targets, track as many as 70 targets, and designate 24 of the targets to the brigade's four GRILL PAN radar systems for engagement.[47]

It seems doubtful, however, that Iran has operational S-300PMU systems, has taken delivery on such units, or has even been able to buy them from Russia. It is also unclear that Russia has sold Iran SV-300 systems or plans to. The Russian Minister of Defense flatly denied any such sales had taken place in February 2006.[48] Even if such systems are delivered, their real-world performance will be uncertain. In the past, Russia has also been careful to control some critical aspects of its weapons exports and sell degraded export versions.

Iran's air forces are only marginally better able to survive in air-to-air combat than Iraq's were before 2003. Iran's command and control system has serious limitations in terms of secure communications, vulnerability to advanced electronic warfare, netting, and digital data transfer. According to the IISS, Iran does still have five operational P-3MP Orions and may have made its captured Iraqi IL-76 Candid AEW aircraft operational. These assets would give it airborne warning and command and control capability, but these are obsolescent to obsolete systems and are likely to be highly vulnerable to electronic warfare and countermeasures, and long-range attack, even with Iranian modifications and updates. There are some reports Iran may be seeking to make a version of the Russian AN-140 AEW aircraft, but these could not be deployed much before 2015.[49]

THE IRANIAN NAVY

The Iranian Navy had some 18,000 men in 2006. According to the IISS, this total included a two-brigade marine force of some 2,600 men and a 2,000-man naval aviation force. It had bases at Bandar-e Abbas, Bushehr, Kharg Island, Bander-e Anzelli, Chah Bahar, Bander-e Mahshahar, and Bander-e Khomeini, most of them opposing the Saudi coast. See Figure 8.5.

The naval forces had 3 submarines, 3 frigates, 2 corvettes, 10 missile patrol craft, 5 mine warfare ships, 52 coastal and inshore patrol craft, and 10 amphibious ships. Its naval aviation branch is one of the few air elements in any Gulf navy, having 5 maritime patrol aircraft and 19 armed helicopters. When combined with the IRGC naval branch, this brought the total maritime strength of Iran to 38,000 men, with significant capabilities for both regular naval and asymmetric naval warfare.

Iran has given the modernization of its naval forces some priority, although its major surface ships are all old vessels with limited refits and aging weapons and fire-control systems. Since the end of the Iran-Iraq War, Iran has obtained new antiship missiles and missile patrol craft from China, midget submarines from North Korea, submarines from Russia, and modern mines. Iran has expanded the capabilities of the naval branch of the IRGC, acquired additional mine warfare capability, and upgraded some of its older surface ships. Iran's exercises have included

Figure 8.5   Iranian Navy's Force Structure Trends, 1990–2006

	1990	2000	2005	2006
Manpower	**14,500**	**20,600**	**18,000**	**18,000**
Active	14,500	20,600	18,000	18,000
Conscripts	0	0	0	0
Submarines	0	5	3	3
SSK (RF Type 877)	0	3	3	3
SSI	0	2	0	0
Destroyers	**3**	**0**	**0**	**0**
Damavand (U.K. Battle)	1	0	0	0
Babr (U.S. Sumner)	2	0	0	0
Frigates	5	3	5	5
Alvand (U.K. Vosper)	3	3	3	3
Bayandor (U.S. PF-103)	2	0	2	2
Patrol and Coastal Combatants	**34**	**64**	**56**	**250+***
Patrol Missile Craft	10	20	10	10
Kaman (Fr Combattante II)	10	10	10	10
Houdong	0	10	0	0
Patrol Inshore	**24**	**42**	**35+**	**85**
Kaivan	3	Some	0	0
Parvin	3	3	3	3
Chaho	3	Some	0	0
Zafar	0	3	3	3
Bogomol	0	1	0	0
China Cat	0	0	3	6
Hovercraft	15	9	14	?†
Mine Warfare	**3**	**7**	**7**	**5**
Sharokh (MSC)	2	1	1	1
Riazi (U.S. Cape)	0	1	2	2
Harischi (MSI)	1	1	0	0
Hejaz (Minelayer)	0	2	2	0
292 MSC	0	2	2	2
Amphibious	**7**	**9**	**10**	**10**
Hengam (LST)	4	4	4	4

Iran Hormuz (LST)	3	3	3	3
Foque (LSL)	0	2	3	3
Landing craft	4+	9+	200+	6
Support	**8**	**25**	**25**	**27**
Maritime Reconnaissance	**0**	**8**	**10**	**8**
P-3F	0	3	5	5
Do-228	0	5	5	5
Antisubmarine Weapons	**9**	**9**	**20**	**10**
SH-3D Sea King	3	3	10	10
AB-212	6	6	10	0
Mine Countermeasures	**2**	**2**	**3**	**3**
RH-53D	2	2	3	3
Transport	**29**	**29**	**18**	**13**
Commander	4	4	4	4
Falcon	1	1	3	3
F-27	4	4	4	4
AB-205 (Heli)	Some	Some	5	5
AB-206 (Heli)	Some	Some	2	2
AB-212	0	0	0	10

*   "+" indicates the numbers listed may be slightly less than the actual units or weapons in stock.

†   All "?" refer to weapons that Iran is believed to possess, though the exact numbers in its possession are unknown.

Source: IISS, *Military Balance,* various editions, including 1989–1990, 1999–2000, 2004–2005, and 2005–2006.

a growing number of joint and combined arms exercises with the land forces and air force.

Iran has also improved its ports and strengthened its air defenses, while obtaining some logistic and technical support from nations like India and Pakistan. In August 2000, the Islamic Republic announced that it had launched its first domestically produced light submarine, which is called the Al-Sabiha 15. It can be used for reconnaissance and laying mines.[50]

Iranian Antiship Missiles and Missile Craft

Iran's depends heavily on its ability to use antiship missiles to make up for its lack of airpower and modern major surface vessels. Iran's Western-supplied missiles are now all beyond their shelf life, and their operational status is uncertain. Iranian forces are now operating the following four systems that Iran has obtained from China:

- **The Seersucker** is a long-range, mobile antiship missile, which is designated the HY-2 or Sea Eagle-2 by the People's Republic of China. It is a large missile with a 0.76-meter diameter and a weight of 3,000 kilograms. It has an 80–90-kilometer range and a 450-kilogram warhead. There are two variants. One uses radar active homing at ranges from the target of 8 kilometers (4.5 nautical miles). The other is set to use passive infrared (IR) homing and a radar altimeter to keep it at a constant height over the water.
- **The CS-801** antiship missile, also called the Yinji (Hawk) missile, is a solid fueled missile. It can be launched from land and ships. It has a range of approximately 74 kilometers in the surface-to-surface mode and uses J-Band active radar guidance. It has a 512-kilogram warhead and cruises at an altitude of 20–30 meters.
- **The CS-802** is an upgraded CS-801. It uses a turbojet propulsion system with a rocket booster instead of the solid fueled booster in the CS-801. It has a range of 70–75 miles, has a warhead of up to 363 pounds, and can be targeted by a radar deployed on a smaller ship or aircraft operating over the radar horizon of the launching vessel.[51]
- **The CS-801K** is a Chinese-supplied, air-launched antiship missile and variant of the CS-801. It too is a sea-skimming, high-subsonic cruise missile and has a range in excess of 20 nautical miles. It has been test-fired by Iran's F-4Es, but Iran may be able to use other launch aircraft. This air delivery capability gives Iran what some analysts have called a "360 degree" attack capability, since aircraft can rapidly maneuver to far less predictable launch points than Iranian combat ships.[52]

Iran has sought to buy advanced antiship missiles from Russia, North Korea, and China, to buy antiship missile production facilities, and possibly even Chinese-made missile armed frigates. Some sources have claimed that Iran has bought eight Soviet-made SS-N-22 "Sunburn" or "Sunburst" antiship missile launch units from Ukraine and has deployed them near the Straits of Hormuz. However, U.S. experts have not seen firm evidence of such a purchase and doubt that Iran has any operational holdings of such systems. The "SS-N-22" is a title that actually applies to two different modern long-range supersonic sea skimming systems—the P-270 Moskit (also called the Kh-15 or 3M80) and the P80 or P-100 Zubi/Onika.

Iran's main launch platforms for antiship missiles include three British-supplied Vosper Mark 5 Sa'am-class frigates—called the *Alvand,* the *Alborz,* and the *Sabalan.* These ships date back to the time of the Shah, and each is a 1,100-ton frigate with a crew of 125–146 and maximum speeds of 39 knots. Each was originally armed with one five-missile Sea Killer Mark II surface-to-surface missile launcher and one Mark 8 4.5″ gun mount. They have since had their Sea Killer's replaced with C-802 antiship missiles and new fire-control radars. The Sea Killer has a relatively effective beam-riding missile with radio command or optical guidance, and a maximum range of 25 kilometers.

All three ships are active, but the *Sabalan* took serious damage from the U.S. Navy during the Tanker War of 1987–1988, and the ships have not had a total refit since the early 1990s. The antisubmarine weapons (ASW) capabilities of these ships seem to be limited or nonfunctioning. Iran has two U.S. PF-103 (Bayandor-class) corvettes called the *Bayandor* and the *Naghdi.* These ships are 900-ton vessels, with crews of 140, two 76-mm guns, and a maximum speed of 18 knots. They were laid down in 1962 and delivered in 1964. The *Bayandor* and the *Naghdi* are probably the most active large surface ships in the Iranian Navy. However, neither is equipped with antiship and antiair missiles, sophisticated weapons systems, sonars, or advanced electronic warfare equipment and sensors.[53]

The rest of Iran's major surface vessels consist of missile patrol boats. These include ten 68-ton Chinese-built Thondor (Hudong)-class fast attack craft or missile patrol boats. The Hudong-class fast attack craft are equipped with I-band search and navigation radars, but do not have a major antiair missile system. Iran ordered these ships for the naval branch of its Iranian Revolutionary Guards Corps in 1992, and all ten were delivered to Iran by March 1996. The vessels have a crew of 28. They carry four antiship missiles and are armed with the CS-801 and CS-802 missiles.

Iran now has at least 100 CS-801s and CS-802s. Iran's missile patrol boats also include 10 275-ton French-made Combattante II (Kaman-class) fast attack boats, out of an original total of 12. These boats are armed with antiship missiles, one 76-mm gun, and have maximum speeds of 37.5 knots. They were originally armed with four U.S. Harpoon missiles, but their Harpoons may no longer be operational. At least 5 had been successfully converted with launchers that can carry 2–4 CS-801/CS-802s. Iran supplied the CS-802s that Hezbollah successfully used against one of Israel's most modern Sa'ar Class 5 missile ships during the fighting in 2006.

Iran has a number of large patrol craft and fast attack craft. The operational ships of this type include three North Korean–supplied 82-ton Zafar-class (Chaho-class) fast attack craft with I-band search radars and armed with 23-mm guns and a BM-21 multiple rocket launcher, two Kavian-class (U.S. Cape-class) 148-ton patrol craft armed with 40-mm and 23-mm guns, and three Improved PGM-71 Parvin-class 98-ton patrol craft supplied in the late 1960s, armed with 40-mm and 20-mm guns.

There are more than 35 other small patrol boats plus large numbers of small boats operated by the IRGC. Most of these craft are operational and can be effective in patrol missions. They lack, however, sophisticated weapons systems or air defenses, other than machine guns and SA-7s and SA-14s. Iran has 5–6 BH-7s and 7–8 SRN-6 Hovercrafst, believed to be operated by the IRGC. About half of these Hovercrafts may be operational. They are capable of speeds of up to 60–70 knots. They are lightly armed and vulnerable, but their high speed makes them useful for many reconnaissance and unconventional warfare missions, and they can rapidly land troops on suitable beaches.

In the early fall of 2006, Iran also demonstrated new naval missile capabilities during its Force of Zolfaghar exercises. These included submarine launched missiles that Iran called the Sagheb, but which seem to have been Chinese YJ-8s.[54] Iran also demonstrated a new missile that it called the Qassed or "Messenger" that its F-4Es could carry in pairs and which Iran said was a 2,000-pound, rocket-assisted, precision-guided standoff weapon that could be used to attack both land and naval targets.

Iranian Mine Warfare Capabilities

Mine warfare, amphibious warfare, antiship missiles, and unconventional warfare offer Iran ways of compensating for the weakness of its conventional air and naval forces. Iran's mine warfare vessels included two to three operational Shahrock-class MSC-292/268 coastal minesweepers (one used for training in the Caspian Sea). Two of these three ships, the *Shahrock* and the *Karkas,* were known to be operational. They are 378-ton sweepers that can be used to lay mines as well as sweep, but their radars and sonars date back to the late 1950s and are obsolete in sweeping and countermeasure activity against modern mines.

Iran had one to two operational Cape-class (Riazzi-class) 239-ton inshore minesweepers and seems to have converted two of its indigenously produced Ajar-class landing ship tanks (LSTs) for mine warfare purposes. Many of its small boats and craft can also lay mines. Both the Iranian Navy and the naval branch of the IRGC are expanding their capability for mine warfare. While Iran has only a limited number of specialized mine vessels, it can also use small craft, LSTs, Boghammers, helicopters, and submarines to lay mines. As a result, it is impossible to determine how many ships Iran would employ to plant or lay mines in a given contingency, and some of its mines might be air dropped or laid by commercial vessels, including dhows.

Iran has a range of Soviet-, Western-, and Iranian-made moored and drifting contact mines, and U.S. experts estimate that Iran has at least 2,000 mines. Iran has significant stocks of antiship mines and has bought Chinese-made and North Korean–made versions of the Soviet mines. It has claimed to be making its own nonmagnetic, acoustic, free-floating, and remote-controlled mines and has had Chinese assistance in developing the production facilities for such mines. It may have acquired significant stocks of nonmagnetic mines, influence mines, and mines with sophisticated timing devices from other countries.[55]

There also are reports that Iran has negotiated with China to buy the EM-52 or MN-52 rocket-propelled mine. The EM-52 is a mine that rests on the bottom until it senses a ship passing over it, and then it uses a rocket to hit the target. The maximum depth of the Straits of Hormuz is 80 meters (264 feet), although currents are strong enough to displace all but firmly moored mines.[56] Combined with modern submarine laid mines and antiship missile systems like the CS-801/802 and the SS-N-22, the EM-52 would give Iran considerable capability to harass Gulf shipping and even the potential capability to close the Gulf until U.S. naval and airpower could clear the mines and destroy the missile launchers and submarines.

Even obsolete moored mines have proven difficult to detect and sweep when intelligence does not detect the original laying and size of the minefield, and free-floating mines can be used to present a constant hazard to shipping. Bottom-influence mines can use acoustic, magnetic, or pressure sensors to detect ships passing overhead. They can use multiple types of sensor/actuators to make it hard to deceive the mines and force them to release, can be set to release only after a given number of ships pass, and some can be set to attack ships only of a given size or noise profile. Such mines are extremely difficult to detect and sweep, particularly when they are spaced at wide intervals in shipping lanes.

Iranian Amphibious Assets

Iran has significant amphibious assets compared to other Gulf countries, and the regular navy and the naval branch of the IRGC operate independent marine forces. These assets are large enough to move a battalion-sized force relatively rapidly; they include three Hengam-class (Larak-class) LST amphibious support ships (displacement of 2,940 tons loaded) that can carry up to six tanks, 600 tons of cargo, and 227 troops; three Iran Hormuz–class (South Korean) LSTs (2,014 tons loaded) that can carry up to nine tanks and berth 140 troops; and three Hormuz-21–class 1, 80-ton LSTs and three Fouque-class 176-ton landing ship logistics (LSLs).

These capabilities are not large enough, however, to sustain large-scale operations across the Gulf. Iran's amphibious ships give it the capability to deploy about 1,000 troops and, theoretically, about 30–40 tanks in an amphibious assault—but Iran has never demonstrated that it has an effective over-the-shore capability. Iran might use commercial ferries and roll-on–roll-off ships if it felt they could survive. Iran has also built up its capability to hide or shelter small ships in facilities on its islands and coastline along the Gulf and has the ability to provide them with defensive cover from antiair and antiship missiles.

Iran has support ships, but these are generally insufficient to sustain "blue-water" operations and support an amphibious task force. It has one Kharg-class 33,014-ton replenishment ship, two Bandar Abbas–class 4,673-ton fleet supply ships and oilers, one 14,410-ton repair ship, two 12,000-ton water tankers, seven 1,300-ton Delva-class support ships, five to six Hendijan-class support vessels, two floating dry docks, and 20 tugs, tenders, and utility craft to help support a large naval or amphibious operation.

Iran's training to date has focused on amphibious raiding, however, and not on operations using heavy weapons or larger operations. Iran lacks the air and surface power to move its amphibious forces across the Gulf in the face of significant air/ sea defenses or to support a landing in a defended area.

Iranian Naval Air

The Iranian Navy's air capability consists of two to three operational P-3F Orion maritime patrol aircraft out of an original inventory of five. According to reports from the Gulf, none of the surviving P-3Fs have fully operational radars, and their crews often use binoculars. It also has up to ten Sikorsky SH-3D ASW helicopters, three RH-53D mine-laying helicopters, and seven Agusta-Bell AB-212 helicopters.

Iran uses air force AH-1J attack helicopters, equipped with French AS-12 missiles, in naval missions, and has adapted Hercules C-130 and Fokker Friendship aircraft for mine-laying and patrol missions. The most significant recent development in Iran's capabilities to use airpower to attack naval targets has been the acquisition of the CS-801K for its regular air force.

Iran's Submarine Forces

Iran has attempted to offset the weakness of its major surface forces by obtaining three Type 877EKM Kilo-class submarines. The Kilo is a relatively modern and quiet submarine that first became operational in 1980. The Iranian Kilos are Type 877EKM export versions that are about 10 meters longer than the original Kilos and are equipped with advanced command and control systems. Each Type 877EKM has a teardrop hull coated with anechoic tiles to reduce noise. It displaces approximately 3,076 tons when submerged and 2,325 tons when surfaced. It is 72.6 meters long, 9.9 meters in beam, has a draught of 6.6 meters, and is powered by three 1,895-horsepower (HP) generator sets, one 5,900 shaft horsepower (SHP) electric motor, and one six-bladed propeller. It has a complement of 52 men and an endurance of 45 days. Its maximum submerged speed is 17 knots, and its maximum surface speed is 10 knots.

Each Kilo has six 530-mm torpedo tubes, including two wire-guided torpedo tubes. Only one torpedo can be wire guided at a time. The Kilo can carry a mix of 18 homing and wire-guided torpedoes or 24 mines. Russian torpedoes are available with ranges of 15–19 kilometers, speeds of 29–40 knots, and warheads with 100-, 205-, and 305-kilogram weights. Their guidance systems include active sonar homing, passive homing, wire guidance, and active homing. Some reports indicate that Iran bought over 1,000 modern Soviet mines with the Kilos and that the mines were equipped with modern magnetic, acoustic, and pressure sensors. The Kilo has a remote antiaircraft launcher with one preloaded missile in the sail, and Soviet versions have six SA-N-5 (Igla/SA-16) surface-to-air missiles stored inside. However, Russia supplied Iran only with the SA-14 (Strela). It can be modernized to carry Chinese YJ-1 or Russian Novator Alfa surface-to-surface missiles.[57]

The Kilo has a maximum surface speed of 10 knots, a maximum submerged speed of about 17 knots, a minimum submerged operating depth of about 30 meters, an operational diving depth of 240 meters, and a maximum diving depth of 300 meters. The submarine also has a surface cruise range of 3,000–6,000 nautical miles and a submerged cruise range of 400 nautical miles—depending on speed and combat conditions.[58]

Iran's ability to use its submarines to deliver mines and fire long-range wake-homing torpedoes gives it a potential capability to strike in ways that make it difficult to detect or attack the submarine. Mines can be laid covertly in critical areas before a conflict, and the mines can be set to activate and deactivate at predetermined intervals in ways that make mining difficult to detect and sweep. Long-range homing torpedoes can be used against tanker-sized targets at ranges in excess of 10 kilometers and to attack slow-moving combat ships that are not on alert and/or that lack sonars and countermeasures.

At the same time, many Third World countries have found submarines to be difficult to operate. For example, Russia delivered the first two Kilos with two 120-cell batteries designed for rapid power surges, rather than power over long periods. They proved to last only one to two years in warm waters vs. five to seven years for similar batteries from India and the United Kingdom. Iran had to turn to India for help in developing batteries that are reliable in the warm waters of the Gulf. Iran has also had problems with the air conditioning in the ships, and their serviceability has been erratic. There are serious questions about crew capability and readiness, and all three submarines already need significant refits.

Iran faces significant operational problems in using its submarines in local waters. Many areas of the Gulf do not favor submarine operations. The Gulf is about 241,000 square kilometers in area and stretches 990 kilometers from the Shatt al-Arab to the Straits of Hormuz. It is about 340 kilometers wide at its maximum width and about 225 kilometers wide for most of its length. While heat patterns disturb surface sonars, they also disturb submarine sonars, and the advantage seems to be slightly in favor of sophisticated surface ships and maritime patrol aircraft.

The deeper parts of the Gulf are noisy enough to make ASW operations difficult, but large parts of the Gulf—including much of the southern Gulf on a line from Al Jubail across the tip of Qatar to about half way up the United Arab Emirates—are less than 20 meters deep. The water is deeper on the Iranian side, but the maximum depth of the Gulf—located about 30 kilometers south of Qeys Island—is still only 88 meters. This means that no point in the Gulf is deeper than the length of an SN-688 nuclear submarine. The keel to tower height of such a submarine alone is 16 meters. Even smaller coastal submarines have maneuver and bottom suction problems, cannot hide in thermoclines, or take advantage of diving for concealment or self-protection. This may explain why Iran is planning to relocate its submarines from Bandar Abbas, inside the Gulf, to Chah Bahar in the Gulf of Oman and is deepening the navy facility at Chah Bahar.[59]

The Strait of Hormuz at the entrance to the Gulf is about 180 kilometers long, but has a minimum width of 39 kilometers, and only the two deep-water channels are suitable for major surface ship or submarine operations. Further, a limited flow of fresh water and high evaporation makes the Gulf extremely salty. This creates complex underwater currents in the main channels at the Straits of Hormuz and complicates both submarine operations and submarine detection. There are some areas with considerable noise, but not of a type that masks submarine noise from sophisticated ASW detection systems of the kind operated by the United States and the United Kingdom. Further, the minimum operating depth of the Kilo is 45 meters, and the limited depth of the area around the Straits can make submarine operations difficult. Submarines are easier to operate in the Gulf of Oman, which is noisy enough to make ASW operations difficult, but such deployments would expose the Kilos to operations by U.S. and British nuclear attack submarines. It is unlikely that Iran's Kilos could survive for any length of time if hunted by a U.S. or British navy air-surface-SSN (nuclear submarine) hunter-killer team.[60]

In any case, the effectiveness of Iran's submarines is likely to depend heavily on the degree of Western involvement in any ASW operation. If the Kilos did not face the U.S. or British ASW forces, the Iranian Kilos could operate in or near the Gulf with considerable impunity. If they did face U.S. and British forces, they might be able to attack a few tankers or conduct some mining efforts, but are unlikely to survive extended combat. This makes the Kilos a weapon that may be more effective in threatening Gulf shipping, or as a remote minelayer, than in naval combat. Certainly, Iran's purchase of the Kilos has already received close attention from the southern Gulf States and convinced them that they must take Iran more seriously.

The Role of the Naval Branch of the IRGC

Iran's unconventional warfare capabilities include the naval branch of the Islamic Revolutionary Guards Corps that operates Iran's land-based antiship missiles and coastal defense artillery. In addition to its land- and sea-based antiship missile forces, the naval guards can use large numbers of small patrol boats equipped with heavy machine guns, grenade launchers, antitank guided weapons, man-portable surface-to-air missiles, and 106-mm recoilless rifles.

The IRGC also uses small launches, and at least 30 Zodiak rubber dinghies, to practice rocket, small arms, and recoilless rifle attacks. Its other small craft were armed with a mix of machine guns, recoilless rifles, and man- and crew-portable anti-tank guided missiles. These vessels are difficult to detect by radar in anything but the calmest seas. Iran bases them at a number of offshore islands and oil platforms, and they can strike quickly and with limited warning. The Naval Branch of the IRGC also has naval artillery, divers, and mine-laying units. It had extensive stocks of scuba equipment and an underwater combat center at Bandar Abbas.[61] Iran is also improving the defenses and port capabilities of its islands in the Gulf, adding covered moorings, more advanced sensors, and better air defenses.

Iran can use IRGC forces to conduct the kind of low-intensity/guerrilla warfare that can be defeated only by direct engagement with land forces and can filter substantial reinforcements into a coastal area on foot or with light vehicles, making such reinforcement difficult to attack. Iran can use virtually any surviving small craft to lay mines and to place unmoored mines in shipping lanes. Its IRGC forces can use small craft to attack offshore facilities and raid coastal targets. Finally, it is important to note the United States did not successfully destroy a single land-based Iraqi antiship missile launcher during the Gulf War, and the IRGC now has many dispersal launch sites and storage areas over a much longer coast. It also has a growing number of caves, shelters, and small hardened facilities. Such targets are sometimes difficult to detect until they are used, and they present added problems because they usually are too small and too numerous to attack with high cost ordnance until it is clear they have valuable enough contents to merit such an attack.

Naval Force Deployments

The main forces of the Iranian Navy are concentrated in the Gulf. Iran gives more importance to the security of its territorial sea in the Gulf area since in this direction it has highly complicated relations with various Arab nations, the United States, and Israel. After the collapse of the Soviet Union, however, Iran's policy toward the Caspian Sea area has changed. According to the contracts between the Soviet Union and

Iran, Tehran was not allowed to station its navy in the Caspian Sea. After the disintegration of the USSR, however, the fourth naval regional forces started representing the Iranian Navy in the Caspian.[62]

The Islamic Republic has almost 3,000 personnel in the Caspian. The forces include up to 50 fighting ships and support vessels, the Marine Corps, coastal guard forces, and the sea aircraft. There are also training vessels in the fleet, including one Shahrokh MSC minesweeper, two Hamzeh ships, and others. Currently, Iran has the second largest fleet in the Caspian after Russia. The fleet, however, is outdated. This is why Tehran has been trying to strengthen its naval forces in the Caspian through various programs. It is reported that the government has numerous plans to modernize its fleet. According to these projects, the future fleet will include several divisions and separate battalions of ships and submarines.[63]

Overall Naval Capabilities

Iran's efforts have steadily improved its capabilities to threaten Gulf shipping and offshore oil facilities, its capability to support unconventional warfare, and its ability to defend its offshore facilities, islands, and coastline. They have not, however, done much to help Iran to act as an effective blue-water navy.

At the same time, the military capability of Iranian naval forces should not be measured in terms of the ability to win a battle for sea control against U.S. and British naval forces or any combination of southern Gulf States supported by U.S. and British forces. For the near future, Iran's forces are likely to lose any such battle in a matter of days. As a result, it is Iran's ability to conduct limited or unconventional warfare, or to threaten traffic through the Gulf, that gives Iran the potential ability to threaten or intimidate its neighbors.

IRAN'S WEAPONS OF MASS DESTRUCTION (WMD) PROGRAM

There is no simple or reliable way to characterize Iran's ability to acquire weapons of mass destruction and the means to deliver them. Iran is clearly attempting to acquire long-range ballistic missiles and cruise missiles, but it has never indicated that such weapons would have CBRN warheads. Iran has never properly declared its holdings of chemical weapons, and the status of its biological weapons programs is unknown.

There have been strong indications of an active Iranian interest in acquiring nuclear weapons since the time of the Shah and that Khomeini revived such efforts after Iraq invaded Iran and began to use chemical weapons. There is, however, no reliable history of such efforts or "smoking gun" that conclusively proves their existence.

The Iranian leadership has consistently argued that its nuclear research efforts are designed for peaceful purposes, although various Iranian leaders have made ambiguous statements about acquiring weapons of mass destruction and Iranian actions strongly suggest that Iran is trying to acquire nuclear weapons. Whether such Iranian deniability is plausible or not is highly questionable, but Iran has been able to find some alternative explanation for even its most suspect activities, and there is no present way to disprove its claims with open source material.

Chemical Weapons

The various claims and counterassertions about Iran's current chemical weapons capabilities are as hard to substantiate as they are to rebut. Open sources are limited and conflicting, and Iranian claims go unchecked. Outside governments have provided some useful summary assessments of Iranian chemical weapons program, but few details.

Official Estimates of Iranian Capability

The CIA has reported that Chinese entities were still trying to supply Iran with chemical warfare (CW)-related chemicals between 1997 and 1998. The U.S. sanctions imposed in May 1997 on seven Chinese entities for knowingly and materially contributing to Iran's CW program remain in effect. In addition, the CIA estimated in January 1999 that Iran obtained material related to chemical warfare from various sources during the first half of 1998. It already has manufactured and stockpiled chemical weapons, including blister, blood, and choking agents and the bombs and artillery shells for delivering them. However, Tehran is seeking foreign equipment and expertise to create a more advanced and self-sufficient CW infrastructure.

The last unclassified U.S. formal assessment of this aspect of Iranian proliferation was released in 2001, and it provided only a broad summary:[64]

Iran has acceded to the Chemical Weapons Convention (CWC) and in a May 1998 session of the CWC Conference of the States Parties, Tehran, for the first time, acknowledged the existence of a past chemical weapons program. Iran admitted developing a chemical warfare program during the latter stages of the Iran-Iraq war as a "deterrent" against Iraq's use of chemical agents against Iran. Moreover, Tehran claimed that after the 1988 cease-fire, it "terminated" its program. However, Iran has yet to acknowledge that it, too, used chemical weapons during the Iran-Iraq War.

Nevertheless, Iran has continued its efforts to seek production technology, expertise and precursor chemicals from entities in Russia and China that could be used to create a more advanced and self-sufficient chemical warfare infrastructure. As Iran's program moves closer to self-sufficiency, the potential will increase for Iran to export dual-use chemicals and related equipment and technologies to other countries of proliferation concern.

In the past, Tehran has manufactured and stockpiled blister, blood and choking chemical agents, and weaponized some of these agents into artillery shells, mortars, rockets, and aerial bombs. It also is believed to be conducting research on nerve agents. Iran could employ these agents during a future conflict in the region. Lastly, Iran's training, especially for its naval and ground forces, indicates that it is planning to operate in a contaminated environment.

In mid-May 2003, the Bush administration released a statement to the Organization for Prohibition of Chemical Weapons in which the United States accused Iran of continuing to pursue production technology, training, and expertise from abroad. The statement asserted that Iran was continuing to stockpile blister, blood, choking, and some nerve agents. This was followed by an unclassified report the CIA released in November 2003 that stated that "Iran is a party to the Chemical Weapons Convention (CWC). Nevertheless, during the reporting period it continued to seek production technology, training, and expertise from Chinese entities that could further Tehran's efforts to achieve an indigenous capability to produce nerve agents. Iran likely has already stockpiled blister, blood, choking, and probably nerve agents—and the bombs and artillery shells to deliver them—which it previously had manufactured."[65]

John R. Bolton, then Under Secretary for Arms Control and International Security at the U.S. Department of State, reported on Iran's chemical program in testimony to the House International Relations Committee Subcommittee on the Middle East and Central Asia in 2005. He reported, however, only in summary terms:[66]

> We believe Iran has a covert program to develop and stockpile chemical weapons. The U.S. Intelligence Community reported in its recent unclassified *Report to Congress on the Acquisition of Technology Relating to Weapons of Mass Destruction and Advanced Conventional Munitions,* also known as the "721 Report," that Iran continues to seek production technology, training, and expertise that could further its efforts to achieve an indigenous capability to produce nerve agents. A forthcoming edition of the 721 report is expected to state that, "Iran may have already stockpiled blister, blood, choking, and nerve agents—and the bombs and artillery shells to deliver them—which it previously had manufactured."
>
> Iran is a party to the Chemical Weapons Convention (CWC). The CWC's central obligation is simple: no stockpiling, no development, no production, and no use of chemical weapons. The overwhelming majority of States Parties abide by this obligation. Iran is not, and we have made this abundantly clear to the Organization for the Prohibition of Chemical Weapons (OPCW). Although Iran has declared a portion of its CW program to the OPCW, it is time for Iran to declare the remainder and make arrangements for its dismantlement and for the destruction of its chemical weapons.

European assessments seem to agree with those of the U.S. Department of Defense (DOD) and the CIA, but there have been only limited public reports. The German Federal Customs Administration published a report in November 2004 that stated, "Iran has an emerging chemical industry. Its CW program obtains support, according to accounts received, from China and India. It probably possesses chemical agents such as sulphur mustards, Tabun, and hydrogen cyanide, possibly also sarin and VC. Iran is attempting to acquire chemical installations and parts thereof, as well as technology and chemical precursors."[67]

Arms Control Estimates of Iranian Capability

Arms control efforts have not provided meaningful transparency, and ratifying the CWC has not guaranteed the end of Tehran's CW programs; it has only meant that if Iran is violating the treaty, it is an "illegal" activity.

Unfortunately, there have been no meaningful inspections or independent analysis of Iran's chemical weapons program. Iran did submit a statement in Farsi to the CWC secretariat in 1998, but this statement consisted only of questions as to the nature of the required compliance. It has not provided the CWC with detailed data on its chemical weapons program. Iran also stridently asserted its right to withdraw from the Convention at any time.

NGO Estimates of Iranian Capability

Some nongovernmental organization (NGO) reporting does provide more detail. A study by the Monterey Institute indicates there are a number of sites in Iran that may be related to Iran's chemical warfare effort:[68]

- **Abu Musa Island:** Iran holds a large number of chemical weapons, principally 155-mm artillery shells, in addition to some weaponized biological agents.
- **Bandar Khomeini:** Allegedly the location of a chemical weapons facility, run by the Razi Chemical Corporation, established during the Iran-Iraq war to manufacture chemical weapons.
- **Damghan:** Either a chemical weapons plant or warhead assembly facility. Primarily involved in 155-mm artillery shells and SCUD warheads.
- **Isfahan:** Suspected location of a chemical weapons facility, possibly operated by the Poly-Acryl Corporation.
- **Karaj:** Located about 14 kilometers from Tehran, this is the site of an alleged storage and manufacturing facility for chemical weapons. Reports suggest that this facility was built with Chinese assistance.
- **Marvdasht:** The Chemical Fertilizers Company is suspected to have been a manufacturing facility for mustard agents during the Iran-Iraq War.
- **Parchin:** The location of at least one munitions factory and is suspected of being a major chemical weapons production facility. Reports of uncertain reliability indicate that the plant was in operation no later than March 1988. In April 1997, a German newspaper reported that, according to the German Federal Intelligence Service, the factories at Parchin were producing primary products for chemical warfare agents.
- **Qazvin:** A large pesticide plant at this location is widely believed to produce nerve gas.
- **Mashar:** Iranian opposition groups have made allegations, of uncertain reliability, that a warhead filling facility is operated at this location.

The Nuclear Threat Initiative summarized what is and is not known about the status of Iran's chemical weapons as follows in January 2006:[69]

Despite its acquisition of precursors from abroad, Iran is allegedly working to develop an indigenous CW production capability. The CIA believes that "Teheran is rapidly approaching self-sufficiency and could become a supplier of CW-related materials to other nations." As of 1996, the Department of Defense claimed that Iran had stockpiled almost 2000 tons of toxic chemical agents and was continuously working on expanding its CW program. Iran has several advanced research institutions employing various chemicals for a variety of reasons, including pesticide production, pharmaceutical research, and other medical studies. Iran has also conducted several military exercises to date that have included defensive chemical and biological weapons maneuvers.

Iran continues to deny any allegations that it is actively pursuing an offensive CW program. In 1996, it held the first regional seminar on the national implementation of the CWC in Tehran so that government authorities could familiarize themselves with their duties and obligations under the treaty. It also held a mock "trial inspection" at the Shahid Razkani chemical factory to allow inspectors to see how such a procedure was conducted. Iran submitted a declaration on its chemical facilities and its past CW stockpile, it has destroyed chemical weapons production equipment in the presence of OPCW inspectors, and it has undergone a number of OPCW inspections of its chemical industrial facilities. Iran continues to play an active role at the Organization for the Prohibition of Chemical Weapons (OPCW), is recognized as a member in good standing, and currently serves on its executive council. Although US and Israeli intelligence agencies continue to insist Iran maintains a stockpile of chemical weapons, no challenge inspections of Iranian facilities have been requested, and none of the allegations made regarding the stockpiling of CW can be verified in the unclassified domain. However, Iran continues to retain a strong incentive for developing a defensive CW program.

Biological Weapons

Any analysis of Iran's biological weapons effort must be even more speculative. In 1997, the U.S. DOD asserted that the Iranian biological warfare (BW) program "is in the research and development [R&D] stage, [but] the Iranians have considerable expertise with pharmaceuticals, as well as the commercial and military infrastructure needed to produce basic biological warfare agents."[70]

The Department updated its findings in 2001 as follows:[71]

> Iran has a growing biotechnology industry, significant pharmaceutical experience and the overall infrastructure to support its biological warfare program. Tehran has expanded its efforts to seek considerable dual-use biotechnical materials and expertise from entities in Russia and elsewhere, ostensibly for civilian reasons. Outside assistance is important for Iran, and it is also difficult to prevent because of the dual-use nature of the materials and equipment being sought by Iran and the many legitimate end uses for these items.
>
> Iran's biological warfare program began during the Iran-Iraq war. Iran is believed to be pursuing offensive biological warfare capabilities and its effort may have evolved beyond agent research and development to the capability to produce small quantities of agent. Iran has ratified the BWC [Biological Weapons Convention].

Since that time, the United States has not significantly updated its unclassified estimates, except to state that such Iranian R&D efforts continue. The problem is whether such statements are a suspicion, a strong probability, or a fact. Iran does have extensive laboratory and research capability and steadily improving industrial facilities with dual-use production capabilities. Whether it has an active weapons development program, however, is a controversial matter.

The reality is that many nations now have the biotechnology, industrial base, and technical expertise to acquire biological weapons. Not only does most civil technology have "dual use" in building weapons, but the global dissemination of biological equipment has made control by supplier nations extremely difficult. Even when such controls do still apply to original sellers, they have little or no impact on the sellers of used equipment, and a wide range of sensitive equipment is now available for sale to any buyer on the Internet.

This makes it almost impossible to disprove a nation's interest in biological weapons. Moreover, there is little meaningful distinction between a "defensive" and an "offensive" capability. Nations can claim to be conducting defensive research, acquiring key gear for defensive purposes, and practicing defensive training and maneuvers.

So far, Iran has not demonstrated any such defensive activities, but there is an active debate over whether it has a biological weapons program.

Possible Early Indicators That Iran Might Have a BW Program

There is a long history of indicators that Iran *might* have some form of BW program. Reports first surfaced in 1982—during the Iran-Iraq War—that Iran had imported suitable type cultures from Europe and was working on the production of mycotoxins—a relatively simple family of biological agents that require only limited laboratory facilities for small-scale production. Many experts believe that the Iranian biological weapons effort was placed under the control of the IRGC, which is known to have tried to purchase suitable production equipment for such weapons.

U.S. intelligence sources reported in August 1989 that Iran was trying to buy two new strains of fungus from Canada and the Netherlands that can be used to produce mycotoxins. German sources indicated that Iran had successfully purchased such cultures several years earlier. Some universities and research centers may be linked to the biological weapons program. The Imam Reza Medical Center at Mashhad University of Medical Sciences and the Iranian Research Organization for Science and Technology were identified as the end users for this purchasing effort, but it is likely that the true end user was an Iranian government agency specializing in biological warfare.

Since the Iran-Iraq War, various reports have surfaced that Iran may have conducted research on more lethal active agents like anthrax, hoof-and-mouth disease, and biotoxins. Iranian groups have repeatedly approached various European firms for equipment and technology that could be used to work with these diseases and toxins.

Unclassified sources of uncertain reliability have identified a facility at Damghan as working on both biological and chemical weapons research and production and believe that Iran may be producing biological weapons at a pesticide facility near Tehran.

Reports also surfaced in the spring of 1993 that Iran had succeeded in obtaining advanced biological weapons technology in Switzerland and containment equipment and technology from Germany. According to these reports, this led to serious damage to computer facilities in a Swiss biological research facility by unidentified agents. Similar reports indicated that agents had destroyed German biocontainment equipment destined for Iran. More credible reports by U.S. experts indicate that Iran might have begun to stockpile anthrax and botulinum in a facility near Tabriz, can now mass manufacture such agents, and has them in an aerosol form. None of these reports, however, can be verified.

The Uncertain Nature of Iran's BW Program Since the Mid-1990s

The CIA reported in 1996, "We believe that Iran holds some stocks of biological agents and weapons. Tehran probably has investigated both toxins and live organisms as biological warfare agents. Iran has the technical infrastructure to support a significant biological weapons program with little foreign assistance." It also reported that Iran has "sought dual-use biotech equipment from Europe and Asia, ostensibly for civilian use," and that Iran might be ready to deploy biological weapons. Beyond this point, little unclassified information exists regarding the details of Iran's effort to "weaponize" and produce biological weapons.

Continuing Alarms and Excursions

Iran announced in June 1997 that it would not produce or employ chemical weapons including biological toxins. However, the CIA reported in June 1997 that Iran had obtained new dual-use technology from China and India during 1996.

Furthermore, the CIA reported in January 1999 that Iran continued to pursue dual-use biotechnical equipment from Russia and other countries, ostensibly for civilian uses. Its BW program began during the Iran-Iraq War, and Iran may have some limited capability for BW deployment. Outside assistance is both important and difficult to prevent, given the dual-use nature of the materials and equipment being sought and the many legitimate end uses for these items.

In 2001, an allegation from the former director of research and development at the Cuban Center for Genetic Engineering and Biotechnology surfaced that claimed Cuba had assisted the Iranian bioweapons program from 1995 to 1998. The authenticity of the director's claims has not been established.[72]

A report produced by an Iranian insurgent group, the Mujahedin-e Khalq (MEK) Organization, asserted in 2003 that Iran had started producing weaponized anthrax and was actively working with at least five other pathogens, including small pox. The MEK was the same organization that produced early evidence of Iran's noncompliance with the terms of the Nuclear Non-Proliferation Treaty (NPT). Iran issued a vehement denial of these charges in a May 16, 2003, press release. The accuracy of either set of statements remains uncertain.

The Possible Role of Outside Suppliers

Russia has been a key source of biotechnology for Iran. Russia's world-leading expertise in biological weapons also makes it an attractive target for Iranians seeking technical information and training on BW agent production processes. This has led to speculation that Iran may have the production technology to make dry storable and aerosol weapons. This would allow it to develop suitable missile warheads, bombs, and covert devices.

In testimony to the Senate Committee on Foreign Relations, John A. Lauder, the Director of the Nonproliferation Center at the CIA, asserted the following in 2000:[73]

> Iran is seeking expertise and technology from Russia that could advance Tehran's biological warfare effort. Russia has several government-to-government agreements with Iran in a variety of scientific and technical fields.
> —Because of the dual-use nature of much of this technology, Tehran can exploit these agreements to procure equipment and expertise that could be diverted to its BW effort.
> —Iran's BW program could make rapid and significant advances if it has unfettered access to BW expertise resident in Russia.

The CIA reported in November 2003, "Even though Iran is part of the BWC, Tehran probably maintained an offensive BW program. Iran continued to seek dual-use biotechnical materials, equipment, and expertise. While such materials had legitimate uses, Iran's biological warfare (BW) program also could have benefited from them. It is likely that Iran has capabilities to produce small quantities of BW agents, but has a limited ability to weaponize them."[74] John R. Bolton, then Under Secretary for Arms Control and International Security at the U.S. Department of State, testified the following to the House International Relations Committee in 2004:[75]

> The U.S. Intelligence Community stated in its recent 721 Report that, "Tehran probably maintains an offensive BW program. Iran continued to seek dual-use biotechnical materials, equipment, and expertise. While such materials had legitimate uses, Iran's biological warfare (BW) program also could have benefited from them. It is likely that Iran has capabilities to produce small quantities of BW agents, but has a limited ability to weaponize them."
> Because BW programs are easily concealed, I cannot say that the United States can prove beyond a shadow of a doubt that Iran has an offensive BW program. The intelligence I have seen suggests that this is the case, and, as a policy matter therefore, I believe we have to act on that assumption. The risks to international peace and security from such programs are too great to wait for irrefutable proof of illicit activity: responsible members of the international community should act to head off such threats and demand transparency and accountability from suspected violators while these threats are still emerging. It would be folly indeed to wait for the threat fully to mature before trying to stop it.

Iran is a party to the Biological Weapons Convention (BWC) and the 1925 Protocol for the Prohibition of the Use in War of Asphyxiating, Poisonous or Other Gases, and of Bacteriological Methods of Warfare. Like the CWC, the central obligation of the BWC is simple: no possession, no development no production and, together with the 1925 Protocol, no use of biological weapons. The overwhelming majority of States Parties abide by these obligations. We believe Iran is not abiding by its BWC obligations, however, and we have made this abundantly clear to the parties of this treaty. It is time for Iran to declare its biological weapons program and make arrangements for its dismantlement.

Possible CBW War-Fighting Capability

These factors make it almost impossible to know how Iran may use any capabilities it does possess. It does not overtly train its forces for offensive chemical warfare, and its current and future war-fighting capabilities are unknown.

Iran has stated its objection to the use of CBW in war on religious grounds—based on Khomeini's statements in the 1980s—and legal obligation under international conventions. Most experts do, however, believe that Iran at least used confiscated Iraqi chemical shells against Iraqi forces. It had definitely instituted its own program to produce chemical weapons and may have used its weapons. The IISS pointed out in its 2005 study of Iran's weapons that "[d]espite a similar record with respect to nuclear weapons and the NPT, Iran conducted undeclared nuclear activities in violation of the treaty for over 20 years. Whether Iran has carried similar activities in violation of its CWC and BWC obligations cannot be determined definitively from the available public information."[76]

It does seem likely that Iran at least retains some capability to make chemical weapons, and it may have inactive or mothballed facilities. There have been no public reports of active production, but this is possible. Iraq produced small lots of mustard gas weapons at the laboratory level before its major production facilities came on-line and showed that it could produce at the batch level with relatively small and easy to conceal facilities. Iran's purchases also indicate that it could have a significant stock of precursors; and some less lethal weapons can be made out of refinery and petrochemical by-products.

Any assessment of Iranian capabilities must also take account of the fact that Iraq began to use chemical weapons against Iran in the early 1980s and that Iran has had at least a quarter of a century in which to react to a real-world threat, six years of which were spent dealing with a nation seeking to acquire chemical, biological, and nuclear weapons to destroy it. Iranian military literature also has extensively reprinted Western and other literature on CBRN weapons, and Iran actively collects such literature on a global basis.

It seems clear that Iran has the technology base to produce mustard gas and non-persistent nerve agents—including reasonable stable agents and binary weapons—and may have the technology to produce persistent nerve agents as well. It probably has technical knowledge of "third generation" and "dusty" agents. It has had the opportunity to reverse engineer captured Iraqi weapons and may have received aid in weapons design from Russian, Chinese, and North Korean sources. It certainly has monitored UN reporting on the Iraqi chemical and biological programs and may have acquired considerable detail on these programs, their strengths and weaknesses, and Iraq's sources abroad.

Iran almost certainly has the ability to make effective chemical artillery shells and bombs and unitary rocket and missile warheads. It can probably design effective cluster bombs and warheads. It may have sprayers for use by aircraft, helicopters, and UAVs. Iran's ability to develop lethal missile warheads is far more problematic. The timing and dissemination problems are far more difficult and may be beyond Iran's current technical skills.

The past history of Iranian efforts at complex program management and systems integration, however, has shown that Iran has serious problems in translating its technical expertise into practice. The knowledge of how to do things rarely leads to similar capability to actually do them, particularly when programs remain concealed and are largely "mothballed" or have low levels of activity.

Testing chemical weapons presents serious problems when the test goes beyond static tests or relative crude measurements of how well given weapons disseminate the agent. It is particularly difficult in the case of missile warheads. It is possible to determine lethality in rough terms from residues, but this requires repeated testing using actual weapons in a variety of real-world conditions. There are no reports of such testing, but it is more than possible that they could be successfully concealed. Unlike most biological weapons, the operational lethality of chemical weapons can be safely tested against live animals. Again, there are no reports of such testing, but it is more than possible that they could be successfully concealed.

The history of actual chemical warfare, however, indicates that the results of such tests can be extremely unrealistic and that operational lethality has rarely approached anything like engineering and test predictions. The "scale-up" of individual weapons results into predictions of real-world results from using large numbers of weapons has produced particularly misleading results. Moreover, as is the case with biological weapons, temperature, weather, sunlight, wind, surface conditions, and a number of external factors can have a major impact on lethality.

These factors, coupled with the difficulty in measuring incapacity or deaths in less than hours to days, also means Iran and other users would have to carry out any chemical campaign with little ability to predict its actual lethality or carry out effective battle damage assessment. Such considerations might not be important, however, when the goal was terror, panic, area denial, forcing an enemy to don protection gear and decontaminate, or accept casualties in addition to other casualties from military operations.

At the same time, all of these factors combine to indicate that even if Iran does have plans and doctrine for using chemical weapons and has made serious efforts to estimate their lethality and effectiveness, such plans are unlikely to survive engagement with reality. Iran's past reports on its military exercises may be propaganda driven, but some of Iran's conventional war-fighting exercises do have a strong element of ideology and wishful thinking and a lack of demanding realism. This could lead military officers and civilian decision makers to make serious miscalculations based on the war they want to fight rather than the war they can fight.

Such considerations would have less impact if Iran chose to use proxies or covert means of attack to strike at high-value targets or for the purposes of terrorism and intimidation. The IRGC has conducted the kind of conventional exercise that could be adapted to such ends, and Iran has long supplied conventional weapons to movements like Hezbollah and Hamas.

Any broader Iran military use of chemical weapons would present a number of problems:

- Chemical weapons are not individually lethal enough to have a major impact on ground battles and take time to be effective. They are best suited to relatively static battles, dominated by ground forces that do not have armored and protected vehicles and which cannot mass airpower effectively. This describes Iran and Iraq in 1980–1988. It does not describe the United States or most of Iran's opponents today. Airpower and sea power are largely immune to the kind of chemical attack Iran could launch, with the possible exception of fixed, targetable area targets—many of which could be denied for any significant time only by large numbers of accurate attacks. Rapidly maneuvering ground forces would be a difficult target for Iran's much more static forces. Nations like the United States would have extensive amounts of detection, protection, and decontamination gear. They also would not have large, static, rear area and support operations near the forward edge of the battle area.

- Iranian artillery tends to be slow moving and lacks the ability to rapidly target and switch fires. It relies heavily on static massed fires. This requires relatively short-range engagement against an equally slow moving or static opponent. In reality, Iran will probably face opponents that maneuver more quickly and have superior intelligence, surveillance, and reconnaissance (IS&R) assets. A repetition of the battlefield conditions of the Iran-Iraq War seems unlikely.

- Chemical weapons could be more effective as area weapons that forced enemy forces to abandon positions, denied the ability to use rear areas, or acted as a barrier to movement. The tactical and maneuver effects were more important in the Iran-Iraq War than using CW as a killing mechanism. They again, however, tend to be most useful against relatively static opponents that do not have air superiority or supremacy.

- Iran has a number of potential long-range artillery rockets and missiles. A single chemical warhead, however, is more a terror weapon than a killing mechanism. Such systems have limited accuracies, and Iran has limited long-range targeting capability against mobile targets. The use of a few chemical rounds would be highly provocative and justify massive escalation by an enemy. As such, it might do more to provoke than terrify, intimidate, or damage. Iran might, however, be able to use persistent nerve and mustard agents to deny the use of a key facility like an air base, key supply facility, mobilization center, oil export facility, or desalination or power plant.

- Effective air strikes require high confidence in the ability to penetrate enemy air defenses and good IS&R assets. In many cases, a chemical weapon would have only marginally greater lethality than a conventional precision-guided weapon or cluster weapon. Again, such use might do more to provoke than terrify, intimidate, or damage.

- The use of chemical weapons against targets at sea presents significant targeting and meteorological problems. These are certainly solvable, but do require exceptional planning and skill. Similarly, firing against coastal targets requires high volumes of CW fire or good meteorological data.

- Covert or proxy use presents serious problems in wartime. Plausible deniability is doubtful, and an opponent simply may not care if it can prove Iran is responsible for any given use of CW.

- Operation lethality is dependent on an opponent's CW defense and decontamination facilities, level of depth, and speed of maneuver. Iran may be dealing with much more sophisticated opponents than the Iraq of the 1980s.

None of these problems and issues mean that Iran could not use chemical weapons effectively under some conditions. They might, however, deter Iran from stockpiling such weapons or using them except under the most drastic conditions. Iran has to understand that their use would tend to make Iran lose the political and information battle and act as a license to its opponent to escalate. While such concerns might well deter Iran under most circumstances, it is also important to understand that wars and drastic crises are not "most circumstances." One inherent problem in any such analysis is that even the most prudent decision maker in peacetime can panic, overreact, or drastically miscalculate in war.

Possible Nuclear Weapons Programs

There is more information available on Iran's nuclear programs than on its chemical and biological programs, but this scarcely eliminates major areas of uncertainty. Estimating Iranian nuclear capabilities is complicated by three key factors:

- First, the United States, the European Union, and the United Nations all agree that Iran has the right to acquire a full nuclear fuel cycle for peaceful purposes under the NPT, but there is no clear way to distinguish many of the efforts needed to acquire a nuclear weapon from such "legitimate" activities or pure research.

- Second, Iran has never denied that it carries out a very diverse range of nuclear research efforts. In fact, it has openly claimed that it is pursuing nuclear technology and has a "national" right to get access to nuclear energy. This has given it a rationale for rejecting Russia's offer to provide Iran nuclear fuel without giving Tehran the technology and the expertise needed to use it for weaponization purposes, and the United States agrees with this position.

- Third, it has never been clear whether Iran does have a "military" nuclear program that is separate from its "civilian" nuclear research. American and French officials have argued that they believe that Iran's nuclear program would make sense only if it had military purposes. Both governments have yet to provide evidence to prove these claims.

If Iran is a proliferator, it has shown that it is a skilled one that is highly capable of hiding many aspects of its programs, sending confusing and contradictory signals, exploiting both deception and the international inspection process, rapidly changing the character of given facilities, and pausing and retreating when this is expedient. It has also shown that denial can be a weapon; by consistently finding an alternative explanation for all its actions, including concealment and actions that are limited violations of the NPT, it can maintain some degree of "plausible deniability" for a long chain of ambiguous actions and events.

Problems in Analyzing Iran's WMD Program: A Case Study

Iran also presents major problems in intelligence collection and analysis. The details of U.S., British, and other intelligence efforts to cover Iran remain classified. At the same time, studies of U.S. and British intelligence failures in covering Iraq have provided considerable insights into the difficulties in covering a nation like Iran, and background discussions with intelligence analysts and users reveal the following general problems in analyzing the WMD threat:

- The uncertainties surrounding collection on virtually all proliferation and weapons of mass destruction programs are so great that it is impossible to produce meaningful point estimates. As the CIA has shown in some of its past public estimates of missile proliferation, the intelligence community must first develop a matrix of what is and is not known about a given aspect of proliferation in a given country, with careful footnoting or qualification of the problems in each key source. It must then deal with uncertainty by creating estimates that show a range of possible current and projected capabilities—carefully qualifying each case. In general, at least three scenarios or cases need to be analyzed for each major aspect of proliferation in each country—something approaching a "best," "most likely," and "worst case."[77]

- Even under these conditions, the resulting analytic effort faces serious problems. Security compartmentation within each major aspect of collection and analysis severely limits the flow of data to working analysts. The expansion of analytic staffs has sharply increased the barriers to the flow of data and has brought large numbers of junior analysts into the process who can do little more than update past analyses and judgments. Far too little analysis is subjected to technical review by those who have actually worked on weapons development, and the analysis of delivery programs, warheads and weapons, and chemical, biological, and nuclear proliferation tends to be compartmented. Instead of the free flow of data and exchange of analytic conclusions, or "fusion" of intelligence, analysis is "stovepiped" into separate areas of activity. Moreover, the larger staffs get, the more stovepiping tends to occur.

- Analysis tends to focus on technical capability and not on the problems in management and systems integration that often are the real-world limiting factors in proliferation. This tends to push analysis toward exaggerating the probable level of proliferation, particularly because technical capability is often assumed if collection cannot provide all the necessary information.

- Where data are available on past holdings of weapons and the capability to produce such weapons—such as data on chemical weapons feedstocks and biological growth material—the intelligence effort tends to produce estimates of the maximum size of the possible current holding of weapons and WMD materials. While ranges are often shown, and estimates are usually qualified with uncertainty, this tends to focus users on the worst case in terms of actual current capability. In the case of Iraq, this was compounded by some 12 years of constant lies and a disbelief that a dictatorship obsessed with record keeping could not have records if it had destroyed weapons and materials. The end result, however, was to assume that little or no destruction had occurred whenever the United Nations Special Commission, the United Nations Monitoring, Verification and Inspection Commission, and the IAEA reported that major issues still affected Iraqi claims.

• Intelligence analysis has long been oriented more toward arms control and counterproliferation rather than war fighting, although the Defense Intelligence Agency and the military services have attempted to shift the focus of analysis. Dealing with broad national trends and assuming capability is not generally a major problem in seeking to push nations toward obeying arms control agreements or in pressuring possible suppliers. It also is not a major problem in analyzing broad military counterproliferation risks and programs. The situation is very different in dealing with war-fighting choices, particularly issues like preemption and targeting. Assumptions of capability can lead to preemption that is not necessary, overtargeting, inability to prioritize, and a failure to create the detailed collection and analysis necessary to support war fighters down to the battalion level. This, in turn, often forces field commanders to rely on field teams with limited capability and expertise and to overreact to any potential threat or warning indicator.

• The intelligence community does bring outside experts into the process, but often simply to provide advice in general terms rather than cleared review of the intelligence product. The result is often less than helpful. The use of other cleared personnel in U.S. laboratories and other areas of expertise is inadequate and often presents major problems because those consulted are not brought fully into the intelligence analysis process and given all of the necessary data.

• The intelligence community does tend to try to avoid explicit statements of the shortcomings in collection and methods in much of its analysis and to repeat past agreed judgments on a lowest common denominator level—particularly in the form of the intelligence products that get broad circulation to consumers. Attempts at independent outside analysis or "B-Teams," however, are not subject to the review and controls enforced on intelligence analysis, and the teams, collection data, and methods used are generally selected to prove given points rather than to provide an objective counterpoint to finished analysis.[78]

Few of these problems have been explicitly addressed in open source reporting on Iran, and it is uncertain from the reporting on past intelligence failures in the intelligence analysis of Iraq before the 2003 invasion that the intelligence community has covered them at the classified level.

Part of the problem lies with the user. Policy-level and other senior users of intelligence tend to be intolerant of analysis that consists of a wide range of qualifications and uncertainties even at the best of times, and the best of times do not exist when urgent policy and war-fighting decisions need to be made. Users inevitably either force the intelligence process to reach something approaching a definitive set of con-clusions or else they make such estimates themselves.

Intelligence analysts and managers are all too aware of this fact. Experience has taught them that complex intelligence analysis—filled with alternative cases, proba-bility estimates, and qualifications about uncertainty—generally go unused or make policy makers and commanders impatient with the entire intelligence process. In the real world, hard choices have to be made to provide an estimate that can actually be used and acted upon, and these choices must be made either by the intelligence community or by the user.[79]

Uncertainty and Credibility of Sources

If one looks at other sources of reporting on Iran, there have been many claims from many corners. First, one source is from opposition groups that are largely asso-ciated with MEK. Their information has proven to be useful at times, yet some of the data they provided has been "too good to be true." The National Council of Re-sistance of Iran (NCRI) revelations about Iran's secret nuclear program did prove to be the trigger point in inviting the IAEA into Tehran for inspections, but their claims about "5,000 centrifuges" were seen by many as an exaggeration or at least an uncon-firmed allegation.[80]

The source of such claims must be taken into account. Mr. Alireza Jafarzadeh is the former President of NCRI, which is associated with MEK—an organization that is considered by the U.S. State Department as a terrorist organization. Its motives are well known, and its information must be considered with a certain level of skepticism. As a former CIA counterintelligence official said, "I would take anything from them with a grain of salt."[81]

NCRI claimed that it relied on human sources, including scientists and civilians working in the facilities or locals who live near the sites. In addition, the NCRI claimed at times that its sources are inside the Iranian regime and added, "Our sour-ces were 100 percent sure about their intelligence."[82] The NCRI did not provide any confirmation about their sources, and their information is considered by some in the U.S. and European governments as less than credible. Another example was NCRI's claim in September 2004 that Tehran allocated $16 billion to build a nuclear bomb by mid-2005. This again was proven to be inaccurate.[83]

Second, U.S. officials have cited "walk-in" sources to prove the existence of an Ira-nian nuclear program. It is unclear who those sources are, but the United States insisted that they were not associated with the NCRI. In November 2004, U.S. offi-cials claimed that a source provided U.S. intelligence with more than 1,000 pages worth of technical documents on Iranian "nuclear warhead design" and missile mod-ifications to deliver an atomic warhead. In addition, it was reported that the docu-ments also included "specific" warhead design based on implosion and adjustments, which was thought to be an attempt at fitting a warhead to Iranian bal-listic missiles.[84]

According to the *Washington Post,* the walk-in source that provided the documents was not previously known to U.S. intelligence. In addition, it was not clear if this source was connected to an exile group. The same source was, apparently, the basis for the comments by then Secretary of State Colin Powell on November 17, 2004, when he said, "I have seen some information that would suggest that they have been actively working on delivery systems...You don't have a weapon until you put it in something that can deliver a weapon...I'm not talking about uranium or fissile material or the warhead; I'm talking about what one does with a warhead."[85]

Press reports indicate that walk-in documents came from one source and were without independent verifications. The uncertainty about this source, reportedly, stopped many in the U.S. government from using the information, and some expressed their surprise when Secretary Powell expressed confidence in the information provided. Some saw it as a reminder of the problems in his presentation to the UN regarding Iraqi WMD and hoped that he had not made those remarks before they were confirmed. Some U.S. officials even went as far as saying that Powell "misspoke" when he was talking about the information.[86]

Other U.S. officials described the intelligence as "weak."[87] Other press reports claimed that the source, who was "solicited with German help," provided valuable intelligence that referred to a "black box," which U.S. officials claim was a metaphor to refer to nuclear warhead design. One U.S. official was quoted by the *Wall Street Journal* as saying the documents represented "nearly a smoking gun," yet the same official claimed that this was not a definitive proof.[88]

Third, there are sources within Iran who have cooperated with the IAEA. According to IAEA reports, Iranian nuclear scientists were interviewed on specific questions. For example, in November 2003, the Agency requested clarification on the bismuth irradiation. The IAEA reported that in January 2004, it "was able to interview two Iranian scientists involved in the bismuth irradiation. According to the scientists, two bismuth targets had been irradiated, and an attempt had been made, unsuccessfully, to extract polonium from one of them."[89]

The credibility of these scientists depends on how much freedom they have to talk about specific issues, their level of involvement, and the nature of the questions posed to them. The nature of access and the type of information provided to the IAEA by Iranian scientists remain uncertain.

Fourth, independent intelligence gathered by the United States, the European Union, and regional powers have no obvious substitute. The IAEA and the UN do not have their own intelligence and have to rely on member states to provide them with the necessary information. These include satellite images, electronic intercepts, human intelligence, and various forms of information gathering and intelligence analysis. The history of the U.S. and the U.K. intelligence provided to UN inspectors in Iraq, however, showed the limited ability of many intelligence agencies to get a full picture of a country's nuclear, biological, chemical, and missile programs.

Key Uncertainties in Iran's Nuclear Developments

While Iran and Iraq are very different cases, much the same level of uncertainty exists. Almost no one believes that Iran has nuclear weapons, is so close to acquiring them, or presents a time-urgent threat. Many believe, however, that it is a matter of when rather than if before Tehran acquires nuclear weapons. That is, once Iran gets the capability to produce the materials necessary to producing a nuclear cycle, Iran would acquire the capabilities to produce a full nuclear weapon.

The previous history has also revealed Iran's attempts to acquire nuclear technology long before the 1979 Revolution. It is also clear from IAEA discoveries that Iran has pursued two key tracks: uranium enrichment and production of plutonium.[90] Both of these tracks can produce the materials that can be used for nuclear reactors and for nuclear weapons. The IAEA, however, does not believe that Iran has yet been successful in achieving either goal. Mohamed ElBaradei, the Director General of the IAEA, was quoted saying, "To develop a nuclear weapon, you need a significant quantity of highly enriched uranium or plutonium, and no one has seen that in Iran."[91]

Plutonium Production

Tehran has followed two different tracks to achieve the capacity to produce plutonium. First, it is building heavy-water production plants, which U.S. officials claim that their only purpose is to supply heavy water that is optimal for producing weapons-grade plutonium. The Iranian government, on the other hand, has claimed that their purpose is for isotope production for its civilian nuclear energy program.[92]

The second track followed the production of light-water power reactors. The main reactor is at Bushehr, which is designed to produce civilian nuclear technology. Bushehr is also the reactor that Russia agreed to supply its fuel and recover the spent fuel from the reactor. The U.S. Under Secretary for Arms Control and International Security, John R. Bolton, claimed that Bushehr would produce enough plutonium per year to manufacture nearly 30 nuclear weapons.[93]

The following chronology by the IAEA shows the history of Iran's plutonium separation experiments:[94]

- **1987–1988:** The separation process was simulated using imported unirradiated UO_2 (DU); dissolution and purification took place in the Shariaty Building at TNRC [Tehran Nuclear Research Center]; pressed and sintered pellets were manufactured using imported UO_2 (DU) at FFL; the UO_2 pellets were further manipulated into aluminum and stainless steel capsules at FFL.

- **1988–1993:** The capsules (containing a total of 7 kilograms of UO_2 in the form of powder, pressed pellets, and sintered pellets) were irradiated in TRR.

- **1991–1993:** Plutonium was separated from some of the irradiated UO_2 targets in the capsules (about 3 kilograms of the 7 kilograms of UO_2) and plutonium solutions produced; these activities were carried out at the Shariaty Building and, after the activities were transferred in October/November 1992, at the Chamaran Building at

TNRC; the research and development related irradiation and separation of plutonium were terminated in 1993.

- • **1993–1994:** The unprocessed irradiated UO_2 was initially stored in capsules in the spent fuel pond of TRR and was later transferred into four containers and buried behind the Chamaran Building.

- • **1995:** In July, purification of the plutonium solution from the 1988–1993 period was carried out in the Chamaran Building; a planchet (disk) was prepared from the solution for analysis.

- • **1998:** In August, additional purification of plutonium from the 1988–1993 period was carried out in the Chamaran Building; another planchet (disk) was prepared from the solution for analysis.

- • **2000:** The glove boxes from the Chamaran Building were dismantled and sent to ENTC [Isfahan Nuclear Technology Center] for storage; one glove box was moved to the Molybdenum Iodine Xenon Facility.

- • **2003:** Due to construction work being carried out behind the Chamaran Building, two containers holding the unprocessed irradiated UO_2 were dug up, moved, and reburied.

In September 2005, the IAEA analysis of Iran's plutonium separation experiments concluded that the solutions that were tested were 12–16 years old, which seemed to corroborate Iran's claims. In addition, the IAEA carried out verification tests for unprocessed irradiated UO_2 targets stored in four containers, and these results also conformed to Iranian claims, although the IAEA argued that the number of targets provided by Iran was much lower than the actual ones it has. The IAEA reported in September 2005, "A final assessment of Iran's plutonium research activities must await the results of the destructive analysis of the disks and targets."[95]

Uranium Enrichment

Many weapons experts believe that the Iranian uranium enrichment program is much more advanced and does not rely on Iran's nuclear reactors. Former Chief UN weapons inspector in Iraq, Hans Blix, has said that Tehran's plans to build a 40-megawatt research reactor at Bushehr, which is considered Iran's main plutonium production facility, should not be the main concern. He argued that the light-water reactor was not ideal for plutonium production. He added, "What is uncomfortable and dangerous is that they have acquired the capacity to enrich uranium of their own uranium that they dig out of the ground...If you can enrich to five percent you can enrich it to 85 percent."[96]

These concerns were further exacerbated following Iranian President Mahmoud Ahmadinejad's announcement on April 11, 2006, that Iran was successful at enriching uranium. "At this historic moment, with the blessings of God almighty and the efforts made by our scientists, I declare here that the laboratory-scale nuclear fuel cycle has been completed and young scientists produced enriched uranium needed to the degree for nuclear power plants [on April 9]." The head of the Atomic Energy Agency of Iran (AEOI) and Iran's Vice President, Gholamreza Aghazadeh, and Iranian nuclear scientists stated Iran's accomplishments and/or goals as follows:[97]

- Started enriching uranium to a level—3.5 percent—needed for fuel on a research scale using 164 centrifuges, but not enriched enough to build a nuclear bomb;
- Produced 110 tons of uranium hexafluoride (UF_6)—this amount is nearly double the amount that Iran claimed to have enriched in 2005;
- Aim[s] to produce a gas high with an increased percentage of U-235, the isotope needed for nuclear fission, which is much rarer than the more prevalent isotope U-238; and
- Plan[s] to expand its enrichment program to be able to use 3,000 centrifuges at the nuclear center at Natanz by the end of 2006.

Mohammad Saeedi, Iran's Deputy Nuclear Chief, reiterated that Iran aimed to expand uranium enrichment to industrial scale at Natanz. In addition to installing 3,000 centrifuges at Natanz by 2006, Saeedi claimed that Iran aims at expanding the total number of centrifuges to 54,000, which would be used to fuel a 1,000-megawatt nuclear power plant.[98]

While some believe that Iran's claims are credible, others speculated that Iran made the announcement to send a message that military strikes or sanctions would not deter Iran from achieving a full nuclear cycle. Much depends on what the announcement really meant. Iran had previously obtained at least 2-percent enrichment from the experimental use of centrifuges and possibly significantly higher levels. The IAEA had previously made it clear that it lacked the data to determine how far Iran had actually progressed. Iran also had reached enrichment levels as high as 8 percent making experimental use of laser isotope separation, although it seemed far from being able to scale such efforts up beyond laboratory tests.

The Iranian claims also said nothing about how efficient the claimed use of a small 164-centrifuge chain was, what its life cycle and reliability was, and about the ability to engineer a system that could approach weapons-grade material. It is at best possible to speculate on how many centrifuges of the P1-type centrifuge derivative involved Iran would need to get a nuclear device and then move on to develop a significant weapons-production capability. It would, however, probably be in the thousands in terms of continuously operating machine equivalents to slowly get the fissile material for a single device or "bomb in the basement," and tens of thousands to support a serious nuclear weapons delivery capability.

One thing was already clear long before these Iranian claims. There was nothing the UN or the United States could do to deny Iran the technology to build a nuclear weapon. The IAEA's discoveries had made it clear Iran already had functioning centrifuge designs, reactor development capability, and plutonium separation capability. It had experimented with polonium in ways that showed it could make a neutron initiator, had the technology to produce high explosive lenses and beryllium reflectors, could machine fissile material, and had long had a technology base capable of performing the same nonfissile of actual weapons designs used by Pakistan in its nuclear weapons design efforts. It also seemed highly likely that it had acquired P2 centrifuge designs and the same basic Chinese design data for a fissile weapon suitable for mounting on a ballistic missile that North Korea had sold to Libya.

As a result, both the claims of the Iranian President that Iran had made a major breakthrough, and President Bush's responding statement that Iran would not be allowed to acquire the technology to build a nuclear weapon, seemed to be little more than vacuous political posturing. Ahmadinejad's statement seemed to be an effort to show the UN that it could not take meaningful action and exploit Iranian nationalism. The Bush statement was a combination of basic technical ignorance on the part of his speech writers and an effort to push the UN toward action and to convince Iran that it could face the threat of both serious sanctions and military action if diplomacy and sanctions failed. It effectively ignored the fact that Iran not only already had the technology, but could disperse it to the point where it was extremely unlikely that any UN inspection effort could find it, even if Iran allowed this, or any military option could seriously affect Iran's technology base—as distinguished from its ability to create survivable large-scale production facilities and openly deploy nuclear-armed delivery systems.

In reality, such developments were at most evolutionary and had been expected. Diplomats and officials from the IAEA were quick to point out that the announcement by Iran should not be a sign of concern and that Iran may face many technical hurdles before it can enrich enough quantities of uranium at high levels to produce a nuclear weapon. One European official said that while the 164-machine centrifuges were more industrial, "...it's not like they haven't come close to achieving this in the past." This assessment has been reflected in reports by the IAEA, which argue that Iran has used centrifuges and laser to enrich uranium throughout the 1990s and even before.[99]

To put such rhetoric in context, most of Tehran's uranium conversion experiments took place between 1981 and 1993 at the Tehran Nuclear Research Center (TNRC) and at the Isfahan Nuclear Technology Center (ENTC). In this case, however, it is clear that some of these activities continued throughout 2002. According to the IAEA, Iran's uranium enrichment activities also received some foreign help in 1991. The IAEA outlined its findings regarding Tehran's uranium enrichment as follows:[100]

In 1991, Iran entered into discussions with a foreign supplier for the construction at Esfahan of an industrial scale conversion facility. Construction on the facility, UCF, was begun in the late 1990s. UCF consists of several conversion lines, principal among which is the line for the conversion of UOC to UF6 with an annual design production capacity of 200 t uranium as UF6. The UF6 is to be sent to the uranium enrichment facilities at Natanz, where it will be enriched up to 5% U-235 and the product and tails returned to UCF for conversion into low enriched UO2 and depleted uranium metal. The design information for UCF provided by Iran indicates that conversion lines are also foreseen for the production of natural and enriched (19.7%) uranium metal, and natural UO2. The natural and enriched (5% U-235) UO2 are to be sent to the Fuel Manufacturing Plant (FMP) at Esfahan, where Iran has said it will be processed into fuel for a research reactor and power reactors....

In March 2004, Iran began testing the process lines involving the conversion of UOC into UO2 and UF4, and UF4 into UF6. As of June 2004, 40 to 45 kg of UF6 had been produced. A larger test, involving the conversion of 37 t of yellowcake into UF4, was initiated in August 2004. According to Iran's declaration of 14 October 2004, 22.5 t of the 37 t of yellowcake had been fed into the process and that approximately 2 t of UF4, and 17.5 t of uranium as intermediate products and waste, had been produced. There was no indication as of that date of UF6 having been produced during this later campaign.

The IAEA inspections found traces of contamination from advanced enrichment effects at Natanz. Iran claimed that these contaminations were from equipment it purchased in the 1980s from abroad (presumably from Pakistan). Reports by the IAEA, however, showed that Iran may have started its enrichment program in the 1970s and that the Iranians were already partially successful at uranium conversion.

Iran has tried two different methods to enrich uranium ever since the time of the Shah. First, Iran's nuclear research has facilities that are dedicated to manufacturing and testing centrifuges. This includes its ultimate goal of producing 50,000 centrifuges in Natanz. Second, Iran also pursued enriching uranium through laser enrichment. According to Mohamed ElBaradei, the Director General of the IAEA, Iran was able to enrich up to 1.2 percent using centrifuges and up to 15 percent using lasers.[101]

Some of Iran's gas centrifuge program depended on help Tehran got from Pakistan. Although reports by the Director General of the IAEA do not mention Pakistan by name, Iran's gas centrifuges could be traced back to the mid-1990s when A.Q. Khan approached an Iranian company and offered it P-1 documentation and components for 500 centrifuges. Iran claimed that it received only the P-1 and not the P-2 design (the P-1 and P-2 refer to two designs for centrifuges by Pakistan). Both Iran and Pakistan would later admit to this transaction and provide the documents to support these allegations.[102]

According to the IAEA, Tehran received P-1 components and documentation in January 1994. Tehran, however, claimed that it did not receive the first of these components until October 1994. Regardless of the month of delivery, there is one more important element that remains unresolved. The IAEA refers to this as the "1987 offer," which reportedly provided Iran with a sample machine, drawings, descriptions, and specifications for production and material for 2,000 centrifuge machines.[103]

In addition, Iran received the P-2 design in 1994/1995 from Pakistan, but all of its components were designed and manufactured in Iran. Furthermore, Iran claimed that it did not pursue any work on the P-2 design between 1995 and 2002 due to shortages in staff and resources at the AEOI and that Tehran focused on resolving outstanding issues regarding the P-1 design. The IAEA, however, was not convinced that Iran did not pursue further development of the P-2 design and called on Iran in September 2005 to provide more information on the history of its P-2 development.[104]

This helps explain why experts have argued that Iran's goal of producing 50,000 centrifuges in Natanz should be considered a sign of serious concern for the international community. For example, David Albright and Corey Hinderstein of the Institute for Science and International Security (ISIS) argued that Iran planned in January 2006 to install centrifuges in modules of 3,000 machines that were designed to produce low enriched uranium for civilian power reactors. If half of these machines, however, were to be used to create highly enriched uranium (HEU), they could produce enough HEU for one nuclear weapon a year. Furthermore, if the Iranians do achieve their ultimate goal of 50,000 centrifuges, Albright and Hinderstein argued, "At 15–20 kilograms per weapon, that would be enough for 25–30 nuclear weapons per year."[105]

A much smaller facility might, however, be adequate. A study by Frank Barnaby for the Oxford Research Group estimates Iran's current centrifuges could produce about 2.5 separative work units (SWUs) a year, with a range of 1.9–2.7 SWUs. If Iran had the P-2, each centrifuge would produce roughly 5 SWUs a year. A fully operational 3,000-centrifuge facility could then produce some 7,500 SWUs or about 40 kilograms of HEU a year, and it would probably take a total capacity of 5,000 machines to keep 3,000 on-line at all times.[106] As is discussed later, the 1,500-centrifuge pilot facility that Iran is now seeking to operate could conceivably produce a single weapon in two to three years.

As for the other enrichment route, Iran acknowledged it had started a laser enrichment program in the 1970s. Iran claimed that it used two different tracks in using laser enrichment: (1) atomic vapor laser isotope separation (AVLIS) and (2) molecular isotope separation (MLIS). Iran, however, depended on key contracts with four (unnamed) different countries to build its laser enrichment program. The following chronology was presented by the IAEA:[107]

- **1975:** Iran signed a contract for the establishment of a laboratory to study the spectroscopic behavior of uranium metal; this project had been abandoned in the 1980s as the laboratory had not functioned properly.

- **Late 1970s:** Iran signed a contract with a second supplier to study MLIS, under which four carbon monoxide (CO) lasers and vacuum chambers were delivered, but the project had ultimately been terminated due to the political situation before major development work had begun.

- **1991:** Iran signed a contract with a third supplier for the establishment of a "Laser Spectroscopy Laboratory " (LSL) and a "Comprehensive Separation Laboratory" (CSL), where uranium enrichment would be carried out on a milligram scale based on the AVLIS process. The contract also provided for the supply of 50 kilograms of natural uranium metal.

- **1998:** Iran signed a contract with a fourth supplier to obtain information related to laser enrichment, and the supply of relevant equipment. However, due to the inability of the supplier to secure export licenses, only some of the equipment was delivered (to Lashkar Ab'ad).

The IAEA seems to be more confident about its findings regarding Iran's laser enrichment developments than gas centrifuges. This is largely due to Iranian cooperation, but it also stems from the fact that Iran had nothing to hide since its foreign contractors failed to deliver on the four contracts Tehran signed between the 1970s and the 1990s.

According to the IAEA, Iran claimed that the laser spectroscopy laboratory and the MLIS laboratory (the first two contracts) were never fully operational.

As for the third contract, the IAEA estimated the contract was finished in 1994, but that CSL and LSL had technical problems and were unsuccessful between 1994 and 2000. Iran responded by claiming that the two labs were dismantled in 2000. In addition, the IAEA concluded, "As confirmed in an analysis, provided to the Agency, that had been carried out by the foreign laboratory involved in the project, the highest average enrichment achieved was 8%, but with a peak enrichment of 13%."

Finally, the fourth contract was signed in 1998, but failed due to the supplier's inability to obtain export licenses. Tehran claimed that it attempted to procure these equipment and parts, but it was unsuccessful.[108]

These failures almost certainly did strain Tehran's ability to effectively use the laser enrichment track to advance its uranium enrichment activities. This may explain why Iran did less to try to conceal its laser enrichment program than conceal the details of its centrifuge program. According to the IAEA, Tehran's declarations largely tracked with the IAEA inspectors' findings. For example, Iran claimed that its enrichment level was 0.8 percent U235, and the IAEA concluded that Iran reached an enrichment level of 0.99 percent ± 0.24 percent U235.[109]

The IAEA findings regarding this aspect of Tehran's enrichment program are summarized in the following two paragraphs:[110]

The Agency has completed its review of Iran's atomic vapor laser isotope separation (AVLIS) program and has concluded that Iran's descriptions of the levels of enrichment achieved using AVLIS at the Comprehensive Separation Laboratory (CSL) and Lashkar Ab'ad and the amounts of material used in its past activities are consistent with information available to the Agency to date. Iran has presented all known key equipment, which has been verified by the Agency. For the reasons described in the Annex to this report, however, detailed nuclear material accountancy is not possible.

It is the view of the Agency's AVLIS experts that, while the contract for the AVLIS facility at Lashkar Ab'ad was specifically written for the delivery of a system that could achieve 5 kg of product within the first year with enrichment levels of 3.5% to 7%, the facility as designed and reflected in the contract would, given some specific features of the equipment, have been capable of limited HEU production had the entire package of equipment been delivered. The Iranian AVLIS experts have stated that they were not aware of the significance of these features when they negotiated and contracted for the supply and delivery of the Lashkar Ab'ad AVLIS facility. They have also provided information demonstrating the very limited capabilities of the equipment delivered to Iran under this contract to produce HEU (i.e. only in gram quantities).

The accuracy of such findings is critical because isotope separation is far more efficient than centrifuge separation, much less costly once mature, uses far less power, and is much harder to detect.[111]

Other aspects of Iranian activity were less reassuring. Following Iran's announcement that it converted 37 tons of yellowcake into UF_4 in May 2005, experts believed that this amount of uranium could "theoretically" produce more than 200 pounds of weapons-grade uranium, which would be enough to produce five to six crude nuclear weapons. The head of Iran's Supreme National Security Council, Hasan Rowhani, was quoted in 1995 saying, "Last year, we could not produce UF_4 and UF_6. We didn't have materials to inject into centrifuges to carry out enrichment, meaning we didn't have UF_6...But within the past year, we completed the Isfahan facility and reached UF_4 and UF_6 stage. So we made great progress."[112]

In February 2006, ahead of the IAEA board meeting, it was reported in the press that a report was circulated to IAEA member states regarding what press reports called "the Green Salt Project." The report largely used information provided by U.S. intelligence. The project name was derived from "green salt," or uranium tetrafluoride. The materials are considered intermediate materials in uranium conversion ore into uranium hexafluoride, UF_4, which is central to producing nuclear fuel.[113]

This project was reportedly started in the spring of 2001 by an Iranian firm, Kimeya Madon, under the auspices of the IRGC. U.S. officials believe that Kimyea Madon completed drawings and technical specifications for a small uranium conversion facility (UCF), and they argue that the drawings provide "pretty compelling evidence" for Iran's clandestine uranium conversion program. In addition, there was evidence that the Iranians envisioned a second UCF. It remains uncertain why the operation of Kimeya Mado stopped in 2003. Some speculated that this was a plan to replace Esfahan in case of a military strike against it. Another view is that Iran scratched the plan after it was revealed that the new UCF was not "as good as what they had" at Esfahan.[114]

Another important development in Iranian activities was the IAEA's discovery of "a document related to the procedural requirements for the reduction of UF6 to metal in small quantities, and on the casting and machining of enriched, natural and depleted uranium metal into hemispherical forms," as the IAEA February 4, 2006, resolution emphasized.[115]

The description of this document first appeared in the IAEA November 15, 2005, reports. This "one-page document" apparently was related to the Pakistani offer in 1987, and the IAEA made the following assessment:[116]

As previously reported to the Board, in January 2005 Iran showed to the Agency a copy of a hand-written one-page document reflecting an offer said to have been made to Iran in 1987 by a foreign intermediary for certain components and equipment. Iran stated that only some components of one or two disassembled centrifuges, and supporting drawings and specifications, were delivered by the procurement network, and that a number of other items of equipment referred to in the document were purchased directly from other suppliers. Most of these components and items were included in the October 2003 declaration by Iran to the Agency.

The documents recently made available to the Agency related mainly to the 1987 offer; many of them dated from the late 1970s and early to mid-1980s. The documents included: detailed drawings of the P-1 centrifuge components and assemblies; technical specifications supporting component manufacture and centrifuge assembly; and technical documents relating to centrifuge operational performance. In addition, they included cascade schematic drawings for various sizes of research and development (R&D) cascades, together with the equipment needed for cascade operation (e.g. cooling water circuit needs and special valve consoles). The documents also included a drawing showing a cascade layout for 6 cascades of 168 machines each and a small plant of 2000 centrifuges arranged in the same hall. Also among the documents was one related to the procedural requirements for the reduction of UF6 to metal in small quantities, and on the casting and machining of enriched, natural and depleted uranium metal into hemispherical forms, with respect to which Iran stated that it had been provided on the initiative of the procurement network, and not at the request of the Atomic Energy Organization of Iran (AEOI).

As noted earlier, the foreign intermediary is believed to have been A. Q. Khan, the Pakistani nuclear scientist. The United Kingdom argued that the document, on casting uranium into hemispheric form, had no other application other than nuclear weapons. Experts agreed with this assessment.[117] IAEA officials, however, were more cautious. One senior IAEA official was quoted as saying that the document "is damaging," but he argued that the handwritten document was not a blueprint for making nuclear weapons because it dealt with only one aspect of the process.[118]

Many experts believe that in order to understand Iran's nuclear program, one must understand its gas centrifuge program—particularly whether Tehran's ability to establish a test run of 1,500 centrifuges at Natanz would give Iran enough capacity to produce HEU. David Albright and Corey Hinderstein of the ISIS argued that Iran may well be on its way to achieving this capacity:

Each P1 centrifuge has an output of about 3 separative work units (swu) per year according to senior IAEA officials. From the A. Q. Khan network, Iran acquired drawings of a modified variant of an early-generation Urenco centrifuge. Experts who saw these drawings assessed that, based on the design's materials, dimensions, and tolerances, the P1 in Iran is based on an early version of the Dutch 4M centrifuge that was subsequently modified by Pakistan. The 4M was developed in the Netherlands in the mid-1970s and was more advanced than the earlier Dutch SNOR/CNOR machines. Its rotor assembly has four aluminum rotor tubes connected by three maraging steel bellows.

With 1,500 centrifuges and a capacity of 4,500 swu per year, this facility could produce as much as 28 kilograms of weapon-grade uranium per year, assuming a tails assay of 0.5 percent, where tails assay is the fraction of uranium 235 in the waste stream. This is a relatively high tails assay, but such a tails assay is common in initial nuclear weapons programs. As a program matures and grows, it typically reduces the tails assay to about 0.4 percent and perhaps later to 0.3 percent to conserve uranium supplies.

By spring 2004, Iran had already put together about 1,140 centrifuge rotor assemblies, a reasonable indicator of the number of complete centrifuges. However, only about 500 of these rotors were good enough to operate in cascades, according to knowledgeable senior IAEA officials. The November 2004 IAEA report stated that from the spring to October 10, 2004, Iran had assembled an additional 135 rotors, bringing the total number of rotors assembled to 1,275. As mentioned above, a large number of these rotors are not usable in an operating cascade.

Iran is believed to have assembled more centrifuges prior to the suspension being re-imposed on November 22, 2004. Without more specific information, it is assumed that Iran continued to assemble centrifuges at a constant rate, adding another 70 centrifuges, for a total of 1,345 centrifuges. However, the total number of good centrifuges is esti-mated at about 700.[119]

These developments also led some observers to question whether Iran received more help from Pakistan than it admitted. Some experts argued that the A.Q. Khan network tended to hand over the "whole package" as was the case with Libya, and they question whether Iran received only the few pages that it shared with the IAEA.[120] These revelations showed how little is known about how advanced Iran's uranium enrichment program is.

Most experts, however, believe that Iran's uranium enrichment program is far more dangerous and far more advanced than its plutonium production activities. They argue that the danger of the enrichment program is that regardless of how high Iran's enrichment level of uranium is, if Iran were able to enrich it at a low level, Iran will have the know-how to enrich it at higher levels and produce the weapons-grade uranium to produce nuclear weapons.[121]

In addition, experts are concerned that Iran may acquire uranium from other nations. For example, during a visit by the Iranian Parliament Speaker, Gholam Ali Haddad-Adel, in early 2006, Iran and Venezuela signed a deal that allowed Iran to explore Venezuela's strategic minerals. Venezuelan opposition figures to President Hugo Chávez claimed that the deal could involve the production and transfer of ura-nium from Venezuela to Iran. The United States, however, downplayed such reports. A State Department official was quoted as saying, "We are aware of reports of pos-sible Iranian exploitation of Venezuelan uranium, but we see no commercial activ-ities in Venezuela."[122]

A Continuing Process of Discovery

It is also clear that there is still much more to learn. As noted earlier, in early 2006, the *New York Times* reported on new U.S. intelligence estimates that suggested Iran's "peaceful" program included a "military-nuclear dimension." This assessment was reportedly based on information provided by the United States to the IAEA and referred to a secret program called the Green Salt Project. This project was started to work on uranium enrichment, high explosives, and on adapting nuclear warheads to Iranian missiles. The report suggested that there was evidence of "administrative interconnections" between weaponization and nuclear experts in Iran's nuclear pro-gram. Tehran argued that these claims were "baseless" and promised to provide fur-ther clarifications on the matter.[123] The IAEA report on Iran's nuclear activities in August 2006 made it clear, however, that Iran was not clarifying any major issues raised relating to its nuclear activities, and it raised new questions about Iran's activities in highly enriching uranium that could not be linked to any contamination of centrifuges imported from Pakistan.

Claims that there was a link between Iran's civilian and military nuclear tracks seem to support the comments made by then Secretary of State Colin Powell in November 2004, yet it remains uncertain if the sources of intelligence were the same. Mr. Powell argued that the U.S. intelligence had information that showed Iranian efforts to adapt their nuclear research to fit their Shahab-3 missile. He argued that it made no sense that Iran would work on advancing its delivery systems unless it were also working on the warheads. Other U.S. officials, however, argued that the information Colin Powell used came from unconfirmed sources with uncertain information and should not be seen as a definitive proof.[124]

The source for this information seems to be a stolen laptop computer, which contained designs of a small-scale uranium gas production facility by Kimeya Madon, an Iranian company. In addition, the documents contained modification to the Shahab-3 missile in a way, U.S. officials believe, to fit a nuclear warhead. U.S. intelligence experts, reportedly, believe that the files on the computer were authentic, but they argue that there was no way to prove it. They argue that while there was the possibility that the document was forged by Iranian opposition groups or fabricated by a third country like Israel, it was unlikely. In addition, the authenticity of the document also seemed to have been confirmed by British intelligence.[125]

What concerns U.S. officials is that, while nowhere on the laptop was there a mention of the word "nuclear," the documents mentioned the names of military officers that were linked to Mohsen Fakrizadeh, who is believed to direct "Project 111." U.S. intelligence believes that this project has been responsible for weaponizing Iran's nuclear research efforts and missile developments. In addition, the United States believes that this project is the successor to Project 110, which used to be the military arm of Iran's nuclear research program. These revelations, however, are "cloaked" with uncertainty, and the United States believes that the only way to know is if Fakrizadeh cooperates with IAEA inspectors.[126]

These concerns about Iranian weaponization efforts were exacerbated by the IAEA's discovery of a document relating to the requirement of reducing UF6 to small quantities of metal as well as casting enriched and natural depleted uranium into hemispherical forms.[127] This is believed to be the first link the IAEA has shown between Iran's military and civilian nuclear program. Many argue that this discovery was the turning point in the IAEA negotiation efforts with Tehran and that the failure to disclose this document early in the inspections was a cause for concern for the Agency.

Press reports have also claimed that there was further evidence of Iran's effort to weaponize its nuclear research. A U.S. intelligence assessment was leaked to the *Washington Post*. According to U.S. officials, Iran's nuclear researchers have completed the drawing of "a deep subterranean shaft." The drawings outlined the plans for a 400-meter underground tunnel with remote-controlled sensors to measure pressures and temperatures. U.S. experts believed that the tunnel was being prepared for an underground nuclear test. One U.S. official was quoted saying, "The diagram is consistent with a nuclear test-site schematic." This assessment was based on the fact that the drawings envisioned a test control team to be so far away— 10 kilometers—from the test site, but the United States believes that the tunnel was still in the drawing stage and no developments have taken place. The evidence for this tunnel and Iranian weaponization efforts were the closest thing to a smoking gun in proving an Iranian nuclear weapons program.[128]

This illustrates the point that Iran can gain as much from concealing and obfuscating its weaponization activities as from hiding or obfuscating the nature of its nuclear program. As long as Iran does not actually test a full nuclear explosion, it can develop and test potential weapons and warhead designs in a wide range of ways. It can also prepare for underground testing and test simulated weapons underground to validate many aspects of the test system—including venting—without exploding a bomb until it is ready for the international community to know it has actually tested a weapon.

It can develop and deploy its missile program with conventional warheads and create considerable confusion over the nature of its warhead and bomb tests, concealing whether it has carried out extensive research on CBRN weaponization as part of what it claims is the testing of conventional weapons. Telemetry can be encrypted, avoided, and made deliberately misleading. The same is true of static explosive testing or the use of air-delivered warheads and bombs. So far, for example, the international community and outside experts have generally failed to explore the rationale for Iran's missile efforts and other weaponization activities. The IAEA and CWC lack any clear mandate for inspection and analysis of such activities, and the BWC does not address the issue.

IRAN'S LONG-RANGE MISSILE ARSENAL

Iran continues to deploy surface-to-surface missiles and has its own systems in development. The number assigned to the army vs. the IRGC is unclear, but the IRGC seems to hold and operate most long-range missiles rather than the army. As Figure 8.6, however, shows, Iran has a variety of short-, medium-, and long-range missiles and while many are based on other missiles such as the SCUD and the CSS, Iran has either developed them further or renamed them.

The Iranian government stated as early as 1999 that it was developing a large missile body or launch vehicle for satellite launch purposes, however, and repeatedly denied that it is upgrading the Shahab series (especially the Shahab-3) for military purposes. Iran also continued to claim that the "Shahab-4" program is aimed at developing a booster rocket for launching satellites into space. In January 2004, Iran's Defense Minister claimed that Iran would launch a domestically built satellite within 18 months. This had still not taken place in June 2006.[129]

In December 2005, the U.S. government announced its belief that Iran had built underground missile factories that were capable of producing Shahab-1s, Shahab-2s, and Shahab-3s, as well as testing new missile designs. It was also believed that Karimi

Figure 8.6 Estimated Iranian Missile Profiles, 2006

Designation	Stages	Progenitor Missiles	Propellant	Range (kilometers)	Payload (kilograms)	IOC (year)	Inventory
Fateh A-110	1	?*	?	210	500	?	?
Ghadr-110	?	?	?	2,500–3,000	?	?	?
M-9 variant	1	CSS-6	?	800	320	?	?
M-11 variant	1	CSS-7	?	400	?	?	?
Mushak-120	1	CSS-8, SA-2	Solid	130	500	2001	200
Mushak-160	1	CSS-8, SA-2	Liquid	160	500	2002	?
Mushak-200	1	SA-2	Liquid	200	500	NA	0
Shahab-1	1	Soviet SSN-4, N. Korean SCUD B	Liquid	300	987–1,000	1995	250–300
Shahab-2	1	Soviet SSN-4, N. Korean SCUD C	Liquid	500	750–989	?	200–450
Shahab-3	1	N. Korean Nodong-1	Liquid	1,300	760–1,158	2002	25–100
Shahab-4	2	N. Korean Taep'o-dong-1	Liquid	3,000	1,040–1,500	NA	0
Ghadr 101	Multi	Pakistan Shaheen-1	Solid	2,500	NA	NA	0
Ghadr 110	multi	Pakistan Shaheen-2	Solid	3,000	NA	NA	0
IRIS	1	China M-18	Solid	3,000	760–1,158	2005	NA
Kh-55	1	Soviet AS-15 Kent, Ukraine	Jet engine	2,900–3,000	200 kgt nuclear	2001	12
Shahab-5	3	N. Korean Taep'o-dong-2	Liquid	5,500	390–1,000	NA	0
Shahab-6	3	N. Korean Taep'o-dong-2	Liquid	10,000	270–1,220	NA	0
Zelifal-1/2/3	?	?	?	?	?	?	?

* All "?" refer to weapons that Iran is believed to possess, though the exact numbers in its possession are unknown.

Source: Adapted from GlobalSecurity.org, available at http://www.globalsecurity.org/wmd/world/iran/missile.htm; the Federation of American Scientists, available at http://www.fas.org/nuke/guide/iran/missile; The Claremont Institute: *Ballistic Missiles of the World*, http://www.missilethreat.com/missiles/index.html. NA = not available.

Industries was housed at one of the secret bases, which is where work is taking place on perfecting Iran's nuclear warheads.[130]

U.S. officials insisted that this information did not come from Iranian opposition sources like the MEK and that it was reliable. They feel Iran has made significant strides in recent years using North Korean, Chinese, and Russian technology. If Iran begins work on the Shahab-5 and the Shahab-6 series, it may acquire delivery systems with the range to make it a global nuclear power, instead of merely a regional one.

Shahab-1/SCUD-B

The Soviet-designed SCUD-B (17E) guided missile currently forms the core of Iran's ballistic missile forces. The missile was used heavily in the latter years of the Iran-Iraq War. In 2006, it was estimated that Iran had between 300 and 400 Shahab-1 and Shahab 2 variants of the Scud B and "Scud C" in its inventory.[131] These seem to be deployed in three to four battalions in a Shahab brigade.

Iran acquired its first Scuds in response to Iraq's invasion. It obtained a limited number from Libya and subsequently a larger number from North Korea. Some 20 such missiles and two MAZ-543P transporter-erector-launchers (TELs) were delivered in early 1985.[132]

It deployed these units with a special Khatam ol-Anbya force attached to the air element of the Pasdaran. Iran fired its first Scuds in March 1985. It fired as many as 14 Scuds in 1985, 8 in 1986, 18 in 1987, and 77 in 1988. Iran fired 77 Scud missiles during a 52-day period in 1988, during what came to be known as the "war of the cities." Sixty-one were fired at Baghdad, 9 at Mosul, 5 at Kirkuk, 1 at Tikrit, and 1 at Kuwait. Iran fired as many as five missiles on a single day, and once fired three missiles within 30 minutes. This still, however, worked out to an average of only about one missile a day, and Iran was down to only 10–20 Scuds when the war of the cities ended.

Iran's missile attacks were initially more effective than Iraq's attacks. This was largely a matter of geography. Many of Iraq's major cities were comparatively close to its border with Iran, but Tehran and most of Iran's major cities that had not already been targets in the war were outside the range of Iraqi Scud attacks. Iran's missiles, in contrast, could hit key Iraqi cities like Baghdad. This advantage ended when Iraq deployed extended-range Scuds.

The SCUD-B is a relatively old Soviet design that first became operational in 1967, designated as the R-17E or R-300E. Its thrust is 13,160 Kg f, its burn time is between 62 and 64 seconds, and it has an Isp of 62-Sl due to vanes steering drag loss of 4–5 seconds. The SCUD-B possesses one thrust chamber and is a one-stage rocket (it does not break into smaller pieces). Its fuel is TM-185, and its oxidizer is the AK-27I.[133]

The SCUD-B has a range of 290–300 kilometers with its normal conventional payload. The export version of the missile is about 11 meters long, 85–90 centimeters in diameter, and weighs 6,300 kilograms. It has a nominal CEP of

1,000 meters. The Russian versions can be equipped with conventional high explosives, fuel air explosives, runway penetrating submunitions, and chemical and nuclear warheads. Its basic design comes from the old German V-2 rocket design of World War II. It has moveable fins and is guided only during powered flight.

The SCUD-B was introduced on the JS-3 tracked chassis in 1961 and appeared on the MAZ-543 wheeled chassis in 1965. The "SCUD-B" missile later appeared on the TEL based on the MAZ-543 (8x8) truck. The introduction of this new cross-country wheeled vehicle gave this missile system greater road mobility and reduces the number of support vehicles required.

The export version of the SCUD-B comes with a conventional high explosive warhead weighing about 1,000 kilograms, of which 800 kilograms are the high explosive payload and 200 are the warhead structure and fusing system. It has a single stage storable liquid rocket engine and is usually deployed on the MAZ-543—an eight-wheel TEL. It has a strap-down inertial guidance, using three gyros to correct its ballistic trajectory, and it uses internal graphite jet vane steering. The warhead hits at a velocity above Mach 1.5.

The following timeline tracks the history of the Shahab-1 (SCUD-B) after it was first introduced in Iran in 1985:

- **1985:** Iran began acquiring SCUD-B (Shahab-1) missiles from Libya for use in the Iran-Iraq War.[134]
- **1986:** Iran turned to Libya as a supplier of SCUD-Bs.[135]
- **1987:** A watershed year. Iran attempted to produce its own SCUD-B missiles, but failed. Over the next five years, it purchased 200–300 SCUD-B missiles from North Korea.[136]
- **1988:** Iran began producing its own SCUD-Bs, though not in large quantities.[137]
- **1991:** It is estimated that at approximately the time of the Gulf War, Iran stopped producing its own SCUD-Bs and began purchasing the more advanced SCUD-Cs (Shahab-2). This is said to be a system with an 800-kilogram warhead and a 500-kilometer range vs. comparable profiles of 1,000 kilograms with a 300-kilometers range for the Scud B or Shahab 1.[138]
- **1993:** Iran sent 21 missile specialists, led by Brigadier General Manteghi, to North Korea for training.[139]

Experts estimate Iran bought 200–300 SCUD-Bs (Shahab 1s) and SCUD-Cs (Shahab 2), or the suitable components for Iranian reverse-engineered systems, from North Korea between 1987 and 1992, and may have continued to buy such missiles after that time.[140]

Israeli experts estimated that Iran had at least 250–300 Scud-B missiles and at least 8–15 launchers on hand in 1997. Most current estimates indicate that Iran now has 6–12 SCUD launchers and up to 200 SCUD-B (R-17E) missiles with 230–310-kilometer range. Some estimates give higher figures. The IISS estimated in 2006 that Tehran had 18 launchers and 300 SCUD missiles.[141] It is, however, uncertain how many of those are SCUD-Bs and how many are SCUD-Cs.

U.S. experts also believe that Iran can now manufacture virtually all of the SCUD-B, with the possible exception of the most sophisticated components of its guidance system and rocket motors. This makes it difficult to estimate how many missiles Iran has in its inventory and how many it can acquire over time, as well as to estimate the precise performance characteristics of Iran's missiles, since it can alter the weight of the warhead and adjust the burn time and improve the efficiency of the rocket motors.

Shahab-2/SCUD-C

Iran served as a transshipment point for North Korean missile deliveries during 1992 and 1993. Some of these transshipments took place using the same Iranian B-747s that brought missile parts to Iran.

Others moved by sea. For example, a North Korean vessel called the *Des Hung Ho,* bringing missile parts for Syria, docked at Bandar Abbas in May 1992. Iran then flew these parts to Syria. An Iranian ship coming from North Korea and a second North Korean ship followed, carrying missiles and machine tools for both Syria and Iran. At least 20 of the North Korean missiles have gone to Syria from Iran, and production equipment seems to have been transferred to Iran and to Syrian plants near Hama and Aleppo.

The SCUD-C is an improved version of the SCUD-B. With superior range and payload, it is another tactical missile first acquired by Iran in 1990. It has an approximate range between 500 and 700 miles, a CEP of 50 meters, and it carries a 700–989-kilogram warhead. It has a diameter of 0.885 meters, a height of 11–12 meters, a launch weight of 6,370–6,500 kilograms, an unknown stage mass, an unknown dry mass, and an unknown propellant mass. In terms of propelling ability, its thrust is unknown, its burn time is unknown, and it has an effective Isp of 231. The SCUD-C possesses one thrust chamber and is a one-stage rocket (it does not break into smaller pieces). Its fuel is Tonka-250, and its oxidizer is the AK 20P.[142]

SCUD-C missile development was successfully completed and ready for production by 1987 (mainly by North Korea) and then distributed to Iran several years later. According to some reports, Iran has created shelters and tunnels in its coastal areas that it could use to store Scuds and other missiles in hardened sites to reduce their vulnerability to air attack.

The missile is more advanced than the SCUD-B, although many aspects of its performance are unclear. North Korea seems to have completed development of the missile in 1987, after obtaining technical support from China. While it is often called a "SCUD-C," it seems to differ substantially in detail from the original Soviet SCUD-B. It seems to be based more on the Chinese-made DF-61 than on a direct copy of the Soviet weapon.

Experts estimate that the North Korean missiles have a range of around 310 miles (500 kilometers), a conventional warhead with a high explosive payload of 700 kilograms, and relatively good accuracy and reliability. While some experts feel the payload of its conventional warhead may be limited for the effective delivery of chemical agents, Iran might modify the warhead to increase payload at the expense of range and restrict the use of chemical munitions to the most lethal agents such as persistent nerve gas. It might also concentrate its development efforts on arming its SCUD-C forces with more lethal biological agents.

It is currently estimated that Iran has 50–150 SCUD-Cs in its inventory.[143] While early development of the SCUB-C tracks closely with that of the SCUD-B, the following timeline tracks the development of Iranian SCUD-C missiles since the Gulf War:

- **1994:** By this year, Iran had purchased 150–200 SCUD-Cs from North Korea.[144]
- **1997:** Iran began production of its own SCUD-C missiles. This is generally considered a technological leap for Iran, and it is believed that a large portion of its production capability and technology came from North Korea.[145]

In spite of the revelations during the 1990s about North Korean missile technology transfers to Tehran, Iran formally denied the fact that it had such systems long after the transfer of these missiles became a fact. Hassan Taherian, an Iranian foreign ministry official, stated in February 1995, "There is no missile cooperation between Iran and North Korea whatsoever. We deny this."[146]

A senior North Korean delegation did, however, travel to Tehran to close the deal on November 29, 1990, and met with Mohsen Rezaei, the former Commander of the IRGC. Iran either bought the missile then or placed its order shortly thereafter. North Korea then exported the missile through its Lyongaksan Import Corporation. Iran imported some of these North Korean missile assemblies using its B-747s and seems to have used ships to import others.

Iran probably had more than 60 of the longer-range North Korean missiles by 1998, although other sources report 100, and one source reports 170. Iran may have five to ten SCUD-C launchers, each with several missiles. This total seems likely to include four North Korean TELs received in 1995.

Iran is seeking to deploy enough missiles and launchers to make its missile force highly dispersed and difficult to attack. Iran began to test its new North Korean missiles. There are reports it fired them from mobile launchers at a test site near Qom to a target area about 310 miles (500 kilometers) away south of Shahroud. There are also reports that units equipped with such missiles have been deployed as part of Iranian exercises like the Saeqer-3 (Thunderbolt 3) exercise in late October 1993.

In any case, such missiles are likely to have enough range-payload to give Iran the ability to strike all targets on the southern coast of the Gulf and all of the populated areas in Iraq, although not the West. Iran could also reach targets in part of eastern Syria, the eastern third of Turkey, and cover targets in the border area of the former Soviet Union, western Afghanistan, and western Pakistan.

Accuracy and reliability do remain major uncertainties, as does the missile's operational CEP. Much would depend on the precise level of technology Iran deployed in the warhead. Neither Russia nor the People's Republic of China seems to have transferred the warhead technology for biological and chemical weapons to Iran or Iraq when they sold them the SCUD-B missile and CSS-8. However, North Korea may have sold Iran such technology as part of the SCUD-C sale. If it did so, such a technology transfer would save Iran years of development and testing in obtaining highly lethal biological and chemical warheads. In fact, Iran would probably be able to deploy far more effective biological and chemical warheads than Iraq had at the time of the Gulf War.

Iran can now assemble SCUD-C missiles using foreign-made components. It may soon be able to make entire missile system and warhead packages in Iran. Iran may be working with Syria in such development efforts, although Middle Eastern nations rarely cooperate in such sensitive areas.

CCS-8 or Tondar 69

Jane's reports that Iran may have some 200 Chinese CCS-8, or M-7/Project 8610 short-range missiles. These are Chinese modifications of the Sa-2 surface-to-air missile for use as a surface-to-surface system. It has a 190-kilogram warhead and a 150-kilometer range. Up to 90 may have been delivered to Iran in 1992, and another 110 may have been delivered later. The system is reported to have poor accuracy.[147]

Shahab-3

Iran appears to have entered into a technological partnership with North Korea after years of trading with the North Koreans for SCUD-Cs throughout the 1990s. The visit to North Korea in 1993 by General Manteghi and his 21 specialists seems a possible date when Iran shifted from procurement to development.

Iran did not have the strike capability to attack Israel with its limited range Scuds. As a result, the Iranians seem to have begun using some of the designs for the North Korean No Dong medium-range ballistic missile (MRBM) in an attempt to manufacture their own version of the missile, the Shahab-3. Between 1997 and 1998, Iran began testing the Shahab-3. While Iran claimed Shahab-3's purpose was to carry payloads of submunitions, it is more likely that Iran would use the Shahab-3's superior range to carry a chemical, nuclear, or biological weapon.

Missile Development

Iran's new Shahab-3 series is a larger missile that seems to be based on the design of the North Korean No Dong 1/A, and No Dong B missiles, which some analysts claim were developed with Iranian financial support. It also has strong similarities to the Ghauri. It is based on North Korean designs and technology, but is being developed and produced in Iran. This development effort is controlled and operated by the IRGC. Iranian officials, however, claimed that the production of the Shahab-3 missiles was entirely domestic. The Iranian Defense Minister, Ali Shamkhani, argued in May 2005 that the production was comprised of locally made parts and that the production was continuing.[148]

As the following timeline shows, the Shahab-3 is a relatively young and constantly evolving system, but it has been tested several times:

- **October 1997:** Russia began training Iranian engineers on missile production for the Shahab-3.[149]

- **1998:** Iran began testing its own Shahab-3s. Problems with finding or making an advanced guidance system hindered many of Iran's tests, however. Meanwhile, Iran begins experimenting with the Shahab-4.[150]

- **July 23, 1998:** Iran launched its first test flight of the Shahab-3. The missile flew for approximately 100 seconds, after which time it was detonated. It is not known if it malfunctioned, because the Iranians did not want to risk discovery.[151]

- **July 15, 2000:** Iran had its first successful test of a Shahab-3, using a new North Korean engine.[152]

- **Summer 2001:** Iran began production of the Shahab-3.[153]

- **July 7, 2003:** Iran completes the final test of the Shahab-3. Allegations emerged that Chinese companies like Tai'an Foreign Trade General Corporation and China North Industries Corporation had been aiding the Iranians in overcoming the missile's final technical glitches.[154] The missile is seen in Iranian military parades and displayed openly.

- **August 11, 2004:** Iran decreases the size of the Shahab-3 warhead, making a move toward being able to mount a nuclear warhead to a Shahab-3. At this point, the modified Shahab-3 is often referred to as the Shahab-3M.[155] The missile had a new, smaller, and "bottleneck" warhead. This kind of warhead has a slower reentry than a cone-shaped warhead and has advantages using warheads containing chemical and biological agents. Some estimated that it had a range of 2,000 kilometers for a 700-kilogram warhead, but this may be a confusion with another solid-fueled system. A second variant may exist with a larger fin, a meter less length, and less than a 1,500-kilometer range.[156]

- **September 19, 2004:** Another test took place, and the missile was paraded on September 21 covered in banners saying "we will crush America under our feet" and "wipe Israel off the map."[157]

- **May 31, 2005:** Iranian Defense Minister Ali Shamkhani claimed that Iran successfully tested a new missile motor using solid-fuel technology with a range of 1,500–2,000 kilometers, and a 700-kilogram warhead. Shamkhani was quoted as saying "Using solid fuel would be more durable and increase the range of the missile."[158] It remains uncertain if this referred to the Shahab-3 or the modified Shahab-3, the IRIS missile.

- **September 2005:** Two new missiles tested, again with a triconic or baby-bottle warhead some 3 meters long. Some experts speculate that it can disperse chemical and biological weapons or is better suited to a nuclear warhead. Others feel it is an airburst warhead, capable of better dispersing chemical and/or biological weapons.

- **September 2006:** Iran is reported to have more than 30 Shahab-3s and 10 TELs, but this is not confirmed.[159]

As of early 2006, there had been some ten launches at a rate of only one to two per year. Roughly 30 percent had fully malfunctioned, and six launches had had some malfunction. Iran had also tested two major payload configurations.[160]

Uncertain Performance[161]

Discussions of the Shahab-3's range-payload, accuracy, and reliability are uncertain and will remain speculative until the system is far more mature. A long-range ballistic missile requires at least 10–30 tests in its final configuration to establish its true payload and warhead type, actual range-payload, and accuracy. While highly detailed estimates of the Shahab-3's performance are available, they at best are rough engineering estimates and are sometimes speculative to the point of being sheer guesswork using rounded numbers.

Its real-world range will depend on both the final configuration of the missile and the weight of its warhead. Various sources now guess that the Shahab-3 has a range between 1,300 and 2,000 kilometers, but the longer-range estimate seems to be based on Iranian claims and assumptions about an improved version, not full-scale operational tests.[162]

U.S. experts believe that the original Shahab-3 missile had a nominal range of 1,100 to 1,300 kilometers, with a 1,200-kilogram payload. The basic system is said to have been 16.5 meters long, have a diameter of 1.58 meters, with a launch weight of 17,410 pounds. Iran has claimed that the Shahab-3 has a range of 2,000 kilometers. This may reflect different estimates of different versions of the missile.

Nasser Maleki, the head of Iran's aerospace industry, stated on October 7, 2004, "Very certainly we are going to improve our Shahab-3 and all of our other missiles." Tehran then claimed in September that the Shahab-3 could now reach targets up to 2,000 kilometers away, presumably allowing the missiles to be deployed a greater distance away from Israel's Air Force and Jericho-2 ballistic missiles.[163]

IRGC Political Bureau Chief Yadollah Javani stated in September 2004 that the modified Shahab—sometimes called the Shahab-3A or Shahab-3M—could be used to attack Israel's Dimona nuclear reactor.[164] Iran performed another test on October 20, 2004, and Iran's Defense Minister, Ali Shamkani, claimed it was part of an operational exercise. On November 9, 2004, Iran's Defense Minister also claimed that Iran was now capable of mass-producing the Shahab-3 and that Iran reserved the option of preemptive strikes in defense of its nuclear sites. Shamkani claimed shortly afterward that the Shahab-3 now had a range of more than 2,000 kilometers (1,250 miles).[165]

One leading German expert stresses the uncertainty of any current estimates and notes that range-payload trade-offs would be critical. He puts the range for the regular Shahab-3 at 820 kilometers with a 1.3-ton payload and 1,100 kilometers with a 0.7-ton payload. (An analysis by John Pike of GlobalSecurity.org also points out that missiles—like combat aircraft—can make trade-offs between range and payload. For example, the No Dong B has a range of 1,560 kilometers with a 760-kilogram warhead and 1,350 kilometers with a 1,158-kilogram warhead.[166]

He feels that an improved Shahab could use a combination of a lighter aluminum airframe, light weight guidance, reduced payload, increased propellant load, and increased burn time to increase range. He notes that little is really known about the improved Shahab-3, but estimates the maximum range of an improved Shahab-3 as still being 2,000 kilometers, that a 0.7–0.8-ton warhead would limit its range to 1,500 kilometers and that a 0.8–1.0-ton warhead would reduce it to 1,200 kilometers. A 1.2-ton warhead would limit it to around 850 kilometers. He feels Iran may have drawn on Russian technology from the R-21 and the R-27. Photos of the system also show progressive changes in cable duct position, fins, and length in 2004 and 2005.[167]

The difference in range estimates may be a matter of Iranian propaganda, but a number of experts believe that Iranian claims refer to the modified Shahab-3D or the Shahab-3M and not the regular Shahab-3. There are reports that such modified versions use solid fuel and could have a range of up to 2,000 kilometers. They also indicate that the standard Shahab-3 remains in production, but the improved Shahab is now called the Shahab-3M.[168]

Much also depends on the missile warhead. In 2004, then U.S. Secretary of State Colin Powell accused Iran of modifying its Shahab-3 to carry a nuclear warhead based on documents the U.S. government had received from a walk-in source. While experts argued that this information was yet to be confirmed, others claimed that Iran obtained "a new nosecone" for its Shahab-3 missile.[169] In addition, other U.S. officials claimed that the source of the information provided "tens of thousands of pages of Farsi-language computer files" on Iranian attempts to modify the Shahab-3 missile to deliver a "black box," which U.S. officials believed "almost certainly" referred to a nuclear warhead. These documents were said to include diagrams and test results, weight, detonation height, and shape, but did not include warhead designs.[170]

Media reporting indicates that the United States was able to examine drawings on a stolen laptop from Iran and found that Iran had developed 18 different ways to adapt the size, weight, and diameter of the new nosecone on it Shahab-3 missile. It was also reported, however, that Iran's effort to expand the nosecone would not work and that Iran did not have the technological capabilities to adapt nuclear weapons into its Shahab-3 missile. U.S. nuclear experts claimed that one reason for this failure was that the project "wasn't done by the A-team of Iran's program."[171]

Some experts believe that new bottleneck warhead tested in 2004 was for the Shahab-3M and makes it more accurate and capable of air-burst detonations, which could be used to more effectively spread chemical weapons. Others believe a smaller warhead has increased its range.

As for other aspects of performance, it is again easy to be precise, but difficult to be correct. One source, for example, reports that the Shahab-3 has a CEP of 190 meters and carries a 750–989–1,158-kilogram warhead. The same source reports that the Shahab-3 has a height of 16 meters, a stage mass of 15,092 kilograms, a dry mass of 1,780–2,180 kilograms, and a propellant mass of 12,912 kilograms. In terms of propelling ability, its thrust is between 26,760–26,600 Kg f, its burn time is 110 seconds, and it has an effective Isp of 226 and a drag loss of 45 seconds. According to this source, the Shahab-3 possesses one thrust chamber. Its fuel is TM-185, and its oxidizer is the AK 27I.[172]

High levels of accuracy are possible, but this remains to be seen. If the system uses older guidance technology and warhead separation methods, its CEP could be anywhere from 1,000 to 4,000 meters. If it uses newer technology, such as some of the most advanced Chinese technology, it could have a CEP as low as 190–800 meters. In any case, such CEP data are engineering estimates based on the ratios from a perfectly located target.

This means real-world missile accuracy and reliability cannot be measured using technical terms like CEP even if they apply to a fully mature and deployed missile. The definition of the term is based on the assumption the missile can be perfectly targeted at launch and performs perfectly through its final guidance phase, and then somewhat arbitrarily define CEP as the accuracy of 50 percent of the systems launched in terms of distance from a central point on the target. True performance can be derived only from observing reliability under operational conditions and by correlating actual point of impact to a known aim point.

A German expert notes, for example, that the operational CEP of the improved Shahab-3 is likely to be around 3 kilometers, but the maximum deviation could be 11 kilometers.[173] In short, unclassified estimates of the Shahab-3's accuracy and reliability available from public sources are matters of speculation, and no unclassified source has credibility in describing its performance in real-world, war-fighting terms.

This is not a casual problem, since actual weaponization of a warhead requires extraordinarily sophisticated systems to detonate a warhead at the desired height of burst and to reliably disseminate the munitions or agent. Even the most sophisticated conventional submunitions are little more than area weapons if the missile accuracy to target location has errors in excess of 250–500 meters, and a unitary conventional explosive warhead without terminal guidance is little more than a psychological or terror weapon almost regardless of its accuracy.

The effective delivery of chemical agents by either spreading the agent or the use of submunitions generally requires accuracies less than 1,000 meters to achieve lethality against even large point targets. Systems with biological weapons are inherently area weapons, but a 1,000-kilogram nominal warhead can carry so little agent that accuracies less than 1,000 meters again become undesirable. Nuclear weapons require far less accuracy, particularly if a "dirty" ground burst can be targeted within a reliable fallout area. There are, however, limits. For example, a regular fission weapon of some 20 kilotons requires accuracies under 2,500–3,000 meters for some kinds of targets like sheltered airfields or large energy facilities.

What is clear is that the Shahab could carry a well-designed nuclear weapon well over 1,000 kilometers, and Iran may have access to such designs. As noted earlier, the Shahab-3 missile was tested in its final stages in 2003 and in ways that indicate it has a range of 2,000 kilometers, which is enough to reach the Gulf and Israel. A.Q. Khan sold a Chinese nuclear warhead design to Libya with a mass of as little as 500 kilograms and a one meter diameter. It is highly probable such designs were sold to Iran as well.

Mobility and Deployment

The Shahab-3 is mobile, but requires numerous launching support vehicles for propellant transport and loading and power besides its TELs.[174] The original version was slow in setting up, taking five hours to prepare for launch.[175] Some five different TELs have been seen, however, and some experts believe the current reaction time is roughly an hour.[176]

The Shahab-3's deployment status is highly uncertain. Some reports have claimed that the Shahab-3 was operational as early as 1999. Reports surfaced that development of the Shahab-3 was completed in June 2003 and that it underwent "final" tests on July 7, 2003. However, the Shahab-3 underwent a total of only nine tests from inception through late 2003, and only four of them could be considered successful in terms of basic system performance. The missile's design characteristics also continued to evolve during these tests. A CIA report to Congress, dated November 10, 2003, indicated that upgrading of the Shahab-3 was still under way, and some sources indicated that Iran was now seeking a range of 1,600 kilometers.

There is an argument among experts as to whether the system has been tested often enough to be truly operational. The CIA reported in 2004 that Iran had "some" operational Shahab-3s with a range of 1,300 kilometers. Some experts feel the missile has since become fully operational and Iran already possesses 25–100 Shahab-3's in its inventory.[177] Iranian opposition sources have claimed that Iran has 300 such missiles. According to other sources, the IRGC operated six batteries in the spring of 2006 and was redeploying them within a 35-kilometer radius of their main command and control center every 24 hours because of the risk of a U.S. or Israeli attack. The main operating forces were deployed in the west in the Kermanshah and Hamadan provinces with reserve batteries farther east in the Fars and Isfahan provinces.[178]

A substantial number of experts, however, believe the Shahab-3 may be in deployment, but only in "showpiece" or "test-bed" units using conventional warheads and with performance Iran cannot accurately predict.

Shahab-3A/3M/3D/IRIS

In October 2004, the Mujahedin-e Khalq claimed that Iran was developing an improved version of the Shahab with a 2,400-kilometer range (1,500 miles). The MEK has an uncertain record of accuracy in making such claims, and such claims could not be confirmed. Mortezar Ramandi, an official in the Iranian delegation to the UN, denied that Iran was developing a missile with a range of more than 1,250 miles (2,000 kilometers).[179]

This new range for the Shahab-3 may have marked a significant move in Iranian technological capability, as some experts believe Iran switched the fuel source from liquid fuel to solid. The possible existence of a Shahab-3 with a solid fuel source created yet another variant of the Shahab-3 series, the Shahab-3D, or the IRIS missile.

Such a development of a solid fuel source might enable the Shahab-3D to enter into space and serve as a potential satellite launch vehicle. Perfecting solid fuel technology would also move Iran's missile systems a long way toward the successful creation of a limited range intercontinental ballistic missile (LRICBM), which is what the Shahab-5 and Shahab-6 are intended to accomplish.[180]

If there is an IRIS launch vehicle, it apparently consists of the No Dong/Shahab-3 first stage with a bulbous front section ultimately designed to carry the IRIS second-stage solid motor, as well as a communications satellite or scientific payload.[181] The IRIS solid fuel missile itself may be the third-stage portion of the North Korean Taep'o-dong 1.[182]

The Shahab-3D alone is not capable of launching a large satellite probe into space, and it is possible that it is a test for the second- and third-stage portions of the upcoming IRBM Ghadr designs and the LRICBM Shahab-5 and Shahab-6.[183]

No test flights of the Shahab-3D have been recorded on video, but it is believed that they have taken place at a space launch facility.[184] The following timeline shows the reported tests of the Shahab-3D/IRIS:

- **July 22, 1998:** First test flight (explodes 100 seconds after takeoff).
- **July 15, 2000:** First successful test flight (range of 850 kilometers).
- **September 21, 2000:** Unsuccessful test flight (explodes shortly after takeoff).
- **May 23, 2002:** Successful test flight.
- **July 2002:** Unsuccessful test flight (missile did not function properly).
- **June 2003:** Successful test flight. Iran declares this was the final test flight before deployment.
- **August 11, 2004:** Successful test flight of Shahab-3M. The missile now has a bottleneck warhead.
- **October 20, 2004:** Another successful test flight of Shahab-3M. Iran now claims the modified missile has a range of 2,000 kilometers.[185]

Shahab-4

Iran may also be developing larger designs with greater range-payload using a variety of local, North Korean, Chinese, and Russian technical inputs. These missiles have been called the Shahab-4, the Shahab-5, and the Shahab-6. As of September 2006, none of these missiles were being produced, and the exact nature of such programs remained speculative.[186]

Some experts believe the "Shahab-4" has an approximate range between 2,200 and 2,800 kilometers. Various experts have claimed that the Shahab-4 is based on the North Korean No Dong 2, the three-stage Taep'o-dong-1 missile, the Russian SS-N-6 SERB, or even some aspects of the Russian SS-4, but has a modern digital guidance package rather than the 2,000–3,000-meter CEP of early missiles like the SS-4.

Russian firms are believed to have sold Iran special steel for missile development, test equipment, shielding for guidance packages, and other technology. Iran's Shahid Hemmet Industrial Group is reported to have contracts with the Russian Central Aerohydrodynamic Institute, Rosvoorouzhenie, the Bauman Institute, and Polyus. It is also possible that Iran has obtained some technology from Pakistan.

One source has provided a precise estimate of some performance characteristics. This estimate of "Shahab-4" gives it an estimated height of 25 meters, a diameter of 1.3 meters, and a launch weight of 22,000 kilograms. In terms of propelling ability, its thrust is estimated to be around 26,000 Kg f and its burn time around 293 seconds. It is said to be a 2/3-stage rocket that possesses three thrust chambers, one for each stage. Its fuel for the first stage is Heptyl, and its oxidizer is inhibited red fuming nitric acid (IRFNA).[187]

Iran has sent mixed signals about the missile development status. In October 2003, Iran claimed it was abandoning its Shahab-4 program, citing that the expected increase in range (2,200 to 3,000 kilometers) would cause too much global tension.[188] Some speculate that Iran may have scrapped its Shahab-4 program because it either was not innovative and large enough and/or to avoid controversy. The reason announced by some Iranians for creating a missile like the Shahab-4 was for satellite launches. The IRIS/Shahab-3D, with its solid fuel source, however, has shown potential for space launches. The improved range and bottleneck warhead design offered by the Shahab-3M (which began testing in August 2004) may make the Shahab-4 simply not worth the effort or controversy.[189]

According to German press reports, however, Iran is moving ahead in its development of the Shahab-4. In February 2006, the German news agency cited "Western intelligence services" as saying that Iran successfully tested the Shahab-4 missile with a range of 2,200 kilometers on January 17, 2006, and the test was announced on Iranian television several days later by the Commander of the IRGC.[190] These reports remain unverifiable.

Shahab-5 and Shahab-6

Israeli intelligence has reported that Iran is attempting to create a Shahab-5 and a Shahab-6, with a 3,000–5,000-kilometer range. These missiles would be based on the North Korean Taep'o-dong-2 and would be three-stage rockets. If completed, the Shahab-5 and the Shahab-6 would take Iran into the realm of LRICBMs and enable Iran to target the U.S. eastern seaboard. The Shahab-5 and Shahab-6 would possess a solid fuel third stage for space entry and liquid fuel for the first stage take units.

It is alleged that Russian aerospace engineers are aiding the Iranians in their efforts. It is believed that the engineers will employ a version of Russia's storable liquid propellant RD-216 in the missile's first stage. The RD-216 is an Energomash engine originally used on the Skean/SS-5/R-14, IRBM, Saddler/SS-7/R-16, ICBM, and Sasin/R-26 ICBM missiles used in the Cold War. These reports remain uncertain, and Israeli media and official sources have repeatedly exaggerated the nature and speed of Iranian efforts.[191]

Neither the Shahab-5 nor the Shahab-6 has been tested or constructed. While no description of the Shahab-6 is yet available, extrapolations for the Shahab-5 have been made based on the North Korean Taep'o-dong 2. The Shahab-5 has an approximate range between 4,000 and 4,300 kilometers. The Shahab-5 has an unknown CEP, and its warhead capacity is between 700 and 1,000 kilograms. It has a height of 32 meters, a diameter of 2.2 meters, and a launch weight of 80,000–85,000 kilograms.

In terms of propelling ability, some experts estimate its thrust to be 31,260 Kg f and its burn time to be 330 seconds. The Shahab-5 is a three-stage rocket that possesses six thrust chambers, four for stage one, and one for the two remaining stages. The Shahab-5 and Shahab-6 would be considered long-range ICBMs.[192]

As of January 2006, Iran had not completed its plans for these missiles, and it had none in its inventory. In February 2006, German press reports, however, claimed that the Federal German Intelligence Service estimated that it was possible for Iran to acquire the Shahab-5 as early as 2007 with a range of 3,000–5,000 kilometers.[193] These estimates, however, are speculative and remain unconfirmed.

Ghadr 101 and Ghadr 110

The uncertainties surrounding Iran's solid fuel problem and the existence or non-existence of the Shahab-3 are compounded by reports of a separate missile development program. The Iranian exile group, NCRI, claimed in December 2004 that the Ghadr 101 and the Ghadr 110 were new missile types that used solid fuel and were, in fact, IRBMs. Their existence has never been confirmed, and conflicting reports make an exact description difficult.

At the time, U.S. experts indicated that the Ghadr is actually the same as the Shahab-3A/Shahab M/Shahab 4, which seemed to track with some Israel experts who felt that Iran was extending the range-payload of Shahab-3 and that reports of both the Gadr and the Shahab-4 were actually decribing the Shahab-3A/3M.[194]

In May 2005, Iran tested a solid fuel motor for what some experts call the Shahab-3D, possibly increasing the range to 2,500 kilometers, making space entry possible, and setting the stage for the Shahab-5 and the Shahab-6 to be three-stage rockets resembling ICBMs.[195] This test showed that Iran had developed some aspects of a successful long-range, solid fuel missile design, but did not show how Iran intended to use such capabilities.

NCRI again claimed in March 2006 that Iran was moving forward with the Ghadr solid fuel IRBM. It also claimed that Iran had scrapped the Shahab-4 because of test failures and performance limitations. It reported that Iran had substantial North Korean technical support for the Ghadr, that it was 70 percent complete, and had a range of 3,000 kilometers. One Israeli expert felt that NCRI was confusing a solid-state, second stage for the liquid-fueled Shahab-4 with a separate missile.[196]

Work by Dr. Robert Schmucker indicates that Iran is working on solid-fueled systems, building on its experience with solid fuel artillery rockets like its Fateh 110A1 and with Chinese support in developing solid fuel propulsion and guidance. The Fateh, however, is a relatively primitive system with strap-down gyro guidance that is not suited for a long-range ballistic missile.[197]

As is the case with longer-range variants of the Shahab, it is probably wise to assume that Iran is seeking to develop options for both solid- and liquid-fueled IRBMs and will seek high range-payloads to ensure it can deliver effective CBRN payloads even if it cannot produce efficient nuclear weapons. It is equally wise to wait for systems to reach maturity before reacting to vague possibilities, rather than real-world Iranian capabilities.

Raduga KH-55 Granat/Kh-55/AS-15 Kent

The Raduga KH-55 Granat is a Ukrainian-/Soviet-made armed nuclear cruise missile first tested in 1978 and completed in 1984.[198] The Russian missile carries a 200-kiloton nuclear warhead, and it has a range of 2,500–3,000 kilometers. It has a theoretical CEP of about 150 meters and a speed of Mach 0.48–0.77.

Its guidance system is reported to combine inertial-Doppler navigation and position correction based on in-flight comparison of terrain in the assigned regions with images stored in the memory of an on-board computer. It was designed to deliver a high-yield nuclear weapon against fixed-area targets and has little value delivering conventional warheads. While it was originally designed to be carried by a large bomber, and its weight makes it a marginal payload for either Iran's Su-24s or F-14As, it has land and ship launch capability. It can also be adapted to use a much larger nuclear or other CBRN warhead by cutting its range, and it may be a system that Iran can reverse engineer for production.[199]

Russian President Boris Yeltsin made further manufacture of the missile illegal in 1992.[200] Still, the Ukraine had 1,612 of these missiles in stock at the end of 1991, and it agreed to give 575 of them to Russia and scrap the rest.[201] The plans to give the missiles to Russia in the late 1990s proved troublesome, however, and an organization was able to forge the documents regarding 20 missiles and listed them as being sold to Russia, while in fact 12 seem to have been distributed to Iran and 6 to China (the other 2 are unaccounted for).[202] It was estimated that the missiles were smuggled to Iran in 2001.[203]

Ukrainian officials confirmed the illegal sale on March 18, 2005, but the Chinese and Iranian governments were silent regarding the matter. While some U.S. officials downplayed the transaction, the U.S. State Department expressed concern that the missiles could give each state a technological boost.[204] The missiles did not contain warheads at the time of their sale, and they had passed their service life in 1995 and were in need of maintenance.[205] It is, however, feared that Iran could learn from the cruise missiles technology to improve its own missile program and the missiles could be fitted to match Iran's Su-24 strike aircraft.[206]

PARAMILITARY, INTERNAL SECURITY, AND INTELLIGENCE FORCES

Iran has not faced a meaningful threat from terrorism. Its internal security forces are focused on countering political opposition. Figure 8.7 shows the force structure of Iran's paramilitary and internal security services. Since 1990, Iran has maintained the same force structure, and its key agencies have not changed since the early years of the Revolution.

The U.S. Department of State described the role of Iran's internal security apparatus as follows:[207]

Several agencies share responsibility for law enforcement and maintaining order, including the ministry of intelligence and security, the law enforcement forces under the interior ministry, and the IRGC. A paramilitary volunteer force known as the Basiji and various informal groups known as the Ansar-e Hizballah (Helpers of the Party of God) aligned with extreme conservative members of the leadership and acted as vigilantes. The size of the Basij is disputed, with officials citing anywhere from 11 to 20 million, and a recent Western study claiming there were 90 thousand active members and up to 300 thousand reservists. Civilian authorities did not maintain fully effective control of the security forces. The regular and paramilitary security forces both committed numerous, serious human rights abuses. According to HRW since 2000 the government's use of plainclothes security agents to intimidate political critics became more

Figure 8.7   Iran's Paramilitary Forces' Force Structure, 1990–2006

	1990	2000	2005	2006
Manpower	1,045,000	1,040,000	1,040,000	1,040,000
Active (interior ministry officers)	45,000	40,000	40,000	40,000
Reserve (includes rev. conscripts, BASU)	1,000,000	1,000,000	1,000,000	1,000,000
Patrol and Coastal Combatants	136	130	130	130
Misc. Boats and Craft	40	40	40	40
PCI	96	90	90	90
Aircraft	?*	?	?	?
Cessna 185/Cessna 310	?	?	?	?
Helicopters	?	24	24	24
UTL Bell/205/206	?	24	24	24

*   All "?" refer to weapons that Iran is believed to possess, though the exact numbers in its possession are unknown.

Source: IISS, *Military Balance,* various editions, including 1989–1990, 1999–2000, 2004–2005, and 2005–2006.

institutionalized. They were increasingly armed, violent, and well equipped, and they engaged in assault, theft, and illegal seizures and detentions.

Iran maintains an extensive network of internal security and intelligence services. The main parts of the domestic security apparatus are made up of the MOIS, the Basij Resistance Force, the Intelligence unit of the IRGC, and the Law Enforcement forces within the Ministry of Interior that largely are responsible for providing police and border control. The leadership of each of these organizations appears to be fragmented and dispersed among several, often competing, political factions. Public information on all Iranian security and intelligence forces is extremely limited and subject to political manipulation.

Key to most paramilitary and intelligence forces in Iran is the IRGC, as it holds control over several other organizations or parts thereof. All security organizations without exception report to the Supreme National Security Council (SNSC), as the highest body in the political chain of command. The phenomenon of the fragmented leadership of the security organizations is reflected in their relationship to the SNSC as different security organizations maintain special ties to certain elements of the SNSC.

In addition, it has to be assumed that other state organizations, most notably the police services, exert varying control over internal security. As with virtually all other organizations, the IRGC is believed to have considerable leverage over these services.[208] The effectiveness of the internal security organizations is unclear and the political will to use them is hard to predict. After local unrest in the Iranian province of Baluchistan in May 2006, police were unable to seize control of the situation against regional tribal forces.[209]

The Ministry of Intelligence and Security (MOIS)

The Ministry of Intelligence and Security (MOIS), or Vezarat-e Ettela' at va Aminat-e Keshvar (VEVAK), was installed following the Revolution to replace the now-disbanded National Organization for Intelligence and Security (SAVAK), which in turn was created under the leadership of U.S. and Israeli officers in 1957. SAVAK fell victim to political leadership struggles with the intelligence service of the IRGC during the Iran-Iraq War. A compromise solution resulted in the creation of MOIS in 1984.

In 2006, the MOIS employed about 15,000 civilian staff. Its major tasks included intelligence about the Middle East and Central Asia and domestic intelligence and monitoring of clerical and government officials[210] as well as work on preventing conspiracies against the Islamic Republic.[211] It can therefore be assumed that the ministry maintains an elaborate domestic service network.

The MOIS staff is believed to maintain a professional service loyalty and therefore is not subject to easy mobilization by military, clergy, or other political forces. Some, however, believe that during President Khatami's rule the MOIS actively sought to rid the organization of hard-line officials.[212] Within Iran's political system there is constant argument about limiting parliamentary control over MOIS, indicating that the control over MOIS can be used as a powerful political instrument. Recently, there were efforts in Iran to extract the counterintelligence unit of MOIS and make it a separate entity. This proposal seems to be favored by Supreme Leader Ayatollah Khamenei and some hard-line legislators.[213]

Until recently, the organization has remained under very limited public disclosure. In the 1990s, ministry personnel were accused of killing political dissidents in Iran. Ensuing investigations have been covered up systematically. Apparently, MOIS has a comparatively large budget at its disposal and operates under the broader guidance of Ali Khamenei.[214] And it seems likely that the details about the ministry's resources are partly undisclosed even to Iranian political officials.

The IRGC Intelligence Branch

As part of the Islamic Revolutionary Guard Corps, the roughly 2,000 staff members of its intelligence force are a largely politicized force with a political mission. According to *Jane's*, their conformity and loyalty to the regime are unquestionable.[215]

The main task of the IRGC Intelligence Branch is to gather intelligence in the Muslim world. As far as domestic security is concerned, the organization targets the enemies of the Islamic Revolution and also participates in their prosecution and trials.[216] In addition, it works closely with the IRGC's Qods Corps, which also operates covertly outside Iran.

The Basij Resistance Force

The IRGC oversaw the creation of a people's militia, a volunteer group, named the Basij Resistance Force (which means Mobilization of the Oppressed), in 1980. Numbering over 1,000,000[217] members, the Basij is a paramilitary force, mostly manned by elderly men, youths, and volunteers who have completed their military service. This force is organized in a regional and decentralized command structure. It has up to 740 regional battalions, each organized into three battalions or four platoons. Each battalion has 300–350 men. It maintains a relatively small active-duty staff of 90,000 and relies on mobilization in the case of any contingency.[218]

The Basij has a history of martyr-style suicide attacks dating back to the Iran-Iraq War, 1980–1988. Today, its main tasks are thought to assist locally against conventional military defense as well as quell civil uprisings. In addition, one of the force's key roles has been to maintain internal security including monitoring internal threats from Iranian citizens and acting as "a static militia force." The state of training and equipment readiness for the Basij is believed to be low. No major weapon systems have been reported for the inventory of the Basij. The Basij derives its legitimization from Article 151 of the Iranian Constitution, which calls upon the government to fulfill its duty according to the Quran to provide all citizens with the means to defend themselves.

The IRGC maintains tight control over the leadership of the Basij and imposes strict Islamic rules on it members. Recent comments by Iranian leaders indicate that the mission of the Basij is shifting away from traditional territorial defense to "defending against Iranian security threats." Furthermore, there are reports of an increased interest in improving the Basij under the leadership of President Ahmadinejad.[219] At the same time, the IRGC leadership questions the effectiveness of the Basij and might loosen its ties to the organization.[220]

In 1993, the Ashura Brigades were created from IRGC and Basij militia units as a response to antigovernment riots. This unit is composed of roughly 17,000 men and women, and its primary purpose is to keep down civil unrest, although there has been some discontent expressed by senior leaders about using IRGC units for domestic contingencies.[221]

The Uncertain Role of the Ministry of Interior

The police forces, which comprise about 40,000 police under the Ministry of Interior (MOI), participate in internal security as well as border protection. The Police-110 unit specializes in rapid-response activities in urban areas to disperse potentially dangerous public gatherings. The maritime police have 90 inshore patrol and 40 harbor boats. In 2003, some 400 women became the first female members of the police force since the 1978–1979 Revolution.[222]

The role of Iran's MOI is unclear, and open source information regarding its structure and forces is limited. The same is true of other organizations in Iran's internal security apparatus. The Ansar-e Hezbollah is a paramilitary force that has gained questionable notoriety. It remains unclear to what extent it is attached to government bodies. Reportedly, the political right in government has repeatedly made use of it to fight and intimidate liberal forces in society. The Ansar-e Hezbollah's military level of training appears to be very poor.[223]

IRAN'S CONTINUING STRATEGIC CHALLENGES

Iran has experienced many serious strategic challenges over the past three decades, which continue to have repercussions until the present time. After the Islamic Revolution of 1979, Iran was left without one of its formerly closest allies, the United States, which has considered Iran an adversarial power since the hostage taking in 1979. In addition to the domestic turmoil created by the Revolution, Iranian oil production and income dropped sharply. Iran went from earning some 17 percent of all OPEC (Organization of the Petroleum Exporting Countries) revenues in the late 1970s to an average of around 10 percent from 1980 to the present.[224] It had to fight a bloody war against Iraq that lasted eight years and came at a great cost to Iran both in terms of human life, strategic prestige, military capability, and economic development.

Following the Iran-Iraq War, the Iranian government failed to manage the nation's finances effectively and implement even basic reforms to develop its economy.

Moreover, Iran suffered from low oil prices during much of the 1990s. This caused Iran's military readiness to decline and its economy to stagnate. While the Gulf War of 1990–1991, and the sanctions on Iraq that followed, greatly weakened a once victorious Iraq, it also triggered a major expansion in the U.S. presence in the Gulf. Iran faced a different threat from the Taliban, which drove millions of Afghanis into Iran as refugees and was violently anti-Shi'ite. While the American military campaigns in Afghanistan and Iraq in 2001 and 2003 largely eliminated such threats, they also led to a massive American military presence on two of Iran's borders.

The "nuclearization" of India and Pakistan did not create a direct threat to Iran, but did change the nature of the balance of power in the region. More significantly, the rise of neo-Salafi Islamic fundamentalism created a direct religious and political challenge to Iran and all Shi'ites. While movements like Al Qa'ida divide over how openly they attack Shi'ites, some key leaders like Abu Musab al-Zarqawi have called for a Sunni jihad against Shi'ites, and others have called Shi'ites polytheists and apostates. Iran increasingly faced a struggle for the future of Islam and one that affected all Shi'ites, including those in Iraq, Lebanon, and Syria—where Iran had direct strategic interests.

The failure of the Israeli-Palestinian peace process and Israeli-Syrian negotiations made it impossible for Iranian "moderates" to back away from hostility to Israel and allowed hard-liners to make the Israeli-Palestinian war of attrition that began in 2000 a rallying call for support of Hezbollah in Lebanon and antipeace Palestinian groups like Hamas and the Palestinian Islamic Jihad (PIJ). It was sometimes unclear how sincere Iran's motives were and whether some of their attacks on Israel were posturing to defuse Arab hostility to Iran. Iran's more extreme statements and actions, however, paralyzed efforts to restore relations with the United States and led President George W. Bush to label Iran part of the "axis of evil" and the United States to call Iran the leading terrorist nation. The election of Ahmadinejad as President in August 2005 made this situation much worse when he questioned the existence of the Holocaust and called for the end of Israel.

Today, Iran faces several severe strategic challenges. Some of these challenges directly impact its internal stability, while others have an indirect impact on its overall strategic posture in the Gulf and beyond. The following list outlines key challenges that Iran faces today and may face in the foreseeable future:

- **Nuclear program, long-range missiles, and proliferation:** Iran has faced growing international pressure to stop those aspects of its uranium enrichment program and other nuclear research and development activities that seem to be tied to the development of nuclear weapons. The difficulty of this challenge to Iran and the international community is that Iran claims that its nuclear program is aimed for peaceful purposes (nuclear energy). While the Islamic republic has the right to achieve a full nuclear cycle under the Nuclear Non-Proliferation Treaty, the United States, the IAEA, and the EU-3 (Britain, Germany, and France) have argued that there are many unknowns about Iran's nuclear intentions. Iran's nuclear program was referred to the United Nations Security Council (UNSC) in early 2006, and Iran was still refusing to comply with UN resolutions at the end of September 2006. Continued Iranian nuclear activity, coupled to its development of long-range missiles, could lead the international community to further isolate Iran through diplomatic or economic sanctions or could provoke preemptive military strikes by the United States or Israel.

- **Iran's involvement in Iraq's internal affairs in the face of a possible division of Iraq or major civil war:** Like all neighboring states, Iran has stakes in ensuring Iraq's stable future. Regional, U.S., and British officials have accused Iran of meddling in Iraq's internal affairs, of supporting Shi'ite militias such as Al-Mahdi Army and the Badr Brigade through its intelligence and security services, and of aiming to create a Shi'ite crescent. From an Iranian perspective, the challenge is not only to answer these allegations, but it must be prepared to deal with Iraq. The threat from Saddam Hussein has been replaced with an insurgency that aims to start a civil war between Iraq's sectarian factions.

- **The U.S. presence in the region:** Many in the region feel that Iran is the clear winner in the case of Iraq, since the Shi'ite majority in Iraq came to power and they are more likely to be more sympathetic to Iran than to their Arab neighbors. While Iran is seen as the winner in the removing of two enemies on its borders (the Taliban in Afghanistan and Saddam Hussein in Iraq), Iran has more than 100,000 U.S. troops on two of its borders (Iraq and Afghanistan). The presence of the U.S. troops in the Gulf is not new, and Iran has had to deal with U.S. support of the GCC states since the Revolution, but the U.S. power projection does act as a deterrent despite the difficulty the United States is facing with the postwar conflict in Iraq.

- **Iran's policy toward neighboring states:** While Iran has evidently ceased to attempt to export its Islamic revolution to neighboring states since the mid-1990s, many Arab Gulf states fear that Iran is seeking hegemony in the Gulf and/or that its expansion of its capabilities for asymmetric warfare in the Gulf and ability to threaten Gulf shipping and energy facilities is a serious threat. Bahrain is concerned over Iran's relations with Bahrain's restive Shi'ite population. Saudi Arabia is concerned over its Shi'ite in its oil-rich Eastern Province. Qatar and Kuwait are concerned over Iranian energy claims, and the United Arab Emirates over the issue of Abu Musa and the Tumbs.

- **The threat from Al Qa'ida and other neo-Salafist extremist groups:** The struggle between Sunnis and Shi'ites is not new in the Gulf, but statements and actions by Al Qa'ida leaders such as Abu Musab al-Zarqawi have led many Shi'ites to see neo-Salafist groups as a key threat. As noted earlier, Iran has not suffered from the threat of terrorism, but such groups can become a threat to Iran's internal stability. The threat from such groups, however, does not have to be direct. An escalation of the attacks that took place in Iraq against Shi'ite holy sites, religious rituals, or leaders that spill over into neighboring states may force Iran to get involved to protect Shi'ites and their holy shrines against such attacks. This has led some Sunni states—notably Egypt, Jordan, and Saudi Arabia—to become steadily more concerned about a Shi'ite crescent of expanding Iranian influence that would include Iran, Iraq, Syria, and Lebanon.

- **Support of proxy groups:** The United States and Israel have accused Iran of supporting proxy groups beyond Iraq. Since the Revolution, Iran has had close relations with groups such as Hezbollah, Hamas, and Palestinian Islamic Jihad. In the "Global War on Terror," while Iran is happy to see the infrastructure of groups such as Al Qa'ida be destroyed, Iran sees Palestinian and Lebanese groups as freedom fighters.

Iran played a major role in supporting Hezbollah before and during its war with Israel in August 2003, and in supporting antipeace Palestinian groups like Hamas and the Palestinian Islamic Jihad. This has been a key factor behind the U.S. designation of Iran as a terrorist state and U.S. sanctions against Iran.

- **Internal political uncertainty:** Iran's political dynamics have been characterized by several factions including reformist, hard-liners, the clerical establishment, and the youth movements. The two key factions, however, that are often talked about as the two rivals are the reformists vs. the hard-liners. The election of Mohammad Khatami as President of the republic in 1997 was seen by many as a turning point in Iran's internal political trends. However, the election of Mahmoud Ahmadinejad in 2005 was a wake-up call to many experts. His political platform had several themes, but the chief items among them were supporting Iran's right to acquire nuclear technology, Persian nationalism, and populism that has not been seen in Iran since the time of Mohammad Mossadeq in the 1950s. It is too early to predict the result of this struggle between the reformists and the hard-liners, and it largely depends on Ahmadinejad's ability to deal with the international scrutiny regarding Iran's nuclear program and domestic economic prosperity.

- **Economic challenges:** Despite high oil prices, Iran's economy is not growing at its potential growth rate. There are several factors behind this. First, the government controls an estimated 80 percent of the economy, and this discourages the growth of a vibrant private sector, puts greater pressure on the government to support a welfare state, and prevents the growth of a business middle class that can demand further economic and political reforms. Iranian budget deficits are a chronic problem in spite of extraordinarily high oil revenues, driven by large-scale state subsidies on foodstuffs and gasoline. The Majlis did try in January 2005 to freeze domestic prices for gasoline and other fuels at 2003 levels, but in March 2006, it reduced the government's gasoline subsidy allocation for FY2006/07 to $2.5 billion vs. a request of $4 billion for 2006, and costs of over $4 billion for imports last year. Iran offers only limited employment opportunities for the country's young and rapidly growing population. The United States estimates that unemployment in Iran is around 11 percent, and it is significantly higher among young people. Inflation is high. Corruption is endemic in state-run, religious foundation, and quasistate monopoly activities which make up a large part of the economy.[225] Iran is attempting to diversify its economy by investing some of its oil revenues in other areas, including petrochemicals production. In 2004, nonoil exports rose by a reported 9 percent. Iran also is hoping to attract billions of dollars worth of foreign investment to the country through creating a more favorable investment climate by reducing restrictions and duties on imports and creating free-trade zones. However, there has not been a great deal of progress in this area. Foreign investors appear to be cautious about Iran, due to uncertainties regarding its future direction under new leadership, as well as the ongoing international controversy over the country's nuclear program.

- **Iran's energy sector suffers from a lack of foreign investment:** Years of sanctions, mismanagement by Iran's government, the steadily declining planning and management capabilities of the National Iranian Oil Company, and rigid foreign investment laws, which tend to be nationalistic in nature, have limited the modernization of Iran's energy sector since the fall of the Shah. This has helped lead to massive declines in its oil production capacity, which in 2006 was averaging around

4.1 million barrels per day vs. 5.6 to over 6.1 million barrels a day during the late 1970s. Iran's economy remains heavily dependent on oil and oil export revenues. While many people associate Iran with being an oil producer, it imports nearly 40 percent of its refined products, and this goes back to Iran's inability and at times unwillingness to attract enough private domestic and foreign investment. The U.S. Energy Information Administration notes that "Iran's existing oilfields have a natural decline rate estimated at 8 percent onshore and 10 percent per year offshore. The fields are in need of upgrading, modernization, and enhanced oil recovery (EOR) efforts such as gas reinjection. Current recovery rates are just 24–27 percent, compared to a world average of 35 percent. Iran also needs to increase its search for new oil, with only a few exploration wells being drilled in 2005."[226]

- **Military reforms:** As the previous sections have shown, Iran's armed services have quantity in Gulf standards, but they do not have the quality. This is due to several reasons, including mismanagement, the arms embargo by the United States, and the lack of enough funds to maintain and purchase new weapons systems. Iran cannot hope to be a viable conventional military power if it continues with the same defense policies. Even smaller countries such as the United Arab Emirates have surpassed Iran in military spending.

This list is not exhaustive, and Iran faces many other internal and external challenges that do not have the same magnitude or strategic importance. The fact remains, however, that Iran now exists between two war theaters (Iraq and Afghanistan), that its politics has led to steadily more concern inside and outside the Gulf, and the United States and its neighbors see it as a potential threat to the security of the Strait of Hormuz, one of the most important strategic waterways in the world and a region where 60 percent of world proven conventional oil reserves exist. Iran also faces two immediate strategic challenges that will preoccupy it for the next several years: dealing with the consequence of its nuclear ambitions and its role in Iraq's future.

Iran's Nuclear Program and Its Strategic Consequences

Iran faces major strategic problems because of an increasingly hostile international reaction to its nuclear enrichment program and failure to fully comply with IAEA inspections. Iran's nuclear file had become a major issue in the UN Security Council by mid-2006, and there seemed to be three different options for international action against Iran: diplomatic, punitive sanctions, or military strikes. No one knows which option is more likely or if any of them will work, but Iran is likely to face this challenge for the next few years—if it does not end its nuclear program.

Economic Sanctions

Iran's traditional economy (carpets, caviars, pistachios, etc.) is an unlikely area for sanctions, since the impact would largely affect farmers and small business without major implications on the Iranian government. Such sectors are also self-sustained, since they are not dependent on imports.

Other sectors, however, are dependent on imports and would be more impacted by economic sanctions. Sectors such as industry, for example, play a major role in Iran's economy. It is estimated that Iran's gross domestic product is 11.8 percent dependent on agriculture, 43.3 percent on industry, and 44.9 percent on services.[227] UNSC members would find it hard to justify the use of sanctions against agricultural products—except for dual-use technologies and fertilizers that can be used in the production of WMD—but industrial sanctions might be a different story.

Iran's heavier industries rely on refined products imports and would suffer from economic sanctions. Iran is an importer of refined products. Since 1982, Iran's dependence on imports of gasoline surged due to the fact that the refineries were damaged by the Iran-Iraq War, the mismanagement of these refineries, and the lack of foreign investment in its refinery sector. According to the International Energy Agency (IEA), Iran's refining sector is inefficient. For example, only 13 percent of the refinery output is gasoline—which is estimated to be half of what European refineries produce.[228]

In 2004, Iran imported an estimated 0.160 million barrels a day (MMBD) of oil equivalent of gasoline (40 percent of its domestic consumption). Iran's dependence on gasoline imports steadily increased in 2005 and 2006. Iran imported an estimated 0.170 MMBD of gasoline (41 percent of its domestic consumption) in 2005, and 0.196 MMBD (43 percent of its domestic consumption) in 2006. It is equally noteworthy that 60 percent of Iran's gasoline is imported from Europe, 15 percent from India, and the rest from elsewhere (Middle East and Asia).[229]

These trends are likely to continue. Iran's domestic demand for gasoline is estimated to increase at approximately 9 percent per year, and the costs of gasoline imports are also steadily increasing. For example, Iran paid an estimated $2.5–$3.0 billion for its gas imports in 2004 and is estimated to pay $4.5 billion in 2005.[230] Other experts, however, estimate that the cost of importing refined products was as high a $10 billion in 2005.[231] This is likely to include jet fuels, diesel, residual oil, kerosene, and other products.

Iran's dependence on gasoline imports is unlikely to change in the near future. It is estimated that Iran is planning to spend $16 billion between 2003 and 2030 to expand its refinery capacity from 1.5 MMBD in 2004 to 1.7 MMBD in 2010, 2.2 MMBD in 2020, and 2.6 MMBD in 2030. However, its total energy demand and consumption of refined products are also estimated to increase at higher rates.[232]

Sanctioning refined products exports to Iran would certainly have an impact on the Iranian economy, but the effectiveness of such a sanctions regimen would be uncertain. Iran can get around the imposed sanctions through unofficial deals and smuggling. In addition, Iran is enjoying high oil revenues and may well use them to fast-track its plans to expand refining capacity. Tehran might use such deals to attract foreign companies and to further complicate a UNSC resolution, since some of these contracts might go to Chinese, Russian, French, German, and British firms.

Some have argued that the first round of sanctions against Iran should target Iranian officials directly. This would include restricting Iranian officials, including the

President, Mahmoud Ahmadinejad, from traveling outside Iran, as well as other top officials and clerics.

These sanctions would have little impact on the general population. They might affect the mobility of Iranian officials, but their impact would be limited. They are hard to enforce outside the European Union and the United States. This may be further complicated by stopping Iranian officials from attending UN meetings in the United States or in the European Union. Middle Eastern and Asian countries might find it hard to comply with these travel restrictions—given the fragile strategic situation in the region.

If the goal is to send a message to the Iranian government and to the world that the world does not approve of Iran's nuclear weapons, then such sanctions might do that. It is questionable, however, whether travel restrictions would change the attitudes or actions of the Iranian government or Iranian public attitudes toward acquiring nuclear technology. The Iranian nuclear research program does not depend on the ability of the Iranian President to visit Paris, and the impact of such sanctions will be only symbolic in the case of Iran.

The historical precedents also are not reassuring. The European Union has maintained travel restrictions and financial sanctions against Zimbabwe. The European Union imposed targeted sanctions that included travel bans, oil embargo, and freezing of financial assets of President Robert Mugabe and 100 other senior Zimbabwean officials. The ban has been extended several times since its inception in February 2002, and it is expected to run out in February 2007. These extensions make either the point that these travel restrictions did not work or that they need a long time to work.

Travel restrictions and financial sanctions combined are also an option that might have more impact. This may, in fact, be the set of sanctions that would arouse the least amount of resistance by UNSC members. Most of the financial assets held in the West belong to the government or the ruling elite of Iran. The combination of freezing assets held in Westerns banks and travel restrictions can have the least impact on the general population and the maximum amount of pressure on the ruling elites.

While U.S. capital markets have been closed to the Iranian government since the Revolution, Iran had alternative sources. Iran relies on loans particularly from European and Asian banks to finance domestic projects in its energy sector.[233] For examples, Iran's shipbuilding and car making sectors are growing faster than Iranian domestic financial institutions. These industries have relied on European banks for investment loans. Some European banks stopped doing business with Tehran, but many other banks continue to finance projects in Iran, including major European banks such as HSBC, BNP Paribas, Deutsche Bank, Commerzbank, Standard Chartered, and Royal Bank of Scotland. Observers have argued that targeting loans from European banks could have a major impact on the Iranian economy, particularly since the Iranian capital market in still small and key industries in Iran cannot survive without investment loans from the outside.[234]

Another option to target Iranian finances is to freeze Iranian assets in European and Asian banks. Iran's financial assets in the United States have been frozen since the Revolution, but Tehran has significant amounts of financial assets in European financial institutions. There are no reliable estimates of how much Iran's hard currency deposits are. It is, however, safe to assume that it is a large amount given the recent surge in oil prices. Some estimates put it at $36 billion in 2005.

The significance of this can be seen through the reaction of the Iranian government following the IAEA referral of Iran's case to the UNSC. In January 2006, the governor of Iran's Central Bank announced that Iran had started transferring its assets out of European banks. It is unclear where the funds have been moved, but there are indications and an initial admission that they may have been transferred to Southeast Asia.[235]

It has also been reported that Iranian government figures have started to move their money from European financial institutions to Dubai, Hong Kong, Malaysia, Beirut, and Singapore. Iranian officials were quoted as saying that as high as $8 billion was moved out of Europe.[236]

Sanctions can reach beyond European financial institutions to include Asian banks and international NGOs such as the World Bank and the International Monetary Fund. This would drain another key source of financial support to the Iranian government. For example, in May 2005, the World Bank approved a $344-million loan to Iran to support the Caspian provinces in managing scarce water resources, $200 million for rebuilding following the Bam earthquake in October 2004, and $359 million in loans to the Government of Iran in order to improve housing, sanitation, and access to clean water in Ahwaz and Shiraz.[237] These loans, however, are focused toward humanitarian projects, but that does not mean that they could not be delayed to force Iran back to the bargaining table.

It is important, however, to keep in mind that the global economy offers many options to Iran, and enforcing such sanctions is not perfect. Iran is not confined to European private and central banks or international organizations to finance its domestic projects. If Iran does build enough incentives for direct foreign investment, no amount of sanctions can stop the flow of money into the country, particularly in its energy sector.

All of these scenarios are hypothetical at this point. It is unclear if the UNSC will actually agree to impose financial restrictions on Iran. In addition, no one can fully predict the response of the Iranian government, the ruling elite in Iran, or the Iranian general population. It is all too clear that freezing the money and restricting the travel of key regime figures is far less disagreeable than preventing investment in Iran's energy sector and causing further tightness in the global energy market. It is also clear that the regime might be more impacted with these restrictions than any broad economic sanctions that have direct implications on the Iranian population.

Military Strikes

Official U.S. policy is to leave all options on the table and emphasize diplomatic activity through the EU3 and the UN. U.S. Vice President Richard B. Cheney reiterated the U.S. policy on March 7, 2006:[238]

The Iranian regime needs to know that if it stays on its present course, the international community is prepared to impose meaningful consequences. For our part, the United States is keeping all options on the table in addressing the irresponsible conduct of the regime...And we join other nations in sending that regime a clear message: We will not allow Iran to have nuclear weapons.

Other U.S. officials also reiterated that preventive military options are still on the table. The U.S. National Security Advisor, Stephen J. Hadley, reiterated that Iran poses a grave threat to U.S. national security. During a presentation of the U.S. national security strategy in March 2006, he said, "We face no greater challenge from a single country than from Iran." Mr. Hadley added, "The doctrine of preemption remains sound...We do not rule out the use of force before an attack occurs."[239]

The U.S. estimates of timelines for Iran's nuclear and missile efforts also leave at least several years in which to build an international consensus behind sanctions and diplomatic pressure and a consensus behind military options if diplomacy fails.

The United States would also have the potential advantage of finding any Iranian smoking gun, improving its targeting and strike options, and being able to strike targets in which Iran had invested much larger assets. The fact Iran can exploit time as a weapon in which to proliferate does not mean that the United States cannot exploit time as a weapon with which to strike Iran.

Iranian Defense against U.S. Strikes

Iran would find it difficult to defend against U.S. forces using cruise missiles, stealth aircraft, standoff precision weapons, and equipped with a mix of vastly superior air combat assets and the IS&R assets necessary to strike and restrike Iranian targets in near real time. For example, each U.S. B-2A Spirit stealth bomber could carry eight 4,500-pound enhanced BLU-28 satellite-guided bunker-busting bombs—potentially enough to take out one hardened Iranian site per sortie. Such bombers could operate flying from Diego Garcia in the Indian Ocean, RAF Fairford in Gloucestershire, United Kingdom, and Whiteman U.S. Air Force (USAF) Base in Missouri.[240]

The United States also has a wide range of other hard target killers, many of which are in development or classified. Systems that are known to be deployed include the BLU-109 Have Void "bunker busters," a "dumb bomb" with a maximum penetration capability of 4 to 6 feet of reinforced concrete. An aircraft must overfly the target and launch the weapon with great precision to achieve serious penetration capability.[241] It can be fitted with precision guidance and converted to a guided glide bomb. The Joint Direct Attack Munition (JDAM) GBU-31 version has a nominal range of 15 kilometers with a CEP of 13 meters in the GPS-aided Inertial Navigation System (INS) modes of operation and 30 meters in the INS-only modes of operation.[242]

More advanced systems include the BLU-116 Advanced Unitary Penetrator (AUP), the GBU-24 C/B (USAF), or the GBU-24 D/B (U.S. Navy), which has about three times the penetration capability of the BLU-109.[243] It is not clear whether the United States has deployed the AGM-130C with an advanced earth penetrating/hard target kill system. The AGM-130 Surface Attack Guided Munition was developed to be integrated into the F-15E, so it could carry two such missiles, one on each inboard store station. It is a retargetable, precision-guided standoff weapon using inertial navigation aided by GPS satellites and has a 15–40-NM range.[244] The United States does, however, have a number of other new systems that are known to be in the developmental stage and can probably deploy systems capable of roughly twice the depth of penetration with twice the effectiveness of the systems known from its attacks on Iraq in 1991.

It is not clear whether such weapons could destroy all of Iran's most hardened underground sites, although it seems likely that the BLU-28 could do serious damage at a minimum. Much depends on the accuracy of reports that Iran has undertaken a massive tunneling project with some 10,000 square meters of underground halls and tunnels branching off for hundreds of meters from each hall. Iran is reported to be drawing on North Korean expertise and to have created a separate corporation (Shahid Rajaei Company) for such tunneling and hardening efforts under the IRGC, with extensive activity already under way in Natanz and Isfahan. The facilities are said to make extensive use of blast-proof doors, extensive divider walls, hardened ceilings, 20-centimeter-thick concrete walls, and double concrete ceilings with earth filled between layers to defeat earth penetrates.[245] Such passive defenses could have a major impact, but reports of such activity are often premature, exaggerated, or report far higher construction standards than are actually executed.

At the same time, the B-2A could be used to deliver large numbers of precision-guided 500-pound bombs against dispersed surface targets or a mix of light and heavy precision-guided weapons. Submarines and surface ships could deliver cruise missiles for such strikes, and conventional strike aircraft and bombers could deliver standoff weapons against most suspect Iranian facilities without suffering a high risk of serious attrition. The challenge would be to properly determine what targets and aim points were actually valuable, not to inflict high levels of damage.

As has been discussed earlier, Iran's air defenses have quantity, but little quality. This would help enable U.S. or Israeli attacks, but this situation could change over the next few years. Iran purchased 20 Russian 9K331 Tor-M-1 (SA-15 Gauntlet) self-propelled surface-to-air missiles in December 2005.[246] Some reports also indicate that Iran is seeking more modern Soviet SA-300 missiles and to use Russian systems to modernize its entire air defense system. If Iran could acquire, deploy, and bring such systems to a high degree of readiness, they would substantially improve Iranian capabilities.

Iran's air forces are only marginally better able to survive in air-to-air combat than Iraq's were before 2003. Iran's command and control system has serious limitations in terms of secure communications, vulnerability to advanced electronic warfare, netting, and digital data transfer. According to the IISS, Iran does still have five operational P-3MP Orions and may have made its captured Iraqi IL-76 Candid AEW aircraft operational. These assets would give it airborne warning and command and control capability, but these are obsolescent to obsolete systems and are likely to be highly vulnerable to electronic warfare and countermeasures, and long-range attack, even with Iranian modifications and updates. There are some reports Iran may be seeking to make a version of the Russian AN-140 AEW aircraft, but these could not be deployed much before 2015.[247]

Iran's air defense aircraft consist of a maximum operational strength of two squadrons of 25 export versions of the MiG-29A and two squadrons of 25–30 F-14As. The export version of the MiG-29A has significant avionics limitations and vulnerability to countermeasures, and it is not clear Iran has any operational Phoenix air-to-air missiles for its F-14As or has successfully modified its I-Hawk missiles for air-to-air combat. The AWG-9 radar on the F-14 has significant long-distance sensor capability in a permissive environment, but is a U.S.–made system in a nearly 30-year-old configuration that is now vulnerable to countermeasures.

Iran might risk using its fighters and AEW aircraft against an Israeli strike. It seems doubtful that Israel could support a long-range attack unit with the air defense and electronic assets necessary to provide anything like the air defense and air defense suppression assets that would support a U.S. strike. A U.S. strike could almost certainly destroy any Iranian effort to use fighters, however, and destroy enough Iranian surface-to-air missile defenses to create a secure corridor for penetrating into Iran and against key Iranian installations. The United States could then maintain such a corridor indefinitely with restrikes.

Iranian Retaliation against U.S. Strikes

This does not mean it would be easy or desirable for the United States to exercise its military options. U.S. forces are preoccupied in Iraq, and the lack of security in Iraq makes a full military attack against Iran all too unlikely. U.S. military options are not risk-free, and the consequences of U.S. strikes are enormous. Tehran has several retaliatory options:

- Retaliate against U.S. forces in Iraq and Afghanistan overtly using Shahab-3 missiles armed with CBR warheads.
- Use proxy groups, including those of Abu Musab al-Zarqawi and Moqtada Al-Sadr, in Iraq to intensify the insurgency and escalate the attacks against U.S. forces and Iraqi security forces.
- Turn the Shi'ite majority in Iraq against the U.S. presence and demand U.S. forces to leave.
- Attack the U.S. homeland with suicide bombs by proxy groups or deliver CBR weapons to Al Qa'ida to use against the United States.
- Use its asymmetric capabilities to attack U.S. interests in the region, including soft targets: e.g., embassies, commercial centers, and American citizens.
- Attack U.S. naval forces stationed in the Gulf with antiship missiles, asymmetric warfare, and mines.
- Attack Israel with missile attacks possibly with CBR warheads.
- Retaliate against energy targets in the Gulf and temporarily shut off the flow of oil from the Strait of Hormuz.

- Stop all of its oil and gas shipments to increase the price of oil and inflict damage on the global and U.S. economies.

Many observers argue that a military strike against Iran could add to the chaos in Iraq and may further complicate the U.S. position in Iraq. While the consequences of U.S. military attacks against Iran remain unclear, the Shi'ite majority in Iraq can (1) ask the United States to leave Iraq, (2) influence Shi'ite militia groups to directly attack U.S. forces, and/or (3) turn the new Iraqi security and military forces against U.S. forces in Iraq.[248]

As has been discussed earlier, Iran has extensive forces suited to asymmetric warfare. These not only include the Revolutionary Guards and elements of the al-Quds force under the Directorate of the Islamic Revolutionary Guards Corps, but elements of the foreign intelligence directorate in the Ministry of Intelligence and Security (Vezarat-e-Ettela'at va Amniat-e Keshvar or VEVAK).[249]

The Iranian surface navy is highly vulnerable, but Iran could position land-based antiship missiles where it could strike at tanker traffic, and mobile firing elements using systems like the HY-2/C-201 Silkworm or Seerseeker (Raad) have ranges of 90 to 100 kilometers and have proved difficult to detect and kill in the past.[250] Iran is reported to have the capability to make or assemble such missiles, modify and upgrade them, have roughly 100 systems in stock, and have eight to ten mobile missile launchers. These are reported to be deployed near the Strait of Hormuz, but may actually be in a number of different locations.[251]

Iran also has three relatively effective Kilo-class submarines, which can use long-range wire-guided torpedoes or release mines. (Reports Iran has advanced "bottom" mines with sensors that release and activate them as they sense ships passing overhead are uncertain.)

The naval branch of the IRGC is reported to have up to 20,000 men. They operate ten Hudong missile patrol boats with C-801K (42–120 kilometers) and C-802 (42–120 kilometers) sea-skimming antiship missiles.[252] The Iranian Air Force has airborne variants of these systems.

They have additional C-14 high-speed catamarans with C-701 antiship missiles and additional North Korean missile boats. They operate some 50 additional patrol boats, including 40 Boghammar Marine boats. Many are so small they are difficult to detect with ship-borne radars. These can be armed with recoilless rifles, RPGs, and small arms to attack or harass ships in or near the Gulf and raid or attack offshore facilities. They can conduct suicide attacks or release floating mines covertly in shipping lanes or near key facilities. Iran can use any commercial ship to release free-floating mines for the same purpose.[253]

Iran made claims in the spring of 2006 that it was testing more advanced weapons for such forces. These included a sonar-evading underwater missile (torpedo?) that IRGC Rear Admiral Ali Fadavi claimed no enemy warship could detect, and "no warship could escape because of its high velocity." Iran also claimed to be testing a new missile called the Kowsar with a very large warhead and extremely high speed to attack "big ships and submarines" that it claimed could evade radar and antimissile missiles. While such tests may have been real, Iran has made so many grossly exaggerated claims about its weapon developments in the past that it seems they were designed more to try to deter U.S. military action and/or reassure the Iranian public than truly being serious real-world capabilities.[254] It followed these actions up in the late summer of 2006 by testing new submarine launched antiship missiles.

In any case, Iran could not close the Strait of Hormuz or halt tanker traffic, and its submarines and much of its IRGC forces would probably be destroyed in a matter of days if they become operational. It could, however, conduct a series of raids to threaten and disrupt Gulf traffic and/or strike at offshore and shore facilities in the southern Gulf or at Iraqi oil facilities in the Gulf. Even sporadic random strikes would create a high risk premium and potential panic in oil markets. Iran could potentially destabilize part of Afghanistan and use Hezbollah and Syria to threaten Israel.

Iran can also use its IRGC asymmetric warfare assets to attack U.S. interests in the region. Iranian officials do not hide the fact that they would use asymmetric attacks against U.S. interests. For example, a Brigadier General in the IRGC and the Commander of the "Lovers of Martyrdom Garrison," Mohammad-Reza Jaafari, threatened U.S. interests with suicide operations if the United States were to attack Iran:[255]

> Now that America is after gaining allies against the righteous Islamic Republic and wants to attack our sanctities, members of the martyrdom-seeking garrisons across the world have been put on alert so that if the Islamic Republic of Iran receives the smallest threat, the American and Israeli strategic interests will be burnt down everywhere.
>
> The only tool against the enemy that we have with which we can become victorious are martyrdom-seeking operations and, God willing, our possession of faithful, brave, trained and zealous persons will give us the upper hand in the battlefield...
>
> Upon receiving their orders, our martyrdom-seeking forces will be uncontrollable and a guerrilla war may go on in various places for years to come...
>
> America and any other power cannot win in the unbalanced war against us.

Iran could seek to create an alliance with extremist movements like Al Qa'ida in spite of their hostility to Shi'ites. It can seek to exploit Arab and Muslim anger against U.S. ties to Israel and the invasion of Iraq on a global level, and it can seek to exploit European and other nations' concerns that the United States might be repeating its miscalculation of the threat posed by Iraq and striking without adequate cause. Unless Iran is far more egregious in its noncompliance, or the United States can find a definitive smoking gun to prove Iran is proliferating, Iran would be certain to have some success in such efforts.

Iran's energy resources are another potential weapon. Shutting off exports would deeply hurt Iran, but would also have an impact on global markets. As Iraq found, energy deals can also sharply weaken support for even diplomatic options, and Russia and China might well oppose any kind of U.S. military strike, regardless of the level of justification the United States could advance at the time.

The Strategic Implications of a Military Strike against Iran

It may be years, or as much as a decade, before all of the implications surrounding Iran's possible efforts to acquire nuclear weapons become clear. As the previous chapters have shown, the strategic implications of whether Iran has any nuclear device are only part of the story. There are many different ways in which Iran can proliferate, deploy nuclear-armed or other CBRN weapons, and use them to deter, intimidate, and strike against other nations. All have only one thing in common: *they are all provocative and dangerous both to any nation Iran may choose to try to influence and target and to Iran.*

Iran's options for war fighting, and the possible response, have already been described in detail. One final point does, however, need to be raised. Even Iranian ambiguity will probably lead Israel and the United States—and possibly India, Pakistan, and Russia—to develop nuclear options to deter or retaliate against Iran. Restraint does not have to stop at the first convincing Iranian threat to use nuclear or highly lethal biological weapons, but it could do so. Any actual Iranian use of such weapons is likely to provoke a nuclear response and may well provoke one targeted on Iranian cities and its population. Iran's effort to limit or control the game will probably end at the first ground zero.

Iranian ambiguity also may trigger Saudi and Egyptian efforts to become nuclear powers. They might show restraint if the United States could provide convincing ballistic and cruise missile defenses and the same form of extended deterrence it once provided to Germany during the Cold War. But these options are speculative and do not yet exist. Saudi Arabia has already said that it has examined nuclear options and rejected them, but this is no certainty and inevitably depends on Iranian action.

The end result is the prospect of a far more threatening mix of CBRN capabilities in the Gulf region and the areas that most models project as the main source of continued world oil and gas exports beyond 2015. It is also the threat of more polarization between Sunni and Shi'ites and broader regional tensions and actions that spill over out of the confrontation over Iran's nuclear activities. None of these prospects are pleasant.

The Future of Iraq

Iran already plays a major role in the political stability (or instability) of Iraq and may take a more aggressive role in trying to shape Iraq's political future and security position in the Gulf. Some believe that the Iranians have abandoned their efforts to export their "Shi'ite revolution" to the Gulf. This view has changed since the invasion of Iraq. Officials across the Arab world, especially in Saudi Arabia and Jordan, have expressed reservations over the lack of rights of Iraqi Sunnis, Kurdish and Shi'ite dominance over the Iraqi government, and a new "strategic" Shi'ite alliance between Iran and Iraq.

Jordan's King Abdullah has claimed that more than 1 million Iranians have moved into Iraq to influence the Iraqi election. The Iranians, King Abdullah argued, have

been trying to build pro-Iranian attitudes in Iraq by providing salaries to the unemployed. The King has also said that Iran's Revolutionary Guards are helping the militant groups fighting the United States in Iraq, and he warned in an interview with
the *Washington Post* of a "Shi'ite Crescent" forming between Iran, Iraq, Syria, and
Lebanon. He was quoted as saying,[256]

> It is in Iran's vested interest to have an Islamic republic of Iraq.
>
> If Iraq goes Islamic republic, then, yes, we've opened ourselves to a whole set of new
> problems that will not be limited to the borders of Iraq. I'm looking at the glass half-full,
> and let's hope that's not the case. But strategic planners around the world have got to be
> aware that is a possibility.
>
> Even Saudi Arabia is not immune from this. It would be a major problem. And then
> that would propel the possibility of a Shi'ite-Sunni conflict even more, as you're taking it
> out of the borders of Iraq.

The same sentiment has been echoed by the former interim Iraqi President, Ghazi
Al-Yawar, a Sunni. "Unfortunately, time is proving, and the situation is proving,
beyond any doubt that Iran has very obvious interference in our business—a lot of
money, a lot of intelligence activities and almost interfering daily in business and
many [provincial] governates, especially in the southeast side of Iraq." Mr. Al-
Yawar, however, asserted that Iraq should not go in the direction of Iran in creating
a religious oriented government. He was quoted in a *Washington Post* interview as
saying, "We cannot have a sectarian or religious government...We really will not
accept a religious state in Iraq. We haven't seen a model that succeeded."[257]

These comments were rejected by both Iran and Iraqi Shi'ites. Iran called King
Abdullah's comment "an insult" to Iraq. Iranian Foreign Ministry Spokesman,
Hamid Reza Asefi, also called on Ghazi Al-Yawar to retract his statement and accused
King Abdullah II and Al-Yawar of wanting to influence the election against Iraqi
Shi'ites. Asefi said, "Unfortunately, some political currents in Iraq seek to tarnish
the trend of election there and cause concern in the public opinion...We expect that
Mr. al-Yawar takes the existing sensitive situation into consideration and avoids
repeating such comments."[258]

What is clear is that Iran has close relations with many Iraqi Shi'ites, particularly
Shi'ite political parties and militias. Some Iraqi groups have warned against U.S.
military strikes against their neighbors. For example, Moqtada Al-Sadr pledged that
he would come to the aid of Iran in the case of a military strike by the United States
against Tehran. Al-Sadr pledged that his militia, Al-Mahdi Army, would come to the
aid of Iran. According to Al-Sadr, Iran asked him about what his position would be if
Iran was attacked by the United States, and he said he pledged that Al-Mahdi Army
would help any Arab or neighboring country if it was attacked.[259]

The London Times in September 2005 identified at least a dozen active Islamic
groups with ties to Tehran. Eight were singled out as having considerable cross-
border influence:[260]

- **Badr Brigade:** A Shi'ite militia force of 12,000 trained by Iran's Revolutionary Guards and blamed for a number of killings of Sunni Muslims. It is thought to control several cities in southern Iraq.

- **Islamic Dawaa Party:** A Shi'ite party that has strong links to Iran. Its leader, Ibrahim al-Jaafari, the present Prime Minister of Iraq, has vowed to improve ties between the two neighbors.

- **Al-Mahdi Army:** Received arms and volunteers from Iran during its battle against U.S. and British troops last year. The group's commander in Basra, Ahmed al-Fartusi, was arrested by British forces in mid-September 2005.

- **Mujahideen for Islamic Revolution in Iraq:** A Tehran-backed militia blamed for the murder of six British Royal Military Police soldiers in Majar el-Kabir in 2003.

- **Thar Allah (Vengeance of God):** An Iranian-backed terror group blamed for killing former members of the ruling Ba'ath Party in Iraq and enforcing strict Islamic law.

- **Jamaat al-Fudalah (Group of the Virtuous):** A paramilitary group that imposes Islamic rules on Shi'ite areas and has attacked shops selling alcohol and music.

- **Al-Fadilah (Morality):** A secret political movement financed by Iran. It is thought to have many members among provincial officials.

- **Al-Quawaid al-Islamiya (Islamic Bases):** An Iranian-backed Islamic movement that uses force to impose Islamic law.

A number of experts believe that Tehran-backed militias have infiltrated Iraqi security forces. In September 2005, Iraq's National Security Adviser, Mouwafak al-Rubaie, admitted that insurgents had penetrated Iraqi police forces in many parts of the country, but he refused to speculate about the extent of the infiltration.[261]

In addition, both the U.S. and the British Ministers of Defense have complained that Iran is actively supporting various militias in Iraq, has supplied advanced triggering and motion detector systems for improvised explosive devices, and is using elements of the al-Quds force to train death squads and militias.[262] Work by Nawaf Obaid and the Saudi National Security Assessment Project indicates the following:[263]

> Iran is insinuating itself into Iraq. The first is through the activities of the al-Quds Forces, the special command division of the Iranian Revolutionary Guard (IRGC). The second approach is by funding and arming Shi'ite militias, the most prominent of which is the SCIRI's 25,000-strong armed wing, the Badr Organization of Reconstruction and Development. Senior members of the Badr Organization and the al-Quds Forces have a closely coordinated relationship. Intelligence reports have indicated that Iranian officers are directing operations under cover in units of the Badr Organization. The Mahdi Army also receives important Iranian assistance, but on a much smaller scale.
>
> The IRGC Commander is General Yahya Rahim-Safavi and the Deputy Commander is General Mohammad Bager Zulgadr. The al-Quds Forces Commander is General Qassem Soleimani. Generals Zulgadr and Soleimani are two most senior officers responsible for Iran's large covert program in Iraq and have a direct link to the Office

of the Leader. Additionally, intelligence estimates have identified four other IRGC generals and nine IRGC colonels that are directly responsible for covert operations in Iraq.

The al-Quds Forces mainly functions as a large intelligence operation skilled in the art of unconventional warfare. Current intelligence estimates puts the strength of the force at 5,000. Most of these are highly trained officers. Within the al-Quds Forces, there is a small unit usually referred to as the "Special Quds Force" which consists of the finest case officers and operatives.

The senior officers attached to this unit conduct foreign covert unconventional operations using various foreign national movements as proxies. The forces operate mainly outside Iranian territory, but maintain numerous training bases inside Iran as well. Al-Quds international operations are divided into geographic areas of influence and various corps. The most important and largest cover Iraq, Saudi Arabia (and the Arabian Peninsula), and Syria / Lebanon. The smaller corps cover Afghanistan, Pakistan/India, Turkey, the Muslim Republics of the former Soviet Union, Europe/North America, and North Africa (Egypt, Tunisia, Algeria, Sudan, and Morocco).

The goal of Iran is to infiltrate all Iraq-based militias by providing training and support to their members. For example, al-Sadr's estimated 10,000-strong Mahdi Army, which gets logistical and financial support from al-Quds, also receives training in IRCG camps in Iran. Moreover, nearly all of the troops in the Badr Organization were trained in these camps as well. In addition, most senior officers acquired their skills in specialized camps under the control of the al-Quds Forces. Intelligence estimates that al-Quds currently operates six major training facilities in Iran, with the main facility located adjacent to Imam Ali University in Northern Tehran. The other most important training camps are located in the Qom, Tabriz, and Mashhad governorates. There are also two similar facilities operating on the Syrian-Lebanese border.

According to a senior general in the Iraqi Defense Ministry and a critic of Iran, the Iranians have set up the most sophisticated intelligence-gathering network in the country, to the extent that they have infiltrated "every major Iraqi ministry and security service." There is also an intelligence directorate that has been set up within the Revolutionary Guard that is under the command of the al-Quds Forces devoted exclusively to monitoring the movements of US and Allied forces in Iraq.

Many members of the newly created police and Iraqi forces are controlled by Shi'ite officers who, in some form or another, previously belonged to SCIRI or other groups affiliated with Iran. Recent intelligence indicates that IRGC officers are currently operating in Iraq in certain Shi'ite militias and actual army and police units. The degree of penetration of these organizations is difficult to assess, and it is virtually impossible to distinguish between Iraqi Shi'ite militias and police units, both of which are profoundly influenced by Iran, and in some cases are under Iranian control.

Iranian manipulation has filtered down to street level as well. Ordinary police and military officers now have a stronger allegiance to the Badr Organization or the Mahdi Army than to their own units. And of course, these organizations are deeply connected to Iran. According to the head of intelligence of an allied country that borders Iraq, "the Iranians have not just pulled off an infiltration, in certain regions in Baghdad and Basra, it's been a complete takeover."

It is not clear just how much Iran is using its security and intelligence forces to destabilize the political situation in Iraq. Iran's political objectives in Iraq remain obscure and partly contradictory. Tehran has stated repeatedly that it supports stability in Iraq. At the same time, several organizations with ties to the Iranian security apparatus are suspected of actively driving a wedge between rivaling factions in Iraq. The IRGC and its affiliates, out of any Iranian government organization, appear to be most strongly involved in assisting terrorist groups in neighboring Iraq.

In December 2004, a group named the Committee for the Commemoration of Martyrs of the Global Islamic Campaign assembled more than 25,000 "martyrdom-seeking volunteers" to fuel the insurgency of Iraqi groups against American forces. The committee maintains close ties to the IRGC from which it probably receives considerable material support. According to Iranian dissident groups, the IRGC is also directly involved in instigating the Iraqi insurgency through its Qods commandos, particularly in southern Iraq. Their number and extent of involvement with Iraqi factions remains unclear, however. Since the beginning of the American military campaign in Iraq, more than 2,000 people—believed to be sponsored directly by Iran—have entered the country to promote militant Islam.[264]

Reports suggest that Iranian sources have tried to establish contact with Moqtada Al-Sadr's organization in Iraq. Al-Sadr in the past spoke out against Iranian influence in Iraq. A relatively close connection between his organization and the Committee for the Commemoration of Martyrs of the Global Islamic Campaign with Iran suggests that destabilizing the political situation in Iraq is an important objective for the Iranian leadership. Apparently, Iranian forces try to gain leverage even over hostile forces in order to further Iraqi factionist politics.

Iran has a strategic interest in a stable Iraqi government. However, at this time, it appears as if Tehran is mobilizing resources to tilt the political climate in its favor, although it understands that this is causing some degree of additional political instability. All of the above concerns could also suddenly become far more serious if Iraq plunges into full-scale civil war or divides along ethnic and sectarian lines. Iran might be virtually forced to intervene on the Shi'ite side, potentially triggering new tensions and conflicts with both Iraq's Sunnis and Sunni states outside Iraq, and raising new issues regarding Iran's attitudes towars Iraq's Kurds, as well as its own Kurdish minority.

Other Challenges

This focus on Iran's nuclear programs and relations with Iraq does not mean that its hostility to Israel, Sunni v.s Shi'ite religious tensions, or its other challenges could not suddenly become the most important issues Iran faces—or simultaneously complicate its other challenges. Iran is also becoming progressively more dependent on high oil prices and export revenues as years go by with governments that all have at least one thing in common—some of the worst economic policies and management in the world compounded by serious social and cultural repression.

It is important to note, however, that many of Iran's strategic challenges owe far more to history, ideology, and political extremism than grand strategic necessity. Iran has every reason to seek better relations with its neighbors and the United States, to reach out to the moderate Gulf and other Islamic regimes that are the natural enemies of neo-Salafi Sunni extremism, and to confine its opposition to Israel to the political support of the Palestinians. Iran has far more to gain from focusing on internal development and regional cooperation than from political or military adventures and would greatly reduce its strategic risks.

Iraq

Iraq's strategic location, its access to water, it rivers, and its fertile soil have long given it strategic importance, and this importance has been vastly increased in the modern era by its status as an oil power. Like Iran, there has been no modern systematic exploration of Iraq's oil and gas resources. The *Oil and Gas Journal* estimates that Iraq contains 115 billion barrels of proven oil reserves, the third largest in the world (behind Saudi Arabia and Canada), concentrated overwhelmingly (65 percent or more) in southern Iraq.

The U.S. Energy Information Agency reports that estimates of Iraq's oil reserves and resources vary widely and that only about 10 percent of the country has been explored. It notes that some experts believe that deep oil-bearing formations located mainly in the vast Western Desert region could yield large additional oil resources (possibly another 100 billion barrels or more), but have not been explored. It cautions, however, that other analysts, such as the U.S. Geological Survey, are not as optimistic, with median estimates for additional oil reserves closer to 45 billion barrels. In August 2004, Iraqi Oil Minister Ghadban stated that Iraq had "unconfirmed or potential reserves" of 214 billion barrels.[1]

At present, Iraq is in the middle of an insurgency that may well lead to a major civil war. There is no way to predict whether Iraq's government can achieve political conciliation, create the security forces it needs to control factional militias and defeat a Sunni insurgency, and move back toward stability and development. It is all too possible that the country may divide or become a group of somewhat hostile federations that separate its Kurds, Arab Sunnis, and Arab Shi'ites.

A PATTERN OF EXTERNAL AND INTERNAL VIOLENCE

Iraq is emerging from centuries of Ottoman control, its creation as an artificial state following World War I, and decades of monarchy and civil war. Modern Iraq was occupied by Britain during the course of World War I. In 1920, Britain carved it out of the ruins of the Ottoman Empire and had it declared a League of Nations mandate under British administration. The result was a Sunni-dominated state with a Shi'ite majority and a Kurdish minority that wanted independence.

The British mandate failed to cope with Iraqi nationalism and led to active rebellion. This rebellion failed in a military sense, in the face of British military action that included the use of poison gas, but it eventually forced Britain to give Iraq independence. A Hashemite monarchy was established that survived a series of coup attempts and a British invasion during World War II.

Hashemite rule could not survive the rise of Arab nationalism, however, and was brutally overthrown in 1958. From that point onward, Iraq was ruled through a series of coups and military dictatorships until the Ba'ath Party seized power. Saddam Hussein consolidated his rule in a new series of bloody purges and executions in 1979 and ruled until he was overthrown in 2003 by the U.S.–led invasion.

Iraq has repeatedly sought to dominate the region politically and militarily. It never, however, has succeeded in having a major political impact on its neighbors, and its Ba'ath Party has done far more to feud with its counterpart in Syria than to have an impact on others. Its long arms race with Iran failed to keep up with the Shah until the Shah fell from power in 1979. This appeared to leave Iraq the dominant power in the Gulf, but its invasion of Iran in 1980 quickly showed that force size was not a measure of military competence and effectiveness. Iraq was forced on the defensive in 1982 and survived only because of European and Russian arms sales and tens of billions of dollars worth of Kuwaiti, Saudi, and other aid.

Iraq did achieve significant victories against an exhausted Iran in 1988, made successful use of mass attack with missiles and poison gas, shattered much of Iran's ground forces, and made it accept a cease-fire largely on the basis of the prewar boundary. Iraq was so deeply in debt and under so much financial pressure, however, that it seized Kuwait in 1990. The resulting Gulf War cost Iraq roughly 40 percent of its forces and led to more than a dozen years of sanctions, a UN arms embargo, UN efforts to fully discover and rid Iraq of the weapons of mass destruction it had built up before the Gulf War, and political and economic struggles over sanctions.

Iraq had to deal with more than outside conflicts. The British used divide and rule techniques that put a Sunni elite firmly in control of a Shi'ite majority that showed little desire for British rule. This Sunni elite remained in power until Saddam Hussein's fall, often exploiting its position at the expense of Iraq's Shi'ites and Kurds. The Kurds repeatedly sought independence and fought a nearly five-year rebellion against the Iraq regime until they lost the support of the Shah. Iraq was, however, forced to concede to many Iranian demands as the Shah's price for abandoning the Kurds when Iraq signed the Algiers Accord in 1975.

The Shi'ites remained largely loyal during the Iran-Iran War, although hundreds of thousands fled Iraq for Iran or deserted. The Kurds did not. Many rebelled and were put down in ruthless attacks using air and artillery strikes on civilians, the use of poison gas, and forced relocations. The aftermath was as violent as the fighting. Marsh Arabs were punished for harboring deserters by seeing their marshes drained and their way of life destroyed. Tribal groups and towns that showed any resistance to the regime were suppressed by force, often using mass executions.

The situation grew worse after Iraq's defeat in the Gulf War in 1991. UN inspectors discovered that Iraq had systematically lied about the nature of its chemical, biological, and nuclear weapons efforts, and missile programs, virtually up to the time of the U.S.–led invasion. While the United States and Britain made almost totally inaccurate estimates of Iraqi activity at the time they struck, this came after more than a decade of constant Iraqi lies and obfuscation. The Shi'ite and Kurdish uprisings in Iraq following Iraq's defeat were put down with savage force and left the Kurds isolated in their own U.S.–secured enclave in the north from 1992 onward. The Shi'ites were largely suppressed, but subject to constant military and security action, with occasional strikes against the regime from Shi'ite exiles based in Iran. Saddam retaliated by supporting the MEK (Mujahedin-e Khalq), a ruthless Iranian terrorist cult, in retaliation. Saddam also encouraged tribalism and Sunni religious action as ways of trying to cement his power.

Iraq's economy was crippled by a combination of massive state mismanagement, corruption, war, civil conflict, and UN sanctions from roughly 1982–2003, a period of over two decades. It was also severely distorted by nepotism and favoritism in ways that favored Sunni elites and compounded the nation's economic problems. At the same time, Iraq had built up a massive military machine during the Iran-Iraq War that it could not afford to pay for or maintain by 1989, and then it lost virtually all military resupply and modernization as a result of the UN arms embargo imposed in the summer of 1990. Iraq's military machine decayed steadily from wear, mismanagement, lack of parts and modernization, and internal security purges for some 13 years.

The fall of Saddam Hussein's regime in March and April 2003 did not make things better. The victorious Coalition was unprepared for the stability and nation-building efforts necessary to offer Iraqis a better way of life, and it was slow to improvise the tools it needed. Iraq's existing political system and governance imploded under the pressure of war and the "de-Ba'athification" of the Iraqi armed forces and government. Much of the secular core of the state was excluded from any meaningful position, even though the vast majority of those involved had simply gone along with Saddam and the Ba'ath Party to survive. Far too many of the exiles who returned and gained positions of power favored their own careers, Shi'ite parties, and religious factions, and a large number had links to Iran and Iranian-sponsored militias. The Kurds sought their own interests.

The end result is not without hope, but there have been three years of growing insurgency, and sectarian and ethnic divisions by Arab Shi'ite, Arab Sunni, Kurd, and other minorities. There is an elected government with a mix of all of Iraq's factions, an ongoing political process, and a serious effort to rebuild Iraqi military and police forces. At the same time, the insurgency is now dominated by Sunni neo-Salafi Islamist extremists who sometimes call for jihad against Shi'ites, mixed with many more moderate Iraqi Sunnis who question whether there is a clear alternative to force in seeking a share of power and wealth. The Shi'ites at a minimum want a share of power that matches their dominant share of the population. Many want revenge for decades of inferiority, and some factions increasingly are using militias and other forces to attack Sunnis in retaliation for the insurgency. The Kurds want at least autonomy and control of Iraq's northern oil fields as a source of wealth.

As a result, Iraq is the most destabilizing single factor in the Gulf, outpacing any other source of national tension like Iranian proliferation and the transnational threat of Islamist extremism. This will disappear if Iraq finds a viable political compromise between its factions, reestablishes effective governance, creates national military and police forces, and can gradually move its economy forward. If it fails in these areas, however, it could divide into some form of federalism or sink into large-scale civil war—potentially dividing Sunni and Shi'ite in support of their respective faction inside Iraq in many other nations in the Gulf. A natural division along such lines between a Shi'ite Iran and the Sunni southern Gulf States, Jordan, and Egypt is just one case in point.

These challenges make predicting the future of Iraq all the more difficult if not impossible. Some things do, however, seem clear. Even if the nation does not become involved in a major sectarian and ethnic civil war, creating a stable Iraq will largely depend on bringing Iraq's factions together, dealing with outside interference, building viable economic and political institutions, and dealing with the presence of foreign troops for many years to come. Any meaningful analysis of Iraq's prospects of stability will also mean successful efforts to build effective internal security and military forces that are free of sectarian manipulations. This would mean examining Iraq's internal security, paramilitary, and military forces' abilities to defeat the insurgency and to ensure security in Iraq's major cities.

IRAQ'S STRATEGIC IMPORTANCE

Iraq has strategic importance for reasons other than oil. Iraq's history, size, and natural resources make it one of the most important nations in the Gulf. As Map 9.1 shows, Iraq borders all the key countries in the Gulf: Iran (1,458 kilometers), Saudi Arabia (814 kilometers), and Kuwait (240 kilometers). In addition, it borders two important countries in the Levant—Syria (605 kilometers) and Jordan (181 kilometers)—as well as Turkey (352 kilometers). In addition, Iraq has a 58-kilometer coastline on the Gulf.

These borders, and Iraq's limited access to the Gulf, have helped lead to territorial disputes and conflicts with its neighbors. Iraq's proxy struggle with Iran during 1970–1975 was largely a broad struggle and fight for control of the Shatt al-Arab on the part of the Shah. The Iran-Iraq War (1980–1988) not only involved an effort to win back what was lost in 1975, but an Iraqi effort to seize Iran's oil rich areas in the southwest which Iraq claimed were Arab, followed by Iranian areas to take "Shi'ite" territory in Iraq's south. Iraq first threatened to invade Kuwait shortly after British forces left in 1932. When it did invade in August 1990, Iraq annexed Kuwait as the "19th province of Iraq" based on claims that can be traced back to the Othman Empire, as well as territorial tensions over claims to oil fields on the

Source: CIA, "Iraq," 2004, available at http://www.lib.utexas.edu/maps/middle_east_and_asia/iraq_pol_2004.jpg

Map 9.1   Iraq

border and Iraq's desire to win secure access to the Gulf. This led to the Gulf War in 1991, when a UN-mandated Coalition forced Saddam Hussein's forces from Kuwait and imposed economic sanctions, the no-fly zones, and political and military isolation of Iraq.

Iraq's energy resources have also been both a curse and a blessing. Its proven oil reserves are estimated to be one of the largest in the world. In 2005, Iraq was estimated to have roughly 10 percent of the world's total proven oil reserves (115 billion barrels of oil).[2] In addition, Iraq was estimated to have approximately 45.01 billion barrels of undiscovered oil reserves. Despite these vast reserves, Iraq's oil production capacity lags behind other countries. This is largely due to failures and mismanagement of Saddam Hussein's regime to modernize Iraq's oil sector, as well as economic sanctions and conflicts that have prevented much needed foreign investments from flowing in.[3]

As has already been touched upon, its sectarian divisions are a source of tension and conflict in the region. Iraq is unique in the sense that it is one of two Arab countries where the majority is actually Shi'ite. Iraq's population is estimated to be 60–65 percent Shi'ites and 32–37 percent Sunnis. Since the creation of the "modern" Iraq, it has, however, been ruled by Sunni government: a Sunni monarchy between 1932 and 1958 and the Ba'ath regime from 1958 until 2003. In addition to these sectarian divisions, Iraq has deep ethnic divisions—the most important of which is between Arabs and the Kurds who dominate northern Iraq and have sought autonomy or independence ever since World War I. The CIA estimates that Iraq's population is Arab, 75–80 percent; Kurdish, 15–20 percent; and Turkoman, Assyrian, or other, 5 percent.[4]

This diversity has caused tensions internally as well as externally. Throughout Saddam Hussein's reign, the Ba'ath government had to fight a war with Iran (a Shi'ite nation), while at the same time it had to pay close attention to the aspirations of its Kurdish and Shi'ite populations. These tensions led to the chemical attacks on the Kurds in Halabjah in 1988 as well as many attacks on the Shi'ites in the south, including following the Shi'ite uprising after the Gulf War in 1991.

Following the toppling of Saddam Hussein's regime in 2003, the sectarian tensions are central in any debate over the future of Iraq. In addition to hundreds of mass graves of Shi'ites and Kurds, almost all of the key destabilizing forces go back to Iraq's ethnic and sectarian divisions. Defeating the insurgency, the ability of Iraq to establish viable political institutions, and reconstruction efforts have been plagued by sectarian divisions.

IRAQI MILITARY DEVELOPMENT

Iraq has gone from being the Gulf's preeminent military power before it invaded Kuwait, and still a major power before the Coalition invasion in 2003, to a power that is just beginning to rebuild its regular military forces. The details of this transition are summarized in Figure 9.1.

Iraq is now concentrating on creating a mix of regular military forces in its Ministry of Defense, a National Police that really consists of security forces in its Ministry of Interior, and more conventional police forces that can defeat an ongoing insurgency and not on creating the heavier combat forces that are necessary to deter and defend against outside enemies. It will need to rebuild such forces in the future, but plans to create them are still highly tentative. Iraq is effectively dependent on the U.S.– and British-led Multinational Force–Iraq (MNF-I) for major armored, artillery, air combat, air mobility, naval, service, and logistic support.

Iraqi security and stability is dependent on the success of these force-building efforts, but force building is equally dependent on Iraqi political conciliation. It is almost totally dependent on three factors for success. One is the success of its political process in uniting the country, bringing Sunnis back into the political fold and

Figure 9.1   Iraq before the Gulf and Iraq Wars vs. Mid-2006

	1990	2002	Mid-2006
Manpower			
Total Active	1,000,000	389,000	264,600
Regular	425,000	375,000	116,100
Reserve	850,000	650,000	0
Other Ministry of Interior Security Forces	0	0	43,800
Paramilitary	40,000	44,000+*	–
Police & Highway Patrol	NA	NA	104,700
Army and Guard[†]			
Manpower	955,000	350,000	114,700
Regular Army Manpower	–	**375,000**	–
Reserve	480,000 (recalled)	650,000	–
Total Main Battle Tanks	**5,500–6,700**	**2,200–2,600**	**77+**
Active Main Battle Tanks	5,100	1,900–2,200	?[‡]
Active AIFV/Reconnaissance, Lt. Tanks	2,300	1,300–1,600	38+
Total Armored Personnel Carriers	**7,100**	**2,400**	**120–200**
Active APCs	6,800	1,800	?
Antitank Guided Missile Launchers	**1,500**	**900+**	**?**
Self-Propelled Artillery	**500+**	**150–200**	**?**
Towed Artillery	**3,000+**	**1,900**	**?**
Multiple Rocket Launchers	**300+**	**200**	**?**
Mortars	**5,000**	**2,000+**	**?**
Surface-to-Surface Missile Launchers	**?**	**56**	**?**
Light Surface-to-Air Launchers	**1,700?**	**1,100**	**?**
Antiaircraft Guns	**?**	**6,000**	**200–300**
Air Force Manpower	**40,000**	**20,000**	**600**
Air Defense Manpower	**10,000**	**17,000**	**0**
Total Combat Aircraft	**513**	**316**	**0**
Bombers	20	6	0
Fighter/Attack	284+	130	0
Fighter/Interceptor	223+	180	0
RRCCE/FGA RECCE	10	5	0

AEW C4I/BM	1	0	0
MR/MPA	0	0	0
OCU/COIN/CCT	0	0	0
Other Combat Trainers	157	73	0
Transport Aircraft§	**63**	**12**	**3**
Tanker Aircraft	**4?**	**2**	**0**
Total Helicopters	**584**	**375**	**10–25**
Armed Helicopters§	160	100	0
Other Helicopters§	424	275	10–25
Major Surface-to-Air Missile Launchers	**600+**	**400**	**0**
Light Surface-to-Air Missile Launchers	**?**	**450**	**0**
Antiaircraft Guns	**–**	**3,000**	**0**
Total Naval Manpower	**5,000**	**2,000**	**800**
Regular Navy	5,000	2,000	–
Naval Guards	0	0	–
Marines	–	–	–
Major Surface Combatants			
Missile	4	0	0
Other	1	0	0
Patrol Craft			
Missile	8	1	0
Other	6	5	3
Submarines	**0**	**0**	**0**
Mine Vessels	**8**	**3**	**0**
Amphibious Ships	**6**	**0**	**0**
Landing Craft	**9**	**–**	**–**
Support Ships	**3**	**2**	**0**

* "+" indicates the numbers listed may be slightly less than the actual units or weapons in stock.

† No accurate counts exist of Iraqi Army equipment because some items are being recovered out of weapons dumps. NA = not available.

‡ All "?" refer to weapons that Iraq is believed to possess, though the exact numbers in its possession are unknown.

§ Includes navy, army, national guard, and royal flights, but not paramilitary.

Source: Adapted by the authors from interviews, IISS, *Military Balance; Jane's Sentinel, Periscope;* and Jaffee Center for Strategic Studies, *Military Balance in the Middle East* (JCSS, Tel Aviv); and U.S. State Department, "Weekly Status Report," data as of June 14, 2006.

undercutting political support for the insurgency. The second is creating a political system and pattern of government that will lead Shi'ite and Kurdish factions to stop using their various militias to attack Sunnis and challenge the authority of the central government. The third is the willingness of the Coalition, and the United States in particular, to keep providing the combat troops and support, military advisors, and money necessary to give Iraq's new forces the time and resources they need to rebuild.

It will, at best, be a close run thing. A report by the U.S. Department of Defense (DOD) makes it clear that even the most optimistic Coalition authorities recognized by mid-2006 that the threat to Iraqi stability had broadened to include a wide range of groups:[5]

- **Sunni and Shi'a Rejectionists** who use violence or coercion in an attempt to rid Iraq of Coalition forces…subvert emerging institutions and infiltrate and co-opt security and political organizations. Beyond this shared goal, Rejectionist groups diverge regarding long-term objectives. Rejectionists continue to employ a dual-track strategy in Iraq, attempting to leverage the political process to address their core concerns. Since the Samarra bombing, sectarian Rejectionist groups, including militant Shi'a militias, have increased attacks against rival sectarian groups and populations. Both Sunni and Shi'a Rejectionists have conducted reprisal ethno-sectarian attacks.

- **Former Regime Loyalists.** Saddam loyalists are no longer considered a significant threat to the MNF-I end state and the Iraqi government. However, former regime members remain an important element involved in sustaining and enabling the violence in Iraq, using their former internal and external networks and military and intelligence expertise involving weapons and tactics. Saddamists are no longer relevant as a cohesive threat, having mostly splintered into Rejectionists or terrorist and foreign fighters.

- **Terrorists and Foreign Fighters.** Terrorists and foreign fighters, although far fewer in number than the Rejectionists or former regime loyalists, conduct most of the high-profile, high-casualty attacks and kidnappings. Many foreign fighters continue to arrive in Iraq via Syria…Al-Qaida in Iraq (AQI) is currently the dominant terrorist group in Iraq. They continue efforts to spark a self-sustaining cycle of ethno-sectarian violence in Iraq…AQI pursues four broad lines of operation: anti-MNF-I, antigovernment, anti-Shi'a, and external operations. Ansar al Sunna (AS) is another significant, mostly indigenous, terrorist group that shares some goals with AQI. Because of similar agendas, AQI and AS tend to cooperate on the tactical and operational levels. Most recently, there have been indications of cooperation between AQI and Rejectionists as well. It is estimated that 90% of suicide attacks are carried out by AQI…The current positive effects of intolerance for Al-Qaida in Iraq (AQI) among Sunni Arabs may be limited if Sunnis perceive a lack of progress in reconciliation and government participation or if increased sectarian violence draws various Sunni insurgency elements closer.

- **Militia Groups.** Militia groups help both to maintain and to undermine security in Iraq, as well as contribute to achieving the goals of their affiliated political parties. In many cases, these militias, whether authorized or not, provide protection for people and religious sites where the Iraqi police are perceived to be unable to provide adequate support. Sometimes they work with the Iraqi police. In some cases, they operate as a power base for militia leaders trying to advance their own agendas. Militia leaders influence the political process through intimidation and hope to gain influence with the

Iraqi people through politically based social welfare programs. Militias often act extra-judicially via executions and political assassinations—primarily perpetrated by large, well-organized Shi'a militia groups and some small Sunni elements. Militias are also sometimes engaged in purely criminal activity, including extortion and kidnapping... Polling data indicate that most Iraqis agree that militias make Iraq a more dangerous place and should be disbanded..... The most prominent militia groups are the Badr Organization—essentially the paramilitary wing of the Supreme Council for the Islamic Revolution in Iraq, but technically its own political party now—and Shi'a cleric Muq-tada al-Sadr's Jaysh al-Mahdi (JAM). The Kurdish Peshmerga is technically an "author-ized armed force," rather than a militia. Shi'a militias have been involved in sectarian violence. Tactics employed by such militias have varied, including death squads, Sharia courts, and campaigns of intimidation. Shi'a militias, including the Badr Organization and Jaysh al-Mahdi (JAM), have been accused of committing abuses against Sunni civilians, exacerbating sectarian tensions. In addition, JAM is implicated in much of the unrest that followed the February 22 Samarra mosque bombing. The Shi'a militias receive arms and other support from Iran, reinforcing Sunni fears of Iranian domina-tion and further elevating ethno-sectarian violence.

These outside threats are compounded by sectarian and ethnic divisions within the government and Iraqi forces—particularly the National Police and regular Iraqi police—which sometimes aid the Sunni insurgents and more often aid violent Shi'ite and Kurdish groups. Endemic corruption in the government and crime throughout civil society add a further mix of problems.

Iraq has had some success in creating unified regular military army units and had 106 battalions in service in September 2006, and some 85 battalions were deployed in some role in counterinsurgency missions, security missions, and efforts to prevent civil war. It is doubtful, however, that the unity of the army, air force, and navy could survive a full-scale civil war.

The National Police or internal security forces were being reorganized in 2006 and had 27 more battalions in active service. However, some elements continued to com-mit abuses and attacks against Sunnis and support Shi'ite militias in such attacks or support the Kurds in their efforts to take control of disputed areas in the north.

The regular police were still weak, corrupt, and divided by sect and ethnic fac-tions. Control often existed at the local and not national level, and actual security came from police recruited locally, other security forces, militias and insurgents—depending on the city and governorate. The MNF-I began a "year of the police" in 2006, but efforts to embed Coalition advisors in police stations and create partner units are still uncertain. Moreover, problems with corruption, crime, and ethnic and sectarian divisions are compounded by large numbers of facilities protection forces, armed security guards, and local security forces—almost all untrustworthy and as much a threat as an asset.

Military Spending and Arms Imports

There are no meaningful data on the cost of Iraqi forces and military imports since the fall of Saddam Hussein's regime in 2003. They have clearly built back from nearly zero to several billion dollars a year, but neither the U.S. aid program nor the Iraqi budget provides detailed accountability, and much of the cost of Iraqi forces is now paid indirectly though U.S. and British support in virtually every aspect of Iraqi operations.

To put the current state of effort in perspective, one must compare Iraqi defense expenditures and arms transfers before the conflict. Even by a conservative estimate, Iraq imported over $150 billion worth of arms and equipment to manufacture and deliver weapons of mass destruction between 1975 and 1991. It spent billions on fighting the Kurds during the early to mid-1970s. It spent over $100 billion more on the Iran-Iraq War, which Saddam Hussein started by invading Iran. It then lost as much as $50 billion more by invading Kuwait—both as the result of attacks on its military equipment, infrastructure, and production facilities by the UN Coalition and of lost economic opportunity costs.

Military expenditures and wartime losses drained Iraq's economy for nearly two decades. Iraq's oil wealth is relative. Measured in constant 1988 dollars, Iraq's gross national product (GNP) peaked during 1979 and 1980, with totals of $118 billion and $120 billion, respectively. The Iran-Iraq War rapidly cut its GNP to $70.4 billion in 1981, and a combination of wartime damage and lower oil prices then cut it to levels of $70 billion throughout the rest of the 1980s. Iraq's GNP was $65.8 billion in 1988, about half of its GNP in 1980. Iraq kept its military expenditures as a per-cent of GNP at around 30 percent from 1978 to 1984 and could sustain these expenditures only through a combination of massive foreign borrowing and aid from southern Gulf States like Kuwait and Saudi Arabia. After 1984, however, Iraq exhausted its borrowing capability, and the Iran-Iraq War grew more threatening. As a result, military spending rose to 52 percent of the GNP in 1985 and stayed near 50 percent for the rest of the 1980s.[6]

By 1989, the year that lay between the Iran-Iraq War and Iraq's invasion of Kuwait, Iraq's economy was experiencing a serious economic crisis. Experts disagree over the economic statistics involved, but not over the seriousness of the crisis. According to the Central Intelligence Agency (CIA), for example, Iraq's GNP was then $35 billion and its per capita income was only $1,940.[7] This level of per capita income is not unusual by Third World standards, but it was low relative to Iraq's economy in 1979 and to the wealth of a far less developed Saudi Arabia—which had a GNP of $79 billion and a per capita income of $4,800.

The International Institute for Strategic Studies (IISS) estimates that Iraq spent $13,990 million in 1987, $12,870 million in 1988, and $8.61 billion in 1990—although there is no way to relate this figure to what Iraq had to spend on the Gulf War, when it had to devote much of its economy to the conflict.[8] While any accurate estimates are impossible, Iraq probably spent over 40 percent of its gross domestic product on military forces during the six months before Desert Storm, and 60 percent on its central government expenditures—including wartime losses. No meaningful military spending data are available for 1991, 1992, and 1993.[9]

Iraq's arms imports were a massive burden on its economy, driven by the arms race with Iran which began in the 1960s, and by the Iran-Iraq War during the period from 1980 to 1988. The Arms Control and Disarmament Agency (ACDA) estimates that Iraq imported $2,400 million worth of arms in 1978, $3,200 million in 1979, $2,400 million in 1980, $4,200 million in 1981, $7,000 million in 1982, $6,800 million in 1983, $9,100 million in 1984, $4,600 million in 1985, $5,700 million in 1986, $5,400 million in 1987, $4,900 million in 1988, and $1,900 million in 1989.[10]

According to a conservative estimate, which ignores all expenditures on weapons of mass destruction and some deliveries of military related goods and services other than actual weapons, Iraq signed at least $30.5 billion worth of new arms agreements between 1983 and 1990.[11] The high volume of new agreements during this period reflects the fact that Iraq established a broad network of suppliers during the 1980s. It shifted away from reliance on the Soviet bloc and bought an increasing number of weapons from Europe and the Third World.

During 1979–1983, the period that covers the fall of the Shah of Iran and the first part of the Iran-Iraq War, Iraq took delivery on $17.6 billion worth of new arms between 1979 and 1983, including $7.2 billion worth of arms from the USSR, $0.85 billion from Poland, $0.4 billion from Romania, $0.04 billion from Czechoslovakia, and $1.5 billion from the People's Republic of China. It obtained $3.8 billion from France, $0.41 billion from Italy, $0.28 billion from the United Kingdom, $0.14 billion from West Germany, and $3.0 billion from other countries.[12]

During the latter half of the Iran-Iraq War, from 1984–1988, Iraq took delivery on $29.7 billion worth of new arms, including $15.4 billion worth of arms from the USSR, $0.75 billion from Poland, $0.65 billion from Bulgaria, $0.675 billion from Czechoslovakia, and $2.8 billion from the People's Republic of China. Iraq obtained $3.1 billion from France, $0.37 billion from Italy, $0.03 billion from the United Kingdom, $0.675 billion from West Germany, and $5.2 billion from other countries.[13] The United States did not transfer significant numbers of weapons to Iraq, but did provide help during the Iran-Iraq War in the form of credits and loans that helped buy weapons and also provided intelligence support.[14]

If one takes the period between 1988 and 1991—which covers the period from the end of the Iran War in August 1988 to the beginning of the embargo on arms shipments to Iraq in August 1990—Iraq ordered only $3.1 billion worth of arms. Some $400 million were ordered from the USSR, $700 million from the People's Republic of China, $500 million from major western European states, $500 million from other European states, and $1.0 billion from other countries. This low rate of new orders was a product of (a) Iraq's growing economic crisis, (b) the arms embargo on Iraq after August 1990, and (c) the fact Iraq was still receiving the backlog from the immense amount of orders Iraq already had placed during the Iran-Iraq War. Yet, Iraq took delivery on $8.9 billion worth of arms during this same period, including $4.1 billion worth of arms from the USSR, $1.0 billion from the People's Republic of China, $1.1 billion from major western European states, $1.7 billion from other European states, and $1.0 billion from other countries.[15]

The overall burden of military spending and arms imports placed on Iraq's economy unquestionably helped lead to Iraq's invasion of Kuwait on August 1,

1990, and to the Gulf War. Iraq had an annual military budget of $12.9 billion in 1990. According to some estimates, Iraq was spending an average of $721 per citizen on military forces, although it had an average per capita income of only $1,950. Although Iraq had cut its rate of new arms orders, it still took delivery on $1,435 million worth of arms and ordered $1,125 million more during the first six months of 1990. This level of expenditure raised Iraq's international debt to at least $40 billion—and some experts feel in excess of $70 billion.[16]

These vast expenditures did not protect Iraq from the consequences of its invasion of Kuwait. The scale of the Iraqi defeat in the Gulf War is indicated by U.S. DOD estimates issued just after the conclusion of the fighting that stated UN Coalition forces had captured more than 50,000 prisoners of war (POWs), destroyed nearly 3,000 Iraqi tanks out of 4,030 in southern Iraq and Kuwait, destroyed about 1,000 out of 2,870 other armored vehicles, and destroyed nearly 1,005 artillery weapons out of 3,110.[17] These estimates compare with Coalition combat losses of 4 tanks, 9 other armored vehicles, and 1 artillery weapon. While such estimates later proved uncertain, they are valid as a broad indication of the scale of the Iraqi defeat at the time of the cease-fire.

In contrast, Iraq's personnel losses were amazingly small compared to these equipment losses—and United States Central Command (USCENTCOM) raised its estimate of Iraqi POWs to 80,000 and Iraqi losses to 3,300 tanks, 2,100 other armored vehicles, and 2,200 artillery pieces on March 3, 1991.[18] While the Defense Intelligence Agency initially gave an estimate of Iraqis killed as high as 100,000, it now seems likely that the total was only about 25,000 to 55,000.[19] Total UN Coalition losses are difficult to estimate because of the unwillingness of several Arab states to provide accurate figures, but the United States lost 147 killed in action or who died later from combat wounds, 121 dead from nonhostile causes, 212 wounded in action, and had 44 missing in action at the time the war ended. According to one estimate, Britain lost 16 killed, 31 wounded in action, and 12 missing. Egypt had 9 killed and 75 wounded. France lost 2 killed and 28 wounded. Italy lost 1 killed. Saudi Arabia lost 29 killed, 53 wounded in action, and 9 missing. Senegal had 8 wounded, and the United Arab Emirates had 6 killed.[20]

It is far harder to provide any meaningful estimate of Iraqi military spending and arms imports after Iraq's defeat. Iraq obviously spent a massive part of its national budget on armed forces and security after 1991, probably between 40 and 50 percent. It also succeeded in smuggling in some arms and spare parts in spite of the UN arms embargo and containment.

Iraq had to spend several billion dollars a year to reconstitute and maintain its forces from 1991–2003. At the time the Coalition invaded, it had built its active military forces back up to some 389,000 men with 650,000 low-grade reserves. The army had some 2,600 main battle tanks, 400 armored reconnaissance vehicles, 1,200 armored infantry fighting vehicles, and some 1,800 armored personnel carriers. It had some 200 self-propelled artillery pieces, 1,900 towed artillery pieces, and some 200 multiple rocket launchers. It had some 164 helicopters in inventory, many armed, but their operational state is unclear.[21] Virtually all were destroyed or damaged in the fighting that followed, by looting after the war, or poor handling and storage. Iraq faced a vastly superior force in qualitative terms and was the subject of attack by some 18,000 precision-guided weapons alone.

There were some 42,000–44,000 men in a wide variety of paramilitary and security forces. Some, like elements of Saddam's Fedayeen, fought well. Most played no role in combat.

The air force had 20,000 men and some 316 combat aircraft. These included 6 bombers and some 130 fighter ground-attack aircraft, 180 fighters, and 5 reconnaissance aircraft, plus several hundred trainers, transport and service aircraft, and support helicopters. Virtually all were permanently damaged beyond repair when Saddam Hussein insisted they be buried to protect them from Coalition air strikes. The massive air defense command had some 17,000 men with 850 surface-to-air missile weapons, many heavy launchers like the SA-2, the SA-3, and the SA-6. It also had large numbers of sensors and command facilities. Almost all were lost due to fighting, looting, and mishandling.

The small Iraqi Navy had some 2,000 men, three minesweepers, six patrol craft, and two support ships. It ceased to play any role early in the war.

Like many intense conventional clashes with high-technology weapons, Iraqi casualties were limited during the main fighting, although the Iraqi body count from the insurgency that followed was so costly that an estimated total of 38,000–43,000 Iraqis had died by late June 2006.[22]

Iraqi Military Manpower

The Iraqi regular military is still very much in formation, although significant numbers of combat elements are coming on-line. In late September 2006, it had a total manning of 130,100 that Coalition forces had trained and equipped with 128,230 in the army and Special Forces, around 740 in the air force, and around 1,130 in the navy. Another 51,910 men were in the Ministry of Interior (MOI) National Police and other security forces, many of which had training and equipment closer to that of Iraq's regular army military forces than normal police forces. Iraq and the MNF-1 had also trained some 120,190 regular police, although an unknown number had deserted and their effectiveness was generally minimal.

These figures, however, were authorized strength and did not take account of substantial numbers of temporary absentees. Manning levels were very much in transition and were climbing rapidly. As of end-2005, Iraqi forces still had only 62 percent of their authorized officers, and 61 percent of their noncommissioned officers (NCOs), but were overmanned with enlisted manpower at 120 percent, much of which was still of limited quality and would have to be cut or be allowed to desert, depending upon its performance in combat. The Iraqi regular military was at 92 percent of its authorized strength as of December 10, 2005.

The sectarian and ethnic composition of the Iraqi security forces (ISF) was a serious issue by the fall of 2005. The debate over federation in drafting the new Constitution had raised the prospect of dividing the country along ethnic and sectarian lines. At the same time, the constant stream of bloody attacks on Shi'ites and Kurds, and horrific suicide bombings, led to increasing talk—and sometimes action—about revenge. The security services in the Ministry of Interior were increasingly found either to tolerate revenge attacks by Shi'ite militias like the Badr Organization or to conduct them.

The new Iraqi Army did not take such reprisals against Sunnis, but the issue of ethnic representation in the army was an increasing concern to the MNF-I, U.S. commanders and officials, and the Iraqi leaders seeking to hold the country together. This prompted a major new recruiting drive targeting Sunni enlistment. Between August and October, 4,000 Sunnis were recruited and were undergoing training by late October, according to one U.S. military official in Baghdad.[23] As of late December 2005, some U.S. commanders in Iraq claimed that the ranks of the Iraqi Army were roughly representative of the national population—about 60 percent Shi'ite, 20 percent Sunni, and 15 to 20 percent Kurdish.

Few Iraqis, or U.S. officers directly within their advisory effort, agreed with this assessment. Major-General Salih Sarhan, a Shi'ite, said that the majority of the soldiers were coming from the south and were Shi'ite as of late December 2005. Nearly all of the Iraqi Army's recent recruits had come from southern Shi'ite cities, including highly religious cities like Karbala and Najaf, where unemployment was high. The 8th and 10th divisions, for example, were almost completely Shi'ite. Meanwhile, the 2nd, 3rd, and 4th divisions in the north were overwhelmingly Kurdish. Sarhan said that the two army divisions in Baghdad were more evenly split.[24]

The elections that came toward the end of the year also seemed to reflect Shi'ite and Kurdish dominance of Iraqi forces. In contrast to the surge in Sunni participation in the political process that led to a high Sunni vote in the December 15, 2005, parliamentary election, Sunni Arab representation in the ISF remained proportionately low. A special tally that consisted mainly of ballots cast by security forces, but also included votes by hospital patients and prisoners, showed that only about 7 percent of votes were cast for the three main Sunni Arab parties. Because Iraqis were overwhelmingly thought to have voted along sectarian lines, many officials believed that this vote reflected low representation of Sunnis in the ISF.

The Kurdish Pesh Merga militiamen seemed to have a disproportionately large representation in the ISF. The special tally revealed that 30 percent of the votes cast went to the principal Shi'ite political alliance and 45 percent of the votes went to the main Kurdish slate of candidates. Lieutenant Colonel Fred Wellman, a spokesman for the military command that oversaw training of Iraqi forces, said that he did not have detailed estimates on the ethnic composition of the ISF, yet admitted that Arab Sunni representation was lagging.[25]

Nevertheless, the May 2006 manning total of 263,400 for Iraqi forces was 14 percent higher than the total reported in February 2006 and 35 percent higher than the total of 171,300 reported in the first quarterly report to Congress, issued in July 2005. As of mid-September 2006, that number had grown to 302,200 total trained and equipped ISF, according to the Department of State's weekly numbers.

Meanwhile, as of August 7, 2006, Coalition forces had closed 48 of their 110 Forward Operating Bases, handing over 31 to the different Iraqi security forces, and 17 to the Ministry of Finance. Thirteen more Forward Operating Bases were scheduled for closure and handover by January 2007.[26]

On September 7, the Iraqi government started to formally take control of its armed forces, beginning with the 8th Army Division, the navy, and the air force. A U.S. military spokesman speculated that further control transfers could take place at a pace of about two divisions per month.[27] The chain of command ran from the Prime Minister to the Defense Minister, to joint headquarters in Baghdad, and finally to the Iraqi ground-forces command. The United States said this self-sufficient line of authority was crucial for self-sufficient Iraqi security forces.[28] As of late August, half of Iraq's ten army divisions were *de facto* in charge of their own territories or in the process of taking over from Coalition forces.[29]

THE IRAQI ARMY

The Iraqi Army effectively went from zero forces in 2003, and one battalion in July 2004, to substantial force deployments by mid-2006, and had completed generating the basic order of battle of a ten-division force. It was years away from fully manning this force with trained personnel and depended on the Coalition for armor, artillery, tactical mobility, air support, and high-technology command and control and intelligence. Nevertheless, Iraqi forces were active in the field.

According to a DOD report to Congress in May 2006, there were two Iraqi divisions, 16 brigades, and 63 Army and National Police battalions with security lead in their areas of responsibility. These areas covered more than 30,000 square miles of Iraq. As of May 6, 2006, the Ministry of Defense (MOD), MOI, or Ministry of Finance had assumed control and responsibility for 34 Forward Operating Bases from Coalition forces.

Figures 9.2 and 9.3 show the overall growth of Iraqi forces after the ouster of Saddam Hussein. Figure 9.4 shows the number of Iraqi Army battalions in combat and Figure 9.5 shows the number of Iraqi units conducting independent and combined operations as of August 2006.

As of May 2006, Iraqi Special Operations Forces (ISOF) had built up to approximately 1,600 trained and equipped personnel organized into the Iraqi Counter-Terrorism Task Force (ICTF), the Iraqi Commandos, a support battalion, and a special reconnaissance unit. The ISOF was to complete force generation by the summer of 2006, according to the DOD's May 2006 Quarterly Report to Congress. The ICTF and Commandos continued to conduct counterinsurgency operations throughout the nation. The ISOF primarily used U.S. equipment, including the M4 carbine, M240 machine guns, M2 heavy machine guns, and up-armored high-mobility multipurpose wheeled vehicles (HMMWVs or Humvees).

Coalition officials partnered with four divisions of the Iraqi Army in the north said that two of those divisions would be ready to take the lead in operations by the end of the summer (2006) and the other two by the end of the year.[32] In a video

Number of Units

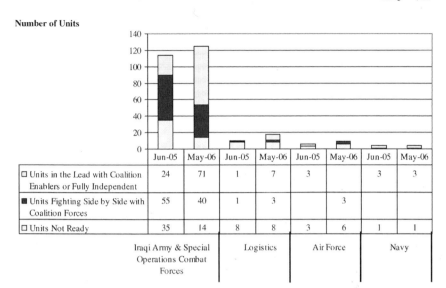

	Jun-05	May-06	Jun-05	May-06	Jun-05	May-06	Jun-05	May-06
☐ Units in the Lead with Coalition Enablers or Fully Independent	24	71	1	7	3		3	3
■ Units Fighting Side by Side with Coalition Forces	55	40	1	3		3		
☐ Units Not Ready	35	14	8	8	3	6	1	1
	Iraqi Army & Special Operations Combat Forces		Logistics		Air Force		Navy	

Category by Percentage

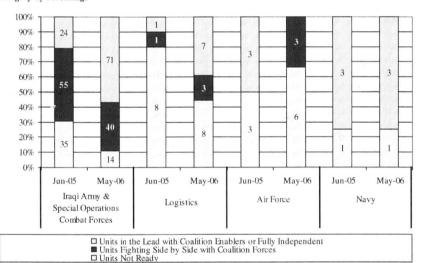

☐ Units in the Lead with Coalition Enablers or Fully Independent
■ Units Fighting Side by Side with Coalition Forces
☐ Units Not Ready

Source: Adapted from "Measuring Security and Stability in Iraq," Report to Congress, May 2006, p. 47.

Figure 9.2 Iraq's Ministry of Defense Forces' Assessed Capabilities

conference with the Pentagon on May 20, 2006, Lieutenant General Peter W. Chiarelli, Commander of Multi-National Corps–Iraq, said that the ISF was on pace to control about 75 percent of the country's battle space by the end of the summer. That same month, Iraqi Prime Minister Nuri al-Maliki said that the Iraqi Army

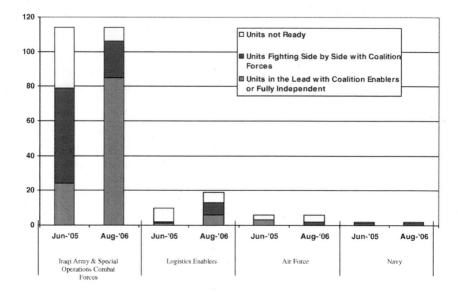

Figure 9.3   Estimated MOD Force Capabilities by Service: Comparison of June 2005 and August 2006

Source: Adapted from U.S. Department of Defense, *Measuring Stability and Security in Iraq,* August 2006, Report to the Congress. Note: +/–5% margin of error.

and police would be able to assume responsibility for security across the entire country by late 2007.

By August the Iraqi Army included approximately 115,000 trained and equipped combat soldiers, including SIB personnel and about 9,600 support forces.[33] General

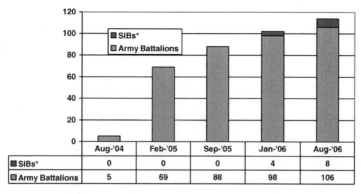

	Aug-'04	Feb-'05	Sep-'05	Jan-'06	Aug-'06
■ SIBs*	0	0	0	4	8
▢ Army Battalions	5	69	88	98	106

*SIBs = Strategic Infrastructure Battalions. Note: Includes special operations battalions and Strategic Infrastructure Battions, but does not include combat support and combat service support units.[30]   Source: Adapted from: US Department of Defense, <u>Measuring Stability and Security in Iraq,</u> August 2006 Report to Congress, p. XX; Note: +/–5% margin of error.

Figure 9.4   Iraqi Army Battalions in Combat: August 2004 to August 2006

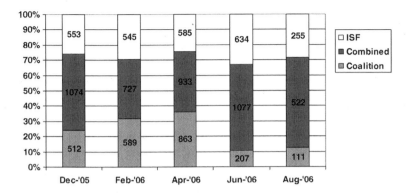

*Includes MOD and National Police units; data includes only those ISF independent operations that are reported to the Coalition. Source: MNF-I. Data as of 15 August 2006.[31]

Figure 9.5 Growth in Independent and Combined Combat Operations (Company Level and Above*)

John Abizaid in early September attested that while Iraqi forces were fighting, they were not yet capable of ensuring their own security.[34] Efforts to increase the independence of Iraqi Army units continued to focus on combat enablers at this time. The three planned Iraqi Training Battalions had been formed and allowed Iraqis to train soldiers independently in sufficient quantities. Army recruits attended a 13-week program of basic instruction followed by military occupational training of a length varying from three to seven weeks, depending on specialty. Specialty schools included the Military Intelligence School, Signal School, Bomb Disposal School, Combat Arms Branch School, Engineer School, and Military Police School. These schools were intended both to contribute to professionalism in the Iraqi Army and to teach the necessary skills for fighting counterinsurgency campaigns.

Although the Motorized Transportation Regiments (MTRs) were approaching full operational capability, a continued lack of competent maintenance personnel hindered their ability to reach full capability. As of August, approximately 80 percent of planned Headquarters and Service Companies (HSCs) had been formed, a third were operational, and the remaining HSCs were scheduled to be completed by December 2006.[35] Meanwhile, training for service and support officers and non-commissioned officers (NCOs) was provided by the Iraqi Army Service and Supply Institute (IASSI) at Taji. By August 2006 the IASSI had trained more than 5,000 officers and NCOs.[36] Iraqi Special Operations Forces at this time were composed of 1,600 soldiers making up the Iraqi Counter-Terrorism Task Force, the Iraqi Commandos, a support battalion, and a special reconnaissance unit.[37]

Equipment Holdings and Issues

At least through 2006, most Iraqi forces remained very lightly equipped by the standard of conventional military forces. The Special Inspector General for Iraq

Reconstruction (SIGIR) Report to Congress issued in April 2006 covered Iraq Relief and Reconstruction Fund (IRRF)-funded activities, as well as information on Iraq Security Forces Fund (ISFF) activity. The following represent the highlights of the security and justice sector report:[38]

- More U.S. funds have been devoted to security and justice than any other reconstruction sector. A total of $11.6 billion has been allocated, combining funds from IRRF 2 and ISFF.
- By the end of this quarter, 82 percent of the $6.35 billion IRRF allocation had been expended, and 31 percent of ISFF funds have been expended.
- Approximately 250,500 military and police personnel have reportedly been trained and equipped.
- More than 600 facilities have been completed—police stations, fire stations, courts, border forts, and army facilities.

According to Multi-National Security Transition Command–Iraq (MNSTC-I), the Iraqi Army had received a number of war zone essentials from Coalition forces by the end of 2005: more than 95,000 assault rifles, 4,400 machine guns, almost 95,000 sets of body armor, more than 3,500 vehicles, 83,000 batons, and more than 105,000 sets of handcuffs.[39] According to Coalition planners, the Iraqi Armed Forces received equally light equipment between January 2006 and May 2006:

- more than 25,000 AK-47s,
- more than 6,200 9-mm pistols,
- nearly 1,300 light and medium machine guns,
- nearly 1,000 light and medium vehicles,
- more than 17,000 sets of body armor,
- more than 15,000 Kevlar helmets, and
- 176 HMMWVs, which were distributed among the divisions and Motorized Transportation Regiments.

There were exceptions. During the same time period, the Iraqi Army's 9th Mechanized Division received 77 Hungarian-donated T-72 tanks and 36 Greek-donated BMP-1 armored personnel carriers. These vehicles were integrated into the 2nd Brigade, comprised of two tank battalions and one mechanized battalion.[40] The 9th Motorized Rifle Division had two mechanized brigades comprising nine maneuver battalions and was to include two battalions of T-72 tanks, two of T-55 tanks, and five of BMP-1 armored personnel carriers.[41] The 1st Mechanized Brigade of this division took over battle space in the Taji area some 25 miles north of Baghdad in January 2006, less than a year after becoming fully operational. It was equipped with T-55s and MTLBs, and largely complete, except for some logistic and supply elements.[42]

By December 2005, the 220,000-strong ISF, including the army and paramilitary police, had received a total of about 600 armored vehicles. They did, however, still have a requirement for nearly 3,000 more, including more than 1,500 armored Humvee utility vehicles.[43]

As a result, equipment deliveries and plans became a growing issue with Iraqi commanders during 2006, with complaints that a lack of proper equipment precluded decisive advantage over relative well-armed and equipped insurgent forces. One criticism was that corruption in the Iraqi Ministry of Defense was largely to blame for the problem. In 2005, the MOD misplaced $1.3 billion that had been allocated to arm the troops. Another complaint from field commanders was that U.S. and Coalition equipment deliveries did not contain the types of heavy equipment necessary to definitely crush the insurgents.[44]

Support Forces

Progress was also being made in creating effective support forces. Combat support and combat service support units continued to be generated to provide critical combat enablers. As of May 2006, these included Operational Regional Support Units, Motor Transport Regiments, Logistics Support Battalions, and Headquarters and Service Companies. Strategic Infrastructure Battalions remain focused on securing critical oil pipelines. In the first quarter of 2006, the train-and-equip mission for these was increased from 4 to 11 battalions to reflect the adjusted Iraqi Army authorization.

While Coalition forces continued to provide matériel movement, life support, and other combat support to the Iraqi Armed Forces, the MOD made progress in building Iraqi logistical capabilities during the first yearly quarter of 2006:[45]

> The National Depot at Taji, which is managed by the civilian component of the ministry, provides strategic and some operational-level supply and maintenance support through its military, civilian, and contractor staff. It provides warehouse facilities for the receipt, storage, and issue of the Iraqi Army and Air Force's national stockholding of most classes of supply and facilities for conducting vehicle overhauls and other 4th-line (i.e. national-level) maintenance support. The National Depot feeds five Regional Support Units (RSUs) that provide maintenance and supply support to nearby units. Four of these RSUs are currently operational, and the fifth is being formed. The national Maintenance Contract, which extends through March 2007, continues to provide a limited interim solution for organizational and intermediate maintenance requirements of the Iraqi Armed forces at ten different locations throughout the country. The capability to provide some routine maintenance is being developed within the support units.

More than 65 percent of personnel in the Iraqi Army's support forces had been trained and equipped, according to the May 2006 DOD Report to Congress, and logistics units continued to increase their capabilities. This number of 65 percent, however, had not changed as of the August 2006 report, raising questions about continued progress in building out the logistical enablers needed for the ISF to be a truly independent and operational force.

THE IRAQI AIR FORCE

The Iraqi Air Force also made progress, although it was scarcely the symbol of Iraqi strength that had existed under Saddam Hussein. It had been a formidable force by regional standards, but Iraqi airpower crumbled under the strain of the Gulf Wars, the U.S.–U.K. enforcement of no-fly zones, and the invasion. Iraq's fighter and surface-to-air inventory had been effectively destroyed. Many fighters had been destroyed on the ground or in the air by Coalition forces. Many of Iraq's more advanced aircraft, such as MiG-29s, were flown to Iran for safekeeping during the Gulf War and have never been returned. Its surface-to-air inventory had been largely destroyed during the interwar period and the invasion, and Iraq destroyed most of its remaining combat aircraft during the invasion by burying and dispersing them in ways that made them permanently inoperable.[46]

Like so much of Saddam Hussein's military buildup, there was no reason that Iraqi forces should now seek anything like the force levels that existed before the invasion. Nevertheless, it was clear that a new Iraqi Air Force did need to emerge, one that eventually had the combat strength necessary to defend the country, as well as deal with country insurgency.

Creating a new Iraqi Air Force, however, was anything but easy, and the new Iraqi Air Force still had serious problems even in operating small numbers of systems in late 2005. The air force was badly short of manning for its dedicated combat, service, and logistic support units. In early September 2005, the service grounded six of the eight surveillance aircraft that it acquired in September 2004. The planes were Jordan Aerospace Industries SAMA CH2000s, equipped with forward-looking infrared sensors. The squadron was left with just two Forward-Looking Infrared (FLIR)-equipped Seeker aircraft, acquired in 2004 from Jordan-based Seabird Aviation.

The grounding, according to a U.S. military adviser to the squadron, was more the product of a contract dispute than the fault of the IAF. While the adviser declined to give specifics on the nature of the dispute, the performance of the aircraft seemed to be in question, with an industry expert citing possible problems related to the CH2000's ability to operate effectively in the heat of the Iraqi summer.[47]

By December, however, the Iraqi Air Force was beginning to operate its C-130Es more effectively and was beginning to deploy the 23rd Transport Squadron from the U.S.–supported Ali Base in southern Iraq to a new permanent base called "New Al Muthana." The Joint Headquarters Center of the Iraqi Headquarters had become more active in mission planning and assignments, the air force was beginning to use encrypted communications, and during one exercise, it flew nine C-130E missions with 117 passengers and 106,000 pounds of cargo during a five-day period.[48]

The IAF also resumed helicopter training in late 2005, after problems with spare parts shortages. These problems had sidelined the training squadrons fleet of Jet

Rangers for several months. The 2nd and 12th squadrons, with UH-1s, were somewhat more active initially, but their UH-1Hs began to be sent back to the United States for reconfiguration into Huey IIs in January 2006.

In early 2006, the Iraqi Air Force had nearly 500 trained and equipped personnel and was developing three airpower capabilities: reconnaissance, battlefield mobility, and air transport. Major assets for these capabilities included the following:[49]

- **Aerial Reconnaissance Fleet**
  - 2 Seabird Seekers
  - 2 SAMA CH-2000s
  - 6 AeroComp Comp Air 7SLs
- **Battlefield Mobility**
  - 4 UH-1H helicopters
  - 5 Bell 206 Jet Ranger helicopters
- **Air Transport Capability**
  - 3 C-130E aircraft

Development of air force personnel capabilities was under way, with the help of Coalition Advisory Support Teams. As of May 2006, the air force had approximately 600 trained and equipped personnel and continued to develop three airpower capabilities: reconnaissance, battlefield mobility, and air transport. The following advancements were also reported:[50]

Iraqi reconnaissance aircraft have a limited capability to perform oil infrastructure reconnaissance and surveillance support for nationwide counter-insurgency operations. The Iraqi Air Force (IAF) reconnaissance aircraft consist of single-engine airplanes used in civilian and commercial markets. One such IAF type, the CH-2000, has continued to experience issues with carbon monoxide presence, which has limited its effectiveness. A temporary fix has been designed, and full operational capability is expected by late May. Another IAF reconnaissance aircraft, the CompAir, awaits the arrival of a US Air Force team, scheduled to be in theater in May, to modify the fleet and return it to operational status.

The IAF has three squadrons of helicopters (2nd Squadron, 4th Squadron, and 12th Squadron) in support battlefield mobility. Sixteen Uh-1H helicopters have returned to the United States for modifications and upgrades to the Huey II configuration. The first seven of these aircraft are scheduled to return to Iraq in January 2007, with the remainder following two to three months later. The 4th Squadron will initially operate 10 Mi-17s procured by the Iraqi MOD. Eight of these 10 have been delivered, but they are awaiting additional armor, weapons mounts, and pilot training and proficiency. These aircraft are expected to be operational by the end of 2006. The 12th Squadron operates five Bell 206 Jet Ranger helicopters, which are used for training purposes.

The 23rd Transport Squadron, with its three C-130E aircraft, completed its move to the new al-Muthanna Air Base early this quarter. This squadron has continued to perform transport, mobility, and humanitarian missions this quarter.

As of August 2006, Iraq's air force remained small with 750 personnel. Increasing the size of the force continued to be a problem because of the difficulty in finding qualified applicants. However, both the 7th Squadron—consisting of five CompAir 7SLs based at Kirkuk Air Base—and the 70th Squadron—consisting of two Seekers and six CH-2000s based at Basrah Air Base—were performing operational missions. These missions mostly consisted of patrolling oil pipeline infrastructure in their respective areas.

By the end of January 2007 the 2nd Squadron based at Taji Air Base was expected to receive its first six Huey IIs and was expected to use them mostly for casualty evacuation. Finally the 23rd Squadron located at the new Al-Muthanna Air Base in Baghdad, consisted of three C-130Es.[51] Overall the air force largely concentrated on reconnaissance, battlefield mobility, and air transport. The control of Iraqi airspace remained a U.S. responsibility, and the Ministry of Defense had not developed plans to procure its own combat aircraft. Figure 9.6 summarizes Iraqi Air Force capabilities as of August 2006.

THE IRAQI NAVY

The Iraqi Navy was still in the process of becoming an effective light coastal defense force in the fall of 2005, although recruiting had improved after it adopted the Direct Recruit Replacement program started by the army. The first such naval

Figure 9.6   Iraqi Air Force Capabilities as of August 2006

	C-130E Hercules Transport Aircraft	CH-2000 Observation Aircraft	SB7L-360 Seeker	Mil Mi-8 Battlefield Helicopters	Bell 206 Jet Ranger Helicopters	Bell UH-1 Helicopters
Number of aircraft	3	6	2	8 (more expected in 2007)	5	16 (upgraded during 2006 in United States to Huey II standard)
Role	Air transport	Patrol oil pipelines and other critical			infrastructure facilities	Patrol oil pipelines and other critical
	infrastructure facilities	Troop transport	Basic rotary-wing training			

Source: U.S. Department of Defense, *Measuring Stability and Security in Iraq*, August 2006 Report to Congress.

training program had begun in May. Its naval infantry battalion was being trained for point defense of oil platforms—a key mission in securing oil exports.

By September 2005, the Iraqi Navy was operating 5 Predator-class patrol boats (PB), 24 fast aluminum boats (dual outboard engines), and 10 rigid hull inflatable boats. The naval forces were further equipped with various small arms and Night Vision Devices. Plans called for the Iraqi Navy to be equipped with 3 Al Faw Class Patrol Boats by December 2005 and with an additional 3 by September 2006. However, design deficiencies (e.g., seawater strainers below the waterline) and construction shortcomings (e.g., poor welding) of one Al Faw boat delivered to date caused delays in fielding the patrol boats.[52]

Iraqi naval forces were also working with U.S. forces in defending Iraq's two oil terminals in the Gulf—the Al Basra Oil Terminal and the Khawr Al Amaya Oil Terminal (KAAOT). The oil exports through these terminals were generating nearly 80 percent of Iraq's revenue—less aid—in late 2005. Iraqi Marines had taken full control of the defense of KAAOT, supported by Coalition ships and naval forces in the area. A total of some 50 Iraqi Marines worked with a total of some 70 U.S. sailors.[53]

Iraqi Coast Guard activity was active enough to lead to a clash with Iranian forces in mid-January 2006. Guard members boarded an Iranian ship in the Shatt al-Arab waterway between Iraq and Iran, some 27 kilometers south of Basra, because they believed it was smuggling oil. Speedboats from the Iranian Navy attacked them, killing one and detaining nine.[54]

In the first months of 2006, the Iraqi Navy had 800 trained and equipped sailors and marines organized into an operational headquarters, two afloat squadrons, and six marine platoons. No significant asset deliveries were made to the Iraqi Navy since early 2005. The navy was operating 5 Predator-class patrol boats, 24 fast aluminum boats, and 10 rigid hull inflatable boats. While the size of the Iraqi Navy did not grow significantly through spring 2006, there were reports of increased command and control capabilities at operational headquarters. However, as with the other services at this time, institutional capacity to execute acquisitions, logistics, and personnel policies remained underdeveloped.[55]

As of May 2006, the Iraqi Navy had 800 trained and equipped sailors and marines organized into an operational headquarters, two afloat squadrons, and six marine platoons. The following advancements were also reported:[56]

> The Iraqi Navy continues to develop capabilities for surface surveillance, maritime interdiction, oil terminal protection, and support operations. The Navy has shown improvement in the command and control capability of the Operational Headquarters as well as the capability to mount a Quick Response Force for board-and-search missions, while maintaining communications with the head-quarters and operating forces.

The Iraqi Navy order of battle included the Patrol Boat Squadron, composed of 5 Predator-class boats; the Assault Boat Squadron, composed of 10 rigid hull inflatable boats; and 24 fast assault boats. Force generation plans in early 2006 called for a total of 6 Al Faw-class patrol boats by September 2006, but the delivery of 3 Al Faw patrol boats continued to be delayed. The procurement of two off-shore support vessels had also been delayed by the MOD until the formation of the new government. The following advancements in training were also reported:[57]

> Training of the Iraqi Navy continues to be conducted by the Iraqi Navy Training Department, with the assistance of the Coalition's Navy Transition Team. Training remains focused on maintaining basic seamanship skills and conducting maritime operations. Afloat Forward Staging Base and visit board search and seizure training continues. Marine training continues to be supported by US Navy Mobile Security Detachments and includes regular marksmanship refresher training.

As of August 2006, Iraqi naval strength stood at around 1,000 sailors and marines, organized into two patrol and assault boat squadrons and a marine battalion. Iraqis regularly served on board U.S. and U.K. ships, and the Iraqi Marines and Navy boats were closely integrated into Coalition operations to protect oil infrastructure.[58]

The Iraqi Navy is examining purchasing larger ships. These could include four Italian 52.8-meter Diciotti patrol vessels. They displace a full load of 427 tons, have a crew of 30, and have an endurance of 1,800 nautical miles at 16 knots. They would have a 25-mm or 30-mm gun. The Iraqi Navy is also examining purchasing another 15 smaller patrol boats and two offshore support vessels.[59] Figure 9.7 summarizes Iraqi naval capabilities as of August 2006.

PARAMILITARY, SECURITY, POLICE, AND INTELLIGENCE FORCES

The Iraqi police had a total of 148,500 men listed as trained and equipped as of June 14, 2006. These include 104,700 police and highway patrol forces, and 43,800 other MOI forces, including the former commando and special security forces. Unlike the regular military, however, these forces presented serious security issues.

Militia infiltration into the Ministry of Interior security and police forces was a steadily growing problem in 2005 and early 2006. Substantial numbers of men from both the Badr Organization and Moqtada Al-Sadr's Al-Mahdi Army joined the force. In the case of the roughly 65,000-strong mix of MOI and police forces in the greater Baghdad area, the men from the Badr Organization tended to go into the MOI special security units and those from Al-Mahdi Army tended to join the police.

Figure 9.7   Iraqi Naval Capabilities as of August 2006

Patrol Boats	Rigid Inflatable Boats	Fast Assault Boats	Offshore Patrol Support Vessels	Al Faw–Class Patrol Boats
5	10	24	Purchase planned	Purchase planned

Source: U.S. Department of Defense, *Measuring Stability and Security in Iraq,* August 2006 Report to Congress.

Both MNF-I and the Iraqi government were slow to react. The Iraqi government and the Coalition continued to claim the situation was improving during much of 2005, although a September 2005 report by the International Crisis Group (ICG) suggested that the process of drafting the Constitution had helped exacerbate the existing ethnic and sectarian divisions between Iraqis and serious problems continued through the formation of a new government in May and June of 2006.[60]

The Ministry of Interior as a "Threat"

Much of the problem began at the top of the MOI. The appointment in May 2005 of Bayan Jabr as the interim head of the Interior Ministry—which oversaw the nation's police and specialized security units—exacerbated all these problems. Jabr was a prominent member of the Supreme Council for Islamic Revolution in Iraq (SCIRI), with close ties to Iran and to the Badr Brigade. It is unclear how many of the growing problems with the special security forces, police, prisons, and militias were really Jabr's fault—he had limited power and freedom of action—but it is clear that no decisive action took place without major pressure on the Minister by the U.S. Embassy and MNF-I.

This situation was made worse by severe understaffing of the Coalition advisory effort to both the Ministry of Interior and the police, a problem that continued until at least early 2006. It was also made worse by the fact that control of the U.S. advisory effort to the MOI was placed under the State Department while control of the advisory effort to the MOD was placed under the Department of Defense. This situation was corrected in October 2005 by putting the MOI under the Department of Defense, but this scarcely meant adequate staffing of the advisory effort, and problems in getting qualified civilian advisors continued to be severe.

Sunni politicians increasingly viewed Jabr's position as particularly troubling and blamed the Ministry for a wave of Sunni-targeted kidnappings, tortures, and murders allegedly carried out by men wearing police uniforms. In late 2005, the Interior Ministry was found to be running secret detention centers in which more than 800 men and boys, mostly Sunnis, were held in horrific conditions. (The Iraqi Constitution authorizes only the Ministry of Justice to run prisons.)[61]

By late 2005, U.S. officials and military sources were complaining that the MOI and Minister Jabr were not informing them of some MOI and police operations and privately acknowledged that they had observed prisoner abuse. Commenting on the futility of filing reports against the incidents, one U.S. official equated it with "trying to put out a forest fire with a bucket of water."[62]

They expressed particular concern about the actions of the MOI's Maghawir or Fearless Warrior special commando units, which were carrying out illegal raids and killings. This 12,000-man force had a number of Sunni officers and had originally been formed under the authority of former Prime Minister Iyad Allawi. Since the new government was formed in April 2005, however, it had recruited larger numbers of new Shi'ite members. Its Commander, General Rashid Flaih Mohammed, was reported to have acknowledged that the unit had had some problems. Sunni police commanders like Brigadier General Mohammed Ezzawi Hussein Alwann, commander of the Farook Brigade, were also purged from the MOI forces, along with junior officers.[63]

The inability to distinguish clearly between different types of Iraqi forces, and imposters from real elements of Iraqi forces, became steadily more serious over time. During the winter of 2005 and 2006, body dumps became a favored tactic for both insurgents and militias. Although this trend existed long before the February 22, 2006, Askariya bombing, it increased thereafter and became part of the cyclical sectarian violence carried out by Shi'ites and Sunnis. It would be almost impossible to catalog all of the discoveries, but finding 10 to 20 corpses at one site was not uncommon, and each day usually resulted in at least one "body dump" being reported. For example, in the period from March 7 until March 21, over 191 bodies were found. On one day in May, it was reported that 51 bodies were found in Baghdad alone. A health official in Baghdad said that there were over 2,500 murders in the capital since the February bombing, excluding mass-casualty bombings.[64]

Efforts did go on, however, to improve the situation. By late spring of 2006, the Iraqi government and its Coalition partners had taken a number of steps to promote respect for human rights within the MOI:[65]

> Iraqi police recruits receive 32 hours of human rights and rule of law training during the ·10-week police basic training program. At the 3-week-long Transition Integration Program, in-service personnel receive 20 hours of human rights and rule of law training. National Police Forces receive 9–15 hours of human rights training during their 6-week courses. Additionally, throughout the country there are numerous programs to train existing MOI security forces in human rights standards, such as embedding civilian advisors and military police into Iraqi police stations.

The fact that many of the MOI forces had become associated with Shi'ite and Kurdish attacks on Sunnis during this period presented another kind of problem. In May 2006, Senior Iraqi leaders were preparing a major restructuring of Baghdad's security brigades that would place all police officers and paramilitary soldiers under a single commander and in one uniform. The move came as part of a wider effort to contain the sectarian violence that was ravaging the city.[66] The one reassuring note was that Sunni Muslims continued to join the security forces in large numbers, a possible sign of success in the effort to include people of Iraq's various religious factions into the military.[67]

While the U.S. government helped the Iraqi government establish an abuse complaint process system that involved the Inspector General, Internal Affairs, and the Public Affairs Office, the MOI still did not have the ability to police itself and eradicate human rights abuses. Human rights violations were particularly egregious at detention centers where there are no places to shower, pray, or prepare food and where plumbing and electrical systems are substandard. The Joint Iraqi Inspection Committee, comprised of Iraqi Inspectors General from various Ministries with the support of the U.S. Embassy and MNF-I, continued its investigation of these detention centers as of spring 2006.

Real vs. Authorized Strength

Figure 9.8 shows the size of Ministry of Interior forces before the growing problems they present in terms of sectarian and ethnic violence led to their reorganization. The number of trained equipped men in the new MOI forces, as of mid-2006, is shown in Figure 9.9. It should be stressed that many of these men had deserted or left. Estimating the actual strength of MOI forces was a major problem. U.S. and Iraqi commanders had long criticized the policy whereby Iraqi soldiers could leave their units whenever they want to. The Iraqi Army does not require its soldiers to sign contracts, so soldiers treat enlistments as temporary jobs. This policy was partially responsible for draining Iraqi ranks to confront the insurgency by as much as 30 to 50 percent.[68]

Growth in Manpower: January 4, 2006 vs. May 31, 2006

January 4, 2006		May 31, 2006	
COMPONENT	TRAINED & EQUIPPED	COMPONENT	TRAINED & EQUIPPED
POLCE	~ 77,500	POLCE	~103,400
HIGHWAY PATROL		HIGHWAY PATROL	
OTHER MOI FORCES	~40,500	OTHER MOI FORCES	~44,300
TOTAL	~118,000*	TOTAL	~145,500

* Unauthorized absence personnel are included in these numbers.

Source: Iraq Weekly Status Report, Bureau of Near Eastern Affairs, US Department of State, January 4, 2006 and May 31, 2006 issues, p. 7.

Manning Realities vs. Goals February 2006

MOI Force	Manning as of Feb. 2006	Manning Goal as of Feb. 2006
Iraqi Highway Patrol	1,800	6,200 (August 2007)
Police Commandos	9,000	11,800 (December 2006)
Mechanized Police	1,500	NA
Public Order Police	8,100	10,600 (May 2006)
Emergency Response Unit	400	700 (June 2006)
Border Police	18,500	28,000 (May 2006)
Dignitary Protection	600	NA

Source: Adapted from U.S. Department of Defense, *Measuring Stability and Security in Iraq,* Report to Congress in Accordance with the Department of Defense Appropriations Act 2006 (Section 9010), February 2006, pp. 49-54.

Figure 9.8   The Manpower of Iraq's Ministry of Interior Forces before Their Mid-2006 Reorganization

Ministry of Interior Forces		Ministry of Defense Forces	
COMPONENT	TRAINED & EQUIPPED	COMPONENT	OPERATIONAL
POLICE	~120,190***	ARMY	~128,230***
NATIONAL POLICE	~24,400	AIR FORCE	~740
OTHER MOI FOCES	~27,510	NAVY	~1,130
TOTAL	~172,100**	TOTAL	~130,100

*Ministry of Interior Forces: Unauthorized absence personnel are included in these numbers; **Ministry of Defense Forces: Unauthorized absence personnel are not included in these numbers; ***Army numbers include Special Operations Forces and Support Forces. Source: Department of State Weekly Iraq Updated, date as of September 13, 2006.

Figure 9.9   MOI and MOD Force Levels as of August 2006

Active recruiting by the militias presented a growing problem, although many who chose the militias over the national army and police scarcely did so out of religious conviction. In violence-prone areas where few jobs are available, young males often have reasons and incentives such as security, money, and general well-being to join the militias over the state-run forces. As one such recruit summed it up, the offer by the Al-Mahdi Army was "an attractive package." Not only did it offer a greater salary, but the organization also promised to take care of his family if something were to happen to him.

The Status of Special Security Forces

The buildup of MOI special security and commando forces and units continued to be significant in 2006. The *New York Times* reported on January 16, 2006, that about 80,000 local police officers across Iraq were certified as being trained and equipped, more than halfway toward the goal of 135,000 by early 2007.[69] As of February 20, 2006, Multi-National Force–Iraq spokesman Major General Rick Lynch said that Iraq's growing security forces planned and carried out more than a quarter of all counterinsurgency operations in Iraq in January, a total of 490 Iraqi-run missions, nearly a 50-percent increase over the September 2005 figure.[70] The Coalition also worked with the Iraqi Public Order Special Police who serve as a bridge between local police and the Iraqi Army in handling terrorist and insurgency threats. Numbering about 9,000 as of February 2006, the Public Order Police operated primarily as a light urban infantry.

As of May 2006, there were around 22,700 trained and equipped National Police (formerly known as "Special Forces" and "Commandos") personnel, an increase of 4,000 since the previous DOD report to Congress in February 2006:[71]

The 1st and 2nd National Police Divisions will reach 95% of equipping and authorized manning by June 2006 and will complete force generation by December 2006. The 1st

National Police Mechanized Brigade continues to provide route security along Route Irish (from the International Zone to Baghdad International Airport), and is currently completing the fielding of 62 Armored Security Vehicles.

Force Size and Readiness

The growing size and the readiness of the elite elements of these forces are shown in Figure 9.10. They presented the problem, however, that some elements were responsible for serious abuses of Shi'ites, and they became a *de facto* part of the problem rather than the solution. Colonel Gordon Davis stated in February 2006 that the composition of these forces was about 20 percent Sunni, many of whom are officers, and claimed this made it unlikely that the group could be infiltrated by vigilantes who carry out ethnic-based attacks. "There are a heck of a lot of strongly willed patriots amongst that group, and if they believed one of their own may be an insurgent or terrorist, then they would pick them out right away because that puts their own lives on the lines, as well as those of their families."[72]

In an April 6, 2006, report to Congress, the DOD addressed the overall progress in the force structure of Iraq's Interior Ministry as follows:[73]

The end-strength force structure for all Ministry of Interior forces is 195,000 trained and equipped personnel manning two division headquarters, nine brigade headquarters, twelve Public Order battalions, twelve Commando battalions, three mechanized battalions, and one Emergency Response Unit. The force structure plan is designed to enable a stable civil-security environment in which a prosperous economy and a democratic and representative government that respects and promotes human rights can evolve. As of March 20, 130,700 Ministry of Interior security personnel, or 67 percent of the authorized end strength of 195,000, have been trained and equipped. This includes 89,000 IPS [Iraqi Police Service] personnel, as described in the next section, and 41,700 other

COMPONENT	IRAQI UNITS ACTIVELY CONDUCTING COUNTERINUSRGENCY OPERATIONS	
	Units fighting side-by-side with Coalition Forces*	Units in the lead with Coalition enablers or fully independent
Public Order Battalions	7	5
Mechanized Battalions	2	1
Police Commando Battalions	9	3
Emergency Response Unit	0	1

Note: * The numbers in this column may decrease as units are assessed into higher levels (i.e., "in the lead" or "fully independent").
Source: *Measuring Stability and Security in Iraq*, Department of Defense report to Congress, February 2006, p. 37.

Figure 9.10   Iraq's Estimated MOI National Police Force Capabilities before the Spring 2006 Reorganization

Ministry of Interior forces, such as 27 National Police Force battalions and one Emergency Response Unit conducting operations with ten of these units "in the lead." There is no specific threshold for the number of Iraqi special police units that must be judged capable of operating independently or in the lead before U.S. force levels can be reduced.

The report went on to outline the progress and the outlook for training and equipping the Iraqi police forces:[74]

The end-strength force structure of the IPS is 135,000 trained and equipped personnel. As of March 20, over 89,000 IPS, or 66 percent of the authorized end strength, have been trained and equipped, an increase of over 14,000 since the December 15, 2005 parliamentary election. These IPS personnel work alongside the 41,700 other Ministry of Interior forces described in the previous section.

The IPS is the primary civilian police organization in Iraq. Their mission is to enforce the law, safeguard the public, and provide internal security at the local level. The IPS is organized into patrol, station, and traffic sections in all major cities and provinces in Iraq and is responsible for providing security in more than 130 districts and at nearly 780 stations throughout Iraq. The scope of their responsibility demonstrates the critical need to ensure the development of professional, capable police forces that utilize modern policing techniques, follow the rule of law, and respect human rights. The Civilian Police Assistance Training Team (CPATT) works closely with the Ministry of Interior to improve the performance and professionalism of these forces. Police Transition Teams mentor and assist the IPS in a role similar to that of the Coalition Military Transition Teams, evaluating their progress and instituting the necessary procedures to continue development of a professional police force.

There is no specific threshold for the number of IPS that must be trained and equipped to maintain law and order and thereby enable U.S. force levels to be reduced.

By August 2006, approximately 24,300 National Police personnel had been trained and equipped, an increase of 1,600 since May of that year. Training for the new recruits consisted of six weeks of training in the police academy in northern Baghdad.

The equipment of the National Police consisted of small arms, medium machine guns, and RPGs, and light trucks, which were used for patrols. The mechanized battalions were equipped with Armored Security Vehicles and REVAs, a South African wheeled APC. By August the National Police had received 92 percent of their authorized equipment. They were expected to reach 96 percent by the end of November, falling short of the goal of reaching 100 percent by that time. They were expected to be fully equipped by the end of December 2006.[75]

Steps toward Reform

By early 2006, Ministry of Interior forces presented a serious problem, particularly among Iraq's Sunni population. So poor was the force's reputation that after the bombing of the Askariya shrine in Samarra on February 22, many Sunnis actually claimed that the perpetrators of the act were MOI forces seeking a pretext for civil war.[76] Among the forces that had gained the mixed reputation as among the most effective, but also the most feared, were the MOI's special security forces and police commandos.

In early 2006, the White House released a fact sheet highlighting the importance of revamping the image and the procedures of MOI forces and elite units:

> The Interior Ministry's Special Police are the most capable Iraqi police force...Many are professional and diverse, but recently some have been accused of committing abuses against Iraqi civilians. To stop abuses and increase professionalism, the Coalition is working with the Iraqi government to make adjustments in the way these forces are trained. Human rights and rule of law training is being increased. A new Police Ethics and Leadership Institute is being established in Baghdad. To improve capabilities, Iraqi Special Police battalions will be partnered with Coalition battalions so that American forces can work with and train their Iraqi counterparts.

Indeed, much attention in the spring and summer of 2006 was placed on reorienting the special MOI forces toward being a more positive force and reducing divisive behavior and the interloping influences of sectarian actors.[77] It was clear that major reforms were still needed. As a result, the Minister of the Interior merged the Police Commandos, the Public Order and Mechanized Police, and the Emergency Response Unit (ERU) to form the Iraqi National Police on April 1, 2006. Under the National Police Headquarters fall the 1st and 2nd National Police Divisions, the 1st National Police Mechanized Brigade, and the ERU. The two police divisions were formed from the Commando Division and the Public Order Division.

The 1st National Police Mechanized Brigade remained a direct supporting unit, and the ERU, previously part of the MOI's Supporting Forces organization, was reassigned as a direct reporting unit to the National Police Headquarters. Two police academies—Camp Solidarity and Camp Dublin—also fell under the National Police Headquarters and provide specialized training and professional development. In addition, the Headquarters was formally recognized to provide command and control, manning, equipping, training, and sustainment for the National Police Forces.

The ERU now reported directly to the National Police Force Headquarters and had more than 400 trained and equipped personnel assigned to it. The goal was for the ERU to become a highly trained, national-level unit similar to the hostage rescue team of the U.S. Federal Bureau of Investigation (FBI). ERU training consisted of two four-week courses that included instruction in handling detainees, human rights, target reconnaissance, physical fitness, and mission planning. Selected personnel received training at the eight-week Explosive Ordnance Disposal course or the six-week Intelligence/Surveillance course.

The Regular Police

The primary organization for local civilian policing in the MOI was the Iraqi Police Service. MNSTC-I's Civilian Police Assistance Training Team was working with the IPS to improve performance and professionalism, and Police Transition Teams were providing mentorship and development roles.

By early 2006, over 80,000 IPS personnel had been trained and equipped, an increase of 13,000 since October 2005. As of early 2006, MNSTC-I was projecting to complete force generation by February 2007.[78]

Increases in Police Strength

As of spring 2006, MOI forces included the IPS and national forces. The IPS consisted of patrol, traffic, station, and highway police assigned throughout Iraq's 18 provinces. National forces consisted of the National Police, the Department of Border enforcement, and the Center for Dignitary Protection.

As of March 2006, the MOI had integrated the former Iraqi Highway Patrol into the respective provincial police departments. This decreased the authorization of MOI forces to 188,000 trained and equipped personnel. The National Police had 28 battalions in the fight with 6 battalions having security lead for their areas of responsibility.

The end result was that the Civilian Police Assistance Training Team (CPATT) had trained and equipped approximately 101,200 IPS personnel as of May 2006, an increase of 18,800 since the previous report. The IPS was organized into patrol, station, traffic, and highway patrol directorates across Iraq and was tasked with enforcing the law, safeguarding the public, and providing internal security at the local level. As of May 2006, the CPATT anticipated that it will have trained and equipped the total authorization of 135,000 personnel by December 2006. More than 225 Iraqi police stations had been constructed and refurbished, 80 more than in February 2006. The CPATT projected that another 225 police stations would be completed by December 2006.

The "Year of the Police"

All of this progress, however, did not affect the fact that problems in the police and other MOI forces were so severe that the Iraqi government and MNF-I not only agreed to the reorganization discussed earlier, but that a comprehensive new approach was needed for training. All elements of the MOI forces needed better training and organization, but the regular police were so large that retraining them was a key challenge to the MOI, the Iraqi government, and the MNF-I.

The fact that the training and overall readiness of the Iraqi National Police remained behind the army, and the presence of militia members or "death squads" operating within or in association with the forces, caused the United States to elevate its efforts to make the police an effective fighting force and unofficially dub 2006 the "year of the police."

President Bush identified these problems in a March speech. He proposed three solutions:

- First, to increase partnerships between U.S. and Iraqi battalions in order that Iraqi units cannot only learn tactical lessons but also that the U.S. forces can "teach them about the role of a professional police force in a democratic system" so that they can conduct their operations "without discrimination."[79]

- Second, he called for further efforts by Iraqi officials in conjunction with their U.S. partners to identify and remove leaders within the police ranks who demonstrate loyalty to a militia. He claimed one success story in this area already. In December 2005, after receiving reports of abuses, the MOI dismissed the Brigade Commander of the Second Public Order Brigade. His replacement subsequently removed more than 100 men with ties to militias.[80]

- Third, to recruit a greater number of Sunni Arabs into what is seen by many as a predominately Shi'ite police force. President Bush noted that a basic training class that graduated in October 2005 was less than 1 percent Sunni. Although it is unclear how much progress has been made in diluting the Shi'ite majority within the ranks, Bush subsequently remarked that the class graduating in April 2006 "will include many more Sunni Arabs."[81]

More than 200 police transition teams were established at the national, provincial, district, and local levels that provided Coalition oversight, mentorship, and training to the police forces. Moreover, the Iraqi Department of Homeland Security Customs and Border Patrol teams mentored MOI forces at points of entry, and the 38 National Police Transition Teams continue to support the development of the National Police units.

Ongoing Reform

The initiative led to the deployment of CPATTs, under MNSTC-I, to lead the MNF-I Year of the Police initiative, and partnering with MOI, to plan, coordinate, and execute the necessary measures to develop the Ministry. Training increasingly focused on leadership development with the Center for Ethics and Leadership initiative as well as efforts to change the Baghdad Police College from focusing on training basic police officers to developing Iraqi police officers. The MOI also improved its internal investigative capability with the Internal Affairs section graduating another group of students to bring the total number of trained Internal Affairs specialists to 25 as of May 2006.

Following the April 1, 2006, reorganization, National Police recruits were to finish basic training programs at the National Police Force Training Academies. Training focused on leader development and "train the trainer" courses to facilitate the transition to Iraqi lead in all areas. The training academy in northern Baghdad accommodated 300–500 students for six weeks of intense training in weapons qualification, urban patrolling techniques, unarmed combat apprehension, use of force, human rights and ethics in policing, introduction to Iraqi law, vehicle checkpoints, and improvised explosive device characteristics and recognition.

Also effective April 1, 2006, National Police Transition Teams (NPTTs) were reassigned to MNC-I to ensure an integrated approach to command and control for the transition teams. This was meant to help ensure a more synchronized effort between Iraqi forces and operational Coalition units. NPTTs provide daily mentorship to the

National Police forces in the field to help develop leadership, plan and execute operations, and otherwise professionalize the force, while emphasizing the importance of human rights and the rule of law.

Equipment and Training

The IPS was equipped with AK-47s, PKCs, Glock pistols, individual body armor, high frequency radios, small pickup trucks, midsize SUVs, and medium pickup trucks. The IPS's logistics capabilities, especially in regard to vehicle maintenance, continued to be a concern, although progress has been made in the effective distribution and improved accountability of supplies and equipment. Forces in the nine key cities are currently approaching 80 percent of their authorized key pacing items.

Deliveries, however, were even lighter than for the regular forces. Equipment deliveries for all MOI forces in the final quarter of 2005 included the following:[82]

- More than 10,000 AK-47 rifles,
- 16,000 pistols,
- 800 light and medium machine guns,
- 4,000 sets of individual body armor,
- 700 Kevlar helmets, and
- More than 65,000 cold weather jackets.

Iraqi police training continued at the Jordan International Police Training Center (JIPTC) and at the Baghdad Police College (BPC) while smaller regional academies complemented these training initiatives. The JIPTC accommodates around 1,500 students per class while the BPC accommodates around 1,000. The ten-week basic course covers the rule of law, human rights, and policing skills in a high-threat environment. Since the previous report, more than 20,000 police personnel have received specialized training on diverse subjects, including interrogation procedures and counterterrorism investigations. Leadership development remained on track to meet the December 2006 goal of having all required officers and NCOs trained.

By July 24, 2006, 71,324 police recruits had passed through the ten-week basic course. Those recruits with prior experience attended the three-week Transitional Integration Program (TIP), in lieu of the longer program. Originally only officers trained during the Saddam regime were eligible for the TIP program, but in July it was extended to include those that lacked formal training, but had at least one year of experience on the force. In addition to the TIP program, the Officer Transitional Integration Program was designed to train officers for leadership and supervisory roles in the IPS. By August 2006, 41,051 officers had graduated from the TIP and OTIP programs.

By August 2006 the CPATT had trained and equipped approximately 113,800 IPS personnel, increasing the force by 12,600 over the three months prior. Although the force was expected to reach the targeted strength of 135,000 by December 2006, it was expected that there would continue to be shortages in some areas and excesses in others.

In an effort to ensure that MOI personnel were committed to the new regime, more than 230,000 MOI employees were screened by the Iraqi Police Screening Service. The process checked fingerprints against records of Ba'ath Party membership and Saddam-era criminal records. Of these checks there were 5,300 possible matches and 74 people were eventually dismissed. Unfortunately there was no test for checking on possible militia allegiance. In addition to the fingerprint checks, over 54,000 police candidates were tested for literacy. Of these candidates 73 percent passed and were enrolled in basic training.

The IPS personnel were equipped with AK-47s, PKC light machine guns, Glock pistols, body armor, high-frequency radios, small and medium pickup trucks, and mid-sized SUVs. In Baghdad and the nine other key cities the IPS personnel were equipped at 99 percent of their authorized equipment by the end of June 2006 and were expected to be fully equipped by mid-August. Overall, however, in the 18 provinces the IPS was equipped only at a 66 percent rate by June and was not expected to be fully equipped until the end of the year.[83]

Dealing with Divided Loyalties

Reorganization and retraining still left open the question of divided loyalties. By the spring of 2006, a recent background check by Iraqi police investigators found more than 5,000 police officers with records of crimes that included attacks on American troops. The results pointed to questions over the initial vetting process for creating the force, as well as continuing problems of quality. A 2006 internal police survey conducted northeast of Baghdad found that 75 percent of respondents did not trust the police enough to tip them off to insurgent activity.

In response to these concerns, the Pentagon announced it was sending 3,000 police trainers across the country in 2006 in an attempt to remake the force and to have a competent functional force of 190,000 police officers by early 2007.[84] According to U.S. Army Colonel Rob Barham, this goal was to follow on a shorter-term goal of 135,000 officers patrolling in all 18 Iraqi provinces by the end of 2006.[85]

Facility Construction

As of spring 2006, work on the Baghdad Police College (formerly the Baghdad Public Safety Training Academy) continued. The project was 80 percent complete and was expected to be finished by July 2006. Renovations on the Al-Zab Courthouse in Kirkuk, which began in October 2005, were 52 percent complete by April, with an estimated completion date of mid-August 2006.

Progress on the Nassriya correctional facility was 28 percent complete and had been hampered due to inadequate workforce levels and security concerns at the site. The facility was expected to be completed in August 2006 and was slated to have a capacity of at least 800 beds, with the possibility of an additional 400 beds.

By April, construction was also completed on the following military facilities:[86]

- Camp India Base, which will support 2,500 Iraqi soldiers in the 4th Brigade of the 1st Division,
- Samawah, which will support 750 Iraqi soldiers in the 2nd Brigade of the 10th Division, and
- Naiad, which will support 250 Iraqi soldiers in the 1st Brigade Headquarters of the 8th Division.

Department of Border Enforcement

Progress also occurred in creating an effective Border Police, a step that was hoped to help stem the infiltration of foreign fighters, smugglers, and Iranian agents. By early 2006, more than 18,500 Border Police had been trained and equipped, up by 1,500 since the last yearly quarter of 2005, but lagging the goal of 24,000 by the December 15, 2005, election. While three border force academies were operational, delays in construction at the Department of Border Enforcement (DBE) was blamed for the slow progress of bringing forces on-line. Construction had been delayed due to weather, remote location, restricted movement, and contractor delays.

By May 2006, the DBE numbered approximately 21,000 trained and equipped personnel, an increase of 2,300 since February 2006. These forces were organized into 5 regions, 12 brigades, and 38 battalions. By August 2006, the DBE had 23,900 trained and equipped personnel. These personnel were organized into 5 regions, 12 brigades, 38 battalions and the staff for 258 border forts. The DBE forces were trained in three academies each with the capacity to train approximately 800 recruits at a time.

Supplying the DBE and the Ports of Entry (POE) were given priority in receiving equipment and this, in addition to the cross-leveling of personnel, managed to raise most units to Level 2 readiness by August. Furthermore, of the 14 land POEs in Iraq, 13 were functional by August 2006. The DBE and POE were expected to have 28,360 trained and equipped personnel by November 2006.[87]

Coalition Border Transition Teams

Members of the 10- to 11-man Coalition Border Transition Teams (BTTs) were trained in various specialties, including logistics and communications, and provided valuable mentorship and support for border force commanders in the areas of personnel management, intelligence, operations, budgeting equipment accountability, and maintenance. The number of BTTs was increased from 15 to more than 25 as part of the Year of the Police initiative. Three academies with a capacity of 800 students each were operational as well.

Such efforts had limits. Although the lack of border control helped allow the passage of foreign fighters and supplies, many came through legal border crossings, and the insurgency was not dependent on smuggling or foreign volunteers. In fact,

Iranian pilgrims were the most frequently intercepted trespassers. Lieutenant General Peter Chiarelli stated, "There is still a lot going over the border...I don't know if you can ever stop it completely."[88]

Border Forces Equipment and Training

During a tour of 2 of the 258 border posts established by Coalition forces, Lieutenant General Peter Chiarelli said that Iraqi border forces were getting "better and better every single day." Yet, he noted that these forces needed better pay and equipment. Some forts lack radios and other standard communication equipment and a few do not have even enough gas on hand to conduct patrols.[89]

The border forces had a force generation and distribution plan calling for the delivery of 85 percent of the key equipment by summer 2006. Standard organization equipment includes small and medium pickup trucks; midsize SUVs, generators; and mobile, base, and handheld radios. Border forces also required personal equipment such as AK-47s, medium machine guns, and individual body armor.

Three DBE academies in al-Kut, Basra, and Sulamaniyah, each with a capacity of approximately 800, were utilized for training border patrol students. Students in the Iraqi Border Patrol Basic Training Course received instruction in law enforcement, human relations, human rights, weapons qualification, combat life saving, vehicle searches, Iraqi border law, arrest and detainee procedures, and small unit patrolling. The curriculum was to be updated to include specialized instruction in first aid, communications, maintenance, and food preparation. After completing the three-week core curriculum, recruits were then tracked according to these four specialties.

The DBE continued to make progress in designating standard organizations, delineating responsibilities, and developing detailed policies and procedures for land POE. As of May 2006, there were 14 land POEs, and 13 of these were functional. Making significant changes in the operation of POEs is difficult because multiple Ministries are involved.

As of August 2006, the DBE and POE were equipped with AK-47s, medium machine guns, body armor, medium pickup trucks, mid-size SUVs, generators, and radios. The DBE had received 81 percent of its authorized equipment by August and was expected to be at 97 percent by the end of the month, falling short of the goal of being 100 percent equipped by this time. By the end of September the goal of being fully equipped was expected to be achieved. The POEs were expected to be fully equipped by the end of December 2006.[90]

Uncertain Progress in Facilities

The border forces were to man 258 border forts. As of May 2006, 244 border posts and forts had been completed, an increase of 74 since February 2006. Layered security effort included border patrols by DBE units, Iraqi Army checkpoints, and Coalition forces.

This progress was, however, sometimes more apparent than real. In spring 2006, the Special Inspector General for Iraq Reconstruction (SIGIR) conducted ground project surveys of 22 border forts located along the Iraq-Iran border. Progress on the completion of these projects was described as thus:[91]

> At the time of the ground survey, 17 were complete or near complete and functional. However, only 7 of the 17 border forts had perimeter security systems, gates, berms, or walls installed. Concrete quality was sometimes poor, and inconsistent surfaces in concrete and plaster finishing were common in the buildings and other structures. Numerous sites lacked retaining walls to prevent degradation of the embankments created by site leveling.
>
> Based on discussions with local personnel at the border forts at the time of the site visits, SIGIR found that the day-to-day users—the border police—were unaware of a plan for maintenance and logistical support for the border posts, and received little if any training in maintaining the generator and septic systems. Logistical needs, such as fuel and water delivery, were lacking at some border posts. The generators lacked protection from drifting snow, and some outdoor electrical fixtures lacked proper insulation against rainwater. SIGIR requested copies of contract documents for the remaining five border forts included in our surveys; however, the MNSTC-I was unable to identify or locate the contract(s) for these projects. As a result, SIGIR was unable to determine the project objectives, SOW [Statement of Work], or design specifications.
>
> All five of these border forts were of poor quality construction and showed no signs of any recent maintenance. Although small generators were located at the five border forts, fuel storage was not available. Electrical and water systems were consistently either inoperable or needed repair.

Other Developments in Border Enforcement

On May 27, 2006, on the second day of his visit to Iraq, Iranian Foreign Minister Manouchehr Mottaki said that Iran and Iraq had agreed to form a joint commission to oversee border issues and that its primary task would be to "block saboteurs" from crossing the 700-mile border. Mottaki went on to say that improved border controls would be part of a wider effort to build close ties between the countries, including $1 billion in Iranian economic assistance to Shi'ite and Kurdish areas of Iraq.[92]

Facilities Protection Forces, Private Security Personnel, and "Ministry Armies"

Iraq and the MNF-I also had problems with a wide range of lighter forces, many of which were corrupt, ineffective, and had elements that either supported the insurgency or rogue Shi'ite operations.

The Facilities Protection Services

L. Paul Bremer, former head of the Coalition Provisional Authority (CPA), established the Facilities Protection Service (FPS) in September 2003 to free American troops from guarding Iraqi government property and to prevent the kind of looting that erupted with the entry of U.S. forces and the overthrow of Saddam Hussein.

Bremer's order put the FPS under the command and pay of the Ministries they protected, not of the Interior and Defense Ministries, which handle the rest of Iraq's security forces. The order also allowed private security firms to handle the contracting of FPS guards for the Ministries.[93]

U.S. and Interior Ministry officials increasingly described the FPS units as militias that answer only to the Ministry or private security firm that employs it. U.S. officials have acknowledged that they have no more control over the FPS than the Interior Ministry does. "Negative. None. Zero," said Lieutenant Colonel Michael J. Negard, a spokesman for the U.S. training of Iraqi forces. Even Interior Ministry Bayan Jabr said in April 2006 that the FPS was "out of control."[94]

In April 2006, Interior Minister Byan Jabr accused the FPS of carrying out some of the killings largely attributed to death squads operating within MOI forces.[95] That same month, oversight of expansion and training of these forces raised further uncertainty. An Inspector General was assigned to audit the $147-million U.S.–overseen FPS program. The report reflected a lack of transparency:[96]

> ...the auditors were never able to determine basic facts like how many Iraqis were trained, how many weapons were purchased and where much of the equipment ended up.
>
> Of 21,000 guards who were supposed to be trained to protect oil equipment, for example, probably only about 11,000 received the training, the report said. And of 9,792 automatic rifles purchased for those guards, auditors were able to track just 3,015.

On May 14, 2006, Ellen Knickmeyer reported in the *Washington Post* that Iraq's Interior Ministry had begun negotiations to bring central authority to the FPS, a unit of 4,000 building guards that U.S. officials say has become the new government's largest paramilitary force, with 145,000 armed men and no central command, oversight, or paymaster.

On May 6, 2006, the private security companies that employ the FPS members agreed to several Interior Ministry proposals intended to bring some measure of central control and oversight to the paramilitary units. The Ministry will issue badges and distinctive seals for FPS vehicles and supervise FPS weapons. Agents of the security companies and the Ministry clarified that FPS members were liable for prosecution for any crimes. The security companies also agreed to bring the FPS under Ministry supervision, but General Raad al-Tamimi of the Interior Ministry did not disclose any details.[97]

The Infrastructure Protection Forces and Other Non-MOD/MOI Paramilitary Elements

The various infrastructure protection forces were placed under the MOD, but were much lower quality forces than the regular military, the MOI security forces, and many of the police. In many cases, they were corrupt, subject to insurgent penetration, and tied to various sects, ethnic groups, and tribes.

While Prime Minister Maliki referred to such forces as having some 150,000 men in May 2006, many were phantom employees, deserters, or virtually inactive. Such units also often sold their uniforms, weapons, and equipment. They also generally reported in *de facto* terms to another Ministry, even when they were formally under the control of the Ministry of Defense.

The two key entities responsible for the security of Iraq's oil infrastructure in spring 2006 were the Strategic Infrastructure Battalions (SIBs) and the Oil Protection Force (OPF). The electric infrastructure is protected by the Electric Power Security Service.

- The SIBs fielded more than 3,400 trained personnel to guard Iraq's critical oil infrastructure, particularly the vast network of pipelines, as of April.
- The OPF, managed by the Ministry of Oil, was responsible for guarding all other Iraqi oil industry assets and facilities.

As reported by SIGIR's April 2006 Report to Congress, the government formed the SIBs to improve infrastructure security. The SIBs were part of the Ministry of Defense, and four SIBs had completed basic training at the time of the report. They were currently conducting security operations to protect oil pipelines and facilities critical to the domestic market and export industry. MNSTC-I equipped the SIBs and helped the Ministry of Defense develop institutional expertise and tradecraft. Developments reported by SIGIR included the following:

> More than 3,400 soldiers have completed training in this area, and training for a second group has already begun. Attacks on Iraq's infrastructure account for only a small portion of total attacks. According to DoD, attacks on infrastructure during this quarter are down by 60%. But, combined with other variables, attacks on critical infrastructure are still expected to have a significant impact on:
> – oil and fuel production
> – revenues derived from crude exports
> Additionally, although the number of infrastructure attacks has recently decreased, the complexity of the attacks has increased: insurgents have become more proficient at targeting critical infrastructure nodes, as well as intimidating personnel who deliver essential services.

These forces had serious problems, however, and were generally ineffective and could not be trusted. In early March 2006, DOD reported that Iraqi police had arrested several SIB guards on suspicion of aiding insurgents in targeting the oil pipeline system. This was the second recent incident in which SIB personnel were arrested in connection with insurgent plots against the oil pipeline infrastructure.[98]

The Oil Ministry, for example, maintained about 20,000 troops to protect refineries and other parts of the country's oil infrastructure. Another example was the Facilities Protection Service, established in 2003 as a 4,000-man force charged with protecting crucial parts of Iraqi utilities, such as power plants and oil refineries.

Between August 2004 and January 2005, that force expanded 15-fold to 60,000 personnel. A contributing factor to the expansion of the force was the U.S. need to free up U.S. troops for combat. Still, some cautioned that the expansion created only another competing militia, whose troops' loyalties were only with the Ministry that paid them.

Intelligence

Iraqi intelligence was still in development at the military and civilian levels in mid-2006. Some independent units were emerging, but most operations were under *de facto* Coalition tutelage or control.

IRAQ'S CONTINUING STRATEGIC CHALLENGES

Iraq faces many strategic challenges, the most serious of which is the risk of division or civil war. Since 2003, the nation has been dealing with many forces that are pulling it apart. The discussion of stability in Iraq has largely focused on the insurgency and the insurgents' ability to inflict death and destruction, but the violence is just one element of the puzzle—albeit an important element.

Iraq is already in a state of civil war and risks break up, far more serious ethnic and sectarian conflict, or violent paralysis. Iraq needs to forge a lasting political compromise among its key factions—Arab-Shi'ites, Arab Sunnis, and Kurds—while protecting other minorities. Political conciliation must also address such critical issues as federalism and the relative powers of the central and regional governments, the role of religion in politics and law, control over petroleum resources and export revenues, the definition of human rights, and a host of other issues.

Iraq must establish both effective governance and a rule of law; not simply deploy effective military, security, and police forces. Legitimacy does not consist of how governments are chosen, but in how well they serve the day-to-day needs of their peoples. Security cannot come through force alone. It must have the checks and balances that can come only when governments and courts are active in the field.

Over time, Iraq must also address its economic and demographic challenges. A nation cannot convert from a corrupt, state-controlled "command kleptocracy" in mid-war. It cannot survive unless it makes such a conversion over time and puts an end to a hopelessly skewed and unfair distribution of income, ends full and partial unemployment levels of 30 to 60 percent, and becomes competitive on a regional and a global level.

The Growing Level of Violence in Iraq

It is not easy to put the level of conflict in Iraq in perspective, and the numbers and trends can easily change radically in the future. No reliable estimates exist of how many Iraqis are killed because many simply disappear, and there is nothing approaching an accurate estimate of wounded. All of the attack counts issued by the Iraqi government and MNF-I are extremely uncertain because many low-level attacks or individual attacks on individuals are never counted, and intimidation and forced moves are not counted. There is no way to separate murders, kidnappings, and violent crimes from insurgent actions and ethnic and sectarian violence. The kind of pressures that have led to more than 130,000 Iraqis (22,977 families) being displaced since the February 22, 2006, bombing of the Mosque in Samarra are largely unreflected in "attack" counts.

Furthermore, efforts to count attacks have a heavy bias toward counting insurgent attacks in Baghdad and the three other provinces where Sunni insurgents are more active. Counts of Kurdish-Arab violence are very uncertain—which has a major impact on the numbers reported in Kirkuk and Mosul. So is intra-Sunni violence in the "Sunni triangle" and intra-Shi'ite violence, particularly in Basra.

The Department of Defense does regularly issue numbers that at least have some value in indicating the rough intensity of the fighting. These numbers do differ in definition over time, which makes trend analysis difficult. It is also important to note that the number of attacks says nothing about the intensity of the attacks or the casualties that result. Some incidents are far more important than others.

Given all these caveats, the data in the Department of Defense quarterly report issued on August 31, 2006, showed the following:[99]

- There had been a massive increase in the Sunni vs. Shi'ite sectarian violence that could trigger an all-out civil war, divide the country, and effectively force the United States to withdraw. Casualties from "Sectarian incidents" rose from less than 200 per month during May 2005 to January 2006, to some 1,200 in February, and averaged around 2,200 per month from March through September. Given the fact that such totals seriously undercount total ethnic and sectarian violence, this more than tenfold increase is a serious warning of the possibility of civil war.

- U.S. reporting indicated that the number of significant attacks per week totaled around 470 per week during the period before the Constitution was signed (February–August 2005) and have risen steadily ever since. They averaged around 540 during the referendum and election period (29-8-05 to 10-2-06), rose to 625 per week during the transition to the new government (11-2-06 to 19-5-06), and reached about 790 per week during the period of government operation (20-5-06 to 11-8-06).

- This was a rise of some 70 percent during the period during which a new Constitution and new government were supposed to bring stability. These attacks concentrated more and more on Iraqi targets and Iraqi civilians, particularly in the Baghdad area—which is the only area where counts of attacks on civilians have anything approaching minimal accuracy. The percentage of attacks on civilians in the Baghdad area rose from 15 percent in April to 22 percent in June, but such counts and percentages are so uncertain that they have limited value.

- The United States reported that almost all attacks were concentrated in four provinces—Anbar, Baghdad, Salah ad Din, and Diyala—with only 37 percent of Iraq's population. For example, this included 81 percent of U.S.–reported attacks during May 20 to August 4, 2006. The problem is that such counts focus heavily on the insurgency and reflect a systematic undercount of ethnic violence, intra-Shi'ite attacks, and attacks outside urban areas where the United States has at least limited confidence in its sources. It simply is not clear what such claims mean.

• There was no correlation between the increase in the number of attacks during these periods and U.S. casualties. U.S. casualties actually dropped during the peak periods from April 1, 2004 to November 28, 2004, when they averaged some 22–24 per day. Since that time, they have consistently remained under 20 per day. The United States also has reported steady increases in improvised explosive device (IED) attacks that have not led to anything approaching proportionate increases in U.S. casualties.

• In contrast, Iraqi government, security, and civilian casualties per day had risen very sharply. These totaled less than 40 per day until the election period began on November 27, 2004. They rose to 45 per day during the election period (27-11-04 to 11-2-05). They rose to around 50 per day during the period before the Constitution was signed (11-2-05 to 28-8-05). They averaged around 48 per day during the referendum and election period (29-8-05 to 10-2-06), rose to 81 per day during the transition to the new government (11-2-06 to 19-5-06), and reached about 118 per day during the period of government operation (20-5-06 to 11-8-06). This is a roughly threefold increase.

The number of attacks on Iraqi infrastructure had steadily gone down, but Iraqi oil facilities and exports continued to experience serious problems, and much of the economic aid effort has been paralyzed or had to be limited to "secure areas."

Infrastructure attacks averaged around 13 per week during April 1, 2004 to June 28, 2004. They dropped to 10 per week during June 29, 2004 to November 26, 2004. They dropped to 5 per week during the election period (November 27, 2004 to February 11, 2005), were 5 per week during the period before the Constitution was signed (February 11, 2005 to August 28, 2005. They dropped to 4 per week during the referendum and election period (August 29, 2005 to February 10, 2006), to 2 per week during the transition to the new government (February 11, 2006 to May 19, 2006), and to 1 per week during the period of government operation (May 20, 2006 to August 11, 2006).

In practical terms, however, all aid and economic activity became steadily more dangerous in spite of this drop in attack numbers. Water and electric power distribution continued to present major problems, and oil exports stayed below 1.7 million barrels a day.[100]

The Dangers of Strategic Uncertainty

Iraq's success or failure in forging political consensus, creating an effective new government, and creating effective security forces will have a major impact on the Gulf and the world. Iraq is a nation with a complex history, which presides in the most strategically important region in the world. In an era when asymmetric warfare and terrorism is threatening international security, energy security, and the threat of a "clash of civilizations," the future of Iraq will have large implications on regional stability and global security. Predicting these implications, however, is equally a useless exercise of imagination.

Many have attempted to predict the future outcome of Iraq, wanted to preempt it through dividing Iraq into three states, or recommended an immediate withdrawal of foreign troops from Iraq. In order, however, to understand Iraq and the prospect of stability in the foreseeable future, one must understand the forces at play and the strategic challenges facing Iraq in the short- to medium-term. The following issues must be dealt with in order to ensure that Iraq does not become involved in a major civil war and is stable in the coming years:

- **Conciliation versus civil war:** Sectarian violence has been the driving force behind the risk of igniting a civil war among Iraq's key factions. Most of the violence has been directed by neo-Salafist elements led by Al Qa'ida against Shi'ites. Iraq's political leaders have urged calm in the face of violence, but emotions run high particularly when the violence is directed against religious gatherings and/or shrines. Shi'ite militia groups such as the Al-Mahdi Army and the Badr Brigade have also been accused of carrying out "revenge" killings against Sunnis. The most dangerous claims have been of the infiltration of Shi'ite militia leaders either at the political level in the Ministry of Interior or at the soldier level in Iraq's security forces. Finally, the Kurdish question may have not spurred the same level of violence that the Sunni-Shi'ite tensions have, but it is all too clear that any attempt by the Kurds to demand autonomy will be met by resistance by both the Sunnis and the Shi'ites and can lead to further violence and enhance the threat of fragmentation in Iraq.

- **Defeating the insurgency and ethnic and sectarian violence:** Characterizing the Iraqi insurgency or defining its composition is not easy. Violence in Iraq has steadily increased on ethnic and sectarian levels. Most estimates, however, show that the insurgency is largely fueled by Sunnis who are dissatisfied with losing power, the Shi'ites control of the government, the occupation by U.S. forces, and with the overall economic and political situation in Iraq. In addition, there are other elements in the insurgency—particularly those led by Al Qa'ida in Iraq—that have attacked and urged more attacks against Shi'ites' holy sites, civilians, and political leaders. Finally, there are the former regime elements that are largely driven by loss of power and an aim for the return of the Ba'ath regime to power. These threats are compounded by a mix of Shi'ite and Kurdish militias and by a wide range of local Sunni, Shi'ite, and Kurdish forces growing out of the sectarian and ethnic fighting. All of these forces and movements must either be defeated or brought into the Iraqi political process on a peaceful basis if the nation is to become stable and secure.

- **Creating effective internal security and armed forces:** For immediate tactical or strategic success against the insurgency, the United States must continue to build Iraq's internal security, paramilitary, and military forces. The focus, however, must be on quality and not quantity. In addition to the usual criteria for ensuring force effectiveness, Iraqi security forces have suffered from the threat of infiltration by both Sunni insurgents as well as Shi'ite militias. This has driven many Iraqis, particularly Sunnis, to mistrust Iraq's security forces and has been a contentious point at the political as well as at the tactical level across sectarian lines. Loyalty cannot be ensured in the best-trained forces, but abuses by Ministry of Interior forces of Sunnis go to the heart of the chance of building force cohesion. In addition, Iraqi security and armed forces have suffered from direct attacks by insurgent groups. Force protection is still a problem for many of the Iraqi units, and it may take time before they are able to act interdependently.

- **Relations with neighboring states:** As noted earlier, Iraq fought two major wars with its neighbors, Iran and Kuwait, and has had hostile relations with two other Gulf States, Jordan and Syria. Since the toppling of Saddam Hussein's regime, Iraqis as well as Coalition officials have accused Iraq's neighboring states of interfering in Iraq's internal affairs. In the case of Iran, it has been accused of supporting Shi'ite militias as well as elements of the insurgency that are fighting against U.S. forces. This has prompted regional officials to accuse Iran of wanting to remake the new Iraq in its own image—a Shi'ite Islamic Republic. This has also forced many Sunnis to accuse Iraqi Shi'ites of working for Iran. However, in the case of Syria, U.S. and Iraqi officials have accused the Syrian government of facilitating the travel of foreign fighters into Iraq. Most of these fighters have joined neo-Salafist groups, namely, Al Qa'ida in Iraq, and have been accused of being behind most of the "spectacular" suicide bombings.

- **Establishing viable political institutions:** Since the overthrow of Saddam Hussein, the political divisions have been drawn across sectarian lines. These divisions have delayed writing key provisions of the Constitution, particularly the role of religion, federalism, and the division of oil revenues. In addition, Sunnis boycotted the first election because they felt underrepresented, which resulted in a win to a religious Shi'ite and nationalist Kurdish groups to score major wins. While Sunnis voted in larger numbers in the proceeding two elections, the challenge for Iraq is not in holding elections, but in establishing sustainable political institutions that transcend sectarian divisions. This includes removing the sense of sectarian favoritism in key Ministries such as the Ministry of Interior, the Ministry of Defense, and the Ministry of Oil. In addition, it means establishing an independent judicial system that is seen fair by all factions. Furthermore, with time, it requires nurturing a culture of citizen participation that is not based on ethnicity, but rather on political ideology that is based on what is best for the citizens of Iraq. Iraq, however, is far from that point, and the political challenge is as important to the future of Iraq as is any counterinsurgency strategy.

- **Building Iraq's economy:** Another important factor that is central to securing Iraq's future is the challenge the Iraqi government is facing in building a free-market economy. Due to the importance of oil revenues to Iraq's economy and the overcentralization policies of Saddam Hussein's regime, Iraq has never had a viable private sector and has never had a real stable currency. Iraq has always dealt with unemployment and underemployment, but the impact of 12 years of economic sanctions and the mismanagement of the reconstruction and aid efforts by the United States have left a large fraction of the Iraqi population unemployed. Perhaps the most prominent among these groups are those who were employed by Iraq's armed forces, who were fired due to the CPA's de-Ba'athification efforts. There are also discrepancies in the levels of development across different regions of Iraq. Under Saddam Hussein, the Sunni area witnessed large investments in infrastructure, while the Kurdish and Shi'ite areas saw minimum investments. The Kurdish region, however, has benefited from the semiautonomy it enjoyed during the 1990s and experienced an inflow of investment and economic development. Following the invasion, due to the relative calmness of the southern and northern regions of Iraq, Shi'ite and Kurdish regions have seen more benefit from Iraq's reconstruction compared to the Sunni regions—albeit on a low scale.

- **Upgrading Iraq's energy infrastructure:** Realistically speaking, no economic development or reform of Iraq can be complete without a large investment and upgrade in Iraq's oil sector. Iraq has suffered from the lack of any meaningful investment since the early 1980s due to mismanagement by the regime, political uncertainties, security risks, and economic sanctions. Iraq's oil fields are using technologies that are outdated, its oil workers have not been trained in industry best practices, and its downstream and upstream management as well as production facilities are worn out. U.S. reconstruction efforts have only begun to address these problems. Iraq's economy will likely continue to depend on its oil revenues, but its production capacity has not kept up either with regional standards or with Iraq's economic and fiscal needs. For the Iraqi government or the Coalition to have any success in dealing with Iraq's economic development problems, these problems in its energy sector must be dealt with.

As this list makes all too clear, Iraq's future largely depends on the Iraqi government's ability to deal with the sectarian divisions, ensure the nation's sovereignty, and ensure Iraq's long-term stability. None of this, however, is possible without sound economic, political, and security policies that aim at dealing with the totality of Iraq's strategic challenges.

Socioeconomic Challenges

Iraq has a long history of economic stagnation despite its vast oil resources. The high oil revenues following the 1970s boom were mismanaged and directed toward defense spending by Saddam Hussein. During the Iran-Iraq War, Iraq's military expenditures reached nearly half of its GNP. According to the U.S. Department of State, Iraq's defense spending as a percentage of GNP was 41.2 percent in 1985, 54.8 percent in 1986, 54.5 percent in 1987, 57.5 percent in 1988, 41.1 percent in 1989, 61.3 percent in 1990, 12.5 percent in 1991, and approximately 4.9–9.7 percent throughout the rest of the 1990s.[101] In the years before the U.S. invasion in 2003, Iraq was estimated to have spent 10 percent of its GNP on defense.[102]

Iraq's high levels of defense spending diverted much needed investment from social and economic development programs, which have suffered for many years from underinvestment. High defense spending is only one of the reasons behind Iraq's economic stagnation. Iraq's economy has also suffered from many years of fiscal mismanagement, oil crashes, economic sanctions, and two major wars, not to mention the U.S. invasion and the subsequent instability and security.

The importance of dealing with these economic challenges, however, goes beyond their economic values. The insurgency in Iraq is partially fueled by the dissatisfaction of the Iraqi population—particularly in the Sunni areas. In addition, it is all too clear that communities that are well-off economically would not risk joining the insurgency since they have a lot to lose. On the other hand, insurgent groups—of all stripes—recruit from unemployed Iraqis who do not see any hope for the future, and who blame the lack of economic and job opportunities on the Iraqi government and the U.S. occupation forces and on the failure of the postconflict reconstruction efforts.

Going forward, to understand the economic challenge Iraq faces, the following are the key areas that the Iraqi government must deal with in order to ensure economic growth and sustainable development:

- **High unemployment rates:** The CIA estimates that Iraq's unemployment rate is around 25–30 percent.[103] This estimate, however, is not based on a survey but rather on a "guesstimate." In fact, no one really knows the actual Iraqi labor force, and there are no meaningful ways to conduct accurate surveys of the labor force, given the security situation in Iraq. What is clear, however, is that estimates of how large the unemployment differ, but at least a third of Iraq's labor force is considered unemployed and some estimate it as high as 60 percent. Regardless of the exact number, a large number of Iraqis are unemployed, and the Iraqi government must find ways to stimulate the labor market, provide job opportunities for its youth, and must deal with its former military personnel who were let go by the de-Bathification campaign. There are no simple ways to deal with it, and Iraq is not alone in the Middle East in suffering from high unemployment, but the Iraqi government has little choice but to find a meaningful and practical solution.

- **Reliance on oil revenues and the public sector:** Part of the problem Iraq faces in creating employment opportunities is the lack of a vibrant private sector. Historically the number one employer in Iraq was the government, which heavily relied on oil revenues, which are estimated to be 95 percent of its export earnings. In addition, the government does not have any meaningful way to impose, reinforce, or collect tax revenues. Due to the volatility of the global oil market and the uncertainty regarding Iraq's oil production levels, Iraq's economic development has been inconsistent. The government must find alternatives to oil and must diversify its sources of revenues. But there is no replacement to a vibrant private sector that empowers the population and that acts as a natural distributor of wealth.

- **Budgetary transparencies:** Most of the Gulf States and, for that matter, most of the developing world suffer from a lack of transparency in their budgetary processes. This has encouraged corruption or, at the very least, the perception thereof. Many Iraqi officials have complained about the plague of corruption in Iraq. The scrutiny has focused on many agencies in Iraq, but particularly on the Ministry of Oil. Part of instilling confidence in the government is reassuring the public that oil revenues are not misused and stolen. Once again, there are no easy answers to this problem, but an honest effort has to be made to provide reporting and to give the Iraqi Parliament the oversight of the use of the money.

- **Establishing a stable currency:** The Iraqi Dinar has been volatile for decades. The sanctions caused a major devaluation of the currency, and ongoing inflationary pressures as well as massive current account deficits have caused the dinar's future to be cloaked with uncertainty. This may be a minor problem in the short-term, but recent history is full of examples when minor inflations and currency devaluation have caused major economic meltdowns. A policy of repatriating Iraqi capital from the West, paying down foreign debt, inviting foreign investment, and curbing down inflationary tendencies can help to stop further currency crashes and to improve the standard of living in Iraq.

These economic challenges are compounded by other social demographic problems. As is the case with its other Gulf neighbors, Iraq faces a youth explosion. As Figure 9.11 shows, approximately 40 percent of Iraq's population is under the age of 14, and more than half (52 percent) are under the age of 20. In addition, the figure shows that approximately 45 percent of Iraq's population is of working age. This distribution does not show the problem Iraq faces in its labor market, but it shows the difficulty it will face in the foreseeable future.

According to UN population estimates, Iraq has experienced major population growth since the 1950s. Iraq's population was estimated to be 5.34 million in 1950, 7.33 million in 1960, 10.11 million in 1970, 14.09 million in 1980, 18.52 million in 1990, 25.08 million in 2000, and 28.81 million in 2005. The same trends are also expected to continue. The UN projects Iraq's population to grow to 32.53 million in 2010, 40.52 million in 2020, 48.80 million in 2030, 56.69 million in 2040, and 63.69 million in 2050.[104]

The insurgents have continued to be successful in attacking the Iraqi economy and the Coalition aid effort, as well as human targets. They have often paralyzed aid efforts, particularly in Sunni or mixed areas where such efforts might win over current or potential insurgents. They have forced a massive reprogramming of aid into short-term, security-oriented activity, and well over 20 percent of aid spending now goes simply to providing security for aid activity. The attacks have done much to discourage or reduce investment and development even in the more secure governorates and have blocked or sharply limited efforts to renovate and improve Iraq's infrastructure. They have largely prevented efforts to expand Iraq's oil exports—its key source of government earnings.

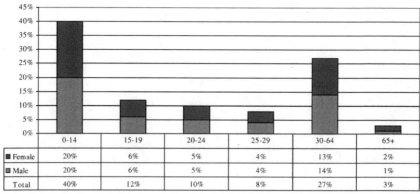

	0-14	15-19	20-24	25-29	30-64	65+
■ Female	20%	6%	5%	4%	13%	2%
■ Male	20%	6%	5%	4%	14%	1%
Total	40%	12%	10%	8%	27%	3%

Source: IISS, *Military Balance 2005-2006*.

Figure 9.11   Iraq's Demographic Distribution, 2006

Insurgents carried out more than 300 attacks on Iraqi oil facilities between March 2003 and January 2006. An estimate by Robert Mullen indicates that there were close to 500 and perhaps as many as 600–700. His breakdown of the number of attacks was as follows: pipelines, 398; refineries, 36; oil wells, 18; tanker trucks, 30; oil train, 1; storage tanks 4; tank farm, 1. In addition, there were at least 64 incidents in which the victims were related to Iraq's petroleum sector, ranging from high-ranking persons in the Oil Ministry to oil workers at refineries, pipelines, and elsewhere in the sector, to contract, military, police, and tribal security people. The number killed in these directed attacks reached at least 100.[105]

The Department of Defense has since reported that a significant cut in attacks on infrastructure and oil facilities took place during February–May 2006, but past damage now combines with the steady deterioration of oil field production and distribution facilities, ongoing problems in security, and corruption and theft to have a major impact.

Oil production dropped by 8 percent in 2005, and pipeline shipments through the Iraqi northern pipeline to Ceyan in Turkey dropped from 800,000 barrels per day before the war to an average of 40,000 barrels per day in 2005. In July 2005, Iraqi officials estimated that insurgent attacks had already cost Iraq some $11 billion. They had kept Iraqi oil production from approaching the 2005 3-million-barrel-a-day goal that the Coalition had set after the fall of Saddam Hussein, and production had dropped from prewar levels of around 2.5 million barrels a day to an average of 1.83 million barrels a day in 2005, and a level of only 1.57 million barrels a day in December 2005.[106]

The impact of insurgent attacks has been compounded by the ability of insurgents —and Iraqi officials and civilians—to steal oil and fuel. The *New York Times* has quoted Ali Allawi, Iraq's Finance Minister, as estimating that insurgents were taking some 40 to 50 percent of all oil-smuggling profits in the country and had infiltrated senior management positions at the major northern refinery in Baji: "It's gone beyond Nigeria levels now where it really threatens national security...The insurgents are involved at all levels." The *Times* also quoted an unidentified U.S. official as saying, "It's clear that corruption funds the insurgency, so there you have a very real threat to the new state...Corruption really has the potential of undercutting the growth potential here." The former Oil Minister, Ibrahim Bahr al-Ulum, had said earlier in 2005, "oil and fuel smuggling networks have grown into a dangerous mafia threatening the lives of those in charge of fighting corruption."[107]

For the quarter ending August 2006, the average number of weekly attacks, including attacks against Coalition forces, the ISF, the civilian population, and infrastructure, had increased 15 percent from the previous period. July 2006 achieved the highest weekly attack levels to that point. The majority (63 percent) of these attacks were directed against Coalition forces. Most attacks against Coalition forces did not involve close engagement, but rather consisted of IEDs, small arms fire, and indirect fire weapons. Despite attracting fewer attacks, the ISF and Iraqi civilians suffered the majority of casualties. Iraqi casualties increased by 51 percent over the previous quarters.[108]

A September 11, 2006, GAO report noted the effect that increasing violence, insecurity, and instability continued to have on Iraqi energy production:

- Iraq's oil production stayed under target levels: during the August 16–22 week, Iraq produced 2.17 million barrels per day, while the Oil Ministry's goal was 2.5 million barrels (the prewar level was about 2.6 million barrels per day).

- Over the same time period, electricity availability averaged around 5.9 hours per day in Baghdad and 10.7 hours nationwide. Electricity output for the week was about 9 percent above the same period in 2005. Major electrical transmission lines have been repeatedly sabotaged.

- Major oil pipelines continue to be sabotaged, shutting down exports. The focus of the U.S. response is to strengthen the Strategic Infrastructure Battalions.[109]

An Aging Energy Sector

Iraqi oil fields have been damaged from overproduction and water encroachment at various times ever since the Iran-Iraq War. This was initially believed to be relatively simple to fix. Stemming Iraq's waterflood problems could increase production by anywhere from 20 to 50 percent, and improved oil recovery techniques and enhanced oil recovery (EOR) methods have the ability to increase recoveries a further 10–15 percent beyond those due to waterflood. Using a conservative estimate of a 10–15-percent increase from waterflood recovery and a 1–6-percent increase from EOR methods, Iraq would still incur a total rise of 50 to 70 billion barrels of recoverable reserves.[110]

The UN found that Saddam Hussein demanded high production at a time that UN economic sanctions precluded Iraq from acquiring the sophisticated computer-modeling equipment and technology required to manage older reservoirs properly. Oil experts working for the UN estimated that some reservoirs in southern Iraq "may only have ultimate recoveries of between 15 percent and 25 percent of the total oil" in the field, as compared with an industry norm of 35 to 60 percent.

The *New York Times* reported the following views of three oil exports about the progress in Iraq's oil industry and the uncertainty it is facing:[111]

- Maury Vasilev, Senior Vice President of PetroAlliance Services, a Russian oil-field company that held discussions with Iraq's Oil Ministry in 2000, concluded that "Kirkuk was of particular concern and particular urgency because of the water content in the wells...there was a question of how much oil they could recover."

- Fadhil Chalabi, a former top Iraqi oil official, claimed in the summer of 2003 that Kirkuk's expected recovery rate had dropped from 30 percent to 15 percent. The *Times* also quoted an unnamed American oil executive as saying in November 2003 that Iraqi engineers told him that they were now expecting recovery rates of 9 percent in Kirkuk and 12 percent in Rumaila without more advanced technology.

- Issam al-Chalabi, Iraq's former Oil Minister, stated in November 2003, "We are losing a lot of oil...[It] is the consensus of all the petroleum engineers involved in the Iraqi industry that maximizing oil production may be detrimental to the reservoirs." An earlier United Nations report on the Kirkuk field issued in 2000 warned of "the possibility of irreversible damage to the reservoir of this supergiant field is now imminent."

The United States ignored these issues in its initial approach to nation building and failed to address them properly after the official end of major combat in Iraq in May 2003. According to the *New York Times,* senior Bush administration officials learned in September 2002, from the Energy Infrastructure Planning Group (EIPG), that Iraq was reinjecting crude oil to maintain pressure in the Kirkuk field. The EIPG was "unequivocal that that practice had to stop and right away." In October 2003, however, Iraq was still reinjecting 0.150 to 0.250 MMBD, down from as much as 0.4 MMBD, and this continued through 2005 due to poor planning and a lack of adequate funding.[112]

In addition, the energy planning task force avoided the issue of reservoir development for political reasons, which included efforts to avoid accusations that the United States planned to steal Iraq's oil, and also because the group had awarded a no-bid contract for fixing Iraq's oil infrastructure to Kellogg, Brown & Root (KBR), a unit of Halliburton, which had an existing Pentagon contract related to war planning and was previously run by Vice President Dick Cheney. It did so, without soliciting bids, making any reserve or reservoir development more controversial.[113]

The historical turbulence that has plagued the Iraqi oil industry was described by the Energy Information Administration (EIA) as follows:[114]

Historically, Iraqi production peaked in December 1979 at 3.7 million bbl/d, and then in July 1990, just prior to its invasion of Kuwait, at 3.5 million bbl/d. From 1991, when production crashed due to war, Iraqi oil output increased slowly, to 600,000 bbl/d in 1996. With Iraq's acceptance in late 1996 of U.N. Resolution 986, which allowed limited Iraqi oil exports in exchange for food and other supplies ("oil-for-food"), the country's oil output began increasing more rapidly, to 1.2 million bbl/d in 1997, 2.2 million bbl/d in 1998, and around 2.5 million bbl/d during 1999–2001. Iraqi monthly oil output increased in the last few months of 2002 and into early 2003, peaking at around 2.58 million bbl/d in January 2003, just before the war....

Throughout most of the 1990s, Iraq did not generally have access to the latest, state-of-the-art oil industry technology (3D seismic, directional or deep drilling, gas injection, etc.), sufficient spare parts, and investment. Instead, Iraq reportedly utilized substandard engineering techniques (i.e., overpumping), obsolete technology, and systems in various states of decay in order to sustain production. In the long run, reversal of all these practices and utilization of the most modern techniques, combined with development of both discovered fields as well as new ones, could result in Iraq's oil output increasing by several million barrels per day.

In spite of the fact that little damage was done to Iraq's oil fields during the war itself, looting and sabotage after the war ended was highly destructive, accounting for perhaps 80 percent of total damage. Starting in mid-May 2003, the U.S. Army Corps of Engineers—which had the lead in restoring Iraq's oil output to pre-war levels—began a major effort to ramp up production in the country. On April 22, 2003, the first oil production since the start of the war began at the Rumaila field, with the restart of an important gas/

oil separation plant (GOSP). As of November 2005 Iraq's Qarmat Ali water injection facility reportedly was operating at only 70 percent of capacity, holding back production from Rumaila and other southern oil fields.

This uncertainty has not subsided following the United States handing sovereignty to the Iraqis, the writing of the Constitution, or the election of a new Iraqi government. The debate and the language of the Constitution may have exacerbated the divisions between Iraq's religious and ethnic factions. Articles 108–111 of the Constitution addressed the Iraqi oil sector, but it left many important details uncertain, such as the control of oil reserves, the distribution of oil revenues, and the future of the Iraqi National Oil Company (INOC).

The United States and the interim Iraqi government have given a high priority to restoring Iraqi oil production and exports since the end of the Iraqi War. As of November 2003, Iraq's Oil Ministry began to call for production levels to rise to 3.0 MMBD in 2004. The United States committed some $2.5 billion in aid to Iraqi oil field repair in fiscal year 2004 (FY2004) funds in 2003 through a contract awarded to KBR. The Congress appropriated another $1.701 billion in FY2004 aid funds in late 2003.

By late March 2004, crude oil production was averaging around 2.4 MMBD and exports around 1.5 MMBD, almost reaching the prewar high of 2.67 MMBD.[115] Both offshore oil export terminals were functioning, and Iraq's pipeline through Turkey to the port of Ceyhan had been restored to limited production.[116] However, an increasingly violent and destabilizing low-intensity conflict in the reconstruction period has caused oil production to fall. In 2005, production averaged only 1.9 MMBD.[117]

The EIA highlighted that the uncertainty surrounding the future of Iraq's oil production capacity did not decrease after the handing over of sovereignty in June 2004, the writing of the Constitution in October 2005, or the election of a new government in December 2005. The EIA Country Analysis Brief: Iraq stated, "As of December 2005, Iraqi production (net of reinjection) was averaging around 1.9 [MMBD], with 'gross' production (including reinjection, water cut, and 'unaccounted for' oil due in part to problems with metering) of about 2.1 [MMBD]. Most analysts believe that there will be no major additions to Iraqi production capacity for at least 2–3 years, with Shell's Vice President recently stating that any auction of Iraq's oilfields was unlikely before 2007."[118]

The war in Iraq continues, along with sabotage and looting. There is also much more to be done than simply restore prewar production. Interim Iraqi Oil Minister Ibrahim Mohammed Bahr al-Uloum warned in November 2003 that it might cost $50 billion to reach production levels of 5.0 MMBD and to compensate for years of underinvestment and cannibalization. He noted this would also require a peaceful environment and several years of intensive work and investment.[119] That same month, Edward C. Chow, a former Chevron executive and visiting scholar with the Carnegie Endowment for International Peace, estimated that it would cost $20 billion to restore Iraqi production to prewar levels.[120]

In addition, the United States and the Iraqi Governing Council found that the cumulative impact of past mismanagement, the Iran-Iraq War, the Gulf War, sanctions, fighting and looting in 2003, and the post–Iraq War insurgency will require billions of dollars in U.S. aid, although estimates of the ultimate cost of fully modernizing Iraq's oil facilities, fixing past neglect, and dealing with reservoir problems are constantly being raised due to inefficient spending and the arising of unforeseen problems.

Furthermore, funds initially appropriated by the United States to aid the Iraqi oil sector have been diverted to security efforts, as the violence has increased and the need for basic infrastructure outside the oil sector has proven to be more expensive than originally estimated. Stuart Bowen, U.S. Special Inspector General for Iraq Reconstruction, noted in a September 2005 presentation to the Foreign Operations Subcommittee of the House Appropriations Committee that $5 billion that had initially been assigned to the infrastructure reconstruction had been shifted to allow for increased security. Consequently, more money would be required to complete minimum requirements for the project.[121]

Other reports criticize the United States for providing funds for much-needed water injection to the damaged southern fields, but neglecting to repair the leaky pipelines carrying the water to the fields. Additionally, delays in the repair of northern field pipelines have forced producers to reinject oil, harming the environment and slowing the whole process. The United States awarded many of these contracts to companies through a no-bid process during the rushed transition to the reconstruction period.[122]

The critical geological assessments have shown particular concern over Iraq's large northern Kirkuk field, which suffers from water seeping into its oil deposits, as well as the major southern oil fields like Rumaila where similar problems are evident. Many of the deficiencies in pipelines and reservoirs stem from years of poor management under Saddam Hussein, rather than being caused by damage from the Iraq War.

Barclays Capital also issued a report in 2005. The report concluded that "the general integrity of Iraqi oil infrastructure appears to us to be heading backwards rather than forwards." Experts believe that attacks against oil facilities have made it difficult to attract foreign investment to rehabilitate Iraq's aging oil infrastructure. In addition, the legal disputes between Iraq's oil provinces and the central government have delayed exploration and production capacity expansion, and some experts contend that there are no visible improvements and that there are no meaningful indications to show that things may get better in the near future.[123]

Political Conciliation vs. Civil War

What has changed since the transfer of power from the CPA to the interim government in June 2004 is the slow and steady evolution of the insurgency toward efforts by Sunni Islamist extremist groups to target Shi'ites, Kurds, and Sunnis in ways that provoke civil conflict.

It is important to recognize that there has been political progress in spite of the violence. The final results for the December 15, 2005, elections gave the Sunnis significant representation, in spite of complaints about fraud. The new Council of Representatives had 275 seats, and the final results for the election, which were certified on February 9, 2006, gave the main parties the following number of seats: Iraq Alliance (Shi'ites), 128 seats; Kurdish coalition, 53 seats; The Iraqi List (Secular "Allawi list"), 25 seats; Iraqi Accordance Front (Sunnis), 44 seats; Iraqi Front for National Dialogue (Sunni), 11 seats. The Shi'ite coalition won 47 percent of the 275 seats, the Kurdish coalition won 21 percent, the Sunni coalition won 21 percent, and Allawi's secular nationalists (with significant Sunni support) won 9 percent.[124] The final 1 percent of the seats went to other parties.[125] As no party won a governing majority of the seats in the Parliament, a coalition government will have to be formed.

More than 12 million Iraqi's voted in the December 2005 election. Sunni turnout increased markedly from the January elections. In Nanawa and Salah ad Din, it grew from 17 percent and 19 percent, respectively, to 70 percent and 98 percent. In al-Anbar Province it grew from 2 percent in January to 86 percent in December. Nationally, voter turnout was 77 percent, an increase from 58 percent in January.[126] Of the 1,985 election complaints received by the Independent Electoral Commission of Iraq, only 3 percent were considered to have possibly affected the results. These complaints amounted to no more than 1 percent of the total vote, which was voided and excluded from the final count.[127]

In the nine months that followed up to September 2006, the Iraqi government took nearly six months to form, and then it could not take a single major step toward political conciliation, dealing with the deep divisions raised by drafting a new Constitution, or halt a steady rise in ethnic and sectarian violence. If the December 2005 election does eventually produce an inclusive national political structure that gives Iraq's Sunnis incentives to join the government and political process, many current Iraqi Sunni insurgents are likely to end their participation in the insurgency and the more extreme elements will be defeated.

No one can deny, however, that there is a serious risk that the political process will fail. The insurgency has found new targets and new opportunities to drive the nation toward a more intense civil war. Voting by sect and ethnic group did not unify the country as much as cement its deep divisions, and Shi'ite violence has come to match or exceed Sunni violence. The formation of a government gave the insurgency a strong incentive to do everything it can to prevent any meaningful unity between Arab Sunnis and Arab Shi'ites and to provoke counterviolence and attacks by Shi'ites that will drive Iraqi Sunnis to support the insurgency. It has often succeeded in exploiting divisions and fault lines within the dominant Shi'ite coalition and trying to provoke the Kurds toward increased separatism. As of this writing, civil violence has overtaken the insurgency as a threat to Iraqi stability, particularly escalating nationwide tension and violence between Arab Shi'ites and Arab Kurds.

So far, the constitutional referendum and the election have not brought added security or stability. Neither have Prime Minister Maliki's plans for national conciliation or calls to limit the powers of the various Arab Shi'ite, Arab Sunni, and Kurdish militias. Efforts at conciliation have led to dialog, but such dialog has also exposed the depth of the sectarian and ethnic divisions in Iraq and raised serious questions as to whether any form of unified or inclusive national government can be effective.

The new government was able to delay an immediate and open confrontation over the issue of federation, and separation along sectarian and ethnic lines, but only deferred an issue that cannot be avoided. As of October 2006, it has not even begun the formal political struggle over some 55 enabling or implementing laws that are necessary to make the Constitution operative that should have already been completed and led to a new referendum.

The key issues that must be dealt with to create a stable political structure and pattern of government in Iraq, and reduce popular support for the various types of insurgents and militias, include the following:

- Whether the nation should be divided into federal components by province: If this happens, it would almost inevitably be along ethnic and sectarian lines although the "Kurdish" provinces have many non-Kurdish minority elements, the "Shi'ite" provinces often have large Sunni minorities, and the "Sunni" provinces lack oil and any economic viability. Soft ethnic cleansing has already begun in many parts of Iraq, including Baghdad. "Federalism" could lead to sweeping, violent struggles over given areas and population movements.

- How the nation's oil resources and revenues should be divided and how new areas should be controlled and developed: The Kurds lack oil reserves in their present areas and clearly want Kirkuk and the northern fields. Shi'ites in the south already talk about controlling the bulk of the nation's proven reserves in central and southern Iraq. The Sunnis have potential reserves but no immediate assets, and the central government gets virtually all of its revenue from oil exports.

- Related issues over how to tax and increase Iraq's revenue base, and who should control its revenues: This includes major debates over the powers of the central government, any federal areas, the provinces, and local governments.

- The future security structure of the country, who will really control the armed forces and security forces, and who will control provincial and local police forces: This is complicated by a major gap between the intent of the present Constitution and the reality of national and local militias. It is further complicated by the fact that the present forces are dominated by Shi'ite and Kurdish elements and could divide along ethnic and sectarian lines if the nation moved toward full-scale civil war.

- Debates over the role of Islamic law in the government and every aspect of civil law: These issues not only have the potential to divide religious and secular Iraqis, but also could lead to struggles over whether Sunni or Shi'ite interpretations should dominate. Both Sunni and Shi'ite Islamist extremists could resort to violence if their views were not adopted.

- Basic issues over governance: These issues include the resulting power of the central government and Ministries vs. provincial and local power.

- Resolving the future of Baghdad, a deeply divided city exempt from being included in any federal area and where soft ethnic cleansing and the relocation of Shi'ites and Sunnis have already become a low-level civil conflict.

- Deciding on how the coming and future budgets should be spent, and how economic aid and development resources should be allocated, in an era where the national budget already exceeds revenues, and massive outside foreign aid and pools of oil-for-food funds will have been expended.
- Societal issues closely linked to religious differences and basic differences over the respective role of secular human rights and law and religious law and custom.

Such issues are explosive at the best of times, but the new government and Council of Representatives must act almost immediately to form a Constitution Review Committee that must try to resolve all of these issues in the middle of an ongoing insurgency and the risk of civil war looming within a four-month period of its formation. It must then win the support of whatever government and mix of the Council of Representatives that exists when it makes its recommendations, and if successful, hold a referendum 60 days later. Every element of this process offers new opportunities to the insurgency if Iraq's political process divides and falters. Every milestone offers new incentives to attack, and every leader that moves toward progress and compromise will be a target.

Insurgent Attacks Push Iraq toward More Intense Civil War

Sunni insurgents intensified their attacks on Shi'ite targets during late 2005 and through 2006 and provoked a steadily escalating level of Shi'ite response. The number of violent sectarian incidents rose from an average of less than 40 per month during May 2005 to January 2006, to 270 in February, and averaged 400–500 during March–September 2006. The number of monthly casualties rose from around 200 per month during May 2005 to January 2006, to 1,200 in February, and over 2,200 during March–September 2006.[128]

Sunni insurgents scored a major victory by attacking the Askariya Shrine in Samarra, a Shi'ite holy landmark, on February 22, 2006, and destroyed its golden dome. The destruction of the shrine, which housed the graves of two revered Shi'ite imams, is a case study in how insurgent attacks helped escalate broader civil violence. The attack caused an unprecedented wave of sectarian violence in Iraq. In the five days that followed, some estimated that over 1,000 Iraqis were killed, that some 300 Sunni and Shi'ite mosques came under attack, and the country seemed to be on the brink of a large-scale civil war.[129] The Iraqi government and MNF-I have put these totals at one-third to one-half these "worst case" estimates, but the fact is that no precise numbers exist, and sectarian attacks continued in the weeks that followed.

Government leaders called for calm, and peaceful demonstrations were held across the Shi'ite dominated south and in ethnically mixed cities such as Kirkuk.[130] At the same time, many statements by participants and average civilians indicate that Shi'ite patience may well be wearing thin. A Shi'ite employee of the Trade Ministry summed up such views as follows: "You have a TV, you follow the news...who is most often killed? Whose mosques are exploded? Whose society was destroyed?" Another Iraqi put it differently: "We didn't know how to behave. Chaos was everywhere." Even the more moderate Shi'ite newspaper, *Al Bayyna al Jadidah,* urged Shi'ites to assert themselves in the face of Sunni violence. Its editorial stated that it was "time to declare war against anyone who tries to conspire against us, who slaughters us every day. It is time to go to the streets and fight those outlaws."[131]

Shi'ite religious leaders also continued to call for calm, but their message was sometimes ambiguous both in words and actions. For example, Moqtada Al-Sadr ordered his Al-Mahdi Army to protect Shi'ite shrines across Iraq and blamed the United States and the Iraqi government for failing to protect the Askariya Shrine saying, "If the government had real sovereignty, then nothing like this would have happened." In a speech from Basra, Al-Sadr also called for restraint and unity among Iraqi's: "I call on Muslims, Sunnis and Shi'ites, to be brothers…Faith is the strongest weapons, not arms." He also publicly ordered his listeners to not attack mosques in retaliation saying, "There is no Sunni mosques and Shi'ite mosques, mosques are for all Muslims…it is one Islam and one Iraq."[132]

Despite Al-Sadr's rhetoric, it appeared that his militia was responsible for at least some of the violence. Amid demonstrations and condemnations from both Sunni and Shi'ite political leaders, Shi'ite militias such as Al-Mahdi Army sought revenge against Sunnis and carried out numerous killings and attacks on Sunni mosques. Sunni groups reciprocated.

Sunni politicians have since made many charges that Sunni mosques in Baghdad and some southern cities were attacked or actively occupied by the Al-Mahdi Army in the days following the attacks.[133] The Association of Muslim Scholars, a hardline Sunni clerical organization, alleged that 168 Sunni mosques were attacked, 10 imams killed, and 15 abducted.[134] The association also made direct appeals to Al-Sadr to intervene and stop the violence, apparently suspecting he was a primary coordinator of the Shi'ite attacks. In early March, however, U.S. government estimates put the number of mosque attacks at 33, only 9 of which were destroyed or sustained significant damage.[135] In some Sunni areas, residents, fearing attacks on their mosques, erected barricades and stood watch. In the Al Moalimin district, armed men patrolled the roof of the Sunni mosque Malik bin Anas.[136]

There is no doubt that the attack and its aftermath threatened progress in forming an inclusive government. Iraqi political figures called on the country to recognize that the attack was an attempt to create a civil war and urged Iraqis to be calm. President Jalal Talabani on the day of the attacks said, "We are facing a major conspiracy that is targeting Iraq's unity…we should all stand hand in hand to prevent the danger of a civil war." President George W. Bush echoed these sentiments saying, "The terrorists in Iraq have again proven that they are enemies of all faiths and of all humanity…the world must stand united against them, and steadfast behind the people of Iraq."[137]

The violence resulted in the announcement by the dominant Sunni party that it would suspend talks to form a coalition government and issued a list of demands. The immediate attention given to these demands by the Iraqi government, and a telephone call from President Bush to each of the leaders of the seven major political factions urging them to reinstitute talks, brought Sunnis back to a meeting with their Shi'ite and Kurdish counterparts. Later that evening, Prime Minister al-Jaafari, accompanied by the leaders of the other major coalitions, announced at a press conference that the country would not allow itself to engage in civil war and that this was a moment of "terrific political symbolism."[138]

The reaction of Iraqi security, military, and police units to the sectarian violence that followed the bombing of the Askariya Shrine was considered by some in the United States and Iraq to be a test of how well these forces could provide security for their own country in a crisis. Opinions differed greatly, however, over whether ISF forces passed this test. The MNF-I has claimed the armed forces played a major role in limiting and halting sectarian violence. Others have claimed they often allowed Shi'ite groups to attack Sunni mosques and that the security forces and police did little to calm the violence. The data that have emerged since the attack tend to support many of the MNF-I claims, but the risks of growing divisions in the Iraqi forces and a tilt toward the Shi'ite and Kurdish sides remain all too real.

The Future of the Insurgency and the Prospect of Large-Scale Civil War

Some claimed by the summer of 2006 that Iraq had already reached the precipice of civil war, seen the dire consequences, and soberly held itself back. For others, sectarian violence marked a trend toward deepening civil conflict. In balance, the risks of large-scale civil war have increased, but it was too soon for pessimistic predictions. Iraqis were drifting toward more intense civil conflict, but the levels of violence were still comparatively limited in most areas. Moreover, for all of the political risks, there are opportunities as well, and many Iraqis in every sectarian and ethnic faction understand the real possibility of further escalation and its potential consequence of dividing the country.

The future of the Sunni insurgency now seems dependent on two factors: first, whether the Iraqi political process succeeds in becoming truly inclusive or whether it heightens the sectarian and ethnic tensions and conflicts that divide Iraq and creates a more intense state of civil war; second, how soon and how well the full range of Iraqi security forces can come on-line and be effective.

Failure in both areas is quite clearly an option. The odds of Iraq drifting into a serious civil war are impossible to quantify, but the risk is clearly serious. At the same time, the insurgency may well divide between its more secular or "nationalist" elements and the Islamist extremist groups.

The "Nationalist" Need for Compromise

Given their present strength, the more nationalistic Sunni insurgents have good reason to seek a political compromise if the Shi'ites and Kurds offer them an inclusive government and acceptable terms. They at best seem capable of paralyzing progress, and fighting a long war of attrition, rather than defeating an Iraqi government that is dominated by a cohesive Shi'ite majority, and which maintains good relations with the Kurds.

The Neo-Salafi insurgents' capacity for extreme violence also does not mean that they dominate Sunni attitudes. Regardless of who is doing the counting, the total for active and passive native Iraqi Sunni insurgents still leaves them a small minority of Iraq's population. Unless the Iraqi government divides or collapses, they cannot bring back Arab Sunni minority rule or the Ba'ath; they cannot regain the level of power, wealth, and influence they once had. They cannot reestablish the form of largely secular rule that existed under Saddam or reestablish Iraq as a country that most Arabs see as "Sunni."

An understanding of these same political and military realities may eventually drive most of the more moderate and pragmatic Sunni insurgents to join the nonviolent political process in Iraq *if* the Shi'ite and Kurdish elements that now dominate the government and political process act to include them and provide suitable incentives.

Such shifts, however, are likely to be slow and uncertain. Historically, most insurgent groups have a much better vision of what they oppose than what they are for, and they have limited interest in pragmatic *realpolitik*. Most Sunni groups are still committed to doing everything—and sometimes anything—they can to drive the Coalition out and break up the peaceful political process almost regardless of the damage done to Iraq and to Sunni areas.

Richard Armitage, the former U.S. Deputy Secretary of State, commented on the insurgency and its lack of realistic political goals as follows: "In Algeria, the so-called insurgents, or in Vietnam, the so-called insurgents, they had...a program and a positive view...In Iraq that's lacking...they only have fear to offer. They only have terror to offer. This is why they're so brutal in their intimidation."[139]

The "Islamist" Need for Civil War

The risk also exists that the Sunni Islamist extremists have become better trained and organized to the point where they are now able to establish themselves as *the* dominant political and military force within the Sunni community—particularly if Iraq's Arab Shi'ites and Kurds mishandle the situation or react to the growing provocation of bloody suicide attacks and other killings by neo-Salafi extremists.[140]

The Sunni Islamist extremists can then try to present themselves as the only legitimate alternative to the occupation, even if they fail to provide a popular agenda. This means they can survive and endure as long as the government is too weak to occupy the insurgency dominated areas and as long as the large majority of Sunnis in given areas does not see a clear incentive to join the government and Iraq's political process.

Much will depend on just how willing Iraqi Shi'ites and Kurds are to forget the past, not to overreact to Sunni Islamist and other attacks designed to divide and splinter the country, and to continue to offer Iraqi Sunnis a fair share of wealth and power. The U.S. position is clear. The United States consistently supported a unified nation and inclusive government. U.S. Ambassador to Iraq, Zalmay Khalilzad, stated in an interview that the Ministries of Defense and Interior must be headed by those who have broad-based support: "The security ministries have to be run by people who are not associated with militias and who are not regarded as sectarian."[141] Later, Ambassador Khalilzad went further and directly tied the future of U.S. economic and military support to the ability of Iraqi leaders to form an inclusive government saying, "We [the United States] are not going to invest the resources of the American people and build forces that are run by people who are sectarian."[142]

The Threat from Shi'ite Death Squads and Militias

While the Islamists have made it one of their goals to ignite civil war between the Sunnis and the Shi'ites, there were more and more reports of revenge killing and anti-Sunni strikes by both the Shi'ite militias and Shi'ite elements in the security forces and police during the rest of 2005, and there were stronger indications that Shi'ite militias were playing a growing role in Iraq's low-level civil war.[143] There are credible reports that hundreds of Sunni bodies have been found in locations like rivers, desert roads, open desert, sewage disposal facilities, and garbage dumps since the new government was formed April 25, 2006.

The Baghdad morgue reported growing numbers of corpses with their hands bound by police handcuffs and reported that it processed 7,553 corpses between January and September 2005, vs. only 5,239 for the same period in 2004. Sunni groups like the Association of Muslim Scholars have published pictures of such corpses and lists of the dead and have claimed there are Shi'ite death squadrons. Then Inspector General of the Ministry of the Interior, General Nori Nori said, "There are such groups operating—yes this is correct." In November, a raid on a secret MOI detention facility in southeastern Baghdad, which was operated by former members of the Badr Brigade, was linked to the death of 18 detainees reported to have died under torture. Some 220 men were held in filthy conditions within this prison and many were subjected to torture.[144]

Minister of Interior Jabr denied any government involvement and claimed that if MOI security forces and police uniforms and cars have been seen, they were stolen. Other sources, however, confirmed that some of the killings of an estimated 700 Sunnis between August and November 2005 involved men who identified themselves as Ministry of Interior forces.[145] This increased the risk that Iraqi forces could be divided by factions, decreasing their effectiveness and leading to the disintegration of Iraqi forces if Iraq were to descend into full-scale civil war.

The killing of at least 14 Sunnis could be clearly traced to MOI arrest records several weeks earlier.[146] U.S. sources also noted that a large number of members of the Badr Organization had joined the MOI forces, including the police and commando units, since the new government was formed in April 2006. The lines between some MOI units and the Badr Organization were becoming increasingly blurred.

During the winter of 2005, and the course of 2006, body dumps became a favored tactic by insurgents and militias. Although this trend existed long before the February 22 Askariya bombing, it increased thereafter and became part of the cyclical sectarian violence carried out by Shi'ites and Sunnis. For example, in the period from March 7 until March 21, over 191 bodies were found.

Common characteristics could be found within these "mystery killings." Increasingly, the victims were relatively ordinary Shi'ites or Sunnis and were not directly working for the government or Coalition forces. Oftentimes, victims were taken from their homes or businesses in daylight by masked gunmen or men wearing police or security force uniforms and driving standard issue trucks. These attributes, and the fact that the bodies were almost always found in the same condition—blindfolded, handcuffed, and shot in the head showing signs of torture—lent credibility to the claim that many of the killings were perpetrated by Shi'ite militias themselves, or elements of security forces dominated by these militias.

The frequency of "extrajudicial killings" was discussed in a UN Human Rights Report and linked to police forces: "A large number of extrajudicial killings, kidnappings and torture were reportedly perpetrated mainly by members of armed militias linked to political factions or criminal gangs. The same methods of execution-style killings are usually used: mass arrests without judicial warrant and extrajudicial executions with bodies found afterwards bearing signs of torture and killed by a shot to the head."

Baghdad, a mixed city, continued to be "ground zero" for much of this violence. More Iraqi civilians were killed in Baghdad during the first three months of 2006 than at any time since the end of the Saddam regime. Between January and March, 3,800 Iraqi civilians were killed, a significant number of which were found tied, shot in the head, and showing signs of torture.[147] According to the Baghdad morgue in May 2006, it received on average 40 bodies a day. Anonymous U.S. officials disclosed that the targeted sectarian killings, or soft-sectarian cleansing, claim nine times more lives than car bombings and that execution killings increased by 86 percent in the nine weeks after the February mosque bombing.[148] These numbers rose steadily though August, dipped only slowly in September, and rose again in October. The number of sectarian incidents and casualties increased more than tenfold between January and the end of August 2006.

Sectarian militias did more than infiltrate the security forces. There have been numerous incidents of the Al-Mahdi Army installing its own members to head hospitals, dental offices, schools, trucking companies, and other private businesses. Rank employees are often fired for no reason. As a Baghdad University professor said, "We are all victims of this new thought police. No longer content to intimidate us with violence, these militias want to control our every move, so they appoint the administrators and managers while dissenters lose their jobs."[149]

Links to the Iraqi Police and Special Security Forces

The number of men who were trained and equipped as regular police expanded from some 31,000 men in July 2004 to nearly 95,000 in July 2005, and 120,000 in September 2006. By that time the number of men "trained and equipped" in the National Police (the reorganized MOI security forces) totaled 24,400, and other

MOI forces totaled 27,510. The reality, however, was very different from what these numbers imply. At least 20 percent—and probably over 20 percent—of the men trained and equipped deserted or were not active. Many were selected with only limited background checks, and large numbers were incapable of properly performing their duties, lacked proper equipment and facilities, and were not properly paid or supplied.

Many of the MOI forces continued to serve Arab Shi'ite or Kurdish causes. Substantial numbers of men from both the Badr Organization and Moqtada Al-Sadr's Al-Mahdi Army joined the forces. In the case of the roughly 65,000-strong mix of MOI and police forces in the greater Baghdad area, the men from the Badr Organization generally tended to go into the MOI special security units and those from Al-Mahdi Army tended to join the police. While both the Iraqi government and Coalition claimed the situation was improving, a September 2005 report by the ICG suggested that the process of drafting the Constitution had helped exacerbate the existing ethnic and sectarian divisions between Iraqis.[150]

While the revelations of large-scale abuses draw the greatest attention, less severe, day-to-day incidents are no less important and can be illustrative of the underlying sectarian tension in Iraq. For example, when several policemen arrived at an Iraqi police station with three suspected insurgents in plastic cuffs, U.S. Sergeant 1st Class Joel Perez had to cut the cuffs because they were too tight and causing the prisoners' hands to swell and turn blue. Later, one of the Iraqi policeman involved confided in a reporter, "They [the insurgents] need to be beaten up. The Americans won't let us . . . I want to have two cars and tie each hand to a different car and break them in half."[151]

This and previous incidents drew comments by both U.S. and Iraqi officials. U.S. military procedure and policy was clarified in a back-and-forth discussion between U.S. Secretary of Defense Donald Rumsfeld and Chairman of the Joint Chiefs of Staff Peter Pace when Pace declared, "it's absolutely the responsibility of every U.S. service member if they see inhumane treatment being conducted to intervene to stop it." Secretary Rumsfeld countered, "I don't think you mean they have an obligation to physically stop it; it's to report it." Pace respectfully reiterated, "If they are physically present when inhumane treatment is taking place, sir, they have an obligation to stop it." Putting prisoner abuse in perspective, former Iraqi Prime Minister Iyad Allawi commented to a British newspaper, "people are doing the same as [in] Saddam's time and worse."[152]

In a February 2006 Department of Defense report to Congress, "Measuring Stability and Security in Iraq," police, military, and justice detention facilities were singled out as being "typically maintained at higher standards than those of the Ministry of Interior facilities." The report also suggested that to correct the "imbalance," joint U.S.–Iraqi "teams should continue to inspect Iraqi detention facilities, with appropriate remediation through Iraqi-led triage and follow-up logistical, security, public relations, and political support."[153] The August 2006 report reflected little or no progress in these areas, or in MNF-I's ability to count the number of police who were actually still active and assess their effectiveness.

At the same time, Sunni Islamic insurgents and some Sunni political figures had every reason to try to implicate the security services. Some of the killings in late November involved key Sunni politicians like Ayad Alizi and Al Hussein, leading members of the Iraqi Islamic Party, a member of the Sunni coalition competing in the December 15, 2005, elections. Shi'ites seemed to have little reason to strike at such targets.[154]

Questionable Loyalties

Regardless, the immediate problem for the Iraqi government became controlling elements of the ISF whose loyalties were clearly not with the national government and, moreover, trying to get these groups to uphold the law rather than engage in or tacitly allow violence. For example, after a public warning was issued on April 7, 2006, by the MOI telling Iraqis not to gather in crowded areas because of specific intelligence indicating that a series of car bombs were likely, it had to similarly warn ISF not to impede this order. The Ministry threatened legal action against "any security official who fails to take the necessary procedures to foil any terrorist attack in his area."[155]

In what may have been the largest incident at the time involving MOI security forces, in early March 2006, gunmen wearing MOI uniforms allegedly stormed a Sunni-owned security firm and abducted 50 of its employees.[156] The Interior Ministry denied its involvement in the event. Later in the same month, investigators discovered and broke up a group of police who ran a kidnapping and extortion ring. Allegedly led by an Iraqi police major general, this group kidnapped individuals, sometimes killing them, and forced their families to pay ransoms that the group members then pocketed.[157] In April, the bodies of three young men were recovered from a sewage ditch. According to co-workers, the three were last seen being arrested by MOI forces after their minibus had been pulled over.[158] In May, two employees of the al-Nahrain television station were kidnapped on their way home by MOI forces according to witnesses. Their bodies were found the next day, along with six other Sunni men. All had been blindfolded, burned with cigarette butts, and severely beaten.[159]

Although the MOI continued to deny that it had any role in the increased sectarian violence since the February shrine bombing, accusations mounted and the accumulation of incidents made this denial more difficult. The consistency and continuation of body dumps, the corpses often exhibiting signs of torture and of being shot execution style, and strings of abductions in which the gunmen wore ISF uniforms furthered tension between Prime Minister al-Jaafari and the United States, which had been pressuring the Prime Minister to rein in the militias. The fear generated within the Sunni community by the merging of Shi'ite militias and the ISF was illustrated by an advisory on a Sunni-run television network, which told its viewers not to allow Iraqi police or soldiers into their homes unless U.S. troops were present.[160]

For some Sunnis, the presence of U.S. forces provided a degree of assurance against abuses of power by Iraqi security forces. In Dora, local leaders agreed that Iraqi forces could conduct raids in mosques only if U.S. soldiers accompanied them. This same rule was later implemented in Baghdad as well. The fact that Sunnis requested the presence of U.S. troops in Islamic holy places during searches, something that earlier would have been inconceivable, was a testament to the depth of sectarian divisions and the genuine distrust between the Shi'ite dominated police forces and Sunni communities.[161] As Ali Hassan, a Sunni, bluntly stated, "We prefer to be detained by Americans instead of Iraqis. Second choice would be the Iraqi army. Last choice, Iraqi police."[162]

These events had an important impact on Iraqi politics and the selection of the new government. In late March 2006, the U.S. administration openly voiced its disapproval of al-Jaafari as the next Prime Minister. Ambassador Khalilzad added that due to his lack of leadership, Shi'ite-led militias were now killing more Iraqis than the Sunni insurgency.[163]

Al-Jaafari's response, in which he warned the United States not to interfere with the democratic process in Iraq, addressed the issue of Shi'ite militias being incorporated in the security forces and his political alliance with Al-Sadr, whose support put him in office. He stated that he favored engaging with Al-Sadr and his followers instead of isolating him and that he viewed the militias as part of Iraq's "*de facto* reality." He continued to voice support for a government that looks past sectarian differences and works toward integrating the militias into the police and the army.[164]

In April, Iraq's Interior Minister Jabr refused to deploy any of the thousands of police recruits trained by the joint U.S.–U.K. Civilian Police Assistance Training Team (CPATT). Although graduates of this program had been available for over three months, Jabr chose to hire those trained outside of the program because he claimed he had no control over CPATT's selection process. The United States was concerned that this was an attempt by the Minister to sustain the sectarian makeup of the forces and continue to incorporate those with allegiance to the Badr Brigade into its ranks.[165]

The UN Assistance Mission for Iraq's Human Rights Report specifically highlighted the threat of militias within the security forces and that it had received information "regarding the actions of some segments of the security forces, in particular the police and special forces, and their apparent collusion with militias in carrying out human rights violations."[166]

There were concerns that even Iraqi brigades that were touted as mixed, in that they struck a balance between Shi'ites and Sunnis within their ranks, were still overwhelmingly Shi'ite. There were reports of at least one soldier who was proudly wearing an Al-Sadr t-shirt under his army uniform. In interviews as well, many of the soldiers privately confided that if they were ever asked to fight Al-Mahdi Army, they would have to quit the Iraqi forces.[167] Brigadier General Abdul Kareem Abdul Rahman al-Yusef, a Sunni, admitted that his brigade was 87 percent Shi'ite and included members of the Badr Organization. Despite this, he still believed that "it's not the time to ask the militias to put down their arms," given that the government cannot provide security to its citizens.[168]

As Lieutenant Colonel Chris Pease, Deputy Commander of the U.S. military's police training programs in eastern Baghdad put it, "We're not stupid. We know for a fact that they're killing people. We dig the damn bodies out of the sewer all of the time. But there's a difference between knowing something and proving something." Captain Ryan Lawrence, an intelligence officer with the 2nd Brigade Special Police Transition Team, displayed similar feelings, "Training and equipping a force, while knowing that at least some element is infiltrated by militias, is a difficult situation."[169]

Pease also admitted that an Iraqi police officer had confided in him the reality and extent of the militia infiltration into ISF. "His assessment was that the militias are everywhere," Pease said, "and his officers weren't going to do anything about that because their units are infiltrated and they know what the cost would be for working against the militias."[170]

This situation did not improve after a new set of political compromises finally led to the selection of Nouri al-Maliki (a Shi'ite) as Prime Minister, and Mahmound Mashhadani (a Sunni) as Speaker, in May 2006. Along with President Jalal Talibani (a Kurd), all of the major factions were now represented, but a new Minister of Defense (Abd al-Qadr Muhammad Jassim al-Mufraji, a Sunni) and a new Minister of the Interior (Jawad al-Bulani, a Shi'ite) were not announced and confirmed until June 8, 2006. The government then remained too divided to function efficiently, Prime Minister Maliki's conciliation plans remained words rather than actions, and internal divisions sharply limited progress in both the MOD and the MOI and in dealing with problems like the militias.

U.S. troops did accompany developing Iraqi military, National Police, and other police units as embedded advisors in their operations. They sought to make them more effective, prevent them from joining in sectarian and ethnic fighting, and to make them treat the local populace and detainees properly. Far too often, however, it was not possible to stop units with Shi'ite and Kudish manpower from taking sides; various units and most of the police were corrupt, desertion rates remained high, and the line between counterinsurgency and revenge became blurred. After a joint U.S.–Iraqi raid in March in which ten Sunnis were rounded up, one U.S. colonel remembered thinking immediately after the action, "Wait a sec, were we just part of some sort of sectarian revenge?"[171]

By October 2006, it was clear that progress in reforming the National and regular police still presented massive problems, and even some of the new army units supposedly "taking the lead" had desertion rates as high as 50 percent. Efforts to secure Baghdad with Iraqi forces in the late spring and summer of 2006 with Iraqi forces had largely failed, and U.S. forces not only had to take the lead, but do most of the actual security work. Indeed, many of the U.S. soldiers who were on their second tour in Iraq returned to a different war. Whereas before the focus was on the Sunni insurgency, it now was about containing the Shi'ite militias and preventing further infiltration into the security forces.[172]

While details of many incidents remained uncertain, the course of a two-day fire fight in the Adhamiyah district, a Sunni neighborhood, in April 2006, illustrates the problems involved. A local Sunni militia took up arms against what it saw as an attack by a Shi'ite "death squad" disguised as a police force. In the process, some locals claimed that the Sunni-dominated army actually fired on the incoming police forces.[173]

The Iraqi government denied claims that Interior Ministry forces were involved. It suggested that insurgent groups, portraying themselves as police and security forces, provoked the violence. It specifically identified those groups as the Islamic Army of Iraq, the 1920 Revolution Brigades, and Al Qa'ida.[174] While such government claims could not be verified, Al Qa'ida in Iraq did issue a statement promising "a new raid to avenge the Sunnis at Adhamiyah and the other areas, and the raid will start with the dawn of Wednesday, if God wishes...The Shiite areas will be an open battlefield for us."[175]

While it was not fully clear if Shi'ite police forces were even present, or if the army was mistaken for a police force as suggested by U.S. claims, the event illustrated the growing distrust between Sunnis and Iraqi security forces that continued to intensify through the late fall of 2006. The threat from Shi'ite death squads, whether real or perceived, caused the townspeople to arm themselves, coordinate action, and attempt to repel the invading police forces.

The Kurdish Question

The January 2005 elections made the Kurds far more powerful relative to other Iraqi factions in military and security terms than their 15 percent of the population might indicate. Iraqi security and stability depends on finding a power-sharing arrangement that gives the Kurds incentives to be part of the political process just as much as it does on developing such arrangements for the Arab Sunnis.

There is no basic political or economic reason such a compromise cannot be found. Unfortunately, however, Iraq has a long history of not finding such compromises on a lasting basis, and Saddam Hussein's legacy left many areas where Kurds were forcibly expelled and Sunni Arabs and minorities were given their homes and property.

Large numbers of Kurds favor independence over political inclusiveness. This helps explain why the Kurdish turnout in the October referendum on the Constitution varied widely. In predominantly Kurdish provinces, participation was much lower than in the January election. Some analysts have suggested the lower turnout was a result of increased voter apathy among a Kurdish population who felt assured the Constitution would pass.

Others noted the increase in dissatisfaction with the central government and the idea of remaining in Iraq among Kurdish populations. Riots and demonstrations protesting the shortages of gas, fuel, and power have become more common in Kurdish cities.[176] Some Kurds may also have felt let down by the Constitution, which did not specifically address the status of Kirkuk or lay out a clear path to secession.[177]

Kurdish Parties and the Kurdish Militias

The two major Kurdish parties, the Kurdish Democratic Party (KDP), headed by Masoud Barzani, and the Patriotic Union of Kurdistan (PUK), headed by Jalal Talabani, retain powerful militias, known collectively as the Peshmerga. Their current strength is difficult to estimate, and some elements are either operating in Iraqi forces or have been trained by U.S. advisors. The Iraqi Kurds could probably assemble a force in excess of 10,000 fighters—albeit of very different levels of training and equipment.

The Kurdish Peshmerga trace their origins to the Iraqi civil wars of the 1920s. They fought against the Saddam Hussein regime during the Iran-Iraq War and supported U.S. and Coalition military action in 2003. The Peshmerga groups of the PUK and the KDP serve as the primary security force for the Kurdish regional government. The PUK and the KDP claim that there are 100,000 Peshmerga troops, and they have insisted on keeping the Peshmerga intact as guarantors of Kurdish security and political self-determination.

Tensions between the Kurds and Other Iraqis

There are serious tensions among the Kurds, the Turcomans, and the Assyrian Christians, as well as between Kurds and Arabs. At a local level, there are many small tribal elements, as well as numerous "bodyguards" and long histories of tensions and feuds. Even if Iraq never divides along national faction lines, some form of regional or local violence is all too possible.

Insurgent activity in the Kurdish areas was particularly intense in the city of Irbil, which has been the site of several suicide bombings. In the summer of 2005, Kurdish security officials and the KDP intelligence service announced the arrest of approximately six insurgent suspects who, the authorities believe, came from six separate and previously unheard of militant organizations. The head of the Irbil security police, Abdulla Ali, stated that there was evidence that the groups had links to international terror groups, established extremist groups in Iraq like Ansar al-Sunna, and even had links to intelligence services from nearby countries.[178] This evidence was not made public, but the Kurdish authorities stated that it appeared as though various groups were working together and, to the anger and disappointment of the Kurdish authorities, that local Kurds were assisting them.

Tension between the Kurds and Iraqi Arabs and other minorities has also been critical in areas like Kirkuk and Mosul. The Kurds claim territory claimed by other Iraqi ethnic groups, and they demand the return of property they assert was seized by Saddam Hussein during his various efforts at ethnic cleansing from 1975 to 2003.

The future of Kirkuk, and the northern oil fields around it, remains the subject of considerable local and national political controversy between the Kurds and other Iraqis. The Kurds claim that over 220,000 Kurds were driven out of their homes by Saddam in the 1970s and fighting in the Gulf War and that over 120,000 Arabs were imported into "Kurdish territory." The Kurds see control of Kirkuk as their one chance to have territorial control over a major portion of Iraq's oil reserves, but

Kirkuk is now roughly 35 percent Kurd, 35 percent Arab, 26 percent Turcoman, and 4 percent other. This makes any such solution almost impossible unless it involves violent means.

There has been armed violence among Kurds, Arabs, and Turcomans, as well as struggles over "soft" ethnic cleansing in the north, and there may well be more violence in the future. Many experts feel that the only reason Kirkuk has been relatively peaceful, and still has something approaching a representative government, is that the Kurds have not been strong enough relative to the other factions in the city to impose their will by intimidation or force.

From August 2005 onward, various reports indicated that Kurdish-dominated government police and military forces in and near the Kurdish zones were using their power to intimidate Arabs through abductions and assassinations. Such activity poses the threat of deepening regional fissures. Likewise, the misuse of power by Coalition-sponsored forces could deepen resentment toward Coalition forces, particularly among the Sunni population.[179]

Other Kurdish actions exacerbated ethnic tension in a struggle for the control of Kirkuk during 2005 and 2006. There were reports that the KDP and PUK systematically kidnapped hundreds of Arabs and Turcomans from the city and transported them to prisons in established Kurdish territory in an apparent bid to create an overwhelming Kurdish majority.[180] This activity allegedly spread to Mosul as well. While some of the abductions had occurred in 2004, reports indicated that there was a renewed effort following the January 30 elections that solidified the two parties' primacy in the Kurdish areas.

According to a leaked State Department cable in mid-June 2005, the abducted were taken to KDP and PUK intelligence-run prisons in Irbil and Sulaymaniyah without the knowledge of the Iraqi Ministry of Defense or the Ministry of the Interior, but sometimes with U.S. knowledge. In fact, the Emergency Services Unit, a special Kirkuk force within the police, was both closely tied to the U.S. military and implicated in many of the abductions, along with the Asayesh Kurdish intelligence service.[181] It should be noted that the head of the Emergency Services Unit is a former PUK fighter.

Kirkuk province's Kurdish governor, Abdul Rahman Mustafa, stated that the allegations were false. However, the State Department cable indicated that the U.S. 116th Brigade Combat Team had known about the activity and had asked the Kurdish parties to stop.[182] According to Kirkuk's Chief of Police, General Turhan Yusuf Abdel-Rahman, 40 percent of his 6,120 officers probably assisted in the abductions, disobeying his orders and following the directives of the KDP and PUK instead. Abdel-Rahman stated, "The main problem is that the loyalty of the police is to the parties and not the police force. They'll obey the parties' orders and disobey us."[183] According to Abdel-Rahman, Provincial Police Director Sherko Shakir Hakim refused to retire as ordered by the government in Baghdad once he was assured that the KDP and the PUK would continue to pay him if he stayed on. The various factions in Kirkuk seem to have agreed on a compromised local government in June 2005, but the city continues to present a serious risk of future conflict.

The issue of Kirkuk took on a new importance after the December 2005 elections. In the months prior, thousands of Kurds erected settlements in the city, often with financing from the two main Kurdish parties. In addition, violence began to rise, with 30 assassination-style killings from October through December. Kurdish political groups were increasingly open about their intent to incorporate Kirkuk into Iraqi Kurdistan and continue to repatriate Kurds into the city in an effort to tip the ethnic balance in their favor. They stated that they sought to accomplish this by the time of the popular referendum in 2007, which is to determine whether the Tamim province will be governed by the Kurdish regional government or from Baghdad.[184]

The future of Kirkuk became a central factor for Kurdish political groups with the new governing coalition after May 2006. So did Kurdish desire to implement Article 58 of the Constitution that stipulates that the question of the "normalization" of Kirkuk must take place by the end of 2007.[185] In fact, the political alliance between Kurds and Shi'ites, once considered natural given their common grievances against the Sunni-dominated Ba'ath Party, was opening up to question.[186]

Kurdish views differ over the increased sectarian violence between Sunni and Shi'ite Arabs. One perspective has its roots in the historical animosity between Kurds and Arabs. A sectarian civil war could bring benefits to the Kurds if, as one individual said, "our enemies [are] killing each other."[187] According to this theory, if civil war breaks out in Iraq, the Kurds will then be justified in breaking away to form an independent Kurdistan. In this situation, the international community would be forced to acquiesce to such a move.[188]

The opposite view is more hesitant and less optimistic. These Kurds worry that although civil war may initially begin in central and southern Iraq, it could spread northward, threatening the stability and relative security they have attained since the 2003 invasion. In fact, there were some reports in the first months of 2006 that Shi'ite militias were migrating north into cities like Kirkuk and moving into mosques in the area as a protection force.[189] If civil war does reach the Kurds, some believe Iraqi Arabs, as well as Turkey, Syria, and Iran, would object to Kurdish separation and that countries, such as Turkey, that have sizable Kurdish populations may intervene militarily to prevent an independent Kurdish nation.[190]

Arab Iraqis have reacted to Kurdish pressure. In April 2006, Shi'ite militias began to deploy to Kirkuk in substantial numbers. According to U.S. embassy officials in the region, Al-Mahdi Army had sent two companies with 120 men each. The Badr Organization extended its reach into the city as well and opened several offices across the Kurdish region. The influx of Shi'ite militias began in the days following the February 22 Askariya bombing. The shift northward was justified by the organizations as a necessary step to protect Shi'ite mosques and families. Yet Shi'ites, many of whom were transferred to the area under Saddam's rule, make up only about 5 percent of the population in the area.[191]

Although Iraqi security officials in Kirkuk maintain that the new militia arrivals have generally kept a low profile, the Kurdish Peshmerga responded by moving nearly 100 additional troops to the area. Moreover, an Al-Sadr associate in the region, Abdul Karim Khalifa, told U.S. officials that more men were on the way and that as many as 7,000 to 10,000 local residents loyal to the Al-Mahdi Army would join in a fight if one were to come.[192]

The Kurdish militias have not yet presented as many problems for Iraqi security and Iraqi force development as the Shi'ite militias, but the deployment of Shi'ite militias into the Kirkuk area makes it clear that this is no guarantee for the future. Kurdish separatism and claims to areas like Kirkuk and Iraq's northern oil fields remain potentially explosive issues. Thousands of Kurdish Peshmerga soldiers were incorporated into the Iraqi Army during the formation of Iraqi forces.[193] Kurdish army units could operate effectively in their relatively ethnically homogenous north; they were often perceived as outsiders in Arab areas.

In the northern city of Balad, a 700-man Kurdish army battalion was confined to its base in March 2006 by an angry and hostile Sunni population. The battalion, sent from Sulaimaniyah to bolster the lone Shi'ite forces comprised of local residents, was resisted by the large Sunni minority in the area so much so that commanders were afraid to let their soldiers leave the base. U.S. officials in the city said that this was because the battalion was mostly former Peshmerga, the armed group that has become the *de facto* army of the regional government in Kurdistan.[194]

In May 2006, a Kurdish-dominated army unit openly clashed with its Shi'ite counterpart. The 1st Battalion, 3rd Brigade, 4th Division hit a roadside bomb in Duluiyah north of Baghdad. Although U.S. and Iraqi officials disagreed over the number of dead and wounded in the incident, the Kurdish division raced its wounded to the U.S. hospital in Balad. According to police reports, when the division arrived members began firing their weapons, ostensibly to clear the way, killing a Shi'ite civilian. As security forces arrived, the Kurdish army unit attempted to leave and take the wounded elsewhere. A Shi'ite army unit from the 3rd Battalion, 1st Brigade tried to stop them and shots were exchanged, killing a member of the 3rd Battalion. As the Kurdish division members attempted to leave in their vehicles, a third army unit attempted to establish a roadblock to stop them. U.S. forces, however, were at the scene to intervene and restore calm.[195]

Uncertain Kurdish Unity

Kurdish unity is always problematic. The Kurds have a saying, "The Kurds have no friends." History shows that this saying should be, "the Kurds have no friends including the Kurds." The Barzani and Talibani factions have fought on several occasions, and there was a state of civil war between them during 1993–1995. PUK forces were able to take control of Irbil in 1994 and put an end to the first attempt to create a unified and elected government that began in 1992. Barzani's KDP collaborated with Saddam Hussein in 1995, when Hussein sent a full corps of troops into Irbil and other parts of the area occupied by Talibani. Tens of thousands of Kurds and anti-Saddam activists fled the area, and the United States did not succeed in brokering a settlement between the two factions until 1998.[196]

Despite the past, and potential future tensions and divisions between the PUK and the KDP, leaders from both parties signed an agreement in January 2006, which allotted 11 ministerial posts to each group. Minority parties were skeptical of KDP-PUK promises to give remaining posts to political factions that did not win a majority and worried that this further isolated them from any future role in the political process.[197]

The present marriage of convenience between the KDP and the PUK has not unified the Kurdish controlled provinces in the north. There were minor clashes between their supporters in 1995, and these political divisions could create future problems for both Kurdish political unity and any agreement on some form of autonomy.

Kurdish frustration with these political parties manifested itself in violent protests in 2006 during ceremonies marking the anniversary of the March 1988 poison gas attack by Hussein at Halabja. Protestors alleged that the PUK and the KDP had misappropriated millions of dollars in foreign aid given to the survivors of the attack.[198] The protestors also complained about the shortage of water and electricity.[199]

The protests, which began at 9 A.M., slowly grew in number and groups began setting fire to tires and throwing rocks at the monument and museum dedicated to those killed under Saddam's rule.[200]

The few dozen PUK guards in front of the monument, who attempted to disperse the crowd by firing into the air, were outnumbered and were forced to retreat. The protestors destroyed museum exhibits with rocks and then attempted to set it on fire. One protestor was killed by the gunfire from the guards and six others were wounded.[201] A regional official, Shahu Mohammed Saed, who according to reports was one of the targets of the peoples' frustration, blamed the riots on Ansar al-Islam.[202] However, there seems to be little indication that this assertion is true.

The Problem of Resources and Oil

The Kurds face the problem that, at present, they have no control over Iraq's oil resources or revenues and no access to any port or lines of communication that are not subject to Iraqi, Turkish, or Iranian interdiction. They have an uncertain economic future since they have lost the guaranteed stream of revenue provided by the UN oil-for-food program; Iraq can now export oil through the Gulf and can potentially reopen pipelines to Syria as a substitute for pipelines through Turkey, and there is far less incentive to smuggle through Kurdish areas now that trade is open on Iraq's borders. The Kurds also face the problem that Iran, Syria, and Turkey all have Kurdish minorities that have sought independence in the past, and any form of Iraqi Kurdish autonomy or independence is seen as a threat to these states.

The Kurds have sought to deal with this problem by opening up the areas they control for independent oil exploration and seeking control of Iraq's northern oil fields to the northwest and southeast of Kirkuk. The future of such efforts, however, remains uncertain.

The Turkish Question

All these problems are still further compounded by the rebirth of Kurdish insurgency in Turkey and by acute Turkish pressure on the Iraqi government, Iraqi Kurds, and MNSTC-I to deny Turkish Kurdish insurgents both a sanctuary and any example that would encourage Kurdish separatism in Turkey. The Turkish Kurdish Worker Party (PKK) is a movement that has often used northern Iraq as a sanctuary and which led to several major division-sized Turkish military movements in the area under Saddam Hussein. While estimates are uncertain, some 6,000 PKK forces seemed to be in Iraq in the spring of 2005, with another 2,000 across the border.[203] These same factors help explain why Turkey has actively supported Iraq's small Turcoman minority in its power struggles with Iraq's Kurds.

The February 2006 visit to Turkey by Prime Minister al-Jaafari created concern among Kurdish politicians and accusations that the trip was carried out in secret.[204]

Relationship with Neighboring States

Many of these problems and difficulties concern the challenges to the prospects of stability in Iraq. If one, however, looks at the implications of an unstable Iraq, one must understand the consequences of the future of Iraq to the Gulf security and the "Global War on Terrorism." All of the Gulf States now face a situation where they cannot predict Iraq's future, whether it will be stable, and whether they will become involved directly or indirectly in a full-scale Iraqi civil war. The southern Gulf States also face the prospect of a new Iranian-Iraqi Shi'ite "axis," real or imagined.

These issues also involve outside states. Most Arab states have actively encouraged Iraqi political unity. Syria, however, has tolerated and supported Sunni neo-Salafi extremist operations on its territory in spite of its Alawite-controlled government. A broader and more intense civil conflict could lead other Arab states to take sides on behalf of the Sunnis—although Bahrain, Lebanon, Oman, Saudi Arabia, and Yemen are just a few of the states that have deep sectarian divisions of their own. Any major divisions within Iraq could reopen the Kurdish issue as it affects Turkey, and possibly Iran and Syria as well.

Creating a "Shi'ite Crescent"?

The most serious wild card in Iraq's immediate neighborhood is Iran. Iran already plays at least some role in the political instability in Iraq and may take a more aggressive role in trying to shape Iraq's political future and security position in the Gulf. As noted in earlier chapters, regional officials have voiced their concerns about Iran's interference in Iraq's internal affairs. The most notable was King Abdullah of Jordan, when he accused Iran of wanting to create a "Shi'ite Crescent" forming between Iran, Iraq, Syria, and Lebanon.[205]

Both Iranian and Iraqi Shi'ites rejected these comments. Jordan's King Abdullah was asked to apologize by Iraqi Shi'ites. The Najaf Theological Center issued a statement, in which it accused the King of meddling in Iraq's internal affairs:[206]

> Distorting the truth and blatantly interfering in Iraqi affairs, provoking tribal sentiments in the region against Iraqi Shi'ites, provoking great powers against Iraqi Shi'ites, intimidating regional countries and accusing them of having links with Iran, displaying a great tendency for ensuring Israel's security and expressing worries about the victory of Shi'ites in the upcoming elections tantamount to insulting millions of people in Iran, who have been insulted just because they follow a religion that the Jordan's king is opposed...
>
> Najaf Theological Center is hopeful that the Jordanian monarch will apologize to the Shi'ites of the region and Iraq, and their religious authorities, because of the inaccurate remarks made against them.

The Arab Gulf States

The Gulf countries, particularly Saudi Arabia, have sought to preserve the unity of Iraq and expressed their fear of Shi'ite dominance of an Arab country that allies itself with Iran. Saudi Arabia has pushed for more Sunni inclusiveness in the constitution-writing process, especially after their lack of participation in the January 2005 elections.

When a draft constitution did not acknowledge Iraq's Arab and Muslim identity, the General Secretary of the Gulf Cooperation Council called the Iraqi Constitution "a catastrophe." The Saudi Foreign Minister, Prince Saud al-Faisal, also warned that if the Constitution did not accommodate the Iraqi Sunni community, it would result in sectarian disputes that might threaten the unity of Iraq.[207]

Prince Saud al-Faisal urged the United States to pressure Iraqi Shi'ites and Kurdish government leaders to work to bring the Iraqi people together. He said, "[Americans] talk now about Sunnis as if they were separate entity from the Shi'ite." Prince Saud reiterated his fear of an Iraqi civil war saying, "If you allow civil war, Iraq is finished forever."[208]

Prince Saud also predicted that a civil war in Iraq could have dire consequences in the region and indicated the Kingdom feared an Iran-Iraq alliance. The Saudi Foreign Minister asserted, "We (US and Saudi Arabia) fought a war together to keep Iran out of Iraq after Iraq was driven out of Kuwait." He added that the U.S. policy in Iraq is "handing the whole country over to Iran without reason." Iranians have established their influence within Iraq, al-Faisal said, because they "pay money... install their own people (and) even establish police forces and arm the militias that are there."[209]

Jordan

Some analysts believed that a limited number of insurgents were crossing into Iraq from the Iraq-Jordan border. Most Arab Jordanians strongly opposed the rise of a Shi'ite-dominated Iraq, although this did not mean support of neo-Salafi extremism. While Abu Musab al-Zarqawi was a Jordanian, the Jordanian government had sentenced Zarqawi to death in absentia on multiple occasions. Though some Jordanians were involved in the insurgency, Jordan has been very cooperative in its efforts to train Iraqi police and to monitor its borders.

The Jordanian government trained many of the new Iraqi security forces and showed it was very much concerned with extreme Islamist elements within its own territory. King Abdullah pledged soon after the fall of Saddam Hussein to train over 30,000 Iraqi military and police within Jordan. On January 13, 2005, the 12th class graduated from its training, bringing the total to almost 10,000 Iraqi security forces trained in Jordan since efforts began.[210]

There have, however, been incidents involving insurgents and terrorists within Jordan's borders. In spring 2004, a plot to create a massive chemical-laced explosion over Amman by radical Islamists was uncovered and disrupted by the Jordanian security forces. On August 19, 2005, Katyusha rockets were fired at two U.S. warships in Jordan's Red Sea Aqaba port. None of the rockets struck the ship. One hit a warehouse, killing a Jordanian soldier; another exploded near a Jordanian hospital, resulting in no casualties; and the third landed outside of Eilat Airport in neighboring Israel, but failed to explode. The Iraqi branch of Al Qa'ida, linked to Jordanian Abu Masab al-Zarqawi, claimed responsibility for the attack. Four days later, Jordanian officials arrested a Syrian man, Mohammed Hassan Abdullah al-Sihly, whom they accused of carrying out the attack. Police said three accomplices slipped across the border into Iraq.[211] Jordanian Interior Minister Awni Yirfas confirmed his government was working with Iraqi authorities in order to capture the militants.[212]

In summer 2005, Jordanian forces broke up an alleged recruitment ring in Amman. According to the main defendant, Zaid Horani, he and several other Jordanians crossed into Syria and boarded buses in Damascus, Syria, that were bound for Iraq as the Coalition forces invaded. Horani apparently returned home and helped to organize a recruitment pipeline for Jordanians interested in joining the insurgency in Iraq. A Syrian, Abu al-Janna, was allegedly the point of contact in Iraq for the Jordanians. Al-Janna reportedly was a central figure in the regional terror network.[213]

A Jordanian, Raad Mansour al-Banna, became the main suspect in the suicide bombing of a police recruitment site in Hilla in February 2005, killing more than 125.[214] On August 21, 2005, Laith Kubba, spokesman for Prime Minister Ibrahim al-Jaafari, accused Jordan of allowing the family of Saddam Hussein to finance the insurgent campaign in Iraq in an effort to reestablish the Ba'ath Party in that country.[215]

As already discussed, none of the bombers involved in the November 9 hotel bombings in Amman were Jordanian, but rather Iraqi nationals. Zarqawi did, however, draw on his connections in Jordan to carry out the attacks. There were over 400,000 Iraqis living in Jordan, some of whom had ties to neo-Salafi extremists in Iraq and were willing to help carry out operations in Jordan. Jordanian officials, including King Abdullah II, refused to rule out the possibility that Jordanians may have been involved in the attacks. In the days immediately following the bombings, Jordanian security officials arrested 12 suspects, mostly Jordanians and Iraqis.

Turkey

The Kurdish issue in northern Iraq has major implications for Turkey. First, Ankara is concerned about activities of Kurdish separatist groups in northern Iraq, whose chief objective is an independent Kurdistan in and around Turkey. Turkey is engaging in heavy diplomacy with both the U.S. and Iraqi administrations to crack down on these organizations and eliminate the Kurdish rebels which were launching attacks into Turkish territory. This long-standing concern is the primary reason for the presence of Turkish intelligence and military units in northern Iraq since the Gulf Operation.

Second, Turkey has consistently opposed strong autonomy for a Kurdish zone within Iraq, out of fear that it would create unrest and aspirations for independence among Turkey's own Kurdish population. Given the rich water supplies in the Kurdish populated regions of Turkey and the colossal irrigation project (the Southeast Anatolian Project) that Turkey has invested in for over four decades, an autonomous Turkish Kurdistan is out of the question for Turkish policy makers.

In summer 2005, Kurdish PKK rebels launched a series of attacks on Turkish forces allegedly from bases in northern Iraq. In two months, more than 50 Turkish security forces were killed in attacks, mostly in the form of planted IEDs, a weapon utilized widely by Iraqi insurgents.

In July 2005, the Turkish Prime Minister threatened cross-border action against the rebels if the attacks did not stop, though such action is generally regarded as extremely provocative and even illegal. Recep Tayyip Erdogan stated, however, "There are certain things that international law allows. When necessary, one can carry out cross border operations. I hope that such a need will not emerge."[216]

There were conflicting reports that the United States, which considers the PKK a terrorist organization, had ordered the Turkish military to capture the organization's leaders. A member of the Turkish military claimed that the United States had agreed to seize the leaders while U.S. military spokesmen were unaware of such an agreement.

The official U.S. position seemed to be that the United States opposed any cross-border action, viewing it as an infringement on sovereignty and likely to incite further violence between the Kurds and the various sects opposed to their independence or autonomy. Furthermore, the United States made it clear that any discussion over the PKK should center on the Iraqi government. U.S. Chairman of the Joint Chiefs of Staff General Richard Myers stated, "I think the difference now is that they [Turkey] are dealing with a sovereign Iraqi government, and a lot of these discussions will have to occur between Turkey and Iraq, not between Turkey and the United States."[217]

Despite the tension in U.S. and Turkish ties, and in Turkey's relations with Iraq and its Kurds, Turkey became deeply involved in postwar reconstruction in Iraq. Turkey also offered to assist with the training of Iraqi police forces. The most recent example of Turkish effort to help the creation of a stable and unified Iraq was the meeting held in April 2005 in Istanbul where all Iraq's neighbors and Egypt and

Bahrain convened to address issues related with cross-border insurgency and terrorist infiltration.

Iran

The role Iran plays in the Iraqi insurgency is controversial. Some sources see Iran as being primarily concerned with having a stable nation on its borders that is Shi'ite dominated, but unified enough so it does not drag Iran into regional problems or force it to deal with an Iraqi civil war. Others feel Iran is seeking a far greater degree of direct influence or wants to use *de facto* control over Iraq to achieve regional hegemony. Virtually all sources agree Iran does not play a passive role and never planned to. Citing Iranian sources, a *TIME* magazine article stated that the Supreme National Security Council of Iran concluded in September 2002, before the U.S. invasion, "It is necessary to adopt an active policy in order to prevent long-term and short-term dangers to Iran."[218]

Iran has active ties to several key Shi'ite political parties. These include key elements in the Shi'ite-based United Iraqi Alliance that emerged as Iraq's most important political coalition in the January and December 2005 elections: the Supreme Council for the Islamic Revolution in Iraq (SCIRI), Al-Da'wa, and Al-Da'wa–Tanzim al-Iraq. The Revolutionary Guard and Iranian intelligence have been active in southern Iraq, as well as other areas, since the early 1980s. They almost certainly have a network of active agents in Iraq at present. There are also some indications that Lebanese Hezbollah has established a presence in Iraq.[219]

Prime Minister Allawi repeatedly expressed his concern over Iran's actions during 2004 and early 2005, as did other senior officials in the Interim Iraqi Government who see Iran as a direct and immediate threat.

Iraqi Interim Defense Minister Hazem Sha'alan claimed in July 2004 that Iran remained his country's "first enemy," supporting "terrorism and bringing enemies into Iraq...I've seen clear interference in Iraqi issues by Iran...Iran interferes in order to kill democracy." A few months later Sha'alan—a secular Shi'ite who is one of Iran's most outspoken critics in Iraq—added that the Iranians "are fighting us because we want to build freedom and democracy, and they want to build an Islamic dictatorship and have turbaned clerics to rule in Iraq."[220] Sha'alan made several points in a briefing on September 22, 2004:

- Iranian intervention and support of Al-Sadr pose major threats; and some infiltration has taken place across the Syria border.
- Iran is behind Al-Sadr. It uses Iranian pilgrims and sends arms, money, and drugs across the border.
- Iraq must have strong border defense forces. "If doors and windows are empty, no amount of cleaning will ever get rid of the dust."

In a study of Iran's role in Iraq, the International Crisis Group noted that an Iranian cleric and close associate of Ayatollah Sistani warned in November 2004, "Iran's policy in Iraq is 100 per cent wrong. In trying to keep the Americans busy they have furthered the suffering of ordinary Iraqis…We are not asking them to help the Americans, but what they are doing is not in the interests of the Iraqi people; it is making things worse. We [Iranians] have lost the trust of the Iraqi people [*Mardom-e Aragh az dast dadeem*]."[221]

In contrast, King Abdullah of Jordan has made a wide range of charges about Iranian interference in Iraq and went so far as to charge during the period before the Iraqi election that Iran was attempting to rig Iraq's election with up to 1,000,000 false registrations. He has since talked about the risk of an Iraqi-Syrian-Lebanese Shi'ite axis or crescent.

In an extraordinary interview aired on Iraqi TV on January 14, 2005, Muayed Al-Nasseri, commander of Saddam Hussein's "Army of Muhammad," claimed that his group regularly received arms and money from both Syria and Iran. "Many factions of the resistance are receiving aid from the neighboring countries," he said. "We got aid primarily from Iran."[222]

On October 13, 2005, the Iraqi Interior Ministry announced that Iraqi security forces had arrested ten Iranian "infiltrators" trying to enter the country illegally. A total of 88 suspected insurgents were arrested in the raid, including one Somali citizen. Iraqi security forces also seized a number of weapons and ammunition caches.[223] In a similar incident in July 2005, Iraqi Border Guards exchanged fire with gunmen crossing into Iraq from Iran. The Iraqi security forces also uncovered a cache of explosives, timers, and detonators.[224] Such incidents, in addition to growing allegations of Iranian involvement by Baghdad and Washington, suggest that Iran may have moved from having the ability to create unrest and violence in Iraq to actively supporting insurgents.

According to what several newspapers claim are classified intelligence reports, British intelligence officials suspect insurgents led by Abu Mustafa al-Sheibani are responsible for the deaths of at least 11 British soldiers in southern Iraq.[225] An investigation of Iranian involvement in Iraq in August 2005 by *TIME* magazine identified al-Sheibani as the leader of the insurgency in the south. According to the magazine, the Islamic Revolutionary Guard Corps had been instrumental in creating the al-Sheibani group and providing it with weapons and training. U.S. intelligence officials also believe the group, estimated to number almost 300 militants, is responsible for at least 37 bombs against U.S. troops in 2005 alone.[226] British officials accused a second Tehran-backed militia group, the Mujahedeen for Islamic Revolution in Iraq, of having killed six British Royal Military Police in Majar el-Kabir in 2003.[227]

In early October 2005, the British government publicly blamed Iran for the deaths of eight British soldiers in southern Iraq. Although British officials had complained to Tehran about ongoing arms smuggling across the porous Iran-Iraq border earlier in the year, this marked the first time London officially implicated Tehran in the deaths of Coalition troops. British officials accused Iran's Revolutionary Guard of supplying advanced-technology "shaped charges" capable of penetrating even the toughest armor to insurgents in Iraq and of trying to further destabilize the country.[228] Echoing British accusations, Defense Secretary Rumsfeld stated that some weapons found in Iraq have "clearly [and] unambiguously" originated from Iran.[229]

A number of experts believe that Tehran-backed militias have infiltrated Iraqi security forces. In September 2005, Iraq's National Security Adviser, Mouwafak al-Rubaie, admitted that insurgents had penetrated Iraqi police forces in many parts of the country, but refused to speculate about the extent of this infiltration.[230] MNF-I, U.S. Embassy, and British Embassy reporting continued to cite this as a problem through the fall of 2006, and Prime Minister Malikis's new government repeatedly raised the issue in its discussions with Iran.

Some reports suggest that between 70 and 90 percent of Basra's police force has been infiltrated by religious and political factions. The Al-Mahdi Army, in particular, is believed to have almost *de facto* control over the police. Not surprisingly, corruption and violence is on the rise within the force. More than 1,300 murders were documented in Basra during the first nine months of 2005, many of them allegedly by men in police uniform.[231] A second Tehran-backed group, the Badr Brigade, controlled the city's Bureau of Internal Affairs up until spring 2005[232]—all in a city not considered an Al-Sadr stronghold, an individual frequently associated with these groups.

There are numerous reports of Iranian-backed groups exerting influence over the lives of everyday Iraqis. Achieving a government job in Basra today is almost impossible without the sponsorship of one of these groups. Teaching posts in local schools and universities are increasingly filled only by those deemed ideologically loyal to Iran.[233] Iranian goods flood local markets and Farsi is becoming the area's second language.[234]

Some U.S. and British officials feel that Iran was backing the insurgency in southern Iraq. The exact level of Iranian influence over the Iraqi insurgency is still unknown, however. Whether the Tehran regime, or elements of it, is encouraging or merely allowing attacks against Coalition troops stationed in southern Iraq is unclear. It should be noted, however, that Iran has repeatedly denied these charges. Moreover, other American experts and some top U.S. officials and commanders are more concerned with the potential role Iran could play in any Iraqi civil conflict, or its influence over a Shi'ite political majority in office, than with direct Iranian support of a Shi'ite insurgency.

As General George Casey put it, "I don't see substantial Iranian influence on this particular government that will be elected in January. I see Iran as more of a longer-term threat to Iraqi security...a long-term threat to stability in Iraq. If you look on the other side, I think Syria is a short-term threat, because of the support they provide to Ba'athist leaders operating inside and outside of Iraq."[235]

In July 2005, Kurdish intelligence officials asserted that Ansar was based primarily in Iran and that attacks in the Kurdish areas could have occurred only with Iranian support. According to an Iraqi Kurdish reporter, the Iranian cities of Mahabad and Saqqiz are centers where Ansar recruited among the Iranian Kurds. Such claims cannot be independently verified.

Iran has not been, and never will be, passive in dealing with Iraq. For example, it sent a top-level official, Kamal Kharrazi, to Iraq on May 17, 2005—only 48 hours after U.S. Secretary of State Condoleezza Rice had left the country. Kharrazi met with Prime Minister al-Jaafari and Foreign Minister Hoshyar Zebari. He also met with other top officials and key members of the Shi'ite parties. His visit was at a minimum a demonstration of Iran's influence in an Iraq governed by a Shi'ite majority, even though some key Iraqi Shi'a parties like Al Dawa have scarcely been strong supporters of Iran. Kharrazi also gave an important message at his press conference, "... the party that will leave Iraq is the United States because it will eventually withdraw ...But the party that will live with the Iraqis is Iran because it is a neighbor to Iraq."[236]

In summer 2005, the Iraqi and Iranian Ministers of Defense, Sadoun Dulaimi and Admiral Ali Shamkhani, met and concluded a five-point military agreement. The meeting, however, produced conflicting statements as to what had been agreed upon. The Iranian Minister, Shamkhani, asserted that as part of the deal Iran would train a number of Iraqi troops. His counterpart, Dulaimi, however, stated that the Iraqi government was satisfied with the Coalition efforts and that Iran would not be training Iraqi troops. Iran would, however, be providing $1 billion in aide that would go toward reconstruction. Dulaimi conceded that some would go to the Ministry of Defense.[237]

Several high-level meetings between Iraqi and Iranian officials took place in the fall of 2005. Iraq's Deputy Minister, Ahmed Chalabi, met with Iranian officials in Tehran only days before traveling to the United States to meet with U.S. Secretary of State Condoleezza Rice. The timing was seen by many as odd given accusations in May 2004 by U.S. officials that Chalabi gave Iran classified information.[238]

In mid-November, Iraq's National Security Adviser, Mouwafak al-Rubaie, traveled to Tehran. While there, he signed a memorandum of understanding with the Iranian government committing the two governments to cooperate on sensitive intelligence-sharing matters, counterterrorism, and cross-border infiltration of Al Qa'ida figures. The agreement took Washington by surprise: U.S. Ambassador to Iraq Zalmay Khalilzad told reporters he found out about the agreement only afterward.[239]

Iraqi President Jalal Talabani traveled to Iran in late November, becoming the first Iraqi head of state to do so in almost four decades. Talabani spent three days in Iran and met with both Iranian President Mahmoud Ahmadinejad and Supreme Leader Ayatollah Ali Khamenei. Al-Rubaie, who accompanied Talabani on the trip, told reporters he asked the Iranians to use their influence with Damascus to secure Syrian cooperation in sealing off the Iraqi border to insurgents.[240] In their meeting, Khamenei told Talabani that foreign troops were to blame for the ongoing violence and urged the Iraqi President to tell the occupiers to go: "The presence of foreign troops is damaging for the Iraqis, and the Iraqi government should ask for their departure by proposing a timetable...the US and Britain will eventually have to leave Iraq with a bitter experience."[241]

According to Talabani, Khamenei promised to support the Iraqi President's efforts to end the insurgency. With regard to Iraq, Khamenei told the official IRNA news agency: "Your security is our own security and Iran honors Iraq's independence and power... We will extend assistance to you in those fields." But Khamenei made a point of denying any responsibility for the violence next door, saying: "Iran considers the United States to be responsible for all crimes and terrorist acts in Iraq and the suffering and misery of the Iraqi people."[242]

Another high-profile Iraqi visit to Tehran took place on November 27 by Vice President Adel Abdul-Mahdi. Abdul-Mahdi met with his Iranian counterpart, Vice President for Executive Affairs Ali Saeedlou to discuss the implementation of accords reached earlier in the month. Together, these visits seemed to mark a sign of improving relations between the two countries in late 2005.

As mentioned above, Iran's influence in Iraq is not just of a political or military nature, but economic as well. In addition to Iranian government aid allotted for reconstruction, Iranian businessmen have reportedly invested heavily in restoring their neighbor's infrastructure. Nonprofit groups headquartered in Iran also helped to provide basic services to Iraqis during the chaos that followed the toppling of Saddam and the dissolution of the Ba'athist government. One nongovernmental organization established in Tehran with ties to the Iranian government, "Reconstruction of the Holy Shrines of Iraq," claims that it has completed more than 300 construction, cultural, and religious projects in the country. Another group, the Organization of Ahl-ul-Bait, whose leadership is comprised of Iranian mullahs, has sent ambulances, doctors, and teachers into Iraq.[243]

New complaints regarding Iranian interference in Iraq were leveled again in March 2006 by Secretary Rumsfeld, who accused Iran of deploying its Revolutionary Guard to Iraq. He said that Iran was "putting people into Iraq to do things that are harmful to the future of Iraq," and that it was something that Tehran would "look back on as having been an error in judgment."[244] That same month, President Bush asserted that "Tehran has been responsible for at least some of the increasing lethality of anti-coalition attacks by providing Shi'a militia with the capabilities to build improvised explosive devices in Iraq."[245]

U.S. Ambassador to Iraq Zalmay Khalilzad made similar allegations. He accused Iran of publicly supporting Iraq's political process while it clandestinely trained and aided Shi'ite militia groups as well as Sunni insurgent organizations such as Ansar al-Sunna. He stated, "Our judgment is that training and supplying, direct or indirect, takes place, and that there is also provision of financial resources to people, to militias, and that there is a presence of people associated with the Revolutionary Guard and with MOIS."[246]

Khalilzad's comments came as the United States and Iran announced that they had agreed to hold direct talks for the first time on how to reduce the violence in Iraq. These talks, scheduled to take place in Iraq, were at the request of SCIRI leader, Abdul al-Hakim, who had solicited Iranian assistance in the past. Ambassador Khalilzad, who had also reached out to Tehran's leaders, was to receive the Iranian negotiators when they arrived.[247]

Both sides came to the talks with minimal expectations. In addition, U.S. officials remained adamant that the discussions would be narrowly focused on Iraqi security issues and would not include the Iranian nuclear program. In statements leading up to the talks, it appeared Tehran saw them as an opportunity to change Washington's behavior, while the United States indicated that Iran's desire to meet was an indication that it was realizing that its defiant posture was not working.

Iran's chief nuclear negotiator, Ali Larijani, made the announcement to the Iranian Parliament saying, "I think Iraq is a good testing ground for America to take a hard look at the way it acts...If there's a determination in America to take that hard look, then we're prepared to help." He went on to indicate that Iran was willing to help the United States in Iraq, but only under the condition that the "United States should respect the vote of the people. Their Army must not provoke from behind the scenes."[248]

Yet, U.S. officials such as Secretary of State Condoleezza Rice emphasized that the negotiations would focus only on Iraq. National Security Advisor Stephen Hadley added optimistically, however, that Iran was "finally beginning to listen."[249]

The announcement of these negotiations drew a strong condemnation from The Iraqi Consensus Front, Iraq's dominant Sunni political party. In a statement it called the negotiations "an obvious unjustified interference," and added, "It's not up to the American ambassador to talk to Iran about Iraq."[250]

None of these pressures or issues faded during the course of 2006. It is also clear that Iran faces a dilemma. It benefits from U.S. support for Iraq to help it deal with the insurgency and provide economic aid. Yet, it fears being "encircled" by the U.S. presence in Iraq, Afghanistan, and the Gulf. Iranian officials have threatened to destabilize Iraq if the United States brings military pressure against Iran because of its alleged nuclear weapons program. A split in Iraq's government could lead some Shi'ite factions to actively turn to Iran for support, and the divisions in Iran's government create the ongoing risk that hard-line elements might intervene in Iraq even if its government did not fully support such action.

Iran also faces the reality that it is "Persian" while Iraq is "Arab," and Iraqi and Iranian Shi'ites do not always share common values and interests. Many of the Iraqi exile groups and militia members who lived in Iran before the fall of Saddam Hussein were never particularly grateful to Iran during the time they had to remain in exile and are not pro-Iranian now. The Ayatollah Sistani, Iraq's preeminent Shi'ite religious leader—as well as virtually all of the influential Iraqi clergy except Al-Sadr —is a "quietest," who opposes the idea that religious figures should play a direct role in politics.

Moreover, the Grand Ayatollah Sistani has rejected the religious legitimacy of a velayat-e faqih or supreme religious leader like Iran's Khameni. The major Iraqi Shi'ite parties that did operate in Iran before Saddam's fall did endorse the idea of a velayat-e faqih while they were dependent on Iran, but have since taken the position that Iraq should not be a theocratic state, much less under the control of an Ayatollah-like figure. Iran's aims in Iraq may not be to secure a religious theocracy akin to its own, but merely to assure a Shi'ite-backed Baghdad government friendly to Tehran.

While the evidence is unclear, there is no firm indication of the existence of any major Iranian effort to destabilize or control Iraq through September 2006.[251] However, the present and future uncertainties surrounding Iran's role can scarcely be ignored. Iran does seem to have tolerated an Al Qa'ida presence in Iran, or at least its transit through the country, as a means of putting pressure on the United States in spite of the organization's hostility toward Shi'ites. Iran may have been active in supporting groups like Al Ansar in the past, or at least turning a blind eye, and may allow cross-border infiltration in Iraq's Kurdish region.

Syria

Both senior U.S. and Iraqi officials feel that Syria may overtly have agreed to try to halt any support of the insurgency, but allows Islamic extremist groups to recruit young men, have them come to Syria, and then cross the border into Iraq—where substantial numbers have become suicide bombers. They also feel Syria has allowed senior ex-Ba'athist cadres to operate from Syria, helping to direct the Sunni insurgency. As has been touched upon earlier, these include top level officials under Saddam Hussein, such as Izzat Ibrahim al-Duri, one of Saddam's vice presidents.

General George Casey, the commander of the Multi-National Force (MNF), has been careful not to exaggerate the threat of foreign interference. Nevertheless, Casey has warned that Syria has allowed Iraqi supporters of Saddam Hussein to provide money, supplies, and direction to Sunni insurgents and continues to be a serious source of infiltration by foreign volunteers.[252] General Casey highlighted Syria's complicity in this regard when testifying before the Senate Armed Services Committee on March 8, 2005:[253]

> There are former regime leaders who come and go from Syria, who operate out of Syria, and they do planning, and they provide resources to the insurgency in Iraq. I have no hard evidence that the Syrian government is actually complicit with those people, but we certainly have evidence that people at low levels with the Syrian government know that they're there and what they're up to.

The U.S. State Department spokesman described Syria's role as follows in the late spring of 2005:[254]

> I think that what we've seen, again, are some efforts, but it certainly isn't enough. We do believe the Syrians can do more. We do believe there's more they can do along the border to tighten controls.
>
> We do believe that there's more that they can do to deal with the regime elements that are operating out of Syria itself and are supporting or encouraging the insurgents there.
>
> And so, again, it's not simply a matter of them not being able to take the actions, at least from our perspective. Part of it is an unwillingness to take the actions that we know are necessary and they know are necessary.

Syria has repeatedly and emphatically denied that it supports or harbors any persons involved in the insurgency in Iraq. After months of American pressure and accusations, however, Syrian authorities delivered a group suspected of supporting the insurgency from Syria to Iraqi officials in February 2005. Among the captives handed over was Sabawi Ibrahim Hassan, Saddam Hussein's half-brother and a leading financier for the insurgency. Syria's Foreign Minister, Farouk al-Sharaa, stated that Syria was doing all that it could, but it needed equipment tailored to policing the borders, such as night vision goggles.[255]

There have also been reports that Zarqawi obtained most of his new young volunteers through Syria and that they were recruited and transited in ways that had to be known to Syrian intelligence. There had also been media reports that Zarqawi's top lieutenants, and perhaps Zarqawi himself, met in Syria for planning sessions.[256] These reports were called into question by U.S. intelligence assessments in June 2005.

U.S. officials and commanders, as well as Iraqi officials, acknowledge that Syria has made some efforts to improve its border security and reduce infiltration. In summer 2005, Syrian security forces fought suspected militants, possibly former bodyguards of Saddam Hussein, for two days near Qassioun Mountain, and a sweep of the border area with Lebanon led to the arrest of some 34 suspected militants. In a high-profile case, Syria arrested a man and his brother's wife whom it accused of facilitating militants' passage into Iraq. The woman admitted on Al Arabiya satellite television that the brothers had crossed into Iraq to join Saddam's Fedayeen prior to the Coalition invasion.[257]

U.S. Central Command Director of Intelligence Brigadier General John Custer acknowledged in July 2005 that Syria had made efforts to improve the situation and faced problems in patrolling the border. Custer stated that Syria had bolstered the forces along the eastern border with units relocated from Lebanon. In comments that seemed to contradict what other intelligence officials had said, Custer stated the following:[258]

I think Syria is intent on assisting the US in Iraq.... [I have] no information, intelligence or anything credible [that Syria] is involved or facilitating in any way [the flow of insurgents into Iraq]...Could they do more? Yes. Are they doing more? Yes. They are working very hard. As troops have been pulled out of Lebanon, we've seen some of those troops go to the border. I am convinced that they are not only doing it along the border but are arresting people as they transit.

The British military attaché in Damascus, Colonel Julian Lyne-Pirkis, inspected the Syrian efforts at the border and agreed with Custer's assessment. Custer suggested that the security environment on the border was a combination of a tradition of lawlessness and lack of Syrian ability to police the area, creating a greater impression of Syrian complicity than there actually was. He stated, "It's not a question of intent—it's simply capacity and capability. You've got a 600-kilometer border there, some of the toughest desert, and you have a thousand-year-old culture of smuggling. Smuggling men now is no different than smuggling men a 1,000 years ago. It's all a smuggling economy."[259] Syria faces problems because its border forces are relatively weak, they lack training and equipment, and much of the border is demarcated only by an earthen beam. At the same time, they feel Syria deliberately turns a blind eye toward many operations and the large number of Islamist extremist volunteers crossing the border.

Some analysts have suggested that the regime in Damascus may view the insurgency in Iraq as a means to "export" their own Islamist extremists who might otherwise take aim at Assad's secular regime (led by an Alawite minority). However, such a view, analysts say, is extremely near-sighted as it is quite possible that extremists in Iraq could cross back into Syria, bringing practical guerrilla warfare experience with them much like the Mujahedeen who fought in the Afghan war brought back to their countries of origin. Such hardened and trained militants could then pose a very serious threat to the ruling regime. As one commentator stated, "They [militants and Syria] may have slept in the same bed to fight the Americans, but what's important for al Qa'ida is that it has entered the bedroom [Syria] and secured a foothold there."[260]

Indeed, such views were supported by classified CIA and U.S. State Department studies in summer 2005. Analysts referred to the return of experienced and trained militants to their country of origin or third-party country as "bleed out" or "terrorist dispersal."[261] The studies sought to compare the returning Mujahedeen from Afghanistan to those who fought in Iraq. Like Syria, those countries could be threatened by the fighters who return with advanced warfare skills.[262] A Marine Corps spokesman pointed out that if nothing else, certain techniques such as the use of IEDs had already been transferred from Iraq to combat zones like Afghanistan. Experts, however, point to the fact that while the Afghan war attracted thousands of foreign fighters, Iraq has yet to do so, meaning that the potential number of returning veterans would be much less.[263]

Saudi Interior Minister Prince Nayef echoed the conclusions of the CIA and State Department studies, pointing out that many of the terrorists who operated in Saudi from May 2003 on were either veterans of the Soviet conflict in Afghanistan or had trained in the camps that operated until Operation Enduring Freedom eliminated them. Nayef and other Saudi officials believe that the Saudis who return from the conflict in Iraq will have skills that are even more lethal than those exhibited by the Afghan war veterans. Nayef stated, "We expect the worst from those who went to Iraq. They will be worse, and we will be ready for them."[264]

Washington's warnings to Damascus over border security intensified during the fall of 2005. On October 7, Syrian President Bashar Assad told the pan-Arab newspaper *Al Hayat*, "They (Americans) have no patrols at the border, not a single American or Iraqi on their side of the border...We cannot control the border from one side."[265] Assad's comments came a day after President Bush and Prime Minister Blair both issued renewed warnings against continued Syrian and Iranian involvement in Iraqi affairs, specifically their roles in giving shelter to Islamic extremists.

A senior U.S. official also suggested that the war might have spread beyond Iraq's borders, telling the *Financial Times*, "We are concerned that Syria is allowing its territory to be part of the Iraqi battlefield. That's a choice the Syrians made. We think that is an unwise choice."[266] In his interview with *Al Hayat*, Assad said the absence of security along the border was hurting Syria and maintained that "controlling it will help Syria because the chaos in Iraq affects us." Assad said his country had arrested more than 1,300 infiltrators from Iraq since the war began.[267] The following day, Assistant Secretary of State David Welch responded by saying the United States was "ask[ing] the Syrian government not to interfere in such matters." Welch went on to say, "It appears that they are not listening and it seems this behavior is not changing."[268] The rhetorical exchanges, however, did not prevent the Syrian Airlines Company from flying its inaugural post-Saddam era flight between Damascus and Baghdad on October 11. It was the first regular flight to operate between the two capitals in a quarter of a century.[269]

The situation has remained roughly the same during the course of 2006, although Iraq is making efforts to create more effective border police. Virtually anyone can go in and out, moving money and small critical supplies, and volunteers can simply enter as ordinary visitors without equipment.

U.S. Customs and Border Protection (CBP) officers are working to train their Iraqi counterparts and have had moderate success in detaining potential insurgents and arms suppliers, and in breaking up smuggling rings. Another U.S. CBP team of officers and border agents was deployed in Iraq on February 1, 2005, to assist further in the training of Iraqis. This may help, but Iraq's border security forces have so far been some of its most ineffective units. Many of its new forts are abandoned and other units that have remained exhibit minimal activity. Yet, even if Iraq's border forces were ready and its neighbors actively helped, border security would still be a problem, in part because they are often vast, uninhabited areas.

This illustrates a general problem for both Iraq and its neighbors. Iraq's borders total 3,650 kilometers in length. Its border with Iran is 1,458 kilometers; with Jordan, 181 kilometers; with Kuwait, 240 kilometers; with Saudi Arabia, 814 kilometers; with Syria, 605 kilometers; and with Turkey, 352 kilometers. Most of these borders are desert, desolate territory, easily navigable water barriers, or mountains. Even Iraq's small 58-kilometer coastline is in an area with considerable small craft and shipping traffic, which presents security problems.

Syria has an Alawite-led regime that is more Shi'ite than Sunni, and while it sees its support of Sunni insurgents as a way of weakening the potential threat from a U.S. presence in Syria, it also maintains ties to Shi'ite factions as well. While it may tolerate and encourage former Iraqi Ba'athist operations in Syria, and transit by Islamist extremists, Syria also maintains ties to elements of formerly Iranian-backed Iraqi Shi'ite groups like the Supreme Council for the Islamic Revolution in Iraq, Al-Da'wa, and Al-Da'wa–Tanzim al-Iraq that it first developed during the Iran-Iraq War. Syria's crackdown on fighters passing into Iraq through its borders, an effort praised by U.S. military officials, was likely the result of broader national security interests and concerns about regime stability.[270] Indeed, despite speculation that the Syrian government was on the brink of reform, indications in early 2006 suggested quite the opposite.

Far from opening the Ba'ath-dominated rule to a multiparty system, Syria implemented new oppressive measures against political opponents and sought methods to co-opt religious elements of society. Fearing the gathering momentum of Islamic political parties such as Hamas and the Muslim Brotherhood—each of which had electoral victories in Palestine and Egypt, respectively—the Ba'ath Party of Syria attempted to head off similar challenges in its state by allowing religious figures a greater role in government and giving them a freer hand to conduct their business among their followers so long as it does not attempt to rival the Syrian government.[271]

Yemen

Yemen is not a Gulf country, but it is a major state on the Arabian Peninsula, and one that has long played a major strategic role in Gulf security. As is shown in Map 10.1, Yemen has coasts on and islands in the Arabian Sea and the Red Sea, and it occupies a strategic position at the Bab al-Mandeb—the narrow strait that controls the entrance to the Red Sea and which every ship passing through the Suez Canal must also traverse:

Yemen shares borders with Oman and Saudi Arabia, and there has been a long history of clashes between Yemen [now a federation of the Yemeni Arab Republic (YAR) and People's Democratic Republic of Yemen (PDRY)], and Oman and Saudi Arabia. Saudi Arabia won a border war with what became the YAR in the 1930s, taking control over the disputed territory—control which is still disputed by some Yemeni nationalists. Saudi Arabia and Egypt nearly came to war when both sides took part in a Yemeni civil war from 1962 to 1967.[1]

South Yemen became a violent Marxist regime when it achieved independence in 1967, and it clashed with Oman as well as North Yemen. South Yemen sponsored a violent Marxist insurgent movement in Oman and provided it with military support and sanctuary during the Dhofar Rebellion, which lasted from 1964 to 1975.[2]

Hundreds of thousands of Yemenis fled from the south to the north over the two decades after South Yemen became independent, and both states had several border wars and became involved in assassinations and covert operations. The regime in the PDRY was so extreme, however, that it provoked a civil war in the late 1980s that led to the collapse of the state and created a political climate that made unification with the YAR both popular and necessary. The two countries were unified as the Republic of Yemen in 1990. A civil war broke out between elements in the north and south in 1994, but the southern secessionist movement lacked broad support and was defeated within a year.[3]

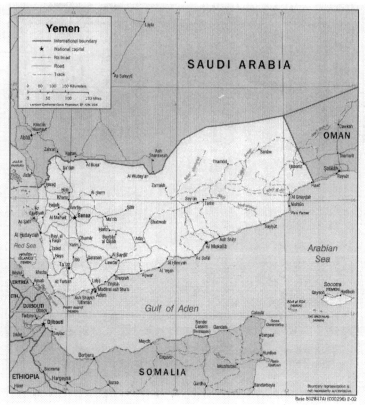

Source: CIA, "Yemen," 2002, available at http://www.lib.utexas.edu/maps/middle_east_and_asia/yemen_pol_2002.jpg

Map 10.1   Yemen

Yemen has resolved its border disputes with Oman and Saudi Arabia; Yemen and Saudi Arabia seem to have reached a stable border agreement in 2000. There still, however, are armed clashes at the tribal level between Yemenis and Saudi security forces. Smuggling from Yemen to Saudi Arabia—including the supply of arms, explosives, and drugs for terrorist organizations—is a continuing problem. So is the long legacy of radicalism in Yemen, tribal and political divisions that limit the central government's internal security capabilities, and the presence of significant Islamist extremist elements including some linked to Al Qa'ida.

The central government has made serious efforts to deal with these problems. Yemen signed a security pact with the United Arab Emirates in 2005, and it began to conduct joint exercises with Saudi Arabia. The security pact with the United Arab Emirates was designed to facilitate stronger anti–Al Qa'ida efforts between the two states, both of which have a long history of combating domestic militants.[4] The first military exercises with the Saudis occurred on March 28, 2005. Though the exercises did not include large numbers of units, they are a symbolic effort to continue to improve relations.[5]

Infiltration of terrorists, illegal immigration, and weapons smuggling from Yemen to Saudi Arabia is, however, a source of tension.[6] The same is true of the steady flow of illegal immigrants seeking jobs in Saudi Arabia. It explains why Saudi Arabia began constructing a security barrier along the Yemeni border in 2004 and why the Kingdom is examining proposals for a much more sophisticated border control system that could cost well in excess of $5 billion.[7]

Religious tensions are also an issue. The population is probably over 90 percent Muslim, with limited numbers of Jews, Christians, and Hindus. It is split, however, between Shaf'i (Sunni) and Zaydi (Shi'ite) Muslims, and there do seem to have been some tribal clashes along sectarian lines.

Internal stability remains a serious problem. Although Yemen is making some progress toward stability, it has a long history of civil war and violence. The central government has tenuous control over many tribal elements, and crimes like kidnappings of foreigners are endemic. Real unemployment, including disguised unemployment, is sometimes put as high as 40 percent, and it is unlikely that it is lower than 35 percent. The population in mid-2005 was 20.7 million, with an extremely high birthrate of 3.45 percent, and 46 percent of the population was under the age of 15 years.

The Yemeni economy cannot support this rapidly growing population. The International Institute for Strategic Studies (IISS) estimates the gross domestic product (GDP) at between $11 and $13 billion.[8] The CIA estimates the GDP at only $17.2 billion, even in purchasing power parity terms, the per capita income at only $800, and estimates that well over 40 percent of the population is below the poverty line. Most workers are employed in agriculture and herding in one of the least productive agricultural sectors in the world because its output is dominated by a low-grade narcotic called Qat.

The CIA estimates that services, construction, industry, and commerce account for less than one-fourth of the labor force, and the real figure may be less than 15 percent. Only remittances from workers overseas and foreign aid allow the nation to function. This economic and demographic instability, coupled with a long history of tolerating the presence of extremist and terrorist movements when they do not directly threaten the regime, makes Yemen a potential threat to both Oman and Saudi Arabia.

MILITARY SPENDING AND ARMS IMPORTS

The CIA estimates that the Yemeni national budget had $5.6 billion in revenues in 2005 and $5.7 billion in expenditures. This limits what Yemen can spend on security and military forces, and Yemen has not been able to benefit from the free or low-cost arms imports it received from the United States and the former Soviet Union (FSU) during the Cold War for well over a decade. According to the IISS, Yemen's military budget has been steadily increasing over the past few years, rising from $482 million in 2001, to $809 million in 2003, $869 million in 2004, and $942 million in 2005.[9] If correct, this represents a 96-percent increase of Yemen's military spending in five years and is much higher than the $374 million to $539 million a year that Yemen spent in the 1990s.[10] It represents a major burden on Yemen's GDP and economy.[11]

As is the case with other countries in the region, Yemen is an arms importer. Figure 10.1 shows the trends in arms deliveries to Yemen by the supplier. It shows that, unlike other Gulf States, Yemen has not been a major recent importer of U.S. arms. At the same time, Figure 10.1 shows Yemen's arms deliveries have nearly doubled from $400 million during 1993–1996 to $700 million during 2001–2004. It is equally important, however, to note that Yemen has relied on Europe, China, and recently Russia for its arms purchases. For example, China delivered $100 million worth of arms to Yemen between 1993 and 1996 and another $100 million between 2001 and 2004. Russia has also emerged as an arms exporter to Yemen. Between 2001 and 2004, Russia delivered $400 million worth of new arms to Yemen.

Figure 10.2, on the other hand, shows the value of recent new arms agreements between Yemen and outside suppliers. The trend of Yemen's new arms agreements is also on the rise. Between 2001 and 2004, Yemen signed several agreements, which the United States and the major western European countries were absent from. Russia signed $600 million worth of new agreements between 2001 and 2004. China signed $100 million, as well as $200 million worth of agreements with other nations during the same period, putting Yemen's total new arms agreements at approximately $900 million.

In spite of the upward trend in both deliveries and new arms agreements, however, Yemen is still not able to fund anything approaching large amounts of more

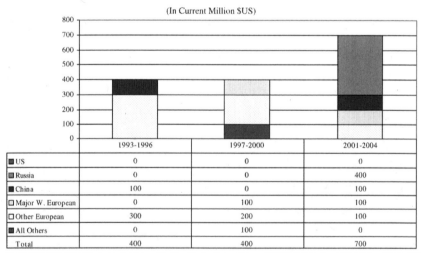

(In Current Million $US)

	1993-1996	1997-2000	2001-2004
US	0	0	0
Russia	0	0	400
China	100	0	100
Major W. European	0	100	100
Other European	300	200	100
All Others	0	100	0
Total	400	400	700

Source: Richard F. Grimmett, *Conventional Arms Transfers To Developing Nations, 1997-2004*, CRS, August 29, 2005; and Richard F. Grimmett, *Conventional Arms Transfers To Developing Nations, 1993-2000*, CRS, August 16, 2001.

Figure 10.1 Yemen's Arms Deliveries by Supplier, 1993–2004

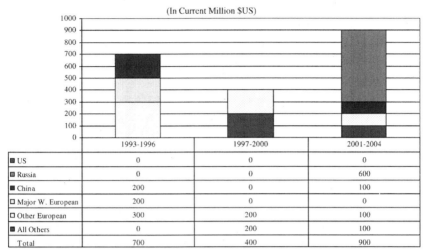

Source: Richard F. Grimmett, *Conventional Arms Transfers To Developing Nations, 1997-2004*, CRS, August 29, 2005; and Richard F. Grimmett, *Conventional Arms Transfers To Developing Nations, 1993-2000*, CRS, August 16, 2001.

Figure 10.2   Yemen's New Arms Agreements by Supplier, 1993–2004

advanced weapons or even recapitalize its existing force structure without significant force cuts or reliance on obsolete equipment. At this point in time, Yemen lacks any clear enemy. Nevertheless, it seems no more capable of making hard trade-offs between force quality and force quantity and bringing force modernization into balance with resources than most other powers in the Middle East North Africa region.

MILITARY MANPOWER

Total Yemeni military manpower was around 66,700 in 2006, with slightly larger paramilitary forces totaling 70,000. These levels of total manning have been typical since the mid-1990s, although Yemen reached totals of 127,000 in the early 1990s. The army had some 60,000 men, the navy, 1,700; the air force, 5,000; and the air defense force, 2,000. There were some 50,000 men in paramilitary roles in the Ministry of the Interior, another 20,000 in tribal levies, and a small coast guard was being created.

Two-year conscripts made up a significant part of the total, although they were a small part of Yemen's potential pool. The CIA estimates that some 237,000 young men became eligible for conscription in 2005. In broad terms, Yemen paid little attention to effective military manpower, lacked effective schools and career development programs, and did not have an effective noncommissioned officer (NCO) corps or mix of technical personnel. As in all countries, there were some outstanding officers and NCOs, but Yemen did a poor overall job in developing suitable manpower quality.

Yemen showed little interest in effective combined arms and joint warfare training and exercises.

THE YEMENI ARMY

The Yemeni Army has some effective battalion-sized elements, but is largely a hollow force better suited to internal security purposes than war fighting. It has a nominal strength of 60,000 men, many of whom are two-year conscripts. It has some 40,000 reserves, with little or no meaningful reserve training.

Figure 10.3 confirms the decreasing trend in the overall manpower of Yemen's conventional army since the consolidation of the state in 1990 and after the brief civil war of 1994. This manning is very limited relative to the total potential manpower pool provided by Yemen's population. As has been noted earlier, Yemen's population is young, 46.5 percent of the population is between ages 0–14.[12] Yemen has approximately 2.8 million men between ages 18–49 who are capable of military service (roughly 13.5 percent of the population).[13] On average, 236,517 men become eligible for military service every year.[14]

At the same time, Yemen faces only limited external conventional military threats. Improved relations with the United Arab Emirates, Saudi Arabia, and Oman have lessened Yemen's need for protection against external threats. Yemen's poor economy has also crippled its military growth. Unlike most other "southern Gulf" countries, the fall of Saddam Hussein did not remove a major conventional threat to Yemen. Iraq was too far away to be a threat, and Saddam and Yemeni President Ali Abdullah Salih had relatively good relations.[15]

The Yemeni Army's force structure is large for its manpower pool. It includes 8 armored brigades, 16 infantry brigades, 6 mechanized brigades, 2 airborne and commando brigades, 1 Special Forces brigade, and a central guard force. Yemen has a number of major combat support units. They include 3 artillery brigades, and 6 air defense brigades with 4 antiaircraft (AA) guns and 1 surface-to-air missile battalion. It has 1 surface-to-surface missile (SSM) brigade with 12 Free Rockets Over Ground (FROGs), 10 SS-21s, and 6/33 SCUD missiles.

The operational status of most of these missiles is uncertain. This order of battle is roughly equivalent to a seven-division force and would normally require about 30 to 50 percent more total manpower than the army possesses.

Armor and Antiarmor Weapons

The army has a mix of a wide variety of equipment types, many of which are obsolete or worn. Figure 10.3 shows that Yemen has 790 main battle tanks (MBTs), including 30 T-34s, 450 T-54/T-55s, 200 T-62s, 50 M-60A1s, and 60 T-72s.[16] *Jane's Sentinel Security Assessment*, however, estimated that Yemen has 763 MBTs, which include 30 T-72s, 75 T-62s, and 106 upgraded T-54/T-55s.[17] Regardless of the exact number, Yemen's MBTs were dominated by older and obsolescent types. There has also been a significant downward trend in numbers. The

Figure 10.3 Yemeni Army's Force Structure Trends, 1990–2006

	1990	2000	2005	2006
Manpower	**134,500**	**101,000**	**100,000**	**100,000**
Active	64,500	61,000	60,000	60,000
Reserve	70,000	40,000	40,000	40,000
Combat Units				
Armored Brigade	4	9	8	8
Mechanized Brigade	4	7	6	6
Infantry Brigade	18	18	16	16
Special Forces Brigade	1	1	1	1
Commando/Airborne	2	2	2	2
Artillery Brigade	8	3	3	3
Surface-to-Surface Missiles Brigades	1	3	1	1
Air Defense	2	4	6	6
Guard/Central Guard Force	1	1	1	1
Main Battle Tanks	**1,195**	**990**	**790**	**790**
T-72	0	30	60	60
M-60A1	140	60	50	50
T-62	100	250	200	200
T-54/T-55	475	500	450	450
T-34	150–480	150	30	30
Armored Infantry Fighting Vehicles	**300**	**200**	**200**	**200**
BMP-1/BMP-2	300	200	200	200
Reconnaissance	**305+***	**200**	**130**	**130**
Saladin	50	0	0	0
Ferret	?†	0	0	0
AML-90	125	100	80	80
BRDM-2	130	100	50	50
Armored Personnel Carriers	**720**	**440**	**710**	**710**
M-113	70	60	60	60
BTR 40/60/152	650	380	650	650
Artillery	**913+**	**1,645+**	**1,153+**	**1,153+**
TOWED 76-mm M-1942	200	0	0	0
TOWED 105-mm M-101A1	90	35	25	25

TOWED 122-mm D-30	120	130	130	130
TOWED 122-mm M-1931/37	30	20	30	30
TOWED 122-mm M-30 M-1938	40	100	40	40
TOWED 130-mm M-46	65	75	60	60
TOWED 15-2mm D-20	0	10	10	10
TOWED 155-mm M-114	12	12	15	15
SP 122-mm 2S1 Carnation	0	0	25	25
Coastal 130-mm SM-4-1	36	36	36	36
MRL 122-mm BM-21	205	184	280	280
MRL 14-0mm BM-14	15	?	14	14
MOR M-43	100	0	0	0
MOR 81-mm	?	600	200	200
MOR 82-mm M-93	?	200	90	90
MOR 107 mm	0	12	12	12
MOR 120 mm	?	100	100	100
MOR 160 mm	0	100	100	100
Antitank Weapons	**?**	**?**	**?**	**?**
Vigiliant	20	0	0	0
MSL AT-3 Sagger	36	35	35	35
MSL M47 Dragon	24	24	24	24
MSL TOW	12	12	12	12
RCL 107-mm B-11	0	?	?	?
RCL 75-mm M-20	?	?	?	?
RCL 82-mm B-10	?	?	?	?
RL 66-mm M-72 LAW	?	?	?	?
RL 73-mm RPG-7Knout	0	0	?	?
GUNS 100-mm M-1944	40	20	20	20
GUNS 100-mm SU-100	30	30	30	30
GUNS 85-mm D-44	30	?	?	?
Air Defense Missiles	**?**	**?**	**1,358**	**1,358**
SAM	?	?	800	800
SA-2	?	0	0	0
SA-13 Gopher	0	?	?	?
SA-14 Gremlin	0	?	?	?

SA-7 Grail	?	?	?	?
SA-9 Gaskin	?	?	?	?
Air Defense Guns	**372**	**470**	**530**	**530**
SP 20-mm M-163 Vulcan	20	20	20	20
TOWED 20-mm M-167 Vulcan	52	40	50	50
23-mm ZSU-23	30	0	0	0
SP 23-mm ZSU-23-4	30	100	50	50
TOWED 23-mm 100ZSU-23-2	0	0	100	100
TOWED 37-mm M-1939	150	150	150	150
TOWED 57-mm S-60	120	120	120	120
TOWED 85-mm KS-12	0	40	40	40
Tactical Surface-to-Surface Missiles	**12**	**28**	**28**	**28**
FROG-7	0	12	12	12
SS-21 Scarab	12	10	10	10
SCUD B Launchers(33 missiles)	0	6	6	6

*   "+" indicates the numbers listed may be slightly less than the actual units or weapons in stock.
†   All "?" refer to weapons Yemen is believed to possess, though the exact numbers in its possession are unknown.
Source: IISS, *Military Balance,* various editions, including 1989–1990, 1999–2000, 2004–2005, and 2005–2006.

Yemeni Army had 1,195 MBTs in 1990. This declined to 990 in 2000 and 790 in 2005–2006.

The downward trend also applied to Yemen's armored reconnaissance (RECCE) vehicles. According to the IISS, Yemen's Army had more than 305 vehicles in 1990. In 2006, Yemen had 130 reconnaissance vehicles (80 AML-90s and 50 BRDM). Yemen had 300 armored infantry fighting vehicles (AIFVs) in 1990, which declined to 200 AIFVs (200 BMP-1/BMP-2s) between 2000 and 2006.

Yemen is estimated to have had 710 armored personal carriers (APCs) in 2006, which is roughly the same number on hand in 1990. However, only around 210 out of the pool of 710 are operational. According to the IISS, this pool included 60 M-113s plus a mix of 150 BTR 40s, 60s, and 152s.[18] According to *Jane's,* Yemen had 70 AML-90s, 10 AML-60-7s, 48 Panhard armored cars, 100 BMP1/2s, 70 M113s, and 180 BTR 40s, 60s, and 152s.[19]

In 2006, Yemen had 12 Tube-Launched Optically Tracked Wire-Guided Missiles (TOWs), 24 Dragons (*Jane's* reports 150 Dragons), and 35 AT-3 Sagger antitank guided weapons. It also had large numbers of rocket launchers, and 75-mm, 82-mm, and 107-mm recoil rifles.[20] *Jane's* estimated that Yemen had 100 82-mm M43 and 450 40-mm M79 antitank weapons.[21] Armor and antiarmor training is limited, while armored maneuver warfare capability and sustainability are low.

Artillery

Yemen has a large pool of some 1,153 artillery weapons—a level that Yemen had maintained since 2000. However, this pool was dependent on towed weapons without modern fire-control systems, artillery radars, and other support equipment.

Yemen had only 25 2S1 122-mm self-propelled artillery weapons, plus 30 worn and obsolescent SU100 100-mm assault guns and 20 100-mm 1944M guns.[22] The IISS estimated that Yemen had 310 towed artillery weapons, including 25 M-101a1 105-mm weapons; 30 M-1931/1937s, 40 M-1938s, and 130 D-30 122-mm weapons; and 60 M-46 130-mm, 10 D-20 152-mm, and 15 M-114 155-mm weapons.[23]

Jane's count was higher, estimating that Yemen had 535 towed weapons. *Jane's* estimated that Yemen has 10 155-mm M114s, 90 122-mm M1938s, 28 122-mm M1931/7s, 92 85-mm D44s, and 70 76-mm 1942s.[24] It also has 36 SM-4-1 coastal defense guns. It has roughly 160–170 operational multiple rocket launchers (MRL), including 150 operational BM-21122-mm weapons out of an inventory of 280, and 14 BM-14 140-mm weapons.[25]

Yemen also had some 502 mortars (81 mm, 82 mm, 107 mm, 120 mm, and 160 mm).[26]

While Yemen had a large inventory of artillery, its artillery forces were even less effective than most other regional forces. Yemen was capable of using artillery in static massed fires, but had very limited capability to maneuver its artillery, support it away from peacetime casernes, rapidly shift fires, or target effectively beyond visual range. It had little or no modern fire-control, counterbattery radar, and fire-management capabilities. Live fire training was very limited.

Antiaircraft Weapons

According to the IISS, Yemen had 530 AA guns. These guns included 50 M-167 and 20 M-163 20 mm, 100 ZSU-23-2 and 50 ZSU-23-4 23 mm, 150 M-1939 37 mm, 120 S-60 57 mm, and 40 KS-12 85 mm.

Jane's estimates, however, differ. Yemen had some 242 AA guns in 2006. These included 100 57-mm SZ-60s, 10 35-mm Oerlikons, 50 ZU-23-2s, 7 ZSU-23-4SPs, 35 14.5-mm ZPU-2 35s, 20 M167 Vulcan self-propelled systems, and 20 M163 Vulcans.[27] It had large numbers of SA-7, SA-9, SA-13, and SA-14 light surface-to-air missiles.

Air defense training and maneuver warfare capability is minimal to limited.[28] Realistic live-fire training is virtually nonexistent.

Ballistic Missiles and Rockets

Yemen has sought ballistic missiles since the 1970s. The Soviet Union was its traditional supplier, but North Korea has since become the primary source. It is believed that Yemen has bought missiles and related items from North Korea for the last ten years. Spain intercepted a North Korean ship on December 9, 2002, that was loaded with 15 complete Scud missiles (possibly SCUD-Cs) as well as fuel and additional warheads. The shipment did not break international law, and the vessel was released after officials stated that the missiles would not be transferred to a third party.

Though it is unclear exactly how many and what type of ballistic missiles Yemen possesses due to the secretive nature of their procurement and the use of many in the 1994 civil war, it is believed that it maintains a variety of weapons. Its tactical SSM strength may have more than doubled between 1990 and 2006, from a total of 12 to 28 missiles.

It is believed that Yemen has up to 12 9k21 FROG 7-TELs (Transporter-Erector-Launchers), approximately 10 9P129 SS-21 Scarabs-TELs, and up to 6 SCUD B/C launchers with approximately 33 missiles.[29] Some of these weapons were delivered in the 1970s, and their effectiveness, especially in light of their performance in the 1994 civil war, is uncertain. A Russian firm has inspected many of Yemen's SS-21s, but both the results and Yemen's upgrade plans remain unknown.[30]

While Yemen may have had some stocks of chemical weapons in the past, it is believed these are limited to token levels, if Yemen retains any at all. Poor training, a lack of live-fire training, lack of long-range targeting and damage assessment capability, and probably reliance on low-grade conventional warheads all seem to sharply limit the effectiveness of this force.

Overall Assessment

The Yemeni Army does not face serious external threats and is probably capable of defeating any major insurrection. It is, however, a low-grade force in virtually every respect, with limited real-world combat capability. Its small number of elite combat units would, however, be somewhat more effective, and the Yemeni Army is large and capable enough to put up considerable resistance in defensive warfare that exploits Yemen's terrain.

THE YEMENI AIR FORCE

The Yemeni Air Force has a nominal strength of 3,000–3,500. It suffers badly from a lack of modernization and foreign support in recent years, although Figure 10.4 shows that Yemen has acquired a few more modern fighters over the past six years. In 2006, the Yemeni Air Force had 75 combat capable aircraft (*Jane's* estimated that number to be 84), of which 40 were in storage. It had 31 fighter

Figure 10.4   Yemeni Air Force's Force Structure, 1990–2006

	1990	2000	2005	2006
Manpower	**3,500**	**3,500**	**3,000**	**3,000**
Active	3,500	3,500	3,000	3,000
Reserve	0	0	0	0
Fighter Interceptor	**66**	**16**	**26**	**31**
J-7M	6	0	0	0
MiG-29SMT Fulcrum	0	5	8	14
MiG-21 Fishbed	60	11	16	15
MiG-29UBT Fulcrum	0	0	2	2
Fighter Ground Attack	**81**	**27**	**40**	**40**
Mig 17	35	0	0	0
Su-20/Su-17 Fitter	45	17	30	30
F5E Tiger II	11	10	10	10
Transport	**14**	**18**	**18**	**18**
An-12 Cub	3	2	2	2
An-24	9	0	0	0
An-26 Curl	4	6	6	6
C-130H Hercules	2	3	3	3
F-27	2	0	0	0
Skyvan 3M	2	0	0	0
Il-14 Crate	4	4	4	4
Il-76 Candid	0	3	3	3
Training Craft	**15+[*]**	**32**	**44**	**44**
MiG 15UTI	3	0	0	0
Su-22	4	0	0	0
F-5B Freedom Fighter	2	2	2	2
L-39C	0	12	12	12
MiG 21 Mongol A	6	4	4	4
Yak-11 Moose	?[†]	14	14	14
Z-242	0	0	12	12
Helicopters	**76**	**25**	**20**	**20**
Ka-26	2	0	0	0
AB-204	2	0	0	0
AB-206	6	0	0	0

Mi-4	5	0	0	0
SA-316	2	0	0	0
Mi-35 Hind	0	8	8	8
ATK AB-47 Bell	0	1	1	1
SPT Mi-8 Hip	53	14	9	9
UTL Bell 212	6	2	2	2

* "+" indicates the numbers listed may be slightly less than the actual units or weapons in stock.
  All "?" refer to weapons that Yemen is believed to possess, though the exact numbers in its possession are unknown.
  Source: IISS, *Military Balance*, various editions, including 1989–1990, 1999–2000, 2004–2005, and 2005–2006.

interceptors, 40 fighter ground attack (FGA) aircraft, 18 transport airplanes, and 44 training craft.

Combat Air Strength

The Yemeni Air Force has lost roughly half of its fighter interceptor strength since the early 1990s. In 1990, it had a total of 66 aircraft. This total dropped to 16 in 2000 and 26 in 2005. In late 2005, Yemen acquired 6 new Mig-29SMT Fulcrums, which brought Yemen's fighter intercept total to 31, including 14 MiG-29SMT Fulcrums, 15 MiG-21 Fishbeds, and 2 Mig-29UBT Fulcrums.

Yemen has also lost roughly half of its FGA aircraft during the last decade. Yemen's FGA total was 81 in 1990, 27 in 2000, and 40 in 2005–2006. Much of the decline was due to the decommissioning of 35 MiG-17s in the early 1990s. In addition, 28 Su-20/Su-17 Fitters (out of a total of 45 in 1990) no longer are listed as operational. The Yemeni Air Force has, however, acquired 13 Su-20/Su-17s. This purchase brought Yemen's total FGA strength in 2006 to 30 Su-20/Su-17s, 10 F5E Tiger IIs, and 2 F5B Freedom Fighters. (The latter may have become a training aircraft, but the IISS still listed them as part of Yemen's combat capable aircraft in 2006.)

Since 1990, Yemen's total number of training aircraft has, however, increased from 15 to 44, the largest increase in Yemen's Air Force structure. The most notable addition has been the purchase of Z-242s from the Czech Republic.

Helicopters and Transport Aircraft

The total number of helicopters operated by the Yemeni Air Force has also been on the decline. In 1990, Yemen reportedly had 76 helicopters, but by 2000 this number declined to 25, and in 2006 it reached 20. Most of the old helicopters that it had in 1990 (including Ka-26, AB-204, AB-206, Mi-4, and SA-316) were decommissioned or were inoperable in the mid-1990s. According to the IISS, in 2006, Yemen had 8 Mi-35 and 9 Mi-8 attack helicopters of unknown readiness and sustainability. In addition, Yemen had several transport aircraft, which are listed in Figure 10.4.[31]

Overall Assessment

Yemen has some effective squadron elements, but cannot operate as a modern air force and has little sustainability. Pilot training is limited, and Yemen lacks anything approaching a modern command and control, battle management, and air control and warning system for its air units and land-based air defenses. Joint warfare capability is token at best.

YEMENI AIR DEFENSE FORCES

Yemen's land-based air defense units have a nominal strength of some 1,500–2,000 men. They are equipped with SA-2, SA-3, and SA-6 heavy surface-to-air missiles, but it is unclear how many are operational or sustainable in combat and few—if any—have been modernized to improve their resistance to jamming and detection. Yemen has large numbers of AA guns and lighter SA-7, SA-9, SA-13, and SA-14 man-portable and vehicle-mounted light surface-to-air missiles (SAMs), but their operational status is unknown.

Figure 10.5 reflects the fact that few unclassified data are available on the Yemeni Air Defense system. Aside from manpower, the ISSS provides little data on most of Yemen's SAM batteries and how many missiles Yemen actually has. *Jane's Sentinel Security Assessment* asserts that Yemen has 100 SAM SA-7s and 12 SAM SA-9 batteries, but it lists all other SAM designations as "not available."

The bulk of Yemen's systems are obsolete to obsolescent. Sensor and command control facilities are limited in modernization and technical effectiveness. Readiness and training are poor, as are most aspects of maintenance and sustainability. Electronic warfare capability is obsolete.

THE YEMENI NAVY

The Yemeni Navy has an important potential role. In addition to its location near the Bab al-Mandeb, Yemen has a 1,030-nautical-mile coastline and major ports at Aden and Al Hudaydah. It has important islands near major shipping channels, including Socottra, Kamaran, and Perim.

In 2006, the Yemeni Navy had 1,700 men and was based on the Indian Ocean and the Red Sea at Aden, Al-Katib, and Al-Hadaidah, with smaller bases at Al Mukalla and on the islands of Perim (Barim) and Socotra (Suqutra). Figure 10.6 shows that the Yemeni Navy has had little modernization over the last decade. Between 2000 and 2005/2006, the fleet shrank in size, and manpower dropped slightly from 1,800 to 1,700.

Surface Combat Forces

Two of the navy's missile patrol boats were Osa II–class vessels in disrepair. One may be decommissioned and the other's SSM system may not function.[32] A

Figure 10.5 Yemeni Air Defense's Force Structure Trends, 1990–2006

	1990	2000	2005	2006
Manpower	?*	**2,000**	**2,000**	**2,000**
Active	?	2,000	2,000	2,000
Reserve	?	0	0	0
Air Defense Missiles	22	0	?	?
SAM SA-2	10	0	0	0
SAM SA-3 Goa	6	?	?	?
SP SA-13 Gopher	0	0	?	?
SP SA-6 Gainful	5	?	?	?
SP SA-9 Gaskin	0	0	?	?
TOWED SA-2 Guideline	0	?	?	?
MANPAD SA-14 Gremlin	0	0	?	?
MANPAD SA-7 Grail	0	0	?	?
Tactical Missiles	**0**	**0**	?	?
AAM AA-2 Atoll	?	?	?	?
AIM-9 Sidewinder	0	?	?	?

* Note: All "?" refer to weapons that Yemen is believed to possess, though the exact numbers in its possession are unknown. In 1990, no figures were available regarding the manpower of the Yemeni Air Defense. At that time, Air Defense was maintained by the Yemeni Air Force, but one can extrapolate that it was near 2,000.

Source: IISS, *Military Balance,* various editions, including 1989–1990, 1999–2000, 2004–2005, and 2005–2006.

385-ton Tarantu–class missile patrol boat was operational, but seems to lack all four of its Styx SS-N-2C antiship missiles.

The navy has three 171-ton Huangfen-class missile patrol boats that should be equipped with relatively effective C-801 ship-to-ship missiles. However, one (the Huangfen 126) was not equipped with missiles, and the Huangfen 128 ran ashore some years ago and was still damaged, though functional.

Smaller patrol boats include two to three 39-ton Zhuk class and six 12-ton Baklan class. There are two Sana'a-class patrol boats, but only one is functioning.[33]

A 804-ton Natya minesweeper is believed to have limited operational status.[34] At least two of five 804-ton Yevgenya class mine-hunters are operational (though it is possible that all are functioning), but probably can be used only for mine-laying purposes. Mine stocks seem to include relatively simple FSU and Chinese types.

The navy is seeking to improve its capabilities through the purchase of ten fast Austal patrol boats, which could help Yemen combat the smuggling of weapons in

Figure 10.6   Yemeni Navy's Force Structure Trends, 1990–2006

	1990	2000	2005	2006
Manpower	**1,500**	**1,800**	**1,700**	**1,700**
Active	1,500	1,800	1,700	1,700
Patrol and Coastal Combatants	**14**	**20**	**18**	**18**
Misc. Boats and Crafts	0	6	6	6
PFI:	8	8	5	5
Sana'a	3	3	2	2*
Zhuk	5	5	3	3
PFM:	6	6	7	8
Huangfen	0	3	3	3
Huangfen with Sardine Tactical SSM	0	0	0	1
Osa II	6	0	2	2
Tarantu l	0	2*	2*	2*
Mine Warfare	**3**	**6**	**6**	**6**
MHC Yevgenya	3	5	5	5
MSO Natya	0	1	1	1
Amphibious Landing Crafts	**6**	**3**	**7**	**7**
LSM Polnochy	4	0	0	0
LST Ropucha	1	1	1	1
LCU PI NS-717	0	0	4	4
LCU Ondatra	2	2	2	2
Logistics and Support	**0**	**2**	**2**	**2**
Toplivo	0	2	2	2

*   One of these boats is inoperative.
Source: IISS, *Military Balance,* various editions, including 1989–1990, 1999–2000, 2004–2005, and
      2005–2006.

its harbors, as well as the entry of terrorist suspects into its country.[35] These ten
Austral patrol boats are reported to have sailed for Yemen on February 9, 2005. They
have a maximum speed of 29 knots and carry two 12.7-mm machine guns and a
twin 25-mm gun mounting.[36]

As part of a Yemeni security pact with the French regarding the Bab al-Mandeb
Strait, the French have agreed to provide support systems for the ten Austal-built
patrol boats, as well as Yemen's six Baklan patrol boats.[37]

Amphibious Forces

Yemen has a number of amphibious ships. These include one NS-722-class LSM, three Deba-class (NS-717) LCUs, and two Ondatra-class (Project 1176) LCUs. The Ropucha-class LST is now a hulk and will be replaced by the NS-722 class.

The NS-722 is 1,383-ton vessel that can carry five T-72 tanks and 111 troops or marines. It is a modern Polish-built ship delivered in May 2002, and it is capable of cadet training and disaster relief operations as well as amphibious missions.

The two Ondatras are 145-ton ships capable of transport of squad-level forces and a major armored vehicle. The three Deba-class ships are modern 221-ton ships capable of lifting 16 tons of cargo and 50 troops. Yemen has possessed two Toplivo tankers whose operational capacity is unknown.[38] *Jane's Fighting Ships* reports that they may be decommissioned, while the IISS *Military Balance* makes no mention of this.[39]

Overall Assessment

Yemen's naval readiness, training, and war-fighting capabilities are minimal. The navy is not capable of independent operations against a regional naval power like Iran, Oman, Saudi Arabia, or Egypt, but could carry out limited asymmetric attacks by mining the Strait of Bab al-Mandeb or shipping routes in the Red Sea. It could also harass shipping traffic.

The purchase of these fast patrol boats illustrates that Yemen is attempting to streamline its navy against threats such as piracy and smuggling, rather than against foreign conventional navies. Between 1990 and 2000, Yemen added six Baklan fast patrol boats and doubled the number of mine-warfare ships from three to six.

The changes are designed to help Yemen use what naval resources it has to defend its islands and the Bab al-Mandeb Strait from unconventional threats. The Yemeni Navy will not be able to carry out the responsibilities inherent in Yemen's geostrategic position along the Horn of Africa and near the Bab al-Mandeb. However, the Yemeni Navy shares the burden of policing this area with the U.S. Navy, which is now in control of the 1,100 strong Combined Joint Task Force–Horn of Africa (CJTF-HOA) in Djibouti. Together, the two navies attempt to curtail the activities of smugglers and terrorists.[40] In addition to counterterrorism, CJTF-HOA also works closely with other Horn of Africa states on issues of economic development, attempting to stabilize the area.[41]

In addition to working with the U.S. Navy, Yemen signed a security pact with France on February 27, 2005, to monitor the Bab al-Mandeb Strait.[42] The agreement primarily includes the French training of Yemeni units in coastal defense and mountain warfare, but it also provides for the sharing of intelligence and threat assessments to the Strait.[43]

In any case, conventional naval warfare is scarcely Yemen's most urgent threat. Asymmetric attacks by groups such as Al Qa'ida are immediate and have been at the center of Yemen's naval strategic planning. Following the attack on the USS *Cole* and the French oil tanker, Yemen's naval forces have worked closely with outside power projectors to improve its naval force structure to deal with this change in the nature of threat.

Yemen is establishing a small coast guard, but it will be capable only of light patrol duties.

PARAMILITARY, SECURITY, AND INTELLIGENCE FORCES

Yemen has large internal security forces, an almost inevitable development in a country with many internal divisions and tensions. The Ministry of the Interior has some 50,000 men, and there are at least 20,000 tribal levies. These troops have seen a great deal of combat during the last several years, as they have clashed with militant insurgents repeatedly as well as dealt with political unrest and violence.

Main Security and Paramilitary Forces

These threats explain Yemen's need to maintain a security force that is almost two-thirds the size of its army. Figure 10.7 shows a steady maintenance of 50,000 Ministry of Interior (MOI) forces for the past six years, with 20,000 tribal levies (reserves) available if needed. There has, however, been a change in these forces over time. Since the mid-1990s, Yemen has come to rely on trained paramilitary forces instead of levies to maintain order, a sign that its internal security has become more regulated.

Yemen's internal security apparatus has several services. Reporting by *Jane's* indicates that they include the following elements:[44]

Figure 10.7   Yemeni Paramilitary's Force Structure Trends, 1990–2006

	1990*	2000	2005	2006
Manpower	75,000	70,000	70,000	70,000
Active/Ministry of Interior Forces	25,000	50,000	50,000	50,000
Reserves/Tribal levies	50,000	20,000	20,000	20,000
Coast Guard (still being established)	0	0	0	?†
PCI	0	5	5	5
French Interceptor (less100 tons)	0	5	5	5

* The number of forces listed for 1990 is the combined figure of Paramilitary troops for North and South Yemen.
† All "?" refer to weapons that Yemen is believed to possess, though the exact numbers in its possession are unknown.
Source: IISS, *Military Balance,* various editions, including 1989–1990, 1999–2000, 2004–2005, and 2005–2006.

- **Central Security Force (CSF):** This is the main paramilitary internal security force in Yemen. It is under the Ministry of Interior and has an estimated strength of approximately 50,000. The CSF is equipped with medium and heavy machine guns as well as armored personnel carriers.

- **Terrorism Combating Department (TCD):** This was established in March 2002. It has been reported that the TCD is under the auspices of the Yemeni Ministry of Interior and has technical and financial help from the United States. The force, reportedly, is equipped with surveillance cameras, electronic intercept capabilities, and a central command center in Sanaa that links terrorist information records to Yemen's airports and seaports. Its total strength remains unknown.

- **Armed tribal levies:** As noted earlier, these levies total 20,000 from tribes that are loyal to the government. They are not as well trained and are not equipped with any meaningful weapons. They act as reserves that can be called upon in case of political or civil insurrection. It is, however, unclear how useful such a force can be in counterterrorism.

- **Coast Guard:** Yemen did not have a coast guard force. As part of its counterterrorism efforts, Yemen has announced that it was building a small coast guard force that will be under the command of the Ministry of Interior to guard its 1,491 miles of coastline. The fact that it is being built under the MOI highlights the focus of Yemen's counterterrorism planning and the importance of its internal security apparatus.

- **Political Security Organization (PSO):** The main purpose of the PSO is to protect Yemen's political elites. It is used for counterintelligence, counterespionage, and also for gathering intelligence on threats against Yemen's government. Its total strength is unknown.

Yemen's internal security largely depends on domestic intelligence and counter-intelligence services to deal with political strife and conduct counterterrorism operations. Most of the trained elements of these counterterrorism forces have been created since 2002. Both the counterterrorism forces and the new coast guard have been supported by outside powers such as the United States, France, and neighboring Saudi Arabia. Their force effectiveness is unknown, however, and it is unclear how well they would operate without foreign assistance.

The absence of a dedicated and well-equipped border guard is a key problem in Yemen's internal security apparatus. Yemen's Army has the responsibility of control-ling Yemen's border, but Yemen's Army is trained to deal with protecting Yemen against conventional armies crossing its borders from Saudi Arabia or Oman. This helps explain Saudi Arabia's concern about Yemen's border control, particularly against weapons smuggling and terrorist infiltration.

Yemen's Struggle against Terrorism

Yemen's most pressing threat is from terrorism organizations operating on its soil, and some estimates indicate Yemen had 5,000 nonstate armed combatants in 2005.[45] This includes tribes that are not under the control of the Yemeni government, but it also includes terrorist organizations with large memberships inside Yemen. Some of the more notable militant organizations that maintained a presence in Yemen include the following:[46]

- **Gama'a al-Islamiyya:** Its strength has been in decline since the late 1990s due to arrests by the Egyptian government (where it is primarily based) and a cease-fire that was signed with the Egyptian government in 1997. Most of its members, however, are believed to be Egyptian.

- **Yemen Islamic Jihad:** This group has close association with Egyptian Islamic Jihad. Its membership is believed to be Yemenis, Egyptians, Algerians, and Saudis. Its leadership is largely composed of fighters from the Afghan war. Its leader, Tariq al-Fasdli, helped the current Yemeni government during the civil war. After the war, the failure of the Yemeni government to incorporate these fighters in the regular Yemeni Army is seen as one of the reasons that these fighters turned against the Yemeni government. Its total strength is unknown, but it is believed that the group enjoys support among the tribes in the south and even some political elite in the Yemeni government.

- **Aden-Abyan Islamic Army (AAIA):** Its strength is unknown, and its membership is largely Yemeni. This group is believed to have been established in 1996 as a splinter group from Al-Jihad, but it first came to prominence in December 1998 by kidnapping 16 Western tourists and killing 4 of them. It is also believed to be behind the attack against the French oil tanker, *Limburg,* in October 2002. The Yemeni government has attempted to combat this group by closing some of its bases and pressuring its leadership. Its total strength in Yemen is unknown, but it is also believed to have international connections with extremist organizations such as Al Qa'ida and British extremist cleric Abu Hamza al-Masri.

- **Al Qa'ida:** Yemen's most troublesome terrorist group, however, has remained Al Qa'ida, even though its presence in Yemen has been reduced by post-9/11 countermeasures. As of February 2005, it was still believed to possess several thousand members worldwide, with potentially thousands of followers in Yemen of multiple nationalities. It has connections with local organizations, as noted earlier, including the AAIA. It is believed to have been behind the USS *Cole* bombing and was involved in helping the AAIA in the bombing against the French oil tanker.

- **Liwa al-Tawhid (Banner of Unity):** This group is believed to be a splinter group, or a subunion between Al Qa'ida and Al-Jihad. It first came to prominence after the assassination of security officials in December 2003. As is the case with most of these splinter groups, determining their actual size given their association is highly uncertain.

As this list reveals, Yemen's internal security is threatened by both the "usual suspects" and by Yemeni splinter groups that have association to transnational groups such as Al Qa'ida. In addition, Yemen's counterterrorism efforts have escalated the tension caused by internal power struggles within Yemen's government and by the brief Yemeni civil war that began in May 1994 and ended the following July. The Yemeni government has been fighting militants since the bombing of the USS *Cole* in October 2000, but these fighters have been a part of Yemen's history since the early 1980s.

Most of these groups have their origins—at least at the leadership level—to fighters in the Afghan war in the 1980s. In response to the Soviet invasion of Afghanistan, Yemen began sending fighters to Afghanistan. When the Soviets withdrew from Afghanistan in 1988, North Yemen welcomed many of them back. These fighters brought their militancy as well as their ties to groups such as Al Qa'ida and Osama bin Laden back to Yemen.[47]

In addition, bin Laden has strong ties to some of the tribes of Hadhramaut, a mountainous region of Yemen, where his father's family is believed to have come from. Using these ties, bin Laden recruited Yemenis for his training camps and is believed to have used the nation as an additional training site starting in 1993.[48] The operations in Yemen included using the Yemeni ports as sources of arms smuggling, an exercise that persists to this day.

The suicide bombing on the USS *Cole* on October 22, 2000, put pressure on the Yemeni government to crack down on the militants. The U.S. government began actively working with Yemen on counterterrorism in an official capacity. Efforts to combat these militants, however, dated back to 1997, when the government acknowledged that the groups posed a serious threat to the state's legitimacy.[49]

One of the most public results of the cooperation between the United States and Yemen was the elimination of six Al Qa'ida members, who were killed by a predator drone while driving in Yemen on November 6, 2002. It has been reported that U.S. forces were tipped off by Yemeni intelligence.[50] Military assistance between the United States and Yemen has also occurred in the exchange of military equipment and spare parts. Yemen received $1.9 million in Foreign Military Financing in 2003. This number increased by 685 percent in 2004 to an estimated $14.9 million.[51]

Internal counterterrorism efforts were further enhanced in early 2005, as the government began enforcing its policy on cracking down on potential terrorist organizations and hotbeds. This included the use of mass arrests, prosecutions that resulted in jail time, and additional heavy guards on various government buildings and embassies.[52]

There were some gaps in the efforts of the Yemeni paramilitary, as two USS *Cole* suspects, Fahd al-Qasaa and Jamal al-Badawi, escaped custody and had to be recaptured in April 2004.[53] Once recaptured, however, each was tried and convicted; Qasaa received 10 years, and Badawi's sentence was reduced from death to 15 years. In addition to prosecuting terror suspects, in April 2005, the Yemeni government began threatening the underground radical schools with shutting them down. It is estimated that these radical schools have as many as 330,000 students.[54]

Yemeni authorities have also claimed that their security forces have thwarted major attacks against western and Yemeni targets. For example, a day before Yemen's presidential election, on September 20, 2006, President Ali Abdullah Saleh announced that terrorist operations were foiled against some American targets and a hotel in Sanaa. These announcements, however, came after two suicide attacks took place on two oil installations in Yemen, causing minor damage and killing one guard.[55]

Pattern of Attacks

The threat from Al Qa'ida to Yemen's internal stability is not over. While there have not been "spectacular" attacks on the scale of the one against the USS *Cole,* attacks against soft targets by extremists groups (Al Qa'ida included), however, continued to occur. The following timeline, based on information adapted from the U.S. National Memorial Institute for the Prevention of Terrorism (MIPT) Knowledge Base, shows major attacks in Yemen between 2001 and 2006:[56]

- **January 23, 2001:** In Aden, a Yemeni, Mohammed Yehia Ali Sattar, hijacked a Yemeni plane carrying U.S. Ambassador Barbara Bodine and 90 other people. Sattar wished to show support for Saddam Hussein by flying to Baghdad airport to protest Iraq's international isolation. He was armed with a gun and possibly a grenade. Sattar was subdued by the members of the crew and was hospitalized with self-inflicted injuries. There were no deaths and no injuries in the attack besides Sattar.

- **January 24, 2001:** In Sanaa, a bomb exploded in front of the house of Brigadier-General Staff Ahmad Shamlan, Commander of the First Defense Brigade of the Presidential Guard. The bomb exploded when a guard opened the gate for the General's car. The attempt is the first to be reported against such a high-ranking security official in the defense brigades of the President.

- **February 12, 2001:** In Hijrat al-Dawagher, a convoy transporting Trade Minister Abdul al-Kumayem and Mahwit's Provincial Governor Abdul Hamid Numan came under attack by gunfire in an ambush by unknown tribesmen.

- **May 19, 2001:** In Radaa, a remote bomb exploded in a gun market, killing 32 and wounding 50. No group claimed responsibility for the explosion, and while terrorism was never ruled out as the cause of the attack, it is also possible the explosion was caused by carelessly stored weapons.

- **September 20, 2001:** In Sanaa, an explosive device detonated near the Sheraton Hotel, where a group of FBI agents was staying. Four people were killed and an unknown number were injured.

- **October 14, 2001:** In Sanaa, a bomb detonated in a garbage bin near the residence of Yemeni President Ali Abdullah Salih. No one was killed or wounded. Police later arrested at least six people in connection with the attack.

- **March 3, 2002:** In Sanaa, a university student tossed two concussion grenades at a wall of the U.S. Embassy the day after Vice President Dick Cheney visited Yemen. There were no injuries.

- **October 6, 2002:** In Mina al Dubah, a Bulgarian was killed and 12 Bulgarians and Frenchmen were wounded in an attack on a French oil tanker, the *Limburg.* The attack was a carried out by a suicide bomber/bombers on a small boat, done in the same style as the USS *Cole.* The AAIA claimed responsibility, though the group admitted that its initial target was a U.S. Navy vessel, not the tanker.

- **December 28, 2002:** In Sanaa, Jarullah Omar, the second ranking official of the Yemeni Socialist Party, was killed as a result of gunshot wounds that he received while attending a conference for the opposition Yemeni Reforms Party.

- **May 14, 2003:** In Sanaa, a bomb exploded in a Yemeni court, injuring a judge and three others. The attack came four days after a different judge at the court sentenced suspected Al Qa'ida militant Abed Abdul Razzah Kamel, 30, to death for killing three Americans who worked at a Christian-run hospital in Jibla.
- **December 4, 2003:** In Shabwa, the Governor of the region, Ali Ahmad al Rasas, was wounded in an ambush, and his brother, Rasas Ahmad, a top intelligence official, was killed by gunmen. The militant group Takfir wal Hijra was blamed for the attack.
- **June 18, 2004:** In Sanna, Hussein Badreddin al-Houthi began a rebellion bearing his name, desiring greater autonomy for his tribe and region. His forces inflicted a total of 400 casualties and almost captured the city before they were repelled by government forces.[57]
- **January 31, 2005:** In the Ma'rib region, armed tribesmen opened fire on Yemeni security forces, resulting in a one-day gun battle. Two soldiers and four attackers were killed, and 16 people were injured. No group claimed responsibility.
- **February 2, 2005:** In Amran two gunmen attacked a Japanese-funded cement factory, wounding two guards. No group claimed responsibility.
- **March 27–28, 2005:** In Nushur, assailants attacked a police patrol, killing between four and seven police officers. The attack was believed to be in retaliation for the killing of Sheikh al-Houthi by the army in late August 2004 and the over 400 civilians who were killed during the fighting. No group claimed responsibility, although it was widely understood that the Faithful Youth Organization, part of the rebellion led by al-Houthi Sr., was responsible.
- **April 3, 2005:** In Sa'dah Governorate, unknown assailants attacked the Sa'dah Security Commander, killing one bodyguard. No group claimed responsibility.
- **April 3, 2005:** In the Talh area, Sa'dah, gunmen fired on the Secretary-General of the Sa'dah local council as he was driving, but failed to kill him. No group claimed responsibility.
- **April 3, 2005:** In Sanaa, an unidentified assailant lobbed a hand grenade out of the window of a passing car at the Central Customs Authority building, killing one civilian and wounding one other. No group claimed responsibility.
- **June 21, 2005:** In Sanaa, one assailant detonated a bomb outside Sana'a University, wounding three civilians, destroying a car, and causing minor damage to the campus. No group claimed responsibility, although authorities have arrested one man, whom they believe was responsible.
- **June 22, 2005:** In Sanaa, assailants armed with automatic weapons fired on the car of a Yemeni Parliament official, killing the official, and wounding two other passengers. No group claimed responsibility, although the Deputy Governor of Al-Baydha Governorate, Abdullah Al-Qawsi, claimed responsibility for the murder.
- **January 17, 2006:** In Zumar, Yehya Mousa, the Yemeni Minister of Justice, was beaten by two masked men and shot in an assassination attempt. Mousa survived the attack, and the assailants are believed to be members of the al-Houthi rebellion.
- **September 14, 2006:** Two nearly simultaneous attacks against two oil installations killed one guard and caused minor damage at those installations. The attack came only several days before Yemen's Presidential elections (September 20, 2006).

- **September 16, 2006:** Yemeni authorities arrested four suspected Al Qa'ida members following a seven-hour siege in Sanna of their holdout. Security forces announced that they found 1,200 pounds of explosives.[58]

What this timeline shows is that before the attacks of "9/11," attacks on foreign diplomatic targets and the Yemeni government assets took place almost on a monthly basis. After 2002, Yemen began seeing major attacks on the government every six months, a noticeable decrease. Political unrest in 2004 and the downward turn of Yemen's economy in 2005 have also brought a higher spurt of violent attacks in Yemen than had been seen since 2001.

Political Unrest

Al Qa'ida and other extremists have not been Yemen's only internal security problem. President Ali Abdullah Salih began facing an internal rebellion led by Hussein Badreddin al-Houthi, a political insider who wanted increased autonomy for his tribe and for his region of Yemen. Al-Houthi disliked President Salih's connection to Washington and opposed U.S. involvement in Iraq. On June 18, 2004, the rebellion assaulted government forces near Sanaa and inflicted hundreds of casualties. The rebels nearly took control of the city.[59]

The rebellion saw a change in leadership when Hussein Badreddin al-Houthi was killed in September 2004. Badreddin al-Houthi, father of the slain Hussein, took over the rebellion in the name of his son. Since that time, al-Houthi Sr. has attempted to broaden his coalition base and has continued fighting.[60] Between March 27 and March 28, 2005, al-Houthi rebels engaged Yemeni troops in a gun battle that killed 400 civilians. In April 2005, the rebels and paramilitary forces fought again, as the paramilitary troops attempted to arrest al-Houthi Sr. There were 250 casualties total.[61]

Groups that take hostages, kidnap, and hold people for ransom are another problem. The primary weapon of these groups, such as the AAIA, is the kidnapping and ransoming of Westerners. In 1998, the AAIA kidnapped 16 Westerners, and in 2005, another group kidnapped 65-year-old German diplomat Juergen Chrobog and his wife, as well as six Italian tourists in January 2006.[62] These groups also attempted bombings of Anglican Churches and Western hotels.[63]

Such groups do not, however, confine themselves to such low-level operations. In October 2002, the AAIA attempted a suicide boat attack on the French oil tanker *Limburg* and killed a Bulgarian crew member and wounded 12 others.[64] The government has repeatedly vowed to crack down on these abductions by arresting and prosecuting the individuals performing the abductions, but the kidnappings have continued despite repeated convictions of offenders.[65] Since this last incident, the AAIA has been relatively quiet, and since the execution of its leader, Zain al-Abidin al-Midhar, in October 1999, it has not been as distinguishable from other Islamic militants.[66]

Yemen's weak economy adds more pressure on internal security.[67] On July 22, 2005, Yemeni troops and tanks dispersed protesters who were angry over the doubling of fuel prices. The protests lasted two days and claimed 36 lives by the time they were dispersed.[68]

YEMEN'S CONTINUING STRATEGIC CHALLENGES

Yemen's primary security needs are internal and are driven by its need for economic reform and social stability. As has been touched upon earlier, 45 percent of the population lives below the poverty line, and unemployment is at least 35 percent.[69] This high unemployment poses a serious risk in light of Yemen's demographic situation. Yemen's population is young—46.5 percent of the population is between ages 0–14, and as the population grows into adulthood, the lack of work and economic opportunities will make the population fertile ground for Al Qa'ida recruitment campaigns and exploitation.

Socioeconomic Challenges

Yemen is an impoverished nation with a young society. The Yemeni economy can scarcely meet its current employment requirement, and if it its economy has not grown sufficiently to employ its youth as they come of age, there will be a demographic/socioeconomic "time bomb."[70]

Figure 10.8 shows the extreme disproportionate nature of Yemen's demographic distribution. Nearly half the population, 47 percent, is between the ages of 0–14. No other groups come close to this percentage. Even the widest category of 30–64 years of age totals only 22 percent. When these young people enter into the workforce in the next decade, the current Yemeni economy will not be able to provide them with work, and they may become a fertile recruiting ground for Al Qa'ida and other militant groups.

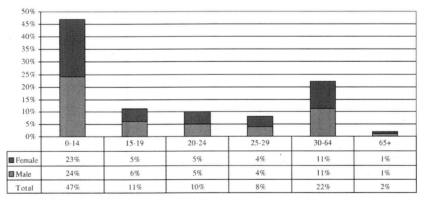

	0-14	15-19	20-24	25-29	30-64	65+
Female	23%	5%	5%	4%	11%	1%
Male	24%	6%	5%	4%	11%	1%
Total	47%	11%	10%	8%	22%	2%

Source: IISS, *Military Balance, 2005-2006*.

Figure 10.8   Yemen's Demographic Distribution, 2006

Yemen's economy also may face decreases in oil revenues due to the depletion of its oil reserves and production capacity. While Yemen is not a major producer compared to its neighbors, oil revenues play an important part in its economy. The depletion of Yemen's oil reserves poses a serious threat to Yemen's financial security, as oil income represenst 60–70 percent of the Yemeni government's total revenue.[71]

Rises in oil prices have helped offset Yemen's oil production plans. Oil revenues were $1.95 billion in 1997, $1.37 billion in 1998, $2.17 billion in 1999, $3.6 billion in 2000, $2.93 billion in 2001, $3.21 billion in 2002, $3.51 billion in 2003, $4.35 billion in 2004, and $5.92 billion in 2005. Yemen's oil production has been falling since 2002.[72] In 2005, Yemen averaged 0.387 million barrels per day (MMBD), approximately 85 percent of what its production level was in 2002.[73] In addition, a 2002 World Bank Survey estimated that by 2008 Yemen's production would fall to less than half of its 2001 level.[74] Yemen's oil revenues have risen this past year because of rising global oil demand and oil prices, but as Yemen's current oil reserves and production decline, prices will not be able to outpace the loss of production, and Yemen's economic woes could become a crisis.[75]

Structural economic reform is difficult, and governmental corruption plagues Yemen's efforts to receive aid and attract foreign direct investment. Foreign investors have been reluctant to give the large amounts of aid or invest in Yemen's economy due to the lack of transparency and the weakness of its judicial system.[76] These risks, however, are further compounded by Yemen's internal insecurity. Foreign companies, including oil and gas multinationals, fear for their workers and investments from attacks by militant groups and the overall political uncertainty in Yemen.

Yemen's judicial system is in need of steady strengthening as well. Yemen is a decentralized state with lawless areas that exist beyond the control of the paramilitary. These regions often use local tribal laws and customs to punish offenders, rather than turn them over to national courts for prosecution.[77] In addition, most of Yemen's rural areas are impoverished. Yemen must continue to aid these rural areas by targeting foreign aid toward their economic development, which will in time strengthen the Republic's influence over them.[78]

Yemen's economy is inefficient, plagued by corruption, experiences slow growth, and has high double-digit inflation and unemployment. The World Bank proposed structural economic reforms on four levels for Yemen. It proposes better economic management, improved structural policies, greater social inclusion, and better public sector management. The economic management refers to monetary policies that can combat inflation and reduce budget deficits.[79]

It also recommends deregulating parts of Yemen's economy to spark growth. The most important recommendation is the proposed reforms on public sector management, specifically corruption and budgetary transparency.[80] It is estimated that Yemen averages $9 million a year in corruption, and this remains one of the largest issues that aid organizations have in funding Yemen's programs.[81] In addition, despite the fact that Yemen desperately needs to combat corruption, some scholars have noted very little desire within the Yemeni government to begin the reforms.[82] Yemen's economy is likely to continue to slide unless it gets serious about structural economic change, and thus far, the government has not taken steps to address all the World Bank's recommendations.

As noted earlier, the Yemeni economy is currently heavily dependent on oil. According to the World Bank, Yemen has the potential to mildly diversify its economy. Yemen has shown economic growth in sectors such as fisheries, tourism, and gasoline exports, and the World Bank believes that these areas can be developed further to diversify Yemen's economy. The World Bank does report, however, that continued long-term growth will continue to be a challenge for Yemen, as it has no industry that can match its oil revenues.[83]

The Bab al-Mandeb

The Bab al-Mandeb is a strategic issue because of its importance as a chokepoint affecting Gulf oil shipments through the Red Sea and shipping through the Suez Canal and the Red Sea. It is situated between Eritrea and Djibouti and Yemen at the southern end of the Red Sea at the entrance to the Gulf of Aden and the Arabian Sea. It is the preferred route for tankers and shipping moving from the Gulf to Europe and the United States. The Energy Information Administration estimates that some 3.2–3.3 MMBD of oil moved through the Bab al-Mandeb in 2003, and recent peaks have brought this total to substantially higher levels.[84]

Any major disruption or closure of the Bab al-Mandeb could prevent tankers carrying Gulf oil from using the Red Sea and the Suez Canal/Sumed Pipeline complex and force them to go around the southern tip of Africa (the Cape of Good Hope), greatly increasing transit time and cost, limiting the tanker capacity now available on world markets. The one alternative is the East-West oil pipeline, which traverses Saudi Arabia and has a capacity of about 4.8 MMBD.

There have not been recent threats to the Bab al-Mandeb or tanker traffic in the Red Sea. Libya did, however, scatter mines in the shipping lanes in the Red Sea in the past, during a period of peak tension with Egypt. While there were reports that South Yemen might try to close the Bab al-Mendab in the 1970s and early 1980s, these reports were largely speculation.

The one tangible set of clashes that affected the security of shipping in the region occurred in December 1995 and August 1996. Yemen and Eritrea disputed control over the Hanish Islands, which are located just north of the Bab al-Mandeb. The issue was, however, resolved by diplomatic means. The two countries agreed to put their case before an international court of arbitration [Permanent Court of Arbitration (PCA)] in October 1996. In October 1998, the PCA ruled that the Hanish Islands are subject to the territorial sovereignty of Yemen. In December of 1999, the PCA issued its ruling on the maritime boundary. Both countries have since accepted these decisions.

Relations with Neighboring States

Relations with Yemen's neighbors, including Oman, the United Arab Emirates, and Saudi Arabia have improved over the past several years and will likely continue to do so. As mentioned earlier, Yemen has been displeased with Saudi Arabia's attempts to build a wall along parts of the Yemeni border where smuggling is prominent, but this dispute has been handled diplomatically and has not strained relations.

Yemen's borders and harbors are porous and scarcely guarded. This has allowed militants fleeing from the U.S. invasion of Afghanistan, as well as weapons, drugs, and explosives smugglers, to move from Yemen into neighboring countries.[85] Militants are also able to move into Oman and Saudi Arabia from Yemen, which makes an unguarded Yemen a potential threat to their internal security. The border treaty signed with Saudi Arabia in 2002 resolved the exact location of the border in contested areas, but the follow-through by Yemen to police its agreed borders has not been forthcoming. Yemen will face increased pressure from its neighbors to control its borders, and if it cannot, then the Saudis will likely continue building walls around the Yemeni border to restrict traffic between the two countries.[86]

The dominating issue for Yemen's neighbors is Yemen's internal security problems. Militants easily can slip into Saudi Arabia and Oman from Yemen, and aside from creating a stronger border guard, the best solution for curbing Yemen's domestic troubles is to aid the Yemeni government's security efforts. This will entail continued peaceful negotiations over issues for the preservation of overall goodwill. By keeping hostilities to a minimum, Saudi Arabia and Oman will allow Yemen to focus its military budget on internal security rather than on conventional forces designed to face external threats.

Ongoing Internal Instability

While Yemen's external threats are minimal, its internal problems are serious and may increase over the coming years. Despite the countermeasures taken by Yemen since the year 2000, the violence caused by Yemen's various factions has not stopped. President Salih is often described as a moderate whose power depends on his ability not to alienate too many groups at once.[87]

As noted earlier, Yemen had a previous history of allowing militants to return from foreign conflicts. Since the USS *Cole* bombing and 9/11, times have changed, and it is likely that President Salih's security forces will attempt to apprehend many of the militants when they return from fighting. With Yemen's unguarded borders, however, there will be large portions of militants that slip through undetected. These militants, having gained experience fighting American forces, can and will destabilize Yemen even further. Unless they are occupied in Iraq for a long period of time, it will be difficult for Yemen's security forces to face even more opponents than already exist.

Al Qa'ida remains strong in Yemen, with a membership that could be in the thousands. In addition, smaller groups also continue to play a key role in Yemen's internal instability. The kidnapping of Westerners remains a problem, and al-Houthi Sr. has not been captured, making his rebellion a continued threat.

The invasion of Iraq has stirred more of Yemen's militants into action, making the job of Yemen's security forces more difficult. In addition, some militants have gone to

Iraq to fight American forces. In whatever way the war in Iraq ends, these militants will return to Yemen after its conclusion, and they could destabilize the state even further.

In order to deal with these challenges, Yemen's internal security forces need to adapt their strategy to deal with these threats. In addition, Yemen's internal economic, social, and political dynamics are likely to adapt over time to lessen the level of poverty in its rural areas and limit Al Qa'ida's ability at recruiting, particularly among its young male population.

Internal stability will likely continue to be Yemen's greatest challenge. Yemen will likely continue to increase its military budget to improve its naval patrolling abilities and to maintain its paramilitary. It is likely that Yemen will continue to need U.S. and French aid in guarding the Horn of Africa. It is even possible that if Yemen does not make a strong effort to eliminate corruption and diversify its economy, then foreign powers may have to take a larger role in ridding Yemen of hostile forces. The following is a summary or checklist of things Yemen will face in the upcoming years:

- **Demographic Time Bomb:** Yemen is a poor country with a young society. Out of its population, 45 percent live below the poverty line, and 46.5 percent of its people are age 14 and below.[88] If Yemen's economy has not grown sufficiently to employ its youth as they come of age, there will be a demographic/socioeconomic crisis. With 35 percent unemployment, Yemen's young and growing population has little hope of finding steady work. While unemployed, these youth become prey to militant groups looking for new members.[89] The high unemployment rate will also likely lead to more protests like the ones that occurred over the loss of subsidies in July 2005.[90]

- **Terrorism and Counterterrorism:** As noted earlier, Yemen faces a threat from terrorist groups of varying size, strength, and organization. Most of them have proven capable of violence on some scale, and they remain a burden for the security forces.[91] Al Qa'ida remains the largest terrorist group in Yemen, as its membership is estimated in the thousands. It has the greatest organizational capability of any militant group, and despite Yemeni antiterrorism efforts, Al Qa'ida is still capable of large-scale attacks.[92] Among key concerns will remain protecting foreign ships from maritime attacks like those that occurred against the *Cole* and the *Limburg*.[93] Yemeni forces will also continue to be concerned with militant groups kidnapping and ransoming Westerners.

- **Militants in Iraq:** Many of the militant groups that reside within Yemen, including Al Qa'ida and the al-Houthi followers, oppose Yemeni cooperation with the United States and the occupation of Iraq.[94] These militants will return to Yemen, and with Yemen's unguarded borders, many can slip through undetected. These militants, having gained experience fighting American and Iraqi forces, can destabilize Yemen.

- **The al-Houthi Rebellion:** The rebellion led by Baddredin al-Houthi has not been put down. The rebels have carried out attacks as recently as January 17, 2006, and al-Houthi will likely remain a strategic challenge for the Yemeni government until he is either appeased or arrested. The rebellion has proven itself capable of launching large-scale assaults when it engaged security forces in June 2004 and in March 2005. It has also shown that it can carry out small-scale attacks like the beating of Justice Minister

Yehya Mousa in January 2006.[95] Yemen will be pressed to resolve the al-Houthi Rebellion, as both the rebels and militant groups stretch the security forces.

- **Economic Reforms:** Yemen's economy is inefficient, plagued by corruption, experiences slow growth, and has high double-digit inflation and unemployment. The World Bank recommends that Yemen create new monetary policies that can combat inflation and shrink deficits. It also suggests that Yemen should deregulate parts of its economy to spark growth. The World Bank also acknowledges that Yemen will need to add greater transparency to its budgetary process in order to curb inflation.[96] Yemen averages $9 million a year in corruption, and this gives pause to foreign investors who do not want to see their investments squandered.[97] The Yemeni government has not taken serious steps to follow the World Bank's proposed reforms. Without economic reform, it will be difficult for Yemen's economy to grow or attract foreign investors.

- **Border Security:** Yemen has extremely limited border checks and patrols. Smugglers and militants exploit this deficiency, and some of Yemen's neighbors like Saudi Arabia fear that militants may migrate from Yemen and take refuge in their countries.[98] The problem of Yemen's inability to control its land borders is compounded by the challenge of controlling its harbors. Several Al Qa'ida suspects have fled Pakistan and Afghanistan and entered the Arabian Peninsula through Yemeni ports.[99] Yemen will continue to face pressure to establish firmer control over who enters its country. In the end, however, Yemen's resources are so limited that neighboring countries and the United States may have to guard the harbors and borders themselves.

In addition to these internal challenges, Yemen continues to suffer from the political uncertainties that plague much of the Middle East and the Gulf. Ali Abdullah Saleh, Yemen's President, has ruled Yemen with an iron fist, but not without challenges. In September 2006, Saleh ran for reelection. His main challenger was Faisal bin Shalman, a former oil minister. Shamlan was part of an opposition umbrella group, the Common Forum, which included people of different ideological persuasions.[100]

While the Common Forum objected to early results that showed Saleh winning by a large margin, many believe that the election was one of the more open ones in Yemen's history. As is the case with many of the countries in the region, elections are just a first step. In addition, regardless of the actual integrity of the procedures, no one believed that Salen would actually lose the election. The key question for Yemen's immediate future, however, is whether allowing an opposition group to nominate a challenge to Saleh was a first step in an array of "internal reforms" or whether it is a one-time policy shift.

Furthermore, many see the role of Ahmad, Saleh's son, who is also the head of the Yemeni Republican Guards and Special Forces, as another key uncertainty in the next several years.[101] It remains a major question whether Yemen will follow Syria (and many believe Egypt in the near future) to allow the transition from father to son and abandon its tradition of a "republic." On the other hand, some experts argue that such transitions might be healthy to ensure internal stability and "evolutionary" reforms in the long run. Regardless, these questions add to the aura of uncertainty facing Yemen in the short-term.

Balancing Internal Security and Conventional Military Needs

Military spending is a serious internal security issue. As noted earlier, Yemen's military budget has doubled over the past five years, rising from $482 million (U.S. dollars) in 2001, to $809 million in 2003, to $942 million in 2005.[102] Most of this increase is believed to have gone toward Yemen's Air Force (i.e., the purchase of the MiGs), to its Navy and the upgrading/purchasing of new patrol boats, and to Yemen's security forces, which deal with Yemen's numerous internal militant groups.

The main purpose of Yemen's conventional military forces now centers around protecting its harbors from illicit activities and attacks, as well as using a modern air force to put down rebellions like those led by Baddredin al-Houthi. However, Yemen desperately needs money for economic and social reform, and funding effective security forces limits Yemen's ability to expand its conventional forces, which are out of date and far weaker than its neighbors.

In addition to maintaining a streamlined and relevant conventional military, Yemen must also maintain and possibly expand its 70,000-man internal security force. Yemen has chosen to meet these demands by doubling its military spending between the years 2001 and 2005 (from $482 million to $942 million).[103] This money has been used to purchase MiG-29 fighters, as well as ten new Austal-class fast patrol boats.

Yemen has not expanded its security forces personnel in recent years, but as terrorist attacks have increased in 2005, and with the threat of insurgents returning from Iraq, Yemen may have to decide to halt further purchases of aircraft or boats for increased paramilitary equipment.[104] It is equally important to note that while counterterrorism forces such as the TCD have been created, their effectiveness remains uncertain. Yemen's internal security forces have been trained to put down political uprisings; the forces often rely on the use of too much force and informal intelligence sources.

Yemen must find a way to maintain (or possibly increase) its internal security force without abandoning needed upgrades to its air force and navy. Not neglecting Yemen's need for patrol craft is especially critical because it is one of Yemen's only ways to counter the smuggling and maritime terrorist attacks that take place around its harbors.

Given Yemen's strategic location, maritime security is of paramount importance to both Yemen's security and to international maritime trade. Control of the seas is something Yemen is attempting to achieve. The purchase of the ten fast Austal patrol boats will help Yemen arrest terror suspects who travel by boat to Saudi Arabia or up the Gulf Coast to Iraq.[105]

It is important to note, however, that the task of policing the geostrategic Horn of Africa and the Bab al-Mandeb Strait is beyond the capabilities of the Yemeni Navy. It would require Yemen's cooperation with neighboring states such as Saudi Arabia as well as outside power projectors in the region such as the United States, France, and Britain. This has started by the signing of a security pact between France and Yemen. The United States Navy also maintains a permanent presence in Djibouti.

Conclusion: The New Balancing Act in the Gulf

It is always tempting to go beyond analysis and try to make policy recommendations. In broad terms, however, the country-by-country studies may do a better job of speaking about the relative need for change than any effort to provide yet another set of well-meaning and ineffective recommendations. There has been major progress in most of the countries analyzed in this book, and it is often clear that regimes not only recognize their problems, but also are working hard to solve at least some of them.

There is a relatively high margin of mid- to long-term risk in the dynamics of Gulf security, but this is scarcely new. The key challenges lie in developments in Iran and Iraq: in the draft of Iranian politics toward hard-line radicalism and in the risks posed by Iranian efforts to proliferate and develop capabilities for asymmetric warfare. They are matched by the risk of the breakup of Iraq, a crippling level of civil war, or simply years of violent sectarian and ethnic tension and failed governance and development.

Neo-Salafi extremism and terrorism are also important risks, and there is the risk of an emerging split between Sunni and Shi'ite and new forms of Shi'ite radicalism. The various divisions within the southern Gulf are important, but are unlikely to be critical to Gulf stability and security unless the United States should cease to be a stabilizing presence, Iraq should implode into division or civil war, or Iran should become far more reckless and adventurous than it is today.

There are no broad regional polices that can change this situation. For all of the talk of the obsolescence of nation-sates, even transnational sources of instability like neo-Salafi extremism still play out on a country-by-country level. Complex security problems require complex (and time-consuming) solutions; they cannot be solved by slogans or the kind of policies or strategies that can be summarized in a fortune cookie.

As long as Gulf security is driven by national differences and values, the list of security problems and issues discussed for each country is to all intents and purposes a list of the need for country-by-country solutions. There is nothing particularly complex or subtle about what needs to be done at the national level. If regimes react intelligently to these realities, their problems can be controlled. If not, they will lead to steadily growing risks of war and steadily more serious internal security problems.

THE NEED FOR MORE EFFECTIVE SECURITY STRUCTURES

It is easy to go call for more unity of effort and collective security structures in the Gulf. In fact, a number of strategic analysts inside and outside the Gulf have done so for decades. If one could only persuade regimes to look beyond their present rivalries and tensions, virtually all analysts agree that it would be desirable for the Gulf States to keep the United States and other outside powers "over the horizon," to avoid proliferation, halt needless military spending, and seek to isolate the Gulf from other regional quarrels and tensions. Political, social, and economic development all offer higher rewards than strategic and military competition. Removing military tensions is a key step in improving the ability to cooperate against extremism and terrorism.

From a purely rational viewpoint, the Gulf Cooperation Council should have become an instant success. There has long been good reason for the southern Gulf States to work with Iraq and every reason for them to find ways of eventually co-opting Iran into a common security concept.

If the southern Gulf States are ever to create truly effective forces, they need to look beyond the national level where there are truly petty tensions and make more effective and collective efforts to improve their conventional forces. The path to more effective security cooperation is also well understood by Gulf military planners. Obvious measures include efforts to do the following:

- Create an effective planning system for collective defense and truly standardized and/or interoperable forces.
- Integrate command, control, communications, computers, and intelligence and sensor nets for air and naval combat, including beyond visual range and night warfare capabilities.
- Create joint air defense and air attack capabilities.
- Establish effective cross-reinforcement and tactical mobility capabilities.
- Set up joint training, support, and infrastructure facilities.
- Create joint air and naval strike forces.
- Deploy joint land defenses of the Kuwaiti/northwestern Saudi borders.
- Prepare for outside or over-the-horizon reinforcement.

- Create common advanced training systems.
- Create improved urban and area security for unconventional warfare and low-intensity combat.
- Emphasize both effective leadership and delegation.
- Place a steadily higher emphasis on officer initiative and truly competitive career selection. Increase reliance on noncommissioned officers and enlisted personnel.
- Balance forces to achieve proper readiness.
- Establish the ability to limit and manage collateral damage.
- Plan for a common effort to deter and defend against the threat of chemical, biological, radiological, and nuclear weapons and covert or long-range delivery.
- Integrate internal security and counterterrorism measures.
- Adopt integrated immigration policies and efforts to reduce dependence on outside labor.
- Accelerate efforts to create a common market, currency, and policies to encourage foreign investment.
- Broaden security efforts for critical infrastructure to allow the "netting" of key national efforts and adopt an integrated approach to energy security, including facilities protection, transnational pipelines, and strategic reserves.

The divisions within the southern Gulf are so serious, and the political dynamics of Iran and Iraq are so unstable, that it makes little sense to talk about including them in a broader regional security structure. This does not, however, mean that the southern Gulf States should not make every effort to create stable diplomatic, security, and economic relations with both northern Gulf States.

Iran and Iraq have clear options that they should pursue on a national basis, and until they do, including them in any meaningful regional structure will be impossible. History has made it all too clear that Iran and Iraq would also have profited far more from focusing on internal development than on an arms race and war, or seeking to dominate the region. Few nations have done as good a job of practicing sheer, self-destructive strategic stupidity so consistently over time.

The benefits Iraq would now gain from moving toward national unity and development are immensely greater than the benefits any group of Iraqis can hope to gain from division, insurgency, or civil war. Iran's efforts to create capabilities for asymmetric warfare and long-range nuclear missile forces do at least as much to threaten it with catastrophic future conflicts as to deter its enemies and strengthen its influence.

As for the United States and Britain, neither thrusting into the Gulf nor being dragged into it has been cost-free. Dealing with the Iran-Iraq War and Iraq's invasion of Kuwait were acts of necessity. Invading Iraq, however, was an optional war and one that may prove to have been a serious strategic mistake. Containing and deterring conflict may be vital national interests for both countries, but intervention and efforts at regime change are a very different thing. It may not be practical to return to an over-the-horizon posture, but it is practical to emphasize cooperation with regional states, helping them build up their capabilities, and strategic restraint coupled to an emphasis on containment and negotiation.

MEETING THE ISLAMIST EXTREMIST CHALLENGE

All the powers in the Gulf confront the reality that transnational religious extremist threats, and violent Neo-Salafi movements like Al Qa'ida, present serious risks. They need to find every practical way they can to improve their cooperation in preventing Islamist extremism from dividing Islam and the region and blocking the political, economic, and social reforms that are critical to true internal and regional security.

For all the reasons cited in this book, progress will be slow. Yet, cooperation in counterterrorism is a critical new priority, as is finding a new balance between regular military forces, the ability to defend against internal security threats and asymmetric warfare, and fund reform. Hard trade-offs need to be made at both the national and regional levels.

At the same time, the preceding analysis is a warning that internal security efforts, and various internal reforms, are likely to be no substitute for a direct effort by the states in the region (and the Islamic world) to directly counter the challenge of Islamic extremism at the religious and political levels. The tendency to avoid such confrontation simply strengthens extremism and the risk of serious sectarian splits among Sunni, Shi'ite, and other Islamic threats. It is Islamic extremism—not some vague, generic form of global terrorism—that is the threat. This threat can be countered only by directly challenging it at the religious and ideological levels.

Furthermore, the West has problems of its own. The efforts of Western nations like the United States to counter such extremism at the ideological level by promoting Western culture and democracy often do more harm than good. Reform needs to be encouraged at the local and national levels and by supporting domestic voices calling for the full mix of political, economic, and social reforms. The West needs to accept that the Gulf will ultimately move at its own pace and in its own way. Outside voices can influence, but not shape the results.

TAKING RESPONSIBILITY VS. CONTINUING EXERCISES IN FUTILITY

It is important to emphasize that all of these security problems do not mean that a great deal of progress is not currently under way in various Gulf states. Military forces are being reformed. Increased internal security efforts are mixed with reform, and there is less repression in the process.

Countries are beginning to openly address the need for trade-offs between security forces and the kind of reforms that bring lasting security. A new round of oil wealth is being used with more wisdom than in the past, particularly in countries like Qatar and Saudi Arabia.

That said, nothing about the history of the region, or its current behavior, fosters great faith that it will make more rapid progress than it is today or will evolve beyond the current level of national tensions that now shape the balance of security efforts in the region. Well-meant strategic rhetoric may pave the road to strategic studies with good intentions, but the reality is almost certain to be that nations will cooperate only in limited areas and when they perceive that immediate threats are so serious that they are forced to act.

The Gulf is scarcely alone in exporting its problems. Every regime and nation finds blaming outside powers and movements irresistible. The extent to which nations focus on exporting their problems rather than solving them is, however, one major factor in shaping failed states. It is a certain indication of failed regimes and failed intellectuals. Unfortunately, the Gulf has far too many leaders and intellectuals who prefer exporting blame to taking responsibility and meaningful practical action. Its history of tension, conflict, and poorly structured national security efforts make it all too clear that far too few in the Gulf have learned that it is results, not rhetoric, that count.

Notes

CHAPTER 1

1. The CIA notes that boundary agreement was signed and ratified with Oman in 2003 for entire border, including Oman's Musandam Peninsula and Al Madhah enclaves, but contents of the agreement and maps showing the alignment have not been published. CIA, "UAE," *The World Factbook, 2006,* https://www.cia.gov/cia/publications/factbook/index.html.

2. CIA, "UAE," *The World Factbook, 2006,* https://www.cia.gov/cia/publications/factbook/index.html.

3. "Iran-Iraq War, 1980–1988," Global Security, http://www.globalsecurity.org/military/world/war/iran-iraq.htm01/03/2005.

4. The U.S. Department of Defense, "'Eagle Resolve' Focused on Reducing WMD Vulnerabilities," Gulf Exercise, May 23, 2005.

5. Richard Nield, "Steady As She Goes," *Middle East Economic Digest* 48, no. 48 (November 26, 2004): 4–6.

6. Brad Bourland, "Saudi Arabia's 2005 Budget; 2004 Performance," *SAMBA Economy Watch* (December 11, 2004).

7. See Col. Ernie Howard, "The Strategic Logic of Suicide Terror," Air University Warfare Studies Institute, April 2004.

8. Department of Defense, Quadrennial Defense Review Report, Washington, Department of Defense, February 6, 2006, http://www.defenselink.mil/qdr/, p. 24.

CHAPTER 2

1. CIA, "Bahrain," *The World Factbook, 2006,* https://www.cia.gov/cia/publications/factbook/index.html.

2. Ibid.

3. "Executive Summary, Bahrain," *Jane's Sentinel Security Assessments: The Gulf States* (December 19, 2005): 3.

4. "Bahrain's Sectarian Challenge," International Crisis Group, Middle East Report no. 40 (May 6, 2005): 1.

5. "Executive Summary, Bahrain," 1; and "Bahrain Background Note," U.S. Department of State, Bureau of Near Eastern Affairs, January 2006, http://www.state.gov/r/pa/ei/bgn/26414.htm.

6. "Executive Summary, Bahrain," 2.

7. "Executive Summary, Bahrain," 3.

8. IISS, *Military Balance* (London: International Institute for Strategic Studies), various editions.

9. Riad Kahwaji, "Bahrain to Scrutinize Future Defense Buys," *Defense News* (February 2, 2004): 3; and IISS, *Military Balance 2005–2006* (London: IISS).

10. "Navy, Bahrain," *Jane's Sentinel Security Assessments: The Gulf States* (November 29, 2004): 1.

11. CIA, "Bahrain."

12. "Security, Bahrain," *Jane's Sentinel Security Assessments: The Gulf States* (November 29, 2004): 13; and "Bahrain Risk: Political Stability Risk," *The Economist Intelligence Unit* (April 22, 2004): 13.

13. IISS, *Military Balance 2005–2006;* and "Army, Bahrain," *Jane's Sentinel Security Assessments: The Gulf States* (November 16, 2005): 4.

14. IISS, *Military Balance 2005–2006;* and "Army, Bahrain," 4.

15. IISS, *Military Balance 2005–2006;* and "Army, Bahrain," 4.

16. "Army, Bahrain," 4.

17. This description is adapted from the *Encyclopedia Astronautica,* available at http://www.astronautix.com/lvs/atacms.htm.

18. IISS, *Military Balance 2005–2006;* and "Army, Bahrain," 5.

19. IISS, *Military Balance 2006* (London: IISS).

20. Damian Kemp, "Bahrain Amiri Air Force Hawk 129 Makes Maiden Flight," *Jane's Defence Weekly* (September 7, 2006).

21. IISS, *Military Balance 2005–2006;* and "Air Force, Bahrain," *Jane's Sentinel Security Assessments: The Gulf States* (November 29, 2004): 5.

22. "Air Force, Bahrain," 5.

23. IISS, *Military Balance 2005–2006.*

24. "Air Force, Bahrain," 5.

25. IISS, *Military Balance 2005–2006.*

26. "Air Force, Bahrain," 5–6.

27. Robin Hughes, "Bahrain, Israel Request FMS Packages for Combat Aircraft," *Jane's Defence Weekly* (August 3, 2005).

28. IISS, *Military Balance 2005–2006.*

29. Ibid.

30. "Navy, Bahrain," 3.

31. IISS, *Military Balance 2006.*

32. "Navy, Bahrain," 1.

33. Ibid.

34. Ibid.

35. IISS, *Military Balance 2006;* and "Security and Foreign Forces, Bahrain," *Jane's Sentinel Security Assessments: The Gulf States* (November 29, 2004): 1.

36. IISS, *Military Balance 2006;* and "Navy, Bahrain," 2.

37. "Security and Foreign Forces, Bahrain," 3.

38. IISS, *Military Balance 2004–2005* (London: IISS); and IISS, *Military Balance 2005–2006.*

39. IISS, *Military Balance 2006;* and "Security and Foreign Forces, Bahrain," 3.

40. IISS, *Military Balance 2005–2006.*

41. "Security, Bahrain," 2.

42. "Bahrain Risk: Political Stability Risk," 4.

43. "Executive Summary, Bahrain," 4.

44. "Security and Foreign Forces, Bahrain," 1–3.

45. U.S. Department of State, "Bahrain: Country Reports on Human Rights Practices—2005," Washington, Bureau of Democracy, Human Rights, and Labor, March 8, 2006, http://www.state.gov/g/drl/rls/hrrpt/2005/61686.htm.

46. CIA, "Bahrain"; and "Executive Summary, Bahrain," 5.

47. "Security, Bahrain," 7.

48. CIA, "Bahrain"; and "Executive Summary, Bahrain," 5.

49. Energy Information Association, "Country Analysis Briefs: Bahrain," 1–3, http://www.eia.doe.gov/emeu/cabs/Bahrain/pdf.pdf.

50. Ibid., 1.

51. "Reforming Bahrain's Labour Market," Crown Prince's Court and the Economic Development Board, September 23, 2004, p. 4.

52. CIA, "Bahrain."

53. IISS, *Military Balance 2005–2006.*

54. "Bahrain Risk: Political Stability Risk," 7.

55. "Security, Bahrain," 13.

56. CIA, "Bahrain."

57. "Bahrain Economy: Fewer Barrels from Saudi Arabia," *The Economist Intelligence Unit* (March 15, 2001): 1.

58. "Executive Summary, Bahrain," 2; and "Bahrain Risk: Political Stability Risk," 6.

59. Kenneth Katzman, "Bahrain: Key Issues for U.S. Policy," Congressional Research Service (CRS), March 24, 2005, p. 6.

60. "Bahrain Risk: Political Stability Risk," p. 6.

61. "Executive Summary, Bahrain," 2.

62. "Bahrain's Sectarian Challenge," 1.

63. "Executive Summary, Bahrain," 4.

64. "Bahrain's Sectarian Challenge," 7–8.

65. "Trouble in Bahrain: Symptoms of a Wider Malaise," *Jane's Islamic Affairs Analyst* (January 30, 2006): 1; and CIA, "Bahrain."

66. "Trouble in Bahrain: Symptoms of a Wider Malaise," 1.

67. "Bahrain Risk: Political Stability Risk," 1.

68. "Bahrain's Sectarian Challenge," 1.

69. Associated Press, "Bahrain's King Swears in New Cabinet, but Reformists Say Changes Don't Go Far Enough," January 15, 2005.

70. Associated Press, "Bahrain's Decision to Register Web Sites Provokes Protest from Press Watchdog," April 28, 2005.

71. MIPT Terrorism Knowledge Database, http://www.tkb.org/MapModule.jsp.

72. "Security and Foreign Forces, Bahrain," 2.

73. "Security, Bahrain," 2.

74. "Security and Foreign Forces, Bahrain," 2.

75. "Bahrain's Sectarian Challenge," 8.

76. Ibid., 7.

77. Ibid., 7.

78. "Executive Summary, Bahrain," 1.

79. "Trouble in Bahrain: Symptoms of a Wider Malaise," 1.

80. "Executive Summary, Bahrain," 1.

81. "Bahrain Risk: Political Stability Risk," 3.

82. "Executive Summary, Bahrain," 3.

83. IISS, *Military Balance 2005–2006;* and Kahwaji, "Bahrain to Scrutinize Future Defense Buys," 3.

84. Kemp, "Bahrain Amiri Air Force Hawk 129 Makes Maiden Flight"; and Hughes; and "Bahrain, Israel Request FMS Packages for Combat Aircraft."

CHAPTER 3

1. CIA, "Kuwait," *The World Factbook, 2006,* https://www.cia.gov/cia/publications/factbook/index.html.

2. Britain took *de facto* control of Kuwait from 1899 until independence in 1961, although the al-Sabah family continued civil rule.

3. Energy Information Association (EIA), "Country Analysis Briefs: Kuwait," http://www.eia.doe.gov/emeu/cabs/kuwait.html.

4. EIA, "Country Analysis Briefs: Kuwait"; and CIA, "Kuwait."

5. Joseph Rohe, "US Grants Kuwait 'Major Non-NATO Ally' Status," *Jane's Defence Weekly* (April 2, 2004).

6. EIA, "Country Analysis Briefs: Kuwait."

7. Ibid.

8. Ibid.

9. Ibid.

10. Riad Kahwaji, "Parliament-MoD Row Delays C4I Deal in Kuwait," *Defense News* (December 1, 2003): 34.

11. CIA, "Kuwait."

12. "Army, Kuwait," *Jane's Sentinel Security Assessment: The Gulf States* (October 24, 2005).

13. According to *Jane's Sentinel Security Assessment: Gulf States,* Kuwait has 1,600 foreign personnel in its army, whereas the International Institute for Strategic Studies (IISS), *Military Balance,* estimated the number is closer to 3,700.

14. "Army: Kuwait."

15. IISS, *Military Balance 2000–2001* (London: IISS).

16. Christopher Foss, "Kuwait Receives Latest Condor 2," *Jane's Defence Weekly* (November 25, 2004).

17. Christopher Foss, "Decision Time Looms for Kuwaiti APC Selection," *Jane's Defence Weekly* (January 25, 2006).

18. Jiri Kominek, "Two Gulf States Weigh Up Heavy Transporter Bids," *Jane's Defence Weekly* (July 2, 2003): 18.

19. "Kuwait-TOW-2A/B Anti-Armor Guided Missiles," Defense Security Cooperation Agency News Release, August 4, 2005, http://www.dsca.mil/PressReleases/36-b/2005/kuwait_05-38.pdf.

20. Smerch 9K58 multiple rocket system, http://www.army-technology.com/projects/smerch/.

21. "Air Force: Kuwait," *Jane's Sentinel Security Assessment: Gulf States* (October 24, 2005).

22. The lower estimates are from the IISS, *Military Balance 2005–2006* (London: IISS), and the higher estimates are from *Jane's Sentinel Security Assessment: The Gulf States* (December 19, 2005).

23. Ed Blanche, "Regional Briefing—Gulf States: Winds of Change," *Jane's Defence Weekly* (February 9, 2005).

24. Katy Glassborow, "General Electric Lands Hornet Engine Contract," *Jane's Navy International* (March 1, 2006).

25. James Murphy, "US Congress Notified of Possible F/A-18 Support Sale to Kuwait," *Jane's Defence Industry* (October 1, 2005).

26. *Jane's* and IISS, *Military Balance,* mostly agree on the number of operational helicopters: the total number, including nonoperational, comes from *Jane's*. For the AS-332 Super Puma, the lower estimate is from *Jane's* and the higher one is from the IISS, *Military Balance*.

27. See http://www.globalsecurity.org/space/systems/patriot.htm.

28. In a December 10, 2004, press release, The U.S. Army claimed,

Patriot missile operations were conducted on an extremely dense and complex battlefield where more than 41,000 sorties were flown by coalition air forces. Forty-one active duty Army and 13 coalition Patriot batteries were deployed to OIF, serving in 8 countries.

Two unfortunate incidents of fratricide or "friendly fire," involving U.S. Navy F/A-18 and British Royal Air Force Tornado aircraft resulted in three fatalities. The U.S. Army regrets the loss of life and expresses condolences to the family members.

In a third incident a U.S. Air Force F-16 fired on a Patriot battery but there were no deaths or injuries. United States Central Command (USCENTCOM) concluded their investigations into these incidents and results are posted on the CENTCOM web site at www.centcom.mil. Application of lessons learned in OIF has already improved upon Patriot's performance and the system will be continuously refined. Improvements include combinations of hardware modifications, software changes and updates to tactics, techniques and procedures.

Some changes include the integration of satellite radio technology at the Battalion Information Coordination Central which provides improved situational awareness through voice and data connectivity with higher headquarters Identification and Engagement Authority as well as enhanced command and control; and software improvements that enable better identification, classification and correlation of airborne objects. In addition the Army continues to explore and evaluate new opportunities to improve performance and reduce the risk of fratricide.

29. Voice of America, http://www.globalsecurity.org/wmd/library/news/iraq/1998/980222b_voa.htm.

30. "Kuwait, Navy," *Jane's Sentinel Security Assessment: The Gulf States* (October 25, 2005).

31. Richard Scott and Robin Hughes, "Kuwait Seeks FMS Deal for Fast Interceptor Boats," *Jane's Defence Weekly* (December 14, 2005); Nick Brown, "Kuwait to Acquire New

Guns for Navy Interceptors," *Jane's Defense Weekly* (July 12, 2006): 20.

32. "Kuwait Selects SINCGARS," *Jane's Defence Weekly* (November 13, 2002).

33. "Kuwait Buys Aerostat," *Jane's Defence Weekly* (December 10, 2003).

34. "News in Brief: Patrol Boats for Kuwait," *Jane's Navy International* (March 1, 2005).

35. U.S. Department of State, "Kuwait: Country Reports on Human Rights Practices—2005," Washington, Bureau of Democracy, Human Rights, and Labor, March 8, 2006, http://www.state.gov/g/drl/rls/hrrpt/2005/61692.htm.

36. "Security and Foreign Forces: Kuwait," *Jane's Sentinel Security Assessment: Gulf States* (June 13, 2005).

37. U.S. Department of State, "Kuwait."

38. "Security and Foreign Forces: Kuwait," *Jane's Sentinel Security Assessment: Gulf States* (June 13, 2005).

39. Ibid.

40. Ibid.

41. Michael Knights, "Northern Gulf Vulnerable to Infiltration by Terrorist Groups," *Jane's Intelligence Review* (October 1, 2005).

42. Ibid.

43. Ibid.

44. "Security and Foreign Forces: Kuwait," *Jane's Sentinel Security Assessment: Gulf States* (June 13, 2005).

45. Stephen Ulph, "Gulf—Islamic Militancy Kicks off in Kuwait," *Jane's Islamic Affairs Analyst* (February 1, 2005).

46. Ibid.

47. Ibid.

48. Knights, "Northern Gulf Vulnerable to Infiltration."

49. Ibid.

50. Ibid.

51. Knights, "Northern Gulf Vulnerable to Infiltration"; and "Security and Foreign Forces: Kuwait," *Jane's Sentinel Security Assessment: Gulf States* (January 4, 2006).

52. Knights, "Northern Gulf Vulnerable to Infiltration"; and "Security and Foreign Forces: Kuwait," *Jane's Sentinel Security Assessment: Gulf States* (January 4, 2006).

53. Knights, "Northern Gulf Vulnerable to Infiltration"; and "Security and Foreign Forces: Kuwait," *Jane's Sentinel Security Assessment: Gulf States* (January 4, 2006).

54. "Security and Foreign Forces: Kuwait," *Jane's Sentinel Security Assessment: Gulf States* (January 4, 2006).

55. Ibid.

56. Knights, "Northern Gulf Vulnerable to Infiltration."

57. "Security and Foreign Forces: Kuwait," *Jane's Sentinel Security Assessment: Gulf States* (January 4, 2006).

58. Ibid.

59. Knights, "Northern Gulf Vulnerable to Infiltration."

60. "Security and Foreign Forces: Kuwait," *Jane's Sentinel Security Assessment: Gulf States* (January 4, 2006).

61. Ibid.

62. Ibid.

63. Ibid.

64. Ulph, "Gulf—Islamic Militancy Kicks off in Kuwait"; and "Security and Foreign Forces: Kuwait," *Jane's Sentinel Security Assessment: Gulf States* (January 4, 2006).

65. Knights, "Northern Gulf Vulnerable to Infiltration."

66. Ulph, "Gulf—Islamic Militancy Kicks off in Kuwait"; and "Security and Foreign Forces: Kuwait," *Jane's Sentinel Security Assessment: Gulf States* (January 4, 2006).

67. Ulph, "Gulf—Islamic Militancy Kicks off in Kuwait."

68. Ibid.

69. "Security and Foreign Forces: Kuwait," *Jane's Sentinel Security Assessment: Gulf States* (January 4, 2006).

70. Ibid.

71. Ibid.

72. Ibid.

73. Ibid.

74. Ibid.

75. "Kuwait—Kuwaiti Court Sentenced 18 Men to Three Years' Imprisonment," *Jane's Terrorism & Security Monitor* (May 18, 2005).

76. "Security and Foreign Forces: Kuwait," *Jane's Sentinel Security Assessment: Gulf States* (January 4, 2006).

77. Knights, "Northern Gulf Vulnerable to Infiltration."

78. Ibid.

79. Ibid.

80. Ibid.

81. "Sheikh-up," *The Economist* (January 21, 2006).

82. Simon Henderson, "Kuwait's Parliament Decides Who Rules," PolicyWatch #1073, The Washington Institute for Near East Policy, January 27, 2006.

83. U.S. Department of State, "Kuwait."

84. Knights, "Northern Gulf Vulnerable to Infiltration by Terrorist Groups."

85. "Seismic Shock in Kuwait," *Jane's Islamic Affairs Analyst* (July 1, 2005).

86. According to *Jane's Islamic Affairs Analyst* ("Seismic Shock in Kuwait"), there are just under 140,000 male voters in Kuwait. According to the U.S. Department of State ("Kuwait"), there are 143,000 male voters.

87. "Seismic Shock in Kuwait."

88. "Kuwait's Elections and Results," *The Estimate* (July 3, 2006): 2.

89. Population Division of the Department of Economic and Social Affairs of the United Nations Secretariat, *World Population Prospects: The 2004 Revision,* http://esa.un.org/unpp/.

90. CIA, *The World Factbook, 2006,* http://www.cia.gov/cia/publications/factbook/geos/ku.html.

91. UN, *World Population Policies 2003* (New York: United Nations, 2004).

92. Andrzej Kapiszweski, "Arab Labor Migration to the GCC States," IOM (September 2003): 14.

93. U.S. Department of State, "Kuwait."

94. Ibid.

95. Ibid.

96. Ibid.

97. Ulph, "Gulf—Islamic Militancy Kicks off in Kuwait."

98. "Security and Foreign Forces: Kuwait," *Jane's Sentinel Security Assessment: Gulf States* (January 4, 2006).

99. "Kuwait's Internal Divisions Exposed," *Jane's Islamic Affairs Analyst* (October 28, 2005).

100. "Security and Foreign Forces: Kuwait," *Jane's Sentinel Security Assessment: Gulf States* (January 4, 2006).

101. Khalid Al-Rodhan, "The Saudi and Gulf Stock Markets," CSIS Report, October 25, 2005, http://www.csis.org/.

102. "Arab Stock Markets Hit by Losses," *Aljazeera.net,* March 14, 2006, http://english.aljazeera.net/NR/exeres/140F02FE-0CEE-4785-B7A4-4DD1976B94D2.htm.

103. "Saudi Blocks Qatar Pipeline," *Jane's Foreign Report* (November 3, 2005).

104. "In Brief: Iran, Kuwait Sign Security MoU," *Jane's Defence Weekly* (March 29, 2006).

105. "Kuwait's Internal Divisions Exposed," *Jane's Islamic Affairs Analyst* (October 28, 2005).

CHAPTER 4

1. This analysis draws heavily upon the Energy Information Agency (EIA) analysis of "World Oil Transit Chokepoints," September 2005, ""http://www.eia.doe.gov/emeu/cabs/World_Oil_Transit_Chokepoints/Hormuz.html.

2. An e-mail message to the authors from Omani officials, September 18, 2006.

3. "Executive Summary: Oman," *Jane's Sentinel Security Assessment: The Gulf States* (December 19, 2005): 3.

4. EIA, "Country Analysis Briefs: Oman," March 2006, http://www.eia.doe.gov/emeu/cabs/Oman/Full.html.

5. "Executive Summary: Oman," 3.

6. An e-mail message to the authors from Omani officials, September 18, 2006.

7. "Executive Summary: Oman," 1.

8. "Security and Foreign Forces: Oman," *Jane's Sentinel Security Assessment: The Gulf States* (September 19, 2005): 2, 4; and IISS, *Military Balance* (London: International Institute for Strategic Studies, 2006).

9. "Executive Summary: Oman," 4.

10. Ibid., 2.

11. U.S. Department of State, Bureau of Near Eastern Affairs, "Background Note: Oman" February 2006, http://www.state.gov/r/pa/ei/bgn/26414.htm.

12. Ibid.

13. Ibid.

14. Ibid.

15. CIA, *The World Factbook, 2006,* https://www.cia.gov/cia/publications/factbook/index.html.

16. U.S. Department of State, "Background Note: Oman."

17. "Executive Summary: Oman," 5.

18. This analysis draws heavily upon EIA, "Country Analysis Briefs: Oman"; other sources include the *Middle East Economic Digest;* and CIA, *The World Factbook.*

19. This analysis draws heavily upon EIA, "Country Analysis Briefs: Oman."

20. CIA, *The World Factbook.*

21. IISS, *Military Balance* (London: International Institute for Strategic Studies), various years. The GDP data for 2005 are from CIA, *The World Factbook, 2005.*

22. U.S. Department of State, "Background Note: Oman."

23. "Armed Forces: Oman," *Jane's Sentinel Security Assessment: The Gulf States* (October 24, 2005): 3.

24. "Executive Summary: Oman," 4.

25. IISS, *Military Balance, 2006.*

26. "Executive Summary: Oman," 5.

27. IISS, *Military Balance, 2006.*

28. IISS, *Military Balance, 2006;* and "Army, Oman," *Jane's Sentinel Security Assessment: The Gulf States* (November 16, 2005): 7.

29. Robin Hughes, "Oman Selects Javelin ATGW," *Jane's Defence Weekly* (January 19, 2005); "Saudi Arabia Continues with Defense Push," *Jane's Defense Weekly* (August 9, 2006): 18.

30. IISS, *Military Balance, 2006;* and "Army, Oman," 7.

31. IISS, *Military Balance, 2006;* and "Army, Oman," 7.

32. "Army, Oman," 7.

33. "Executive Summary: Oman," 3.

34. Robin Hughes, "Oman Receives First Block 50+ F-16," *Jane's Defence Weekly* (August 17, 2005).

35. Robin Hughes, "Omani F-16s to Get Reconnaissance Pods," *Jane's Defence Weekly* (February 11, 2004).

36. "PANTERA Pods for Oman and Poland," *Jane's Defence Weekly* (January 7, 2004).

37. IISS, *Military Balance, 2006.*

38. IISS, *Military Balance, 2006;* and "Air Force, Oman," *Jane's Sentinel Security Assessment: The Gulf States* (October 24, 2005): 4.

39. IISS, *Military Balance, 2006;* and "Navy: Oman," *Jane's Sentinel Security Assessment: The Gulf States* (October 24, 2005): 3.

40. Robin Hughes, "Oman and UAE Bolster Coastal Protection," *Jane's Defence Weekly* (February 11, 2004).

41. Richard Scott, "Oman Chooses VL MICA Missile for OPVs," *Jane's Defense Weekly* (July 26, 2006): 19.

42. "Army: Oman," 3.

43. IISS, *Military Balance, 2006;* and Christopher Foss, "Oman Gets Chinese Armoured Personnel Carriers," *Jane's Defence Weekly* (September 24, 2003).

44. MIPT Terrorism Knowledge Base, http://www.tkb.org/MapModule.jsp.

45. James Boxell, "VT Poised to Land £400 Order to Supply Oman Order," *Financial Times Companies UK* (April 14, 2006).

46. MIPT Terrorism Knowledge Base.

47. "Security and Foreign Forces: Oman," 1–2.

48. U.S. Department of State, "Oman: Country Reports on Human Rights Practices—2005," March 8, 2006, http://www.state.gov/g/drl/rls/hrrpt/2005/61696.htm.

49. MIPT Terrorism Knowledge Base.

50. "Security and Foreign Forces: Oman," 1.

51. "Executive Summary: Oman," 2; and CIA, *The World Factbook, 2006.*

52. U.S. Department of State, "Country Reports on Terrorism 2005," April 2006, p. 141, http://www.state.gov/documents/organization/65462.pdf.

53. "Security and Foreign Forces: Oman," 2.

54. "Oman Risk: Political Stability Risk," *The Economist Intelligence Unit* (April 22, 2004): 5.

55. "Executive Summary: Oman," 4.
56. Ibid.
57. "Security and Foreign Forces: Oman," 7.
58. Ibid.
59. Ibid., 9.
60. "Executive Summary: Oman," 3.
61. "Security and Foreign Forces: Oman," 8.
62. "Executive Summary: Oman," 5; and "Security and Foreign Forces: Oman," 10.
63. U.S. Department of State, "Oman: Country Reports on Human Rights Practices."
64. "Security and Foreign Forces: Oman," 9–10.
65. "Executive Summary: Oman," 5.
66. "Security and Foreign Forces: Oman," 11.
67. Economist Intelligence Unit, Online Database, Country Data 2005, http://eiu.com.
68. EIA, "Country Analysis Briefs: Oman."
69. "Security and Foreign Forces: Oman," 9.
70. "Security and Foreign Forces: Oman," 8.
71. "Executive Summary: Oman," 3; and "Oman Risk," 5.
72. "Executive Summary: Oman," 3.
73. "Security and Foreign Forces: Oman," 2.
74. "Oman Risk," 6.
75. "Executive Summary: Oman," 3.
76. Ibid., 2.
77. "Oman Risk," 2.
78. "Executive Summary: Oman," 4.

CHAPTER 5

1. U.S. Department of State, *World Military Expenditures and Arms Transfers, 1999–2000* (Washington, DC: U.S. Department of State, June 2002).
2. "Executive Summary: Qatar," *Jane's Sentinel Security Assessment: Gulf States* (May 3, 2005).
3. CIA, *The World Factbook, 2006,* https://www.cia.gov/cia/publications/factbook/index.html.
4. CIA, *The World Factbook, 2006.*
5. Richard F. Grimmett, "Conventional Arms Transfers to Developing Nations, 1997–2004," Congressional Research Service, RL33051, August 29, 2005.
6. U.S. Department of State, *World Military Expenditures and Arms Transfers, 1999–2000.*
7. Ed Blanche, "Regional Briefing—Gulf States: Winds of Change," *Jane's Defence Weekly* (February 9, 2005).
8. Ibid.
9. "Security and Foreign Forces: Qatar," *Jane's Sentinel Security Assessment: Gulf States* (May 3, 2005).
10. "Armed Forces: Qatar," *Jane's Sentinel Security Assessment: Gulf States* (May 3, 2004).
11. CIA *The World Factbook, 2006.*
12. IISS, *Military Balance, 2005–2006* (London: International Institute for Strategic Studies).
13. "Air Force: Qatar," *Jane's Sentinel Security Assessment: Gulf States* (May 3, 2005).

14. Vivek Raghuvanshi, "India to Buy Mirage 2000-5 Aircraft from Qatar," *Defense News* (October 25, 2004): 24.

15. IISS, *Military Balance,* 2006.

16. "Air Force: Qatar."

17. Ibid.

18. Ibid.

19. "Navy: Qatar," *Jane's Sentinel Security Assessment: Gulf States* (May 3, 2005).

20. Richard Scott, "Qatar Orders Fast Interceptor Craft," *Jane's Defense Weekly* (February 12, 2003).

21. "Navy: Qatar."

22. "Security and Foreign Forces: Qatar."

23. "Executive Summary: Qatar."

24. "Security and Foreign Forces: Qatar."

25. Michael Knights, "Southern Gulf Co-operation Council Countries Brace for Terrorist Attacks," *Jane's Intelligence Review* (November 1, 2005).

26. "GCC Dismantles Peninsula Shield," *Jane's Foreign Report* (January 19, 2006).

27. "Saudi Blocks Qatar Pipeline," *Jane's Foreign Report* (November 3, 2005).

28. "Bridge over Saudi's Troubled Waters," *Jane's Foreign Report* (September 15, 2005).

29. Ibid.

30. "GCC Dismantles Peninsula Shield."

31. "Security and Foreign Forces: Qatar."

32. Energy Information Association, Department of Energy, "Country Analysis Briefs: Qatar, March 2006, http://www.eia.doe.gov/emeu/international/qatar.html#Reports.

33. Michael Knights, "Gulf States Face New Security Challenges," *Jane's Intelligence Review* (May 1, 2005).

34. Mary Anne Weaver, "Democracy by Decree: Can One Man Propel a Country into the Future?" *The New Yorker,* November 20, 2000.

35. "Executive Summary: Qatar."

36. Ibid.

37. Ibid.

38. Weaver, "Democracy by Decree."

39. "All That Jazeera," *The Economist* (June 21, 2003); also, "The World through Their Eyes—Arab Satellite Television," *The Economist* (February 26, 2005).

40. "Saudi Blocks Qatar Pipeline."

41. Knights, "Southern Gulf Co-operation Council Countries Brace."

42. "Executive Summary: Qatar."

43. Knights, "Southern Gulf Co-operation Council Countries Brace."

44. "Qatar Economic Forum Eyes Billions," *Aljazeera.net,* March 12, 2006, http://english .aljazeera.net/NR/exeres/725AFCF0-57F2-4EF7-8129-230D000C9CF5.htm.

45. Knights, "Southern Gulf Co-operation Council Countries Brace."

46. Ibid.

47. Ibid.

48. Ibid.

49. Ibid.

50. Ibid.

51. Population Division of the Department of Economic and Social Affairs of the United Nations Secretariat, *World Population Prospects: The 2004 Revision,* http://esa.un.org/unpp/.

52. Ibid.

53. CIA, "Qatar," *The World Factbook,* January 10, 2006, https://www.cia.gov/cia/publications/factbook/index.html.

54. This was estimated by the authors.

55. "Security and Foreign Forces: Qatar."

56. IISS, *The Military Balance 2005–2006,* 206.

57. CIA, "Qatar," *The World Factbook.*

58. Knights, "Southern Gulf Co-operation Council Countries Brace."

59. Ibid.

CHAPTER 6

1. CIA, *The World Factbook, 2006,* https://www.cia.gov/cia/publications/factbook/index.html.

2. Population Division of the Department of Economic and social Affairs of the United Nations Secretariate, *World Population Prospects: The 2004 Revision,* http://esa.un.org/unpp/.

3. Authors' estimate based on the CIA, *The World Factbook, 2006.*

4. P. K. Abdul Ghafour, "Security Body to Draw Out Domestic, Foreign Policies," *Arab News,* October 18, 2005, www.arabnews.com.

5. "NSC Given Wide Powers," *Arab News,* October 19, 2005, www.arabnews.com.

6. Ibid.

7. U.S. Department of State, *Annual Report on Military Expenditures, 1999,* submitted to the Committee on Appropriations of the U.S. Senate and the Committee on Appropriations of the U.S. House of Representatives, July 27, 2000, in accordance with section 511(b) of the Foreign Operations, Export Financing, and Related Programs Appropriations Act, 1993.

8. IISS, *Military Balance* (London: International Institute for Strategic Studies), various editions.

9. Ibid. This number includes the National Guard

10. The FY1988 budget was planned to have a $10 billion deficit, with $8 billion in foreign borrowing. It involved the first foreign borrowing in 25 years and the first increase in taxes in 8 years—all on foreign businesses. The actual budget reached a $15–17-billion deficit by the year's end, with some $10 billion in financing. See *Economist* (January 16, 1988): 59; and *Defense News* (January 18, 1988): 4.

11. This is based on various editions of the CIA, *The World Factbook.* Some of the differences between these estimates may, however, reflect differences in the CIA definition of GDP and military expenditures.

12. *Report on Allied Contributions to the Common Defense, March 2001, June 2002, July 2003,* Report to the U.S. Congress by the Secretary of Defense, http://www.defenselink.mil/pubs/allied.html.

13. Interview with an official of the Office of the Secretary of Defense, February 2001.

14. *Defense News* (November 20–26, 1995): 27.

15. Richard F. Grimmett, *Conventional Arms Transfers to the Third World, 1985–1992,* Washington, Congressional Research Service, CRS-93-656F, July 19, 1993, 59, 69; *Conventional Arms Transfers to the Third World, 1989–1996,* Washington, Congressional Research Service, CRS-97-778F, August 13, 1997, 53, 65; and *Conventional Arms Transfers to the Third World, 1992–1996,* Washington, Congressional Research Service, CRS-RL30640, August 18, 2000, 47–49, 58–60.

16. James Boxell, "Saudis in $19bn Eurofighter Deal," *Financial Times* (August 18, 2006).

17. Grimmett, *Conventional Arms Transfers to the Third World, 1989–1996,* 53, 65–66.

18. Richard F. Grimmett, *Conventional Arms Transfers to the Third World, 1996–2003,* Washington, Congressional Research Service, CRS-RL32547, August 26, 2004, 53, 51–61.

19. Richard F. Grimmett, *Conventional Arms Transfer to Developing Nations, 1996–2000,* Washington, Congressional Research Service, CRS RL32547, August 26, 2004, 50, 61.

20. See Arms Control and Disarmament Agency (ACDA), "High Costs of the Persian Gulf War," *World Military Expenditures and Arms Transfers, 1987* (Washington, DC: GPO, 1988), 21–23; ACDA printout dated May 14, 1996; and Richard F. Grimmett, *Trends in Conventional Arms Transfers to the Third World by Major Supplier, 1982–1989,* Congressional Research Service, Library of Congress, Washington, 90-298F, June 19, 1990.

21. Estimates based on data provided by Richard F. Grimmett of the Congressional Research Service.

22. ACDA, *World Military Expenditures and Arms Transfers, 1989* (Washington, DC: GPO, 1990), Table II; ACDA printout dated May 14, 1996; ACDA, *World Military Expenditures and Arms Transfers, 1996* (Washington, DC: GPO, 1997), Table II; and U.S. Department of State, Bureau of Arms Control, *World Military Expenditures and Arms Transfers, 1998* (Washington, DC: GPO, 2000).

23. These data are all taken from the 1988–1996 editions of Richard F. Grimmett *Conventional Arms Transfers to Developing Nations,* Congressional Research Service.

24. Grimmett, *Conventional Arms Transfer to Developing Nations, 1996-2000,* 50, 61.

25. Ibid.

26. Boxell, "Saudis in $19bn Eurofighter Deal."

27. "Saudi Arabia in Talks with Russia over Weapons Sales," *The Peninsula* (September 10, 2006).

28. Authors' estimate based on the CIA, *The World Factbook, 2006.*

29. Robin Hughes, "Saudi Arabia Continues with Defense Push," *Jane's Defense Weekly* (August 9, 2006): 18.

30. IISS, *Military Balance,* various editions.

31. "Army, Saudi Arabia," *Jane's Sentinel Security Assessment: The Gulf States* (November 16, 2005).

32. The IISS reports 90 GCT-1s, but Giat reports the sale of only 51.

33. Hughes, "Saudi Arabia Continues with Defense Push," 18.

34. Robin Hughes, "SANG to Expand Its Capabilities," *Jane's Defense Weekly* (July 26, 2006), 7.

35. David Long, *The Kingdom of Saudi Arabia* (Gainesville: University Press of Florida, 1997).

36. "Security and Foreign Forces, Saudi Arabia," *Jane's Sentinel Security Assessment: The Gulf States* (August 8, 2005): 11–12.

37. Hughes, "SANG to Expand Its Capabilities," 7.

38. Robin Hughes, "Modernization Drive for Saudi National Guard," *Jane's Defense Weekly* (December 3, 2003).

39. *Jane's Defense Weekly* (August 7, 2002): 16.

40. Richard Scott, "Sawari II Frigates Set Sail," *Jane's Navy International* (January 1, 2005).

41. See *naval-technology.com,* www.naval-technology.com/projects/al_riyadh/.

42. Scott, "Sawari II Frigates Set Sail."

43. Ibid.

44. Richard Scott, "New Saudi Frigates to Receive Oto Melara Guns," *Jane's Defence Weekly* (November 27, 2002).

45. Christopher Cavas, "Saudi Arabia Eyes Heavily Armed, Aegis LCS, *Defense News* (September 25, 2006): 1.

46. Scott, "New Saudi Frigates to Receive Oto Melara Guns."

47. *Periscope,* "Nations/Alliances/Geographic Regions Middle/East/North Africa—Saudi Arabia."

48. J.A.C. Lewis, "Saudis Move Closer to NH 90 Purchase for Navy," *Jane's Defence Weekly* (December 24, 2003).

49. Ibid.

50. Based on *Jane's Fighting Ships,* 1996–1997, 1999–2000, and 2000–2001; IISS, *Military Balance,* 1996–1997, 1999–2000, and 2001–2002.

51. USCENTCOM, *Atlas, 1996,* MacDill Air Force Base, USCENTCOM, 1997; and the IISS, *Military Balance,* various editions.

52. USCENTCOM, *Atlas, 1996,* MacDill Air Force Base, USCENTCOM, 1997; IISS, *Military Balance,* various editions.

53. Andrew Chuter and Pierre Tran, "Saudi Aircraft Moves Prompt Speculation about Ties with UK," *Defense News* (April 25, 2005): 4.

54. Ibid.

55. Chuter and Tran, "Saudi Aircraft Moves Prompt Speculation," 4; see also http://www .answers.com/main/ntquery?method=4&dsid=2222&dekey=RAF+Tornado +GR4&gwp=8&curtab=2222_1; and http://www.globalsecurity.org/military/world/europe/ tornado.htm (accessed May 6, 2005).

56. Chuter and Tran, "Saudi Aircraft Moves Prompt Speculation," 4; see also http://www .answers.com/main/ntquery?method=4&dsid=2222&dekey=RAF+Tornado +GR4&gwp=8&curtab=2222_1; and http://www.globalsecurity.org/military/world/europe/ tornado.htm (accessed May 6, 2005).

57. Jean-Pierre Neu, "Saudis Pledge to Buy French Jets in 6.0 Deal," *The Financial Times* (April 15, 2005).

58. J. Lewus, "France, Saudi Arabia on Verge of Closing Major Arms Deal," *Jane's Defense Weekly* (September 13, 2006): 5.

59. Neu, "Saudis Pledge to Buy French Jets."

60. P.K. Abdul Ghafour, "No Arms Deals during French Visit, Says Saud," *Arab News* (April 18, 2005).

61. Chuter and Tran, "Saudi Aircraft Moves Prompt Speculation," 4.

62. Boxell, "Saudis in $19bn Eurofighter Deal."

63. Riad Kahwaj, "Saudi Crown Prince Confirms Typhoon Deal with U.K.," *Defense News* (December 28, 2005).

64. Tim Ripley, "Saudis Opt for Typhoon Buy," *Jane's Defense Weekly* (January 4, 2006).

65. Ibid.

66. *Defense News* (September 9, 1996): 26.

67. *Defense News* (March 17, 1997): 3; Associated Press, May 12, 1997; *Jane's Defense Weekly* (July 30, 1997): 17.

68. Patrick Clawson, "Nuclear Proliferation in the Middle East: Who Is Next after Iran?" The Washington Institute for Near East Policy.

69. Ed Blanche, "Gulf-Saudi Arabia's Nuclear Footprint," *Jane's Islamic Affair Analyst* (September 1, 2003).

70. See *GlobalSecurity.org*, http://www.globalsecurity.org/wmd/world/saudi/.

71. "President Hu Arrives in Saudi Arabia for State Visit," *Xinhua* (April 22, 2006), http://www.chinadaily.com.cn/china/2006-04/22/content_574220.htm; and Richard L. Russell, "Oil for Missiles," *Wall Street Journal* (January 25, 2006), http://www.opinionjournal.com/editorial/feature.html?id=110007866.

72. Associated Press, May 12, 1997, 0251.

73. U.S. experts have never monitored a test of the conventional version of the missile. CEP stands for circular error probable and is an indication of a missile's accuracy. The figure represents the radius of a circle in which half the warheads are expected to fall. It should be noted, however, that the theoretical figures apply only to missiles that operate perfectly up to the point which the missile has left the launcher and at least iis first booster and guidance system are operating perfectly. Operational CEPs can be only "guesstimated," but will be much lower. Missiles generally do not have fail-safe warheads. A substantial number will have partial failures and deliver their warheads far from their intended targets. *Jane's Defense Weekly* (October 1, 1990): 744–46; Fred Donovan, "Mideast Missile Flexing", *Arms Control Today* (May 1990): 31; Shuey, Lenhart, Snyder, Donnelley, Mielke, and Moteff, *Missile Proliferation: Survey of Emerging Missile Forces*, Washington, DC, Congressional Research Service, Report No. 88-642F, February 9, 1989.

74. *Jane's Defense Weekly* (October 1, 1990): 744–46; *Jane's Defense Weekly* (July 30, 1997): 17; Donovan, "Mideast Missile Flexing," 31; Shuey, Lenhart, Snyder, Donnelley, Mielke, and Moteff, *Missile Proliferation*.

75. Associated Press, May 12, 1997, 0251; *Jane's Defense Weekly* (July 30, 1997): 17.

76. *Jane's Defense Weekly* (October 1, 1988): 744–55; *Jane's Defense Weekly* (July 30, 1997): 17; Associated Press, May 12, 1997, 0251.

77. *Jane's Defense Weekly* (October 1, 1990): 744–46.

78. *Washington Times,* October 4, 1988, A-2; *Christian Science Monitor,* October 8, 1988, 2.

79. Shuey, Lenhart, Snyder, Donnelley, Mielke, and Moteff, , *Missile Proliferation*, 64–65.

80. The warhead could also be enhanced with submunitions, a proximity fuse to detonate before impact to give an optimum burst pattern and widen the area covered by shrapnel, and a time delay fuse to allow the warhead to fully penetrate a building before exploding. Shuey, Lenhart, Snyder, Donnelley, Mielke, and Moteff, *Missile Proliferation*, 23–24.

81. *Jane's Defense Weekly* (July 30, 1997): 17.

82. Prince Nayef is 68 years old. Like Fahd, Abdullah, and Nawaf, he is a son of King Abdul Aziz.

83. "Security and Foreign Forces, Saudi Arabia."

84. *Gulf Daily News,* August 30, 2004, http://www.gulf-daily-news.com/arc_Articles.asp?Article=90497&Sn=WORL&IssueID=27163.

85. Ed Blanche, "Saudi Extremists Target Intelligence Chiefs," *Jane's Intelligence Review* (February 1, 2004).

86. See Simon Henderson, "The Saudis: Friend or Foe?," *Wall Street Journal,* October 22, 2001, as provided by e-mail in *publications@washingtoninstitute.org;* also see *The Estimate* XIII, no. 16 (September 7, 2001): 1.

87. P. K. Abdul Ghafour, "Prince Muqrin New Intelligence Chief," *Arab News,* October 23, 2005, www.arabnews.com.

88. *Arab News,* July 8, 2001, Jeddah, http://www.arabnews.com/article.asp?ID=3823.

89. The Kingdom of Saudi Arabia's Experience in Fighting Drug and Arms Smuggling and the Relationship between Terrorism and Arms, Tables 5 and 6, a working paper submitted at the Counter-Terrorism International Conference, Riyadh, 5–8/2/2005.

90. Ibid.

91. *Defense News* (November 11, 1991): 36; *Washington Technology* (September 24, 1992): 1.

92. "Security and Foreign Forces, Saudi Arabia," *Jane's Sentinel Security Assessment: The Gulf States,* posted December 23, 2004.

93. Jonathan Fenby, "Chirac Takes Charge to Clinch E7BN Franco-Saudi Arms Deal," *Sunday Business Group,* May 2, 2004, 7.

94. Herve Gattegno, "The Saudi Contract that Pits Mr. Chirac against Mr. Sarkozy," *Le Monde,* April 15, 2005.

95. Ibid.

96. Fenby, "Chirac Takes Charge," 7.

97. Ibid.

98. Douglas Barrie, Michael A. Taverna, and Robert Wall, " Singapore Sling: Eurofighter Typhoon Drops from Singaporean Short List, Faces Potential Competition in Saudi Arabia," *Aviation Week & Space Technology* (April 25, 2005).

99. "Dassault Steps up Negotiating Sale of Rafale Airplanes to Riyadh," *Le Monde,* April 16, 2005.

100. Barrie, Taverna, and Wall, "Singapore Sling."

101. Timothy J. Burger, "The Great Wall of Arabia," *TIME,* September 4, 2006.

102. This analysis draws heavily on interviews; various annual editions of the IISS, *Military Balance;* and *Jane's Sentinel: The Gulf States, 1997* (London: Jane's Publishing, 1997).

103. This text is modified from text provided in the U.S. Department of State, "1999 Country Reports on Human Rights Practices,"http://www.state.gov/www/global/human_rights/1999_hrp_report/saudiara.html; and U.S. Department of State, "Saudi Arabia: Country Reports on Human Rights Practices—1999," released by the Bureau of Democracy, Human Rights, and Labor, February 25, 2000.

104. U.S. Department of State, "Country Reports on Human Rights Practices," various editions, especially U.S. Department of State, "Saudi Arabia: Country Reports on Human Rights Practices—1999."

105. U.S. Department of State, "Country Reports on Human Rights Practices—1999," http://www.state.gov/g/drl/rls/hrrpt/1999/426.htm.

106. Ibid.

107. The Ministry of Islamic Affairs funds the Mutawaa'in, and the general president of the Mutawaa'in holds the rank of cabinet minister. The Ministry also pays the salaries of imams (prayer leaders) and others who work in the mosques. During 1999, foreign imams were barred from leading worship during the most heavily attended prayer times and prohibited from delivering sermons during Friday congregational prayers. The government claims that its actions were part of its Saudisation plan to replace foreign workers with citizens.

108. Associated Press, New York, March 18, 2002, 0650; Associated Press, March 25, 2002, 1225; Reuters, March 12, 2002, 0430.

109. These comments are based on an English transcript and summary provided in e-mail form by the Saudi Embassy in Washington on December 5, 2002.

110. Mahmoud Ahmad, "Prince Naif Curbs Power of Virtue Commission," *Arab News,* May 25, 2006, www.arabnews.com.

111. Associated Press, New York, December 30, 2001, 1928; Reuters, December 29, 2001, 1802; *Saudi Arabia* 18, no. 10 (October 2001): 1–4.

112. *Gulf News,* February 19, 2004, http://www.gulf-news.com/Articles/news.asp ?ArticleID=111432.

113. Souhail Karam, "Al-Qaeda Vows More Attacks after Saudi Oil Raid," Reuters, February 25, 2006.

114. "Five Al-Qaeda Militants Arrested in Riyadh Raid," *Arab News,* January 18, 2006, www.arabnews.com.

115. Samir Al-Saadi, "40 Terror Suspects Held in Sweep," *Arab News,* March 30, 2006, www.arabnews.com.

116. "Saudi Arabia's Ambitious al-Qaida Fighter," *Dateline NBC,* July 11, 2005, http:// msnbc.msn.com/id/8304825/.

117. "Saudi Arabia Says May Overcome Terrorism in 2 Years," Reuters, November 20, 2005.

118. "Saudi Arabia's Ambitious al-Qaida Fighter."

119. "Saudi Says Stops Nearly One Mln at Borders," Reuters, September 21, 2004.

120. Anthony H. Cordesman and Nawaf Obaid, "Saudi Petroleum Security: Challenges and Responses," CSIS, November 30, 2004.

121. Ibid.

122. Aramco, "Abqaiq Emergency Center Upgraded," November 28, 2002.

123. "Bin Laden Tape Urges Oil Attack," *BBC News,* December 16, 2004, http://news .bbc.co.uk/1/hi/world/middle_east/4101021.stm.

124. Paul Marriott, "Oil Back above $60," Reuters, December 7, 2005.

125. "Iraq Pipeline Watch," February 25, 2006, http://www.iags.org/iraqpipelinewatch .htm.

126. "Nigerian Militants Claim Attacks," *BBC News,* February 20, 2006, http://news.bbc .co.uk/2/hi/africa/4730754.stm.

127. Christopher Dickey, "Saudi Storms," *Newsweek,* October 3, 2005.

128. Donna Abu Nasr, "Al-Qaeda Threatens More Saudi Attacks," Associated Press, February 25, 2006.

129. Karam, "Al-Qaeda Vows More Attacks."

130. Febe Armanios, "Islam: Sunnis and Shiite," Congressional Research Service, February 23, 2005.

131. "Gulf Shiites Want Non-Sectarian Rule in Iraq," Agence France-Presse, January 26, 2005; see also Armanios, "Islam: Sunnis and Shiite."

132. Anthony H. Cordesman and Nawaf Obaid, "Saudi Counterterrorism Efforts," Center for Strategic and International Studies, Working Draft, Revised on February 2, 2005.

133. Anthony H. Cordesman and Nawaf Obaid, "Saudi Counterterrorism Efforts," Center for Strategic and International Studies, Working Draft, revised on February 2, 2005.

134. "Bahrain's Sectarian Challenge," The International Crisis Group, Middle East Report #40, May 6, 2005.

135. GlobalSecurity.org, "Hezbollah," http://www.globalsecurity.org/military/world/para/ hizballah.htm..

136. Assad Abboud, "Iraq Charter Rattles Nervous Arab Regimes," Associated Press, October 11, 2005.

137. Robin Wright and Peter Baker, "Iraq, Jordan See Threat To Election From Iran," *The Washington Post,* December 8, 2004, http://www.washingtonpost.com/wp-dyn/articles/A43980-2004Dec7.html.

138. Robert Gibbons, "Saudi Says U.S. Policy Handing Iraq over to Iran," Reuters, September 21, 2005, http://in.today.reuters.com/news/newsArticle.aspx?type=worldNews&storyID=2005-09-21T030042Z_01_NOOTR_RTRJONC_0_India-216835-1.xml.

139. Suleiman al-Khalidi, "Iraq Blasts Saudi Arabia for Anti-Shiite Remarks," Reuters, October 2, 2005.

140. "The Shiite Question in Saudi Arabia," International Crisis Group, Middle East Report No. 45, September 19, 2005.

141. "Iran FM Puts off Visit to Saudi amid Iraq Row," Agence France-Presse, October 5, 2005.

142. Todd Pitman, "A Wily Politician Known for Playing His Cards Close to His Chest," Associated Press, February 22, 2005, http://www.newsobserver.com/24hour/world/story/2171685p-10260756c.html.

143. Dominic Evans, "Saudi Sees Iraq Constitution Tilting Power to Iran," Reuters, October 13, 2005.

144. Ma'ad Fayad, "Q & A with Iraqi Interior Minister Bayan Jabr," *Asharq Alawsat,* October 10, 2005, http://www.aawsat.com/english/news.asp?id=2085&section=3.

145. For detailed discussion on the evolving nature of the insurgency, see Anthony H. Cordesman, "Iraq's Evolving Insurgency," Center for Strategic and International Studies (CSIS), December 9, 2005, http://www.csis.org/media/csis/pubs/051209_iraqiinsurg.pdf.

146. Transcript of Briefing with Major General Rick Lunch, MNFI, October 6, 2005, http://www.mnf-iraq.com/Transcripts/051005b.htm.

147. "Control of Iraq-Syria Border Re-established, Major General Says," Press Release, The Bureau of International Information Programs, U.S. Department of State, Washington, DC, December 1, 2005.

148. Fayad, "Q & A with Iraqi Interior Minister Bayan Jabr."

149. Nawaf Obaid and Anthony H. Cordesman, "Saudi Militants in Iraq: Assessment and Kingdom's Response," Center for Strategic and International Studies, September 19, 2005, http://www.csis.org/media/csis/pubs/050919_saudimiltantsiraq.pdf.

150. Jonathan Finer, "Among Insurgents in Iraq, Few Foreigners Are Found," *The Washington Post,* November 17, 2005, http://www.washingtonpost.com/wp-dyn/content/article/2005/11/16/AR2005111602519.html; "Israeli, Irishman Among Foreign Fighters in Iraq: US" *Daily Times,* October 21, 2005, http://www.dailytimes.com.pk/default.asp?page=2005%5c10%5c21%5cstory_21-10-2005_pg7_40.

151. "Aid Money Falls Short of Pledges," *The Seattle Times,* July 13, 2004, http://seattletimes.nwsource.com/html/nationworld/2001978174_iraqdig13.html.

152. Obaid and Cordesman, "Saudi Militants in Iraq."

153. Reuven Paz, "Arab Volunteers Killed in Iraq: An Analysis," *PRISM Series of Global Jihad* 3, No. 1/3 (March 2005), www.e-prism.org.

154. Murad Al-Shishani, "The Salafi-Jihadist Movement in Iraq: Recruitment Methods and Arab Volunteers," *Terrorism Monitor,* 3, no. 23 (December 2, 2005), Figure 1, http://www.jamestown.org/terrorism/news/article.php?articleid=2369842.

155. Fayad, "Q & A with Iraqi Interior Minister Bayan Jabr."

156. Dominic Evans, "Saudi Arabia Says Ready to Beat Militants from Iraq," Reuters, July 10, 2005.

157. Barbra Slavin, "Iraq Coming Apart, Saudi Official Warns," *USA Today,* September 22, 2005, http://www.usatoday.com/news/world/2005-09-22-saudi-warning-iraq_x.htm.

158. Joel Brinkley, "Saudi Warns US Iraq May Face Disintegration," *New York Times,* September 23, 2005.

159. Ibid.

160. Nawaf Obaid, "Meeting the Challenge of a Fragmented Iraq: A Saudi Perspective," CSIS, April 6, 2006, http://www.csis.org/media/csis/pubs/060406_iraqsaudi.pdf.

161. P.K. Abdul Ghafour, "Naif Raps West on N-Policy," *Arab News,* February 2, 2006, http://www.arabnews.com/?page=1&section=0&article=77201&d=2&m=2&y=2006.

162. Walter Pincus, "Push for Nuclear-Free Middle East Resurfaces," *Washington Post,* March 6, 2005, A24.

163. Edmund O. Sullivan, "The UAE Flexes Its Regional Muscles," *Middle East Economic Digest* (January 2006).

164. Simon Henderson, "Map Wars: The UAE Reclaims Lost Territory from Saudi Arabia," The Washington Institute for Near East Studies, Policy Watch #1069, January 19, 2006, http://www.washingtoninstitute.org/templateC05.php?CID=2431.

165. P.K. Abdul Ghafour, "Cabinet OKs Anti-Terror Pact," *Arab News,* October 4, 2005.

166. Final Report on the Counterterrorism International Conference," Riyadh, February 5–8, 2005, http://www.ctic.org.sa/.

167. "Saudi King Abdullah Vows Gradual Reform," Associated Press, April 1, 2006.

168. EIA, "OPEC Fact Sheet," various editions, http://www.eia.doe.gov/emeu/cabs/opec.html.

169. Saudi Arabia National Security Assessment Project.

170. P.K. Abdul Ghafour, "Census Finds Expat Numbers below Estimate," *Arab News,* November 26, 2004.

171. The General Statistics Department announced new population statistics on November 26, 2004. It stated that preliminary results of this year's general census estimate the total number of expatriates in the Kingdom at 6.14 million, the Saudi Press Agency reported. This figure is much lower than the 8.8 million official figures given earlier by the labor minister.

The census, which started Sept. 15, put the Kingdom's total population at more than 22 million. The department added that there are 8,285,662 male Saudis, who represent 50.1 percent of the total Saudi population, while the number of Saudi females is 8,243,640. According to the last census taken in 1992, the population of Saudi Arabia amounted to 12,304,000 Saudis and 4,625,000 foreigners. Riyadh and Jeddah had populations of more than 2 million each.

172. Abdul Wahab Bashir, "Jobless Figure Put at 180,433," *Arab News,* January 13, 2005.

173. "Saudi Business Women to Participate in Dubai Conference," *Arab News,* November 24, 2004.

174. Javid Hassan, "Move to Saudize Ten More Job Catgories," *Arab News,* January 6, 2005.

CHAPTER 7

1. The United Arab Emirates was formed when the United Kingdom decided to leave its positions east of Suez and granted the Trucial States on the southern Gulf Coast control of their defense and foreign affairs that had been ceded to Britain in a series of nineteenth century

treaties. Six of these states—Abu Zaby, 'Ajman, Al Fujayrah, Ash Shariqah, Dubayy, and Umm al Qaywayn—merged to form the United Arab Emirates (UAE) in 1971. They were joined by Ra's al Khaymah in 1972, after Iran seized control of the Tumbs and Abu Musa from Ra's al Khaymah.

2. U.S. Department of State, United Arab Emirates: Country Reports on Human Rights Practices—2005, Washington, DC: Bureau of Democracy, Human Rights, and Labor, March 8, 2006, http://www.state.gov/g/drl/rls/hrrpt/2005/61701.htm; and CIA, *The World Factbook, 2006* https://www.cia.gov/cia/publications/factbook/index.html.

3. CIA, *The World Factbook, 2006.*

4. Data taken from CIA, *The World Factbook, 2006.*

5. "Armed Forces: United Arab Emirates," *Jane's Sentinel Security Assessment: Gulf States* (October 21, 2005).

6. "Gulf States Indulge in Defence Spending Bonanza," *Jane's Foreign Report* (March 2, 2006).

7. IISS, *Military Balance, 2005–2006* (London: International Institute for Strategic Studies).

8. CIA, *The World Factbook, 2006.*

9. U.S. Department of State, "UAE," *World Military Expenditures and Arms Transfers, 1999–2000* (Washington, DC: U.S. Department of State).

10. CIA, *The World Factbook, 2006.*

11. U.S. Department of State, "UAE."

12. IISS, *Military Balance, 2005–2006.*

13. Jiri Kominek, "Two Gulf States Weigh up Heavy Transporter Bids," *Jane's Defense Weekly* (July 2, 2003): 18.

14. Ed Blanche, "United Arab Emirates Builds Armed Forces against a Volatile Backdrop," *Jane's International Defense Review* (January 11, 2005).

15. Ibid.

16. Robin Hughes, "UAE Requests Javeline ATGW Package," *Jane's Defense Weekly* (December 1, 2004).

17. Blanche, "United Arab Emirates Builds Armed Forces."

18. See http://www.globalsecurity.org/military/world/russia/9k58.htm.

19. See http://www.fas.org/nuke/guide/russia/theater/r-11.htm.

20. Blanche, "United Arab Emirates Builds Armed Forces."

21. Ibid.

22. "IDEX: UAE Orders 500 High Mobility Tactical Vehicles," *Jane's Defence Weekly* (February 23, 2005).

23. Martin Bayer, "Schröder Seals German Deals with UAE," *Jane's Defence Weekly* (March 16, 2005).

24. Helmoed-Romer Heitman, "UAE Orders RG-31 Mine-Protected 4x4 Armoured Personnel Carriers," *Jane's Defence Weekly* (November 16, 2005).

25. Christopher F. Foss, "UAE Considers ARV Upgrade," *Jane's Defence Weekly* (November 15, 2005).

26. "Air Force: United Arab Emirates," *Jane's Sentinel Security Assessment: Gulf States* (October 21, 2005).

27. Robin Hughes, "UAE 'Close' to Apache Upgrade Signature," *Jane's Defence Weekly* (December 7, 2005); Robin Hughes, "UAE to Equip Apaches with Longbow FCRs," *Jane's Defense Weekly* (August 16, 2006): 17.

28. Riad Kahwaji, "UAE Doubles Mirage Orders, Halts Swiss Hawks Purchase," *Defense News* (June 23, 2003): 1.

29. Andrew Chuter, "Trainer Aircraft Makers Court UAE Air Force," *DefenseNews.com*, December 15, 2003.

30. Riad Kahwaji, "A Year of Decisions for UAE Air Force," *Defense News* (February 21, 2005): 15.

31. Blanche, "United Arab Emirates Builds Armed Forces."

32. Ibid.

33. Riad Kahwaji, "UAE Seeks E-20 Deal, Upgrade of Ex-Libyan CH-47s," *Defense News* (December 1, 2003): 32.

34. Riad Kahwaji, "Unrealized Ambitions, Export Restrictions, Cost Put Net-Centric Systems beyond Reach of Most Mideast States," *Defense News* (October 18, 2004): 30.

35. Kahwaji, "A Year of Decisions," 15.

36. Kahwaji, "UAE Seeks E-20 Deal," 32.

37. Robin Hughes, "UAE Upgrades ex-Libyan Chinooks," *Jane's Defence Weekly* (June 22, 2005).

38. "IDEX: UAE Places Order for Eight AB139 Helicopters," *Jane's Defence Weekly* (February 23, 2005).

39. Andrew Koch, "Emirates Look for New UAVs," *Jane's Defence Weekly* (May 18, 2005).

40. Blanche, "United Arab Emirates Builds Armed Forces."

41. Sam Dagher, "UAE Military Air Flight Center Could Become Regional Force," *Defense News* (December 9, 2003).

42. Miroslav Gyürösi, "UAE Pantsir Chassis Displayed," *Jane's Missiles and Rockets* (August 1, 2005).

43. Riad Kahwaji, "Iraq War Stalls GCC Missile Defense Plans," *Defense News* (December 1, 2003): 1.

44. "EADS to Upgrade UAE Radar Systems," *Jane's Defence Weekly* (December 17, 2003).

45. *Jane's Sentinel Security Assessment: The Gulf States* (August 27, 2004).

46. Nick Brown, "Keel Laid for Baynunah-Class Corvette in Abu Dhabi," *Jane's Defense Weekly* (July 12, 2006): 20.

47. Riad Kahwaji, "Abu Dhabi Shipyard Raises Export Profile," *Defense News* (March 3, 2003): 25.

48. Richard Scott, "Selection of Baynunah Corvette Equipment Confirmed," *Jane's Defense Weekly* (November 4, 2004).

49. Nick Brown, "Steel Cutting for UAE Baynunah Corvette Begins," *Jane's Defence Weekly* (January 25, 2006).

50. Blanche, "United Arab Emirates Builds Armed Forces."

51. Ibid.

52. Scott, "Selection of Baynunah Corvette."

53. Helmoed-Romer Heitman, "Avitronics Laser Warner for UAE Corvette," *Jane's Defense Weekly* (December 22, 2004).

54. Alex Pape, "Germany Agrees to UAE Minehunter Sale," *Jane's Defence Weekly* (February 15, 2006).

55. Damian Kemp, "Dubai Air Show: Alenia Revises Bid for UAE ASW Patrol Aircraft," *Jane's Defence Weekly* (November 30, 2005).

56. Blanche, "United Arab Emirates Builds Armed Forces."

57. Ibid.

58. U.S. Department of State, "United Arab Emirates: Country Reports on Human Rights Practices—2005."

59. Ibid.

60. "UAE Orders Rohde & Schwarz Radios for Coast Guard," *Jane's International Defence Review* (April 1, 2005).

61. William Wallis, "Dubai Sees Future as Ally, Entrepôt, and Playground," *Financial Times* (March 7, 2006).

62. Simon Henderson, "UAE after Sheikh Zayed: Tension between Tribe and State," PolicyWatch #915, The Washington Institute for Near East Policy, November 12, 2004.

63. This argument is drawn from Christopher M. Davidson, "After Shaikh Zayed: The Politics of Succession in Abu Dhabi and the UAE," *Middle East Policy* XIII, no. 1 (Spring 2006): 55.

64. Davidson, "After Shaikh Zayed," 55.

65. Simon Henderson, "Succession Politics in the Conservative Arab Gulf States: The Weekend's Events in Ras Al-Khaimah," PolicyWatch #769, The Washington Institute for Near East Policy, July 17, 2003.

66. This estimate is drawn from the International Energy Agency's *World Energy Outlook 2005,* 263.

67. "Abu Musa Island: Iran Special Weapons Facilities," *GlobalSecurity.org,* http://www.globalsecurity.org/wmd/world/iran/abu-musa.htm.

68. Blanche, "United Arab Emirates Builds Armed Forces."

69. Ed Blanche, "Country Briefing: United Arab Emirates—Packing a Bigger Punch," *Jane's Defence Weekly* (November 16, 2005).

70. "Gulf States at Odds with Iran," *Jane's Foreign Report* (January 12, 2006).

71. Hassan M. Fattah, "Gulf States Join Call for Tougher Action toward Tehran," *The New York Times,* February 1, 2006.

72. Blanche, "United Arab Emirates Builds Armed Forces."

73. "Gulf States at Odds with Iran."

74. "GCC Dismantles Peninsula Shield," *Jane's Foreign Report* (January 19, 2006).

75. "Free Trade Ruffles Feathers in the Gulf," *Jane's Foreign Report* (January 12, 2006).

76. Ibid.

77. Blanche, "United Arab Emirates Builds Armed Forces."

78. "GCC Dismantles Peninsula Shield."

79. Edmund O. Sullivan, "The UAE Flexes Its Regional Muscles," *Middle East Economic Digest* (January 2006).

80. Simon Henderson, "Map Wars: The UAE Reclaims Lost Territory from Saudi Arabia," The Washington Institute for Near East Studies, Policy Watch #1069, January 19, 2006, http://www.washingtoninstitute.org/templateC05.php?CID=2431.

81. "Oil at Heart of Renewed UAE-Saudi Border Dispute," *Jane's Foreign Report* (August 4, 2005).

82. *Landmine Monitor Report 2005,* http://www.icbl.org/lm/2005/.

83. Wallis, "Dubai Sees Future."

84. CIA, "United Arab Emirates," *The World Factbook,* January 10, 2006, https://www.cia.gov/cia/publications/factbook/index.html.

85. Population Division of the Department of Economic and Social Affairs of the United Nations Secretariat, *World Population Prospects: The 2004 Revision.*

86. Ibid.

87. CIA, "United Arab Emirates."

88. Andrzej Kapiszweski, "Arab Labor Migration to the GCC States," IOM (September 2003): 14.

CHAPTER 8

1. CIA, "Iran," *The World Factbook, 2006,* https://www.cia.gov/cia/publications/factbook/index.html.

2. BP, *Statistical Review of World Energy,* June 2005.

3. Energy Information Agency (EIA), "OPEC Revenues Fact Sheet," Department of Energy, Washington, January 2006, http://www.eia.doe.gov/emeu/cabs/OPEC_Revenues/OPEC.html.

4. CIA, "Iran."

5. IISS, *Military Balance, 2005–2006,* 2006; CIA, "Iran."

6. IISS, *The Military Balance,* various editions; "Iran," *Jane's Sentinel Security Assessments: The Gulf States,* various editions.

7. There are reports that the lighter and smaller formations in the regular army include an Airmobile Forces group created since the Iran-Iraq War, and which includes the 29th Special Forces Division, which was formed in 1993–1994, and the 55th paratroop division. There are also reports that the regular army and IRGC commando forces are loosely integrated into a corps of up to 30,000 men with integrated helicopter lift and air assault capabilities. The airborne and Special Forces are trained at a facility in Shiraz. These reports are not correct. Note that detailed unit identifications for Iranian forces differ sharply from source to source. It is unclear that such identifications are accurate, and now dated wartime titles and numbers are often published, sometimes confusing brigade numbers with division numbers.

8. No reliable data exist on the size and number of Iran's smaller independent formations.

9. The estimates of Iran's AFV and APC strength are based on interviews with Israeli, British, and U.S. civilian experts; and the IISS, "Iran," *Military Balance;* "Iran," *Jane's Sentinel: The Gulf States.*

10. Christopher Foss, "Iran Reveals Up-Armored Boraq Carrier," *Jane's Defence Weekly* (April 9, 2003), http://jdw.janes.com (accessed January 8, 2004). Labeled 42.

11. Lyubov Pronina, "U.S. Sanctions Russian Firm for Alleged Iran Sales," *Defense News* (September 22, 2003): 12. Labeled 43.

12. Amir Taheir, "The Mullah's Playground," *Wall Street Journal,* December 7, 2004, A10.

13. Doug Richardson, "Iran's Raad Cruise Missile Enters Production," *Jane's Missiles and Rockets.*

14. *Jane's Defence Weekly* (January 15, 2003), http://jdw.janes.com (accessed January 8, 2004). Labeled 45.

15. *International Defense Review,* 7/1996, 23–26; Anthony H. Cordesman, *Iran's Weapons of Mass Destruction,* CSIS, April 1997.

16. Robin Hughes, "Iran and Syria Advance SIGINT Cooperation," *Jane's Defense Weekly* (July 19, 2006): 41.

17. "Iran Enhances Existing Weaponry by Optimizing Shahab-3 Ballistic Missile," *Jane's Missiles and Rockets* (January 20, 2004).

18. Reports that the IRGC is operating F-7 fighters do not seem to be correct.

19. Reuters, June 12, 1996, 17:33.

20. See *TIME,* March 21, 1994, 50–54; *TIME,* November 11, 1996, 78–82; also see *Washington Post,* November 21, 1993, A-1; *Washington Post,* August 22, 1994, A-17; *Washington Post,* October 28, 1994, A-17; *Washington Post,* November 27, 1994, A-30; *Washington Post,* April 11, 1997, A-1; *Washington Post,* April 14, 1997, A-1; *Los Angeles Times,* November 3, 1994, A-1, A-12; *Deutsche Presse-Agentur,* April 17, 1997, 11:02; Reuters, April 16, 1997, BC cycle; Reuters, April 17, 1997, BC cycle; *The European,* April 17, 1997, 13; *The Guardian,* October 30, 1993, 13; *The Guardian,* August 24, 1996, 16; *The Guardian,* April 16, 1997, 10; *New York Times,* April 11, 1997, A1; Associated Press, April 14, 1997, 18:37; *Jane's Defense Weekly* (June 5, 1996): 15; Agence France-Presse, April 15, 1997, 15:13; BBC, April 14, 1997, ME/D2892/MED; Deustcher Depeschen via ADN, April 12, 1997, 0743; *Washington Times,* April 11, 1997, A22.

21. Riad Kahwaji and Barbara Opall-Rome, "Hizbollah: Iran's Battle Lab," *Defense News* (December 13, 2004): 1, 6.

22. Taheir, "The Mullah's Playground," A10.

23. The estimates of such holdings of rockets are now in the thousands, but the numbers are very uncertain. Dollar estimates of what are significant arms shipments are little more than analytic rubbish, based on cost methods that border on the absurd, but significant shipments are known to have taken place.

24. The reader should be aware that much of the information relating to the Quds is highly uncertain. Also, however, see the article from the Jordanian publication *Al-Hadath* in FBIS-NES-96-108, May 27, 1996, 9; and in *Al-Sharq Al-Awsat,* FBIS-NES-96-110, June 5, 1996, 1, 4; A. J. Venter, "Iran Still Exporting Terrorism," *Jane's Intelligence Review* (November 1997): 511–516.

25. *New York Times,* May 17, 1998, A-15; *Washington Times,* May 17, 1998, A-13; *Washington Post,* May 21, 1998, A-29.

26. Venter, "Iran Still Exporting Terrorism," 511–516.

27. For typical reporting by officers of the IRGC on this issue, see the comments of its acting commander in chief, Brigadier General Seyyed Rahim Safavi, speaking to reporters during IRGC week (December 20–26, 1995). FBIS-NES-95-250, December 25, 1995, IRNA 1406 GMT.

28. "Armed Forces, Iran," *Jane's Sentinel Security Assessment: The Gulf States* (October 7, 2004).

29. The range of aircraft numbers shown reflects the broad uncertainties affecting the number of Iran's aircraft which are operational in any realistic sense. Many aircraft counted, however, cannot engage in sustained combat sorties in an extended air campaign. The numbers are drawn largely from interviews; *Jane's Intelligence Review,* Special Report No. 6, May 1995; "Iran," *Jane's Sentinel: The Gulf Staffs,* various editions; the IISS, "Iran," *Military Balance,* various editions; Andrew Rathmell, *The Changing Balance in the Gulf* (London, Royal United Services Institute, 1996), Whitehall Papers 38; Dr. Andrew Rathmell, "Iran's Rearmament: How Great a Threat?," *Jane's Intelligence Review* (July 1994): 317–22; *Jane's World Air Forces* (CD-ROM).

30. *Wall Street Journal,* February 10, 1995, 19; *Washington Times,* February 10, 1995, A-19.

31. *Periscope,* Nations/Alliances/Geographic Regions/Middle East/North Africa, Plans and Programs. Labeled 69.

32. Reports that the IRGC is operating F-7 fighters do not seem to be correct.

33. Reuters, June 12, 1996, 17:33.

34. *Jane's All the World's Aircraft, 2002–2003* (London: Jane's Information Group), 259–63.

35. Robert Hewson, "Iran's New Combat Aircraft Waits in the Wings," *Jane's Defence Weekly* (November 20, 2002): 15. Labeled 43; *Jane's All the World's Aircraft, 2002–2003*, 259–63.

36. *Jane's All the World's Aircraft, 2002–2003*, 259–63.

37. Hughes, "Iran and Syria Advance SIGINT Cooperation," 41.

38. *Jane's Defense Weekly* (September 4, 1996): 4.

39. "Iran Reveals Shahab Thaqeb SAM Details," *Jane's Defense Weekly* (September 4, 2002), http://jdw.janes.com (accessed January 9, 2004). Labeled 44.

40. Based on interviews with British, Israeli, and U.S. experts; and Anthony H. Cordesman, *Iran and Iraq: The Threat from the Northern Gulf* (Boulder, CO: Westview, 1994); Anthony H. Cordesman and Ahmed S. Hashim, *Iran: the Dilemmas of Dual Containment* (Boulder, CO: Westview, 1997); IISS, "Iran," *Military Balance*, various editions; "Iran," *Jane's Sentinel: The Gulf States*, various editions; USNI Data Base; Anoushiravan Ehteshami, "Iran's National Strategy," *International Defense Review* (April 1994): 29–37; "Military Technology," *World Defense Almanac: The Balance of Military Power*, XVII, no. 1-1993, ISSN 0722-3226, pp. 139–42; and working data from the Jaffee Center for Strategic Studies; Rathmell, "Iran's Rearmament," 317–22; Ahmed Hashim, "The Crisis of the Iranian State," Adelphi Paper 296, London, IISS, Oxford, July 1995, 7–30, 50–70; Rathmell, *The Changing Military Balance in the Gulf*, 9–23; Michael Eisenstadt, *Iranian Military Power, Capabilities and Intentions* (Washington, DC: Washington Institute, 1996), 9–65; and Anoushiravan Ehteshami, "Iran Strives to Regain Military Might," *International Defense Review* (July 1996): 22–26.

41. Robert Hewson, "Iran Stages Large-Scale Exercises to Underline Defense Capabilities," *Jane's Defense Week* (September 15, 2006): 5.

42. Alon Ben David, "Iran Launches New Surface to Air Missile Production," *Jane's Defense Weekly* (February 15, 2006).

43. See http://www.globalsecurity.org/military/world/russia/sa-15.htm; "Russia May Deliver Iranian Tor-M1s Earlier than Expected," *Jane's Missiles and Rockets* February 1, 2006.

44. Lyubov Provina, "Russian Arms Sale to Iran Draws US Scrutiny," *DefenseNews.com*, December 12, 2005; Ben David, "Iran Launches New Surface to Air Missile Production."

45. For full details, see http://www.globalsecurity.org/military/world/china/qw-1.htm.

46. Reuters, January 5, 1997, 7:00:32 PST; http://www.globalsecurity.org/military/world/russia/s-300pmu2.htm; http://www.globalsecurity.org/military/world/russia/s-300pmu.htm.

47. See http://www.globalsecurity.org/military/world/russia/s-300v.htm.

48. "No S-300 Deal with Iran, Says Russian Defense Minister," *Jane's Missiles and Rockets* (March 1, 2006).

49. Michael Knights, "Iran's Conventional Forces Remain Key to Deterring Potential Threats," *Jane's Intelligence Review* (February 1, 2006).

50. "Iran", *Jane's* (October 29, 2001).

51. *World Missiles Briefing*, Teal Group Corporation.

52. *Jane's Defense Weekly* (June 25, 1997): 3; Associated Press, June 17, 1997, 1751; United Press, June 17, 1997, 0428; *International Defense Review* (June 1996): 17.

53. *Jane's Fighting Ships, 2002–2003* (London, Jane's Information Group), 336–43.

54. Hewson, "Iran Stages Large-Scale Exercises," 5; Ali Akbar Dareini, "Iran Test-fires Sub-to-Surface Missile in Persian Gulf," *Philadelphia Inquirer*, August 28, 2006.

55. *Washington Times*, March 27, 1996, A-1.

56. *Defense News* (January 17, 1994): 1, 29.

57. *Jane's Fighting Ships, 2002–2003*, 336–43.

58. Only two torpedo tubes can fire wire-guided torpedoes. *Defense News* (January 17, 1994): 1, 29.

59. *Jane's Fighting Ships, 2002–2003*, 336–43.

60. See David Miller, "Submarines in the Gulf," *Military Technology* (June 1993): 42–45; David Markov, "More Details Surface of Rubin's 'Kilo' Plans," *Jane's Intelligence Review* (May 1997): 209–15.

61. In addition to the sources listed at the start of this section, these assessments are based on various interviews, various editions of the IISS, *Military Balance;* the *Jaffee Center Middle East Military Balance;* "Iran," *Jane's Sentinel Security Assessments: The Gulf States;* and *Jane's Defense Weekly* (July 11, 1987): 15.

62. A. Kozhikhov and D. Kaliyeva, "The Military Political Situation in the Caspian Region," Central Asia's Affairs, No. 3.

63. Ibid.

64. U.S. Department of Defense, The Office of Secretary of Defense, *Proliferation: Threat and Response,* 2001, 36, http://www.defenselink.mil/pubs/ptr20010110.pdf.

65. CIA, *Unclassified Report to Congress on the Acquisition of Technology Relating to Weapons of Mass Destruction and Advanced Conventional Munitions,* November 2003, http://www.cia.gov/cia/reports/721_reports/pdfs/721report_july_dec2003.pdf.

66. John R. Bolton, "Iran's Continuing Pursuit of Weapons of Mass Destruction," *Testimony Before the House International Relations Committee Subcommittee on the Middle East and Central Asia,* June 24, 2004, http://www.state.gov/t/us/rm/33909.htm.

67. Quoted in the IISS, *Iran's Strategic Weapons Programs: A Net Assessment,* IISS Strategic Dossier, 2005, 67.

68. Merav Zafary, "Iranian Biological and Chemical Weapons Profile Study," Center for Nonproliferation Studies, Monterey Institute of International Studies, February 2001.

69. "Iran: Chemical Overview," Nuclear Threat Initiative, revised in January 2006, http://www.nti.org/e_research/profiles/Iran/Chemical/#fnB15.

70. U.S. Department of Defense, The Office of Secretary of Defense, *Proliferation: Threat and Response,* 1997, http://www.defenselink.mil/pubs/prolif97/.

71. U.S. Department of Defense, *Proliferation: Threat and Response,* 2001, 36.

72. "Iran," *Jane's Sentinel Security Assessment: The Gulf States' Armed Forces* (October 7, 2004).

73. Statement by John A. Lauder, to the Senate Committee on Foreign Relations on Russian Proliferation to Iran's Weapons of Mass Destruction and Missile Programs, October 5, 2000, http://www.cia.gov/cia/public_affairs/speeches/2000/lauder_WMD_100500.html.

74. CIA, *Unclassified Report to Congress on the Acquisition of Technology Relating to Weapons of Mass Destruction and Advanced Conventional Munitions,* July–December 2003, http://www.cia.gov/cia/reports/721_reports/pdfs/721report_july_dec2003.pdf.

75. Bolton, "Iran's Continuing Pursuit."

76. IISS, *Iran's Strategic Weapons Programs,* 82–83.

77. Earlier unclassified CIA reports on problems like the ballistic missile threat often projected alternative levels of current and future capability. The qualifications and possible futures are far less well defined in more recent reports. For example, see CIA, "Unclassified Summary of a National Intelligence Estimate, Foreign Missile Developments and the Ballistic Missile

Threat Through 2015," National Intelligence Council, December 2001, https://www.cia.gov/cia/publications/factbook/index.html.

78. There is no way to determine just how much the Special Plans Office team set up within the office of the Secretary of Defense to analyze the threat in Iraq was designed to produce a given conclusion or politicized intelligence. The Department has denied this and stated that the team created within its policy office was not working Iraqi per se, but on global terrorist interconnections. It also stated that the Special Plans Office was never tied to the Intelligence Collection Program—a program to debrief Iraqi defectors—and relied on CIA inputs for its analysis. It states that it simply conducted a review, presented its findings in August 2002, and its members returned to other duties. See Jim Garamone, "Policy Chief Seeks to Clear Intelligence Record," American Forces Information Service, June 3, 2003; and Douglas J. Feith, Under Secretary of Defense for Policy, and William J. Luti, Deputy Under Secretary of Defense for Special Plans and Near East and South Asian Affairs, "DoD Briefing on Policy and Intelligence Matters," June 4, 2003, http://www.defenselink.mil/transcripts/2003/tr20030604-0248.html.Some intelligence experts dispute this view, however, and claim the team's effort was used to put press on the intelligence community. Such "B-teams" also have a mixed history. They did help identify an intelligence community tendency to underestimate Soviet strategic nuclear efforts during the Cold War. The threat analysis of missile threats posed to the United States by the "Rumsfeld Commission," however, was a heavily one-sided assessment designed to justify national missile defense. Also see Greg Miller, "Pentagon Defends Role of Intelligence Unit on Iraq," *Los Angeles Times,* June 5, 2003; and David S. Cloud, "The Case for War Relied on Selective Intelligence," *Wall Street Journal,* June 5, 2003.

79. Some press sources cite what they claim is a deliberate effort to ignore a September 2002 DIA report on Iraqi chemical weapons capabilities called "Iraq-Key WMD Facilities-An Operational Support Study." See James Risen, "Word that US Doubted Iraq Would Use Gas," *New York Times,* June 18, 2003; and Tony Capaccio, "Pentagon 2002 Study Reported No Reliable Data on Iraq Weapons," *USA Today,* June 6, 2003.

In fact, the unclassified excerpts from the DIA report show that DIA was not stating that Iraq did not have chemical weapons, but rather that it had "[n]o reliable information on whether Iraq is producing and stockpiling chemical weapons, or where Iraq has—or will—establish its chemical weapons facilities." The report went on to say, "although we lack any direct information, Iraq probably possess CW agent in chemical munitions, possibly include artillery rockets, artillery shells, aerial bombs, and ballistic missile warheads. Baghdad also probably possess bulk chemical stockpiles, primarily containing precursors, but that also could consist of some mustard agent of stabilized VX."

If anything, the report is a classic example of what happens when intelligence reports do state uncertainty and of how the user misreads or misuses the result.

80. Alireza Jafarzadeh, "Iranian Regime's Plan and Attempts to Start Uranium Enrichment at Natanz Site," Statement at the National Press Club, Washington, DC, January 10, 2006.

81. "Iran Says It Will Resume Uranium Conversion Today," *Global Security Newswire,* August 11, 2005, http://www.nti.org/d_newswire/issues/2005/8/1/6860ebe5-d0a1-428e-829d-6005c7b26698.html.

82. Dafna Linzer, "Powell Says Iran Is Pursuing Bomb," *Washington Post,* November 18, 2004, A01.

83. "UN Atomic Agency Seeks to Visit Key Iranian Defense Site: Diplomats," Agence France-Presse, September 10, 2004.

84. Dafna Linzer, "Nuclear Disclosure on Iran Unverified," *Washington Post,* November 19, 2004, A01.

85. Linzer, "Powell Says Iran Is Pursuing Bomb," A01.

86. Linzer, "Nuclear Disclosure on Iran Unverified," A01.

87. Sonni Efron, Tyler Marshall, and Bob Drogin, "Powell's Talk of Arms Has Fallout," *Los Angeles Times,* November 19, 2004.

88. Carla Anne Robbins, "As Evidence Grows Of Iran's Program, US Hits Quandary," *Wall Street Journal,* March 18, 2005, 1.

89. International Atomic Energy Agency (IAEA), *Implementation of the NPT Safeguards Agreement in the Islamic Republic of Iran: Report by the Director General,* November 15, 2004, 18, http://www.iaea.org/Publications/Documents/Board/2004/gov2004-83_derestrict.pdf.

90. John R. Bolton, "Preventing Iran from Acquiring Nuclear Weapons," Remarks to the Hudson Institute, Washington, DC, August 17, 2004.

91. Dafna Linzer, "Strong Leads and Dead Ends in Nuclear Case Against Iran," *Washington Post,* February 8, 2006, A01.

92. Bolton, "Preventing Iran from Acquiring Nuclear Weapons."

93. Ibid.

94. IAEA, *Implementation of the NPT Safeguards Agreement in the Islamic Republic of Iran: Report by the Director General,* September 2, 2005, Annex 1, p. 14, http://www.iaea.org/Publications/Documents/Board/2005/gov2005-67.pdf.

95. Ibid., 7.

96. "Iran far from Nuclear Bomb-Making Capacity: Ex-UN Weapons Chief Blix," Agence France-Presse, June 23, 2005.

97. Ali Akbar Dareini, "Iran Hits Milestone in Nuclear Technology," Associated Press, April 11, 2006.

98. Ali Akbar Dareini, "Iran to Move to Large Scale Enrichment," Associated Press, April 12, 2006.

99. Nazila Fathi and Christine Hauser, "Iran Marks Step in Nuclear Development," *New York Times,* April 11, 2006.

100. IAEA, *Implementation of the NPT Safeguards Agreement in the Islamic Republic of Iran: Report by the Director General,* November 15, 2004.

101. Bolton, "Preventing Iran from Acquiring Nuclear Weapons."

102. IAEA, *Implementation of the NPT Safeguards Agreement in the Islamic Republic of Iran: Report by the Director General,* September 2, 2005.

103. Ibid.

104. Ibid.

105. David Albright and Corey Hinderstein, "Iran's Next Steps: Final Tests and the Construction of a Uranium Enrichment Plant," Institute for Science and International Security, Issue Brief, January 12, 2006, http://www.isis-online.org/publications/iran/irancascade.pdf.

106. Dr. Frank Barnaby, "Iran's Nuclear Activities," Oxford Research Group, February 2006.

107. IAEA, *Implementation of the NPT Safeguards Agreement in the Islamic Republic of Iran: Report by the Director General,* September 1, 2004, Annex, p. 7, http://www.iaea.org/Publications/Documents/Board/2004/gov2004-60.pdf.

108. Ibid.

109. Ibid.

110. IAEA, *Implementation of the NPT Safeguards Agreement in the Islamic Republic of Iran: Report by the Director General,* September 1, 2004, p. 7.

111. Barnaby, "Iran's Nuclear Activities."

112. Ali Akbar Dareini, "Iran Confirms Uranium-to-Gas Conversion," Associated Press, May 9, 2005.

113. Elaine Sciolino and William J. Broad, "Atomic Agency Sees Possible Link of Military to Iran Nuclear Work," *New York Times,* February 1, 2006, 1.

114. Dafna Linzer, "Strong Leads and Dead Ends in Nuclear Case Against Iran," *Washington Post,* February 8, 2006, A01.

115. IAEA, *Implementation of the NPT Safeguards Agreement in the Islamic Republic of Iran: Resolution Adopted on 4 February 2006,* February 4, 2006, http://www.iaea.org/Publications/Documents/Board/2006/gov2006-14.pdf.

116. IAEA, *Implementation of the NPT Safeguards Agreement in the Islamic Republic of Iran: Report by the Director General,* November 18, 2005, 11, http://www.iaea.org/Publications/Documents/Board/2005/gov2005-87.pdf.

117. Ian Traynor, "Papers Found in Iran Are Evidence of Plans for Nuclear Weapon Manufacture, Says UK," *The Guardian,* November 25, 2005, http://www.guardian.co.uk/iran/story/0,,1650423,00.html.

118. "Iran Hands over Suspected Atom Bomb Blueprint: IAEA," Agence France-Presse, November 18, 2005.

119. David Albright and Corey Hinderstein, "The Clock Is Ticking, But How Fast?," Institute for Science and International Security, Issue Brief, March 27, 2006, http://www.isis-online.org/publications/iran/clockticking.pdf.

120. "Iran Hands Over Suspected Atom Bomb Blueprint."

121. "Iran far from Nuclear Bomb-Making Capacity."

122. Kelly Hearn, "Iranian Pact with Venezuela Stokes Fears of Uranium Sales," *Washington Times,* March 13, 2006, 1.

123. Sciolino and Broad, "Atomic Agency Sees Possible Link," 1.

124. Linzer, "Powell Says Iran Is Pursuing Bomb," A01.

125. Linzer, "Strong Leads and Dead Ends," A01.

126. Ibid.

127. IAEA, *Implementation of the NPT Safeguards Agreement in the Islamic Republic of Iran: Resolution Adopted on 4 February 2006,* February 4, 2006.

128. Linzer, "Strong Leads and Dead Ends," A01.

129. "Iran Enhances Existing Weaponry."

130. "US Consultancy Claims Iran Has Built Underground Missile Factories," *Jane's Missiles and Rockets* (December 8, 2005).

131. "Iran: Missiles" *GlobalSecurity.org,* http://www.globalsecurity.org/wmd/world/iran/missile.htm.

132. Robin Hughes, "Long-Range Ambitions," *Jane's Defense Weekly* (September 13, 2006): 22–27.

133. Federation of American Scientists, "SCUD-B/Shahab-1," December 1, 2005, http://www.fas.org/nuke/guide/iran/missile/shahab-1.htm.

134. Kenneth Katzman, *Commission to Assess the Ballistic Missile Threat to the United States,* 1998, http://www.globalsecurity.org/wmd/library/report/1998/rumsfeld/pt2_katz.htm.

135. Ibid.

136. Ibid.

137. Ibid.

138. Ibid.

139. Paul Beaver, "Iran's Shahab-3 IRBM 'Ready for Production,'" *Jane's Missiles and Rockets* (June 1, 1998).

140. Hughes, "Long-Range Ambitions," 22–27.

141. IISS, *The Military Balance 2005–2006.*

142. Federation of American Scientists, "Shahab-2," December 1, 2005, http://www.fas
.org/nuke/guide/iran/missile/shahab-2.htm.

143. "Iran: Missiles."

144. Katzman, *Commission to Assess the Ballistic Missile Threat.*

145. Ibid.

146. "Flashpoints: Iran," *Jane's Defense Weekly* (March 4, 1995): 18.

147. Hughes, "Long-Range Ambitions," 22–27.

148. "Iran Says Shahab-3 Missile Entirely Iranian, Production Ongoing," Agence France-
Presse, May 5, 2005.

149. Katzman, *Commission to Assess the Ballistic Missile Threat.*

150. Ibid.

151. "Iran Tests Shahab-3 Ballistic Missile," *Jane's Missiles and Rockets* (August 1, 1998).

152. "Shahab 3/Zelzal 3," *Global Security.org,* www.globalsecurity.org/wmd/world/iran/
shahab-3.htm.

153. David Isby, "Shahab-3 Enters Production," *Jane's Missiles and Rockets* (November 26,
2001).

154. Ed Blanche, "Shahab-3 Ready for Service, Says Iran," *Jane's Missiles and Rockets* (July
23, 2003).

155. "Shahab-3/Zelzal 3."

156. Hughes, "Long-Range Ambitions," 22–27.

157. Farhad Pouladi, "Iran Vows to Continue Nuclear Drive at all Costs," Agence France-
Presse, September 22, 2004.

158. "Iran 'Tests New Missile Engine,'" *BBC News,* May 31, 2005, http://news.bbc.co.uk/
2/hi/middle_east/4596295.stm.

159. Hughes, "Long-Range Ambitions," 22–27.

160. Dr. Robert H. Schmucker, "Iran and Its Regional Environment," Schmucker Technologies, Pease Research Institute Frankfurt, March 27, 2006, www.hsfk.de and http://www
.hsfk.de/static.php?id=3929&language=de.

161. For further details on the history and nature of the Shahab and Iran's programs, see
Andrew Feickert, "Missile Survey,: Ballistic and Cruise Missiles of Selected Foreign Coun-
tries," Congressional Research Service, RL30427 (regularly updated); the work of Kenneth
Katzman, also of the Congressional Research Service; the "Missile Overview" section of the
Iran Profile of the NTI (http://www.nti.org/e_research/profiles/Iran/Missiles/); and the work
of Global Security, including http://www.globalsecurity.org/wmd/world/iran/shahab-3.htm.

162. Ed Blanche, "Iran Claims Shahab-3 Range Now 2,000km,"*Jane's Missiles and Rockets*
(November 1, 2004).

163. "Iran Boasts Shahab-3 Is in Mass Production,"*Jane's Missiles and Rockets* (November
19, 2004).

164. "Iran Threatens to Abandon the NPT," *Jane's Islamic Affairs Analyst* (September 29,
2004).

165. Douglas Jehl, "Iran Reportedly Hides Work on a Long-Range Missile," *New York Times,* December 2, 2004.

166. "Iran: Missiles Development," *GlobalSecurity.org,* http://www.globalsecurity.org/wmd/world/iran/missile-development.htm.

167. See the work of Dr. Robert H. Schmucker, "The Shahab Missile and Iran's Delivery System Capabilities," Briefing to the James Shasha Institute Conference on a Nuclear Iran, May 30–June 2, 2005; and Schmucker, "Iran and Its Regional Environment."

168. IISS, *Iran's Strategic Weapons Programs,* 102.

169. Efron, Marshall, and Drogin, "Powell's Talk of Arms Has Fallout."

170. Carla Anne Robbins, "US Gives Briefing on Iranian Missile to Nuclear Agency," *Wall Street Journal,* July 27, 2005, 3.

171. Linzer, "Strong Leads and Dead Ends," A01.

172. Federation of American Scientists, "Shahab-3," December 1, 2005, http://www.fas.org/nuke/guide/iran/missile/shahab-3.htm.

173. See the work of Schmucker, "The Shahab Missile"; and Schmucker, "Iran and Its Regional Environment."

174. Federation of American Scientists, "Shahab-3D," December 1, 2005, http://www.fas.org/nuke/guide/iran/missile/shahab-3d.htm.

175. Doug Richardson, "Iran Is Developing an IRBM, Claims Resistance Group," *Jane's Rockets and Missiles* (December 14, 2004).

176. Hughes, "Long-Range Ambitions," 22–27.

177. "Iran: Missiles."

178. "Iran Moves Its Shahab 3 Units," *Jane's Missiles and Rockets* (April 1, 2006).

179. Douglas Jehl, "Iran Is Said to Work on New Missile," *International Herald Tribune,* December 2, 2004, 7.

180. "Iran: Missiles Development."

181. Federation of American Scientists, "Shahab-3D."

182. "Iran: Missiles Development."

183. Federation of American Scientists, "Shahab-3D."

184. Ibid.

185. IISS, *Iran's Strategic Weapons Programs,* 102.

186. Hughes, "Long-Range Ambitions," 22–27.

187. Federation of American Scientists, "Shahab-4," December 1, 2005, http://www.fas.org/nuke/guide/iran/missile/shahab-4.htm.

188. Richardson, "Iran Is Developing an IRBM."

189. Federation of American Scientists, "Shahab-4."

190. "Western Intelligence Confirms Iranian Missile Developments—German Report," *BCC Monitoring International Report,* February 6, 2006, available through Lexus Nexus.

191. Federation of American Scientists, "Shahab-5," December 1, 2005, http://www.fas.org/nuke/guide/iran/missile/shahab-5.htm.

192. Federation of American Scientists, "Shahab-4."

193. "Western Intelligence Confirms Iranian Missile Developments."

194. Andrew Koch, "Tehran Altering Ballistic Missile," *Jane's Defense Weekly* (December 8, 2004).

195. "Iran Tests Shahab-3 Motor," *Jane's Missiles and Rockets* (June 9, 2005).

196. Robin Hughes, "Iranian Resistance Group Alleges Tehran Is Developing New Medium Range Missile," *Jane's Defense Weekly* (March 22, 2006).

197. Schmucker, "Iran and Its Regional Environment."

198. Federation of American Scientists, "KH-55 Granat," www.fas.org/nuke/guide/russia/bomber/as-15.htm.

199. Hughes, "Long-Range Ambitions," 22–27; http://www.globalsecurity.org/wmd/world/russia/as-15-specs.htm; http://www.globalsecurity.org/wmd/world/russia/kh-55.htm; and http://www.globalsecurity.org/wmd/world/iran/x-55.htm.

200. Federation of American Scientists, "KH-55 Granat."

201. "Cruise Missile Row Rocks Ukraine," *BBC News*, March 18, 2005, http://news.bbc.co.uk/2/hi/europe/4361505.stm.

202. Bill Gertz, "Missiles Sold to China and Iran," *Washington Times*, April 6, 2005, http://washingtontimes.com/national/20050405-115803-7960r.htm.

203. Ibid.

204. Paul Kerr, "Ukraine Admits Missile Transfers," Arms Control Association, May 2005, http://www.armscontrol.org/act/2005_05/Ukraine.asp.

205. "Ukraine Investigates Supply of Missiles to China and Iran," *Jane's Missiles and Rockets* (May 1, 2005).

206. "18 Cruise Missiles Were Smuggled to Iran, China," Associated Press, March 18, 2005.

207. U.S. Department of State, "Iran: Country Reports on Human Rights Practices—2005," http://www.state.gov/g/drl/rls/hrrpt/2005/61688.htm.

208. *Jane's Sentinel Security Assessment: The Gulf States: Armed Forces, Iran* (October 21, 2005).

209. Alex Vatanka and Fatemeh Aman, "The Making of an Insurgency in Iran's Baluchistan Province, *Jane's Intelligence Review* (June 1, 2006).

210. *Jane's Sentinel Security Assessment: The Gulf States: Armed Forces, Iran.*

211. Daniel Byman, Shahram Chubin, Anoushiravan Ehteshami, and Jerrold D. Green, *Iran's Security Policy in the Post-Revolutionary Era* (Washington, DC: RAND, 2006), 32.

212. Ibid.

213. *GlobalSecurity.org, [MOIS] Vezarat-e Ettela'at va Amniat-e Keshvar VEVAK,* http://www.globalsecurity.org/intell/world/iran/vevak.htm.

214. GlobalSecurity.org, *Ministry of Intelligence and Security,* http://www.globalsecurity.org/intell/world/iran/vevak.htm.

215. *Jane's Sentinel Security Assessment: The Gulf States: Armed Forces, Iran.*

216. *GlobalSecurity.org, Qods (Jerusalem) Force Iranian Revolutionary Guard Corps (IRGC–Pasdaran-e Inqilab),* http://www.globalsecurity.org/intell/world/iran/qods.htm.

217. *Jane's Sentinel Security Assessment: The Gulf States: Armed Forces, Iran.*

218. Ibid.

219. *GlobalSecurity.org, Niruyeh Moghavemat Basij Mobilisation Resistance Force,* http://www.globalsecurity.org/intell/world/iran/basij.htm.

220. Byman et al., *Iran's Security Policy in the Post-Revolutionary Era,* 39.

221. *Globalsecurity.org, Qods (Jerusalem) Force.*

222. Congressional Research Service, *Country Profile: Iran,* March 2006.

223. *GlobalSecurity.org, Ansar-i Hizbullah Followers of the Party of God,* http://www.globalsecurity.org/intell/world/iran/ansar.htm.

224. EIA, "OPEC Revenue Fact Sheet, January 2006, http://www.eia.doe.gov/emeu/cabs/OPEC_Revenues/OPEC.html.

225. EIA, "Iran Country Brief," August 2006, http://www.eia.doe.gov/emeu/cabs/Iran/Background.html.

226. Ibid.

227. CIA, "Iran," *The World Fact Book, 2006.*

228. IEA, *World Energy Outlook 2005, Middle East and North Africa Insights,* OECD/IEA, Paris, 2005, 361.

229. EIA, "Country Analysis Briefs: Iran," January 2006, http://www.eia.doe.gov/emeu/cabs/Iran/pdf.pdf.

230. Ibid.

231. Daniel Altman, "Quandary over Iran Sanctions," *International Herald Tribune,* January 24, 2006.

232. IEA, *World Energy Outlook 2005, Middle East and North Africa Insights,* 568.

233. Christian Oliver and Alireza Ronaghi, "Iran's Powerful Bazaar Braced for Atomic Storm," Reuters, February 7, 2006.

234. Christian Oliver, "Iran Bravado on UN Sanctions May Ring Hallow," Reuters, February 1, 2006.

235. Nazila Fathi and Andrew E. Kramer, "With Threat of Sanctions, Iran Protects Some Assets," *New York Times,* January 21, 2006, 5.

236. "Iran Denies Shifting Assets in Europe," *Gulf Daily News,* January 20, 2006, http://www.gulf-daily-news.com/Story.asp?Article=133050&Sn=BUSI&IssueID=28306.

237. World Bank, "Iran," http://web.worldbank.org/WBSITE/EXTERNAL/COUNTRIES/MENAEXT/IRANEXTN/0,,menuPK:312962~pagePK:141159~piPK:141110~theSitePK:312943,00.html.

238. Steven R. Weisman, "Cheney Warns of 'Consequences' For Iran on Nuclear Issue," *New York Times,* March 8, 2006.

239. Peter S. Canellos, "As A Threat from Iran Increases, US May Lack Preemptive Options," *Boston Globe,* March 21, 2006.

240. Global Security reports that the Guided Bomb Unit-28 (GBU-28) bomb was developed in 1991, and it can penetrate hardened targets before exploding, capable of penetrating 100 feet of earth or 20 feet of concrete. The GBU-28 is laser guided and uses an 8-inch artillery tube as the bomb body. It is fitted with GBU-27 LGB kits and is 14.5 inches in diameter and almost 19 feet long. The operator illuminates a target with a laser designator and then the munition guides to a spot of laser energy reflected from the target. Global Security notes that the bomb is nominally a 5,000-pound bomb, but may actually weigh 4,700 pounds.

F-117s dropped two weapons during the Gulf War. The bomb was modified after the conflict, and F-15s used the weapon in Kosovo. It is not clear that the B-2 or U.S. aircraft would now use this weapon. The Hard and Deeply Buried Target Defeat System (HDBTDS) program has made major progress in recent years.

The fuzing of the weapon is believed to have been improved and possibly some aspects of its penetration capability. It has been tested against rock as well as soil. Global Security indicates that Guided Bomb Unit-28C/B, also known as BLU-122 or Enhanced Paveway III, provides an improved aerial delivery capability for the BLU-113 P3I warhead and possesses a Global Positioning System aided laser guidance capability with improved lethality, survivability, and penetration over the 28B/B weapons system and is compatible with F-15E and B-2A aircraft platforms (http://www.globalsecurity.org/military/systems/munitions/gbu-28.htm). The B-2 Spirit bomber has also tested simulated nuclear earth penetrator modifications of the B61-11 (http://www.globalsecurity.org/wmd/library/news/usa/1998/n19980326_980417.html).

241. http://www.globalsecurity.org/military/systems/munitions/blu-109-specs.htm.

242. http://www.globalsecurity.org/military/systems/munitions/jdam.htm.

243. http://www.globalsecurity.org/military/systems/munitions/blu-116.htm.

244. http://www.globalsecurity.org/military/systems/munitions/agm-130.htm.

245. Robin Hughes, "Tehran Takes Steps to Protect Nuclear Facilities," *Jane's Defense Weekly* (January 25, 2006).

246. Ben David, "Iran Launches New Surface to Air Missile Production."

247. Knights, "Iran's Conventional Forces Remain Key."

248. Ellen Knickmeyer and Omar Fekeiki, "Iraqi Shi'ite Cleric Pledges to Defend Iran," *Washington Post,* January 24, 2006, A13.

249. Michael Knights, "Deterrence by Punishment Could Offer Last Resort Option for Iran, *Jane's Intelligence Review* (April 1, 2006).

250. This would require remote targeting. Surface-radar coverage of a large ship from a ground-mounted radar is about 26–32 nautical miles.

251. It is unclear what version of the missile Iran has and what modifications it may have made. China made a wide range of variants of the system. Global Security describes them as follows (http://www.globalsecurity.org/military/world/china/c-201.htm):

- HY-2A terminal guidance radar of the prototype missile was modified into a passive infrared target seeker which effectively raised the concealment and antijamming capabilities of the missile. The interception performance of this missile within guidance range can realize omnidirectional attacks on ship targets at sea.

- HY-2B conical scanning terminal guidance radar of the prototype missile was modified to an advanced monopulse system radar that improved its resistance sea waves interference and various forms of electronic jamming.

- HY-2C terminal guidance radar of the prototype missile was modified into a television-equipped target seeker which was able to effectively raise the concealment and antijamming capabilities of the missile as well as increase its hit probability.

- HY-2G uses a high precision radio altimeter so that the level flight altitude of the missile can be lowered to 30–50 meters, raising penetration capabilities. The basic HY-2 uses active radar homing, while HY-2G adds a radio altimeter to permit a lower penetration altitude.

252. http://www.globalsecurity.org/military/world/china/c-802.htm.

253. IISS, *Military Balance, 2005–2006;* Knights, "Deterrence by Punishment."

254. Al Akbar Dareini, "Iran Rolls Out Yet Another Missile," *Chicago Tribune,* April 4, 2006; "Iran Says Has Tested 2nd Missile," *CNN.com,* April 4, 2006; Ali Ronaghi, "Iran Says Fires Sonar-Evading, Underwater Missile," *Washingtonpost.com,* April 2, 2006, 1:03 P.M.

255. "Iran Suicide Bombers to "Burn Down" US Interest," *Iran Focus,* February 13, 2006, http://www.iranfocus.com/modules/news/article.php?storyid=5753.

256. Robin Wright and Peter Baker, "Iraq, Jordan See Threat to Election from Iran," *The Washington Post,* December 8, 2004, http://www.washingtonpost.com/wp-dyn/articles/A43980-2004Dec7.html.

257. Ibid.

258. *MEHR News,* "Remarks of Jordanian King an Insult to Iraqi Nation: Iran," December 11, 2004, http://www.mehrnews.ir/en/NewsDetail.aspx?NewsID=137699.

259. Knickmeyer and Fekeiki, "Iraqi Shi'ite Cleric Pledges to Defend Iran," A13.

260. Richard Beeston, "Two Years on, Iran Is the Only Clear Winner of War on Saddam," *Times* (London), September 23, 2005.

261. ABC TV News, Baghdad e-mail, September 20, 2005.

262. Robin Hughes, "Rumsfeld Alleges IRGC Al Qods Infiltrating Iraq," *Jane's Defense Weekly* March 15, 2006.

263. Nawaf Obaid, "Meeting the Challenge of a Fragmented Iraq: A Saudi Perspective," CSIS, April 6, 2006, http://www.csis.org/media/csis/pubs/060406_iraqsaudi.pdf.

264. Matthew Levitt, Statement before the U.S. House of Representatives, Committee on International Relations, Joint Hearing before the Subcommittee on the Middle East and Central Asia and the Subcommittee on International Terrorism and Nonproliferation of the Committee on International Relations House of Representatives, 109th Congress, 1st Session, February 16, 2005, wwwa.house.gov/international_relations/109/98810.PDF, 15.

CHAPTER 9

1. EIA, "Country Analysis Briefs: Iraq," June 2006, http://www.eia.doe.gov/emeu/cabs/Iraq/Full.html.

2. BP, *Statistical Review of World Energy 2006,* June 2006.

3. Ibid.

4. CIA, *The World Fact Book, 2006,* https://www.cia.gov/cia/publications/factbook/index.html.

5. "Measuring Stability and Security in Iraq," May 26, 2006, Report to Congress in Accordance with the Department of Defense Appropriations Act 2006, 30–35.

6. Arms Control and Disarmament Agency (ACDA), *World Military Expenditures and Arms Transfers, 1989* (Washington, DC: GPO, 1990), 51.

7. CIA, *The World Factbook, 1991,* 148–49.

8. IISS, *Military Balance,* 1990–1991 and 1991–1992 editions.

9. Estimate based on recent reporting and ACDA, *World Military Expenditures and Arms Transfers, 1989,* Table I.

10. ACDA, *World Military Expenditures and Arms Transfers, 1990,* Table II.

11. Richard F. Grimmett, *Conventional Arms Transfers to the Third World, 1983–1990,* Washington, Congressional Research Service, CRS-9 1-578F, August 2, 1991, p. CRS-54.

12. ACDA, *World Military Expenditures and Arms Transfers, 1985* (Washington, DC: GPO, 1985), 134.

13. ACDA, *World Military Expenditures and Arms Transfers, 1989,* 117.

14. *Los Angeles Times,* February 24, 1992, A1; *Los Angeles Times,* February 24, 1992, p. A-1.

15. Richard F. Grimmett, *Conventional Arms Transfers to the Third World, 1984–1991,* Washington, Congressional Research Service, CRS-92-577F, July 20, 1991, pp. CRS-58, CRS-70; Kenneth Katzman, "Iraq's Campaign to Acquire and Develop High Technology," Congressional Research Service, CRS-92-611F, August 3, 1991. U.S. reporting on this subject is inconsistent. ACDA, *World Military Expenditures and Arms Transfers, 1990* (Washington, DC: GPO, 1992), 133, indicates that Iraq imported a total of $22,750 million worth of arms during 1985–1989, including $13,000 million from the Soviet Union, $1,700 million from France, $20 million from the United Kingdom, $1,600 million from the People's Republic of China, $90 million from West Germany, $2,900 million from other Warsaw Pact countries,

$1,500 million from other European countries, $420 million from other Middle Eastern countries, $20 million from other East Asian states, $1,300 million from Latin American, and $200 million from other countries in the world.

16. U.S. Air Force, "Reaching Globally, Reaching Powerfully: The United States Air Force in the Gulf War," Washington, USAF, September, 1991, 3–4.

17. Department of Defense press release, February 28, 1991. USCENTCOM raised the number of Iraqi POWs to 80,000 and Iraqi losses to 3,300 tanks, 2,100 other armored vehicles, and 2,200 artillery pieces in a press release made on March 3, 1991.

18. USCENTCOM press release of March 3, 1991. The U.S. lost 182 killed to all causes during the war from January 16 to March 1, 1991; Department of Defense press release, March 3, 1991.

19. The U.S. Defense Intelligence Agency (DIA) estimated on June 4, 1991, that 100,000 Iraqi soldiers died, 300,000 were wounded, 150,000 deserted, and 60,000 were taken prisoners of war. DIA noted, however, that these estimates could be 50 percent or more in error (Department of Defense press release, June 6, 1991). Later studies have steadily reduced the number of killed and wounded and increased the number of deserted. These estimates do not include losses in the Shi'ite and Kurdish uprisings that followed the cease-fire.

20. Reuters, March 4, 1991.

21. Estimates by author based on material in *Jane's* and in the IISS, "Iraq," *Military Balance, 2003–2004.*

22. Iraq Body Count, accessed June 23, 2006, http://www.iraqbodycount.net/.

23. Tom Lasseter, "Shiite Troops' Thirst for Revenge Threatens Iraq," *Philadelphia Inquirer,* October 13, 2005, 1.

24. Ann Scott Tyson, "Departing U.S. Commander Reports Progress in Baghdad," *Washington Post,* December 31, 2005, 12.

25. Richard A. Oppel, Jr., "Iraq Vote Shows Sunnis Are Few in New Military," *New York Times,* December 27, 2005, 1.

26. "Measuring Stability and Security in Iraq," August 2006, Report to Congress in Accordance with the Department of Defense Appropriations Act 2006 (Section 9010), 63.

27. "Iraqis to Begin Taking Control of Forces," *USA Today,* September 7, 2006.

28. Rowan Scarborough, "U.S. Says Iraq Poised to Take Control of Its Ground Forces," *Washington Times,* August 29, 2006, 5.

29. Solomon Moore, "Iraq Army Battles Shiites," *Los Angeles Times,* August 29, 2006, 1.

30. "Measuring Stability and Security in Iraq," August 2006 (Section 9010), 52.

31. Ibid., 53.

32. David I. McKeeby, "Iraqi Army, Police Continue Denying Terrorists Safe Haven (Forces in Northern Iraq Will Lead Operations by 2007, Says U.S. Commander)," Washington file, U.S. Department of State, May 8, 2006.

33. "Measuring Stability and Security in Iraq," August 2006 (Section 9010), 52.

34. Richard Lardner, "Sobering Talk on Iraq War," *Tampa Tribune,* September 7, 2006.

35. "Measuring Stability and Security in Iraq," August 2006 (Section 9010), 54.

36. Ibid.

37. Ibid.

38. Special Inspector General for Iraq Reconstruction, "April 2006 Report to Congress," 21.

39. Gina Vavallaro, "Small Teams with Big Jobs," *Defense News* (February 13, 2006): 48.

40. U.S. Department of Defense, "Measuring Stability and Security in Iraq," February 2006 (Section 9010), 41–42.

41. Greg Grant, "T-72s to Bolster Iraqi Military," *Defense News* (October 24, 2005): 34.

42. John J. Pistons, "Iraqi Mechanized Brigade Takes the Lead in Taji," *The Advisor* (January 7, 2006): 3–4.

43. Rowan Scarborough, "Iraqi Army Needs Armored Vehicles," *Washington Times*, December 27, 2005, 1.

44. Michael Hastings and Scott Johnson, "We Want Better Weapons," *Newsweek*, February 20, 2006.

45. U.S. Department of Defense, "Measuring Stability and Security in Iraq," May 2006, Report to Congress in Accordance with the Department of Defense Appropriations Act 2006 (Section 9010), 52.

46. "US Strives to Resurrect Iraq's Broken Air Force," *Flight International* (October 4, 2005).

47. Andrew Chuter, "New Surveillance Planes Grounded by Iraq Air Force," *Defense News* (October 3, 2005): 4.

48. Lt. Colonel Herb Phillips, "Exercises Test Air Force," *The Advisor* (December 17, 2005): 6.

49. U.S. Department of Defense, "Measuring Stability and Security in Iraq," February 2006 (Section 9010), 45–46.

50. US Department of Defense, "Measuring Stability and Security in Iraq," May 2006 (Section 9010), 56.

51. "Measuring Stability and Security in Iraq," August 2006 (Section 9010), 54.

52. U.S. Department of Defense, "Report to Congress Measuring Stability and Security in Iraq," submitted to Congress pursuant to the section entitled "Measuring Stability and Security in Iraq" of House Conference Report 109-72 accompanying H.R. 1268, Emergency Supplemental Appropriations Act for Defense, the Global War on Terror, and Tsunami Relief, 2005, Public Law 109–13, October 2005.

53. Louis Hansen, "With the 5th Fleet, Iraq's Crude Navy," *Virginian Pilot*, December 6, 2005.

54. BBC News, January 17, 2006, 15:16.

55. U.S. Department of Defense, "Measuring Stability and Security in Iraq," February 2006 (Section 9010), 44–45.

56. U.S. Department of Defense, "Measuring Stability and Security in Iraq," May 2006 (Section 9010), 55–56.

57. Ibid., 56.

58. Tim Ripley, "Country Briefing Iraq," *Jane's Defence Weekly* (July 5, 2006): 28.

59. Niall Chorney, "Iraq, Italy Verge on Signing deal for Patrol Vessels," *Jane's Defense Weekly* (September 13, 2006): 18.

60. International Crisis Group, "Unmaking Iraq: A Constitutional Process Gone Awry," Middle East Briefing No. 19, September 26, 2005.

61. Jonathan Steele, "Iraq's Interior Ministry Refusing to Deploy US-Trained Police," *The Guardian*, April 4, 2006.

62. Dan Murphy, "Abuse 'Widespread' In Iraqi Prisons; A US Military Doctor Says US Troops Intervene When They Can, but Iraqi's Run the Jails," *Christian Science Monitor*, December 7, 2005.

63. Solomon Moore, "Killings Linked to Shi'ite Squads in the Iraqi Police Force," *Los Angeles Times,* November 29, 2005, 1.

64. Dan Murphy, "Death Squads Deepen Division in Baghdad; Bombs Sunday Killed at Least 30; Some 45 Men Were Found Slain in the Capital," *Christian Science Monitor,* May 8, 2006.

65. U.S. Department of Defense, "Measuring Stability and Security in Iraq," May 2006 (Section 9010), 58.

66. Dexter Filkins, "Iraq Set to Unify Security Forces to Battle Chaos," *New York Times,* May 11, 2006, 1.

67. Rowan Scarborough, "General Says Iraq Army Is 'Willing,' But Not Ready," *Washington Times,* May 3, 2006, 3.

68. "Commanders Protest Policy that Lets Iraqi Troops Quit," Associated Press, April 14, 2006.

69. Eric Schmitt, "2,000 More M.P.'s Will Help Train the Iraqi Police," *New York Times,* January 16, 2006.

70. Hastings and Johnson, "We Want Better Weapons."

71. U.S. Department of Defense, "Measuring Stability and Security in Iraq," May 2006 (Section 9010), 59.

72. U.S. Department of State missive, February 17, 2006.

73. U.S. Department of Defense, Report to Congress, pursuant to U.S. Policy in Iraq Act, Section 1227 of the National Defense Authorization Act for FY2006, April 6, 2006, 22.

74. Ibid., 22–23.

75. "Measuring Stability and Security in Iraq," August 2006 (Section 9010), 47.

76. Christopher Allbritton, "Why Iraq's Police Are a Menace," *TIME,* March 20, 2006.

77. "U.S. Military Warily Eyes Iraqi Forces," *NewsMax.com Wires,* April 25, 2006.

78. U.S. Department of Defense, "Measuring Stability and Security in Iraq," February 2006 (Section 9010), 47–48.

79. "Strategy for Victory: Defeating the Terrorists and Training Iraqi Security Forces," Office of the Press Secretary, White House, March 13, 2006.

80. Ibid.

81. Ibid.

82. U.S. Department of Defense, "Measuring Stability and Security in Iraq," February 2006 (Section 9010), 47.

83. "Measuring Stability and Security in Iraq," August 2006 (Section 9010), 45.

84. Michael Moss, "How Iraq Police Reform Became Casualty of War," *New York Times,* May 22, 2006.

85. David I. McKeeby, "Iraqi Police Facing Challenges, Making Progress," *Washington File,* U.S. Department of State, May 2, 2006.

86. Special Inspector General for Iraq Reconstruction, "April 2006 Report to Congress," 25.

87. "Measuring Stability and Security in Iraq," August 2006 (Section 9010), 47.

88. Borzou Daragahi and James Rainey, "Amid Iraq Violence, Kurds Unify Their Government," *Los Angeles Times,* May 8, 2006.

89. Ibid.

90. "Measuring Stability and Security in Iraq," August 2006 (Section 9010), 48.

91. Special Inspector General for Iraq Reconstruction, "April 2006 Report to Congress," 173.

92. John F. Burns, "Iran and Iraq to Join to Seal Border against Insurgents," *New York Times,* May 28, 2006.

93. Ellen Knickmeyer, "Iraq Begins to Rein in Paramilitary Force," *Washington Post,* May 14, 2006.

94. Ibid.

95. Ibid., A16.

96. Dexter Filkins, "Armed Groups Propel Iraq toward Chaos," *New York Times,* May 23, 2006, http://www.nytimes.com/2006/05/24/world/middleeast/24security.html ?pagewanted=4&_r=1.

97. Knickmeyer "Iraq Begins to Rein in Paramilitary Force."

98. Special Inspector General for Iraq Reconstruction, "April 2006 Report to Congress," 28–29.

99. U.S. Department of Defense, "Measuring Stability and Security in Iraq," August 2006, 30–37.

100. U.S. Department of State, "Weekly Progress Report," September 20, 2006, 22.

101. U.S. Department of State, *World Military Expenditures and Arms Transfers, 1999–2000,* June 2002, http://www.state.gov/t/vci/rls/rpt/wmeat/1999_2000/.

102. IISS, *Military Balance,* various editions.

103. CIA, *The World Factbook, 2006,* https://www.cia.gov/cia/publications/factbook/index.html.

104. Population Division of the Department of Economic and Social Affairs of the United Nations Secretariat, *World Population Prospects: The 2004 Revision.*

105. Robert K. Mullen, The Energy Incident Data Base, February 2006.

106. Charles Kraul, "Decline in Oil Output Dims Iraqi Recovery," *Washington Post,* January 25, 2006, 2.

107. Ellen Knickmeyer, "Graft Alleged in Oil Protection Effort," *Washington Post,* February 5, 2006, A17; Robert F. Worth and James Glanz, "Oil Graft Fuels the Insurgency, Iraq and U.S. Say," *New York Times,* February 5, 2006.

108. "Measuring Stability and Security in Iraq," August 2006 (Section 9010), 31.

109. General Accounting Office, "Stabilizing Iraq: An Assessment of the Security Situation," September 11, 2006, 9.

110. Mahendra K. Verma, Thomas S. Ahlbrandt, and Mohammad Al-Gailani, "Petroleum Reserves and Undiscovered Resources in the Total Petroleum Systems of Iraq: Reserve Growth and Production Implications," *GeoArabia* 9, no. 3 (2004).

111. Jeff Gerth, "Oil Experts See Long-Term Risks to Reserves," *New York Times,* November 30, 2003, A-1.

112. Ibid.

113. Ibid.

114. EIA, "Country Analysis Briefs: Iraq," December 2005, http://www.eia.doe.gov/emeu/cabs/iraq.html.

115. Robin Wright and Ellen Knickmeyer, "U.S. Lowers Sights on What Can Be Achieved in Iraq," *Washington Post,* August 14, 2005, A01.

116. *Wall Street Journal,* March 15, 2004; U.S. Department of Defense, *Draft Working Papers, Iraq Status,* March 4, 2004, Washington.

117. EIA, "World Crude Oil Production (Including Lease Condensate), 1997–Present," July 2005, http://www.eia.doe.gov/emeu/ipsr/t11a.xls.

118. EIA, "Country Analysis Briefs: Iraq," December 2005.

119. Glen C. Carey, interview with Iraqi Oil Minister Ibrahim Mohammed Bahr al-Uloum, "Iraq Keeps Eye on Goal of 3 Million Barrels a Day," *USA Today*, November 20, 2003.

120. Gerth, "Oil Experts See Long-Term Risks," A-1.

121. Reuters, September 7, 2005, 22:54, http://www.alertnet.org/thenews/newsdesk/N07207597.htm.

122. Christian T. Miller, "Missteps Hamper Iraqi Oil Recovery," *Los Angeles Times*, September 26, 2005, 1.

123. Jim Krane, "Production Lags, Report Says," Associated Press, December 9, 2005.

124. ABC TV News, February 10, 2006.

125. "Measuring Stability and Security in Iraq," February 2006, 9.

126. Ibid., 7.

127. Ibid., 8.

128. Background information provided by MNF-I source on September 29, 2006.

129. Ellen Knickmeyer and Bassam Sebti, "Toll in Iraq's Deadly Surge: 1,300; Morgue Count Eclipses Other Tallies Since Shrine Attack," *The Washington Post*, February 27, 2006, A1.

130. Jonathan Finer and Bassam Sebti, "Sectarian Violence Kills over 100 in Iraq; Shi'ite-Sunni Anger Flares Following Bombing of Shrine," *Washington Post*, February 24, 2006, A1.

131. Sabrina Tavernise, "Violent Cycle of Revenge Stuns Iraqis," *New York Times*, February 24, 2006.

132. ABC TV News, February 27, 2006.

133. Finer and Sebti, "Sectarian Violence Kills Over 100 in Iraq" A1.

134. Nelson Hernandez, "Diplomacy Helped to Calm the Chaos; U.S.-Kurdish Campaign Sought to Steer Sunnis, Shi'ites from Brink of Civil War," *The Washington Post*, February 27, 2006, A11.

135. David I. McKeeby, "U.S. General Praises Iraqi Government's Security Efforts (Insurgents Continue Targeting Civilians to Inflame Sectarian Violence)," U.S. State Department, March 2, 2006.

136. Tavernise, "Violent Cycle of Revenge Stuns Iraqis."

137. Alexandra Zavis, "Dozens of Bodies Found, Sunni Bloc Suspends Talks with Rival Parties in Wake of Shrine Attack," Associated Press, February 23, 2006.

138. Hernandez, "Diplomacy Helped to Calm the Chaos," A11.

139. Richard L. Armitage, interview with Pan-Arab print reporters, December 21, 2005, www.state.gov.

140. Jeffrey White, "Resistance Strategy in the Trans-Election Period," PolicyWatch #945, The Washington Institute for Near East Policy, January 24, 2005.

141. David Ignatius, "America's Message to Iraq," *The Washington Post*, January 25, 2006, A19.

142. Hamza Hendawi, "U.S. Ambassador Warns Iraq against Creating a Sectarian Government; Attacks Kill 24," Associated Press Worldstream, February 20, 2006.

143. For example, see Moore, "Killings Linked to Shi'ite Squads," 1; Dexter Filkins, "Sunnis Accuse Iraqi Military of Kidnappings and Slayings," *New York Times*, November 29, 2005, 1.

144. Murphy, "Abuse Widespread in Iraqi Prisons," 1; Moore, "Killings Linked to Shi'ite Squads," 1.

145. Filkins, "Sunnis Accuse Iraqi Military of Kidnappings and Slayings," 1.

146. Moore, "Killings Linked to Shi'ite Squads," 1.

147. Louise Roug, "Targeted Killings Surge in Baghdad; Nearly 4,000 Civilian Deaths, Many of Them Sunni Arabs Slain Execution-Style, Were Recorded in the First Three Months of the Year," *Los Angeles Times,* May 7, 2006, 1.

148. Ibid., 1.

149. Daniel McGrory. "Exodus of the Iraqi Middle Class." *Times* (London), May 11, 2006.

150. International Crisis Group, "Unmaking Iraq."

151. Jeremy Redmon, "Iraqi Police Fear Danger in Ranks: Recruits Learn the Basics as U.S. Soldiers Share Risks," Atlanta Journal-Constitution, February 23, 2006, 1.

152. Murphy, "Abuse 'Widespread' In Iraqi Prisons."

153. "Measuring Stability and Security in Iraq," February 2006, 11.

154. Jonathan Finer and Nasser Nouri, "Sunni Politicians Killed, 4 Abductions Confirmed," *Washington Post,* November 29, 2005, A-16.

155. Associated Press article e-mailed to author on April 7, 2006.

156. Sinan Salaheddin, "Iraqi Interior, Defense Ministers Agree to Conduct only Joint Raids," Associated Press, March 12, 2006.

157. Rick Jervis, "General: Kidnap Ring Run by Cops; Iraqi Officers Held in Investigation," *USA Today,* March 15, 2006, 1.

158. Richard A. Oppel, Jr., "Dozens of Security Force Recruits Are Killed by Iraqi Insurgents," *New York Times,* April 25, 2006.

159. Leila Fadel, "Violence Tied to Iraqi Security Continues; Some Say Attackers Pose as Interior Forces. What is More Certain: Killings and Abductions Go On," *Philadelphia Inquirer,* May 9, 2006.

160. Edward Wong and Kirk Semple, "Civilians in Iraq Flee Mixed Areas as Killings Rise," *New York Times,* April 2, 2006.

161. Ellen Knickmeyer, " On Baghdad Patrol, a Vigilant Eye on Iraqi Police; U.S.-Trained Allies Are Often Suspects," *Washington Post,* May 15, 2006, A1.

162. Ibid.

163. Edward Wong, "Beleaguered Premier Warns U.S. to Stop Interfering in Iraq's Politics," *New York Times,* March 30, 2006, A14.

164. Ibid.

165. Steele, "Iraq's Interior Ministry Refusing to Deploy US-Trained Police."

166. UN Assistance Mission for Iraq, "Human Rights Report," January 1–February 28, 2006, 1.

167. E-mail correspondence between Ben Gilbert and author.

168. Aamer Madhani, "On The Ground, It's a Civil War; The debate over What to Call Iraq's War Is Lost on Many Iraqis as Shadowy Shiite Militias and Sunni Insurgents Wage Their Deadly Conflict," *Chicago Tribune,* April 14, 2006, 1.

169. Ibid.

170. Ibid.

171. Jeffrey Gettleman, "In Iraqi Divide, Echoes of Bosnia for U.S. Troops," *New York Times,* April 16, 2006.

172. Ibid.

173. Bushra Juhi, "Baghdad District Calm after Gunbattles," Associated Press, April 19, 2006; Nelson Hernandez and Bassam Sebti, "Mystery Hangs over Baghdad Battle; Conflicting Accounts Obscure Even Identity of Combatants in 2 Days of Street Fighting," *Washington*

Post, April 19, 2006, A10; Steve Negus, "Fears Grow over Sunni Backing for Insurgency," *Financial Times,* April 19, 2006, 7; and Robert H. Reid, "Sunni Clerics Call for Calm amid Sectarian Clashes in Northern Baghdad," Associated Press, April 19, 2006.

174. Qassim Abdul-Zahra, "Al-Jaafari Clear the Way for Shiites to Replace Him as Prime Minister," Associated Press, April 20, 2006.

175. Hernandez and Sebti, "Mystery Hangs Over Baghdad Battle," A10.

176. "Out of Bloodiness, a Certain Hope," *The Economist* (October 20, 2005).

177. Adam Wolfe, "Iraq's Future Still in Doubt as Elections Approach," Power and Interest News Report, October 24, 2005.

178. James Glanz, "Kurdish Suspects Reveal International Links, Officials Say," *Washington Post,* July 11, 2005.

179. Ibid.

180. Steve Fainaru and Anthony Shadid, "Kurdish Officials Sanction Abductions in Kirkuk," *Washington Post,* June 15, 2005, A01.

181. Ibid.

182. Ibid.

183. Quoted in Fainaru and Shadid, "Kurdish Officials Sanction Abductions in Kirkuk," A01.

184. Edward Young, "Kurds Are Flocking to Kirkuk, Laying Claim to Land and Oil," *New York Times,* December 29, 2005.

185. Steve Negus, "Kirkuk Dispute Bedevils Iraq's Political Crisis," *Financial Times,* March 11, 2006.

186. Robert F. Worth, "In Placid Iraqi Kurdistan, Strife to the South Elicits Little Sympathy," *New York Times,* March 23, 2006

187. Ibid.

188. Ibid.

189. Author's e-mail correspondence with Kimberly Johnson of *USA Today,* April 4, 2006.

190. Worth, "In Placid Iraqi Kurdistan"; and Patrick Cockburn, "Battle for Baghdad 'Has Already Started,'" *Independent,* March 25, 2006.

191. Jonathan Finer, "Shiite Miltias Move into Oil-Rich Kirkuk, Even as Kurds Dig in; Control of Iraqi City Has Long Been in Dispute," *Washington Post,* April 25, 2006, A16.

192. Ibid.

193. "Clashes Erupt between two Iraqi Army Battalions Following Insurgent Attack," Associated Press, May 12, 2006.

194. David Axe, "Sunni Suspicions of Kurds, Shi'ites Undermine Army," *Washington Times,* March 15, 2006, 11.

195. "Clashes Erupt between two Iraqi Army Battalions."

196. Toby Dodge, *Iraq's Future: The Aftermath of Regime Change* (London: International Institute of Strategic Studies, 2005), 51–52, Adelphi Paper 372.

197. "Iraqi Kurdish Leaders Comment on Unification of Kurdish Region," FRE/RL Iraq Report, vol. 9, no. 4, January 27, 2006. Translated by Petr Kubalek.

198. Aamer Madhani, "Offensive Targets Rebels; Airborne Assault Drops Troops on Insurgent Camps," *Chicago Tribune,* March 17, 2006, C1.

199. Richard Boudreaux, "U.S.-Iraqi Offensive Targets Insurgents; The Major Assault near Samarra Occurs as the New Parliament Holds Its Inaugural Session," *Los Angeles Times,* March 17, 2006, A1.

200. Madhani, "Offensive Targets Rebels," C1.

201. Madhani, "Offensive Targets Rebels," C1; and Kirk Semple, "Sunni Leaders Say U.S.-Iran Talks Amount to Meddling," *New York Times,* March 18, 2006, A3.

202. Boudreaux, "U.S.-Iraqi Offensive Targets Insurgents," A1.

203. Karl Vick, "In Turkey, New Fears that Peace Has Passed," *Washington Post,* May 10, 2005, A12.

204. Negus, "Kirkuk Dispute Bedevils Iraq's Political Crisis."

205. Robin Wright and Peter Baker, "Iraq, Jordan See Threat to Election from Iran," *The Washington Post,* December 8, 2004, http://www.washingtonpost.com/wp-dyn/articles/A43980-2004Dec7.html.

206. *Iran Daily,* December 12, 2004, http://www.iran-daily.com/1383/2161/html/.

207. Salah Nasrawi, "Iraqi Constitution Angers Sunnis," Associated Press, August 28, 2005.

208. Robert Gibbons, "Saudi Says, US Policy Handing Iraq over to Iran," Reuters, September 21, 2005.

209. Ibid.

210. Alfred B. Prados, "Jordan: U.S. Relations and Bilateral Issues," March 22, 2005, Congressional Research Service, 8.

211. Challis McDonough, "Jordanian Police Arrest Suspect in Aqaba Attack," *Voice of America,* August 23, 2005, http://www.voanews.com/english/2005-08-23-voa23.cfm.

212. Dale Gavlak, "Jordan Seeks Arrest in Aqaba Rocket Attack," *Los Angeles Times,* August 27, 2005, http://www.latimes.com/news/nationworld/world/wire/sns-ap-jordan-aqaba-attack,1,282074.story?coll=sns-ap-world-headlines.

213. James Glanz, "In Jordanian Case, Hints of Iraq Jihad Networks," *New York Times,* July 29, 2005.

214. Ibid.

215. Richard A. Oppel, Jr., "Iraq Accuses Jordan of Allowing Financing of Insurgency," *New York Times,* August 22, 2005.

216. Quoted in Umit Enginsov and Burak Ege Bekdil, "U.S. Warns Ankara against Cross-Border Raids on Kurds," *DefenseNews,* July 25, 2005, 36.

217. Ibid.

218. Michael Ware, "Inside Iran's Secret War for Iraq," *TIME,* August 15, 2005.

219. Daniel Byman, "Iran, Terrorism and Weapons of Mass Destruction," Congressional Testimony to the Subcommittee on the Prevention of Nuclear and Biological Attacks of the Homeland Security Committee, September 8, 2005, 6.

220. See International Crisis Group, "Iran in Iraq: How Much Influence?" Crisis Group Middle East Report No. 38, March 21, 2005, 6; and Doug Struck, "Official Warns of Iranian Infiltration," *The Washington Post,* July 26, 2004; Associated Press, December 15, 2004; and Annia Ciezadlo, *Christian Science Monitor,* December 16, 2004.

221. International Crisis Group, "Iran in Iraq: How Much Influence?" Crisis Group Middle East Report No. 38, March 21, 2005, http://www.crisisgroup.org/home/index.cfm?id=3328&l=1. Text drawn from Crisis Group interview, Mashhad, November 2, 2004.

222. Translation of the Al Fayhaa TV interview by The Middle East Media Research Institute, *Special Dispatch Series,* No. 849, January 19, 2005.

223. Al-Sharqiyah TV News Report, "Iraqi Security Forces Arrest 10 Iranian 'Infiltrators'; Six Car Bombs Defused," BBC Monitoring Middle East, October 13, 2005.

224. Richard Beeston, "Two Years On, Iran Is the Only Clear Winner of War on Saddam," *Times* (London), September 23, 2005.

225. "Surge in Violence Linked to Iran," *Times* (Australian), September 21, 2005, 10.

226. Ware, "Inside Iran's Secret War For Iraq."

227. Beeston, "Two Years On."

228. Michael Evans and Richard Beeston, "Iran Blamed for Deaths of Eight Britons in South Iraq," *Times* (London), October 6, 2005, http://www.timesonline.co.uk/article/0,,7374-1813246,00.html.

229. Ware, "Inside Iran's Secret War for Iraq."

230. ABC TV News Baghdad e-mail, September 20, 2005.

231. Adrian Blomfield, "UK Troops Left Isolated as Mahdi Army Weaves a Web of Official Corruption," *London Daily Telegraph,* September 22, 2005.

232. Ibid.

233. Al-Sharq al-Awsat Web site, "Pan-Arab paper quotes Iraqi "figures" on role, aims of Iran, Syria," BBC Monitoring Middle East, October 7, 2005.

234. Beeston, "Two Years On."

235. Thomas E. Ricks, "General: Iraqi Insurgents Directed from Syria," *Washington Post,* December 17, 2004, 29.

236. John F. Burns, "Registering New Influence, Iran Sends a Top Aide to Iraq," *New York Times,* May 18, 2005.

237. Andy Mosher, "Iraqi Official Says Iran Will Not Train Troops," *Washington Post,* July 12, 2005, A16.

238. "Iraq Deputy Prime Minister Visits Iran," UPI, November 6, 2005.

239. "Administration Fears Weak Iraq Could Become "Tehran's Playground," *The White House Bulletin,* November 21, 2005.

240. "Iraqi President on Landmark Iran Visit," Agence France-Presse, November 21, 2005.

241. "Iraq's Talabani Says Iran Promises Support against Insurgents," AFX International Focus, November 23, 2005.

242. "Iran's Leader Urges Iraqis to Tell Occupiers to Go," Reuters, November 22, 2005.

243. Jay Solomon, Farnaz Fassihi, and Philip Shishkin, "Iran Plays Growing Role in Iraq, Complicating Bush's Strategy: Tehran's Influence on Politics, Daily Life Could Give It Leverage in Nuclear Debate; Help for Shi'ite TV Stations," *Wall Street Journal,* February 14, 2006, 1.

244. Robert Burns, "Rumsfeld Accuses Iran of Sending Paramilitary Forces into Iraq," Associated Press, March 8, 2006.

245. Stephen Dinan, "Bush Says Iran Bmobs Used In Iraq; Seeks to Boost Support for Three-Year-Old War," *Washington Times,* March 14, 2006, 1.

246. Jonathan Finer and Ellen Knickmeyer, "Envoy Accuses Iran of Duplicity on Iraq; Fighters Receive Support, Khalilzad Says," *Washington Post,* March 24, 2006, A12.

247. Michael Slackman and David E. Sanger, "U.S. and Iranians Agree to Discuss Violence in Iraq," *New York Times,* March 17, 2006, A1.

248. Ibid.

249. Ibid.

250. Semple, "Sunni Leaders Say U.S.-Iran Talks Amount to Meddling," A8.

251. International Crisis Group, "Iran in Iraq: How Much Influence?"

252. Ricks, "General: Iraqi Insurgents Directed from Syria," 29; Bill Gertz, "Commander Says Syria Must Curb Terrorist Support," *Washington Times,* December 17, 2004.

253. Quoted in Rowan Scarborough, "Bomb Makers' Skills in Iraq Seen as Eroding," *Washington Times,* March 9, 2005, 6.

254. Briefer Tom Casey, U.S. Department of State Daily Briefing, May 9, 2005.

255. Richard Beeston and James Hider, "Following the Trail of Death: How Foreigners Flock to Join Holy War," *Financial Times,* June 25, 2005.

256. Jeffrey Flieshman, "Zarqawi Reportedly Called for a Shift in Strategy," *Los Angeles Times,* May 19, 2005; Jonathan Finer, "Violence Blamed on Zarqawi Allies," *Washington Post,* May 19, 2005, A24.

257. Hassan M. Fattah, "Syrians Clash with Fighters Linked to the Insurgency," *New York Times,* July 5, 2005.

258. Quoted in Tony Capaccio, "Syria Increasing Efforts to Seal Border with Iraq," *Bloomberg.com,* July 6, 2005.

259. Ibid.

260. Quoted in Albert Aji and Zeina Karam, "Syria May Have Its Own Terrorists," *Washington Times,* July 7, 2005, 17.

261. Warren P. Strobel, "Iraq Is No. 1 Extremist Training Spot, Studies Say," *Philadelphia Inquirer,* July 5, 2005.

262. Ibid.

263. Ibid.

264. Quoted in Dominic Evans, "Saudi Arabia Says Ready to Beat Militants from Iraq," Reuters, July 10, 2005.

265. Associated Press, "Syria's Assad Quoted as Accusing US of not Doing Anything to Control Iraqi Dorder," October 7, 2005.

266. Christopher Adams, Edward Alden, and Guy Dinmore, "US and UK Warn Iran and Syria on Terror, Iraqi Affairs," *Financial Times,* October 7, 2005, 7.

267. Associated Press, "Syria's Assad."

268. Salah Nasrawi, "Top US Diplomat Warns of Syria's Behavior in Middle East," Associated Press, October 9, 2005.

269. BBC Monitoring Middle East, "Iraqi TV Reports First Syrian Flight to Baghdad," October 11, 2005.

270. Times Staff Writer, "U.S. General Praises Syria for Border Tightening," *Los Angeles Times,* March 17, 2006.

271. Michael Slackman, "Syria Imposing Stronger Curbs on Opposition," *New York Times,* April 5, 2006, A1.

CHAPTER 10

1. U.S. Department of State, "Background Note: Yemen," http://www.state.gov/r/pa/ei/bgn/35836.htm.

2. U.S. Department of State, "Background Note: Oman," http://www.state.gov/r/pa/ei/bgn/35834.htm.

3. For more details, see the CIA country profile on Yemen, https://www.cia.gov/cia/publications/factbook/index.html.

4. "Yemen Signed a Security Pact with the United Arab Emirates," *Jane's Terrorism and Security Monitor* (April 15, 2005).

5. "Saudi Arabia, Yemen in First Joint Exercises," *Jane's Defence Weekly* (April 6, 2005).

6. Michael Knights, "Internal Politics Complicate Counterterrorism," *Jane's Intelligence Review* (February 1, 2006): 2.

7. Mohammed bin Sallam, "Yemen Tells Saudi It Defies Treaty: Wall Opposed by Waliyah Tribes," *Yemen Times,* February 7, 2004, http://www.yementimes.com/article.shtml ?i=710&p=front&a=3.

8. IISS, *Military Balance, 2005–2006*; CIA, *The World Factbook, 2006.*

9. IISS, *Military Balance, 2005–2006*; CIA, *The World Factbook, 2003.*

10. These IISS estimates track in broad terms with CIA estimates.

11. This trend analysis is based on the declassified data base use for U.S. Department of State, *World Military Expenditures and Arms Transfers, 1999–2000,* (Washington, DC: State Department, June 2002).

12. CIA, *The World Factbook, 2006,* https://www.cia.gov/cia/publications/factbook/index. html.

13. CIA, *The World Factbook, 2006*

14. Ibid.

15. Knights, "Internal Politics Complicate Counterterrorism," 6.

16. IISS, *Military Balance,* 1990, 2000, 2005, and 2006.

17. "Army: Yemen," *Jane's Sentinel Security Assessment: The Gulf States,* November 16, 2005, 5.

18. IISS, *Military Balance,* 1990, 2000, 2005, and 2006.

19. "Army, Yemen," *Jane's Sentinel Security Assessment: The Gulf States,* 5.

20. IISS, *Military Balance,* 1990, 2000, 2005, and 2006, "Army, Yemen," *Jane's Sentinel Security Assessment: The Gulf States,* 6.

21. "Army, Yemen," *Jane's Sentinel Security Assessment: The Gulf States,* 6.

22. IISS, *Military Balance,* 1990, 2000, 2005, and 2006.

23. Ibid.

24. "Army, Yemen," *Jane's Sentinel Security Assessment: The Gulf States,* 6.

25. IISS, *Military Balance,* 1990, 2000, 2005, and 2006.

26. Ibid.

27. "Army, Yemen," *Jane's Sentinel Security Assessment: The Gulf States,* 6.

28. IISS, *Military Balance,* 1990, 2000, 2005, and 2006.

29. Ibid.

30. Joseph Bermudez, "Yemen Continues Ballistic Missile Procurement Programme," *Jane's Intelligence Review* (April 1, 2003).

31. IISS, *Military Balance,* 1990, 2000, 2005, and 2006.

32. "Yemen Patrol Forces," *Jane's Fighting Ships* (April 12, 2005).

33. IISS, *Military Balance,* 1990, 2000, 2005, and 2006, "Navy: Yemen," *Jane's Sentinel Security Assessment: The Gulf States,* June 13, 2005, 3.

34. "Yemen Patrol Forces."

35. Ian Bostock, "Yemen Orders Patrol Boats," *Jane's Defence Weekly* (June 18, 2003).

36. Richard Scott, "New Patrol Boats Headed for Yemen," *Jane's Defence Weekly* (February 23, 2005).

37. J.A.C. Lewis, "Yemen, France Sign Security Pact to Monitor Bab el Mandeb Strait," *Jane's Defence Weekly* (March 9, 2005).

38. IISS, *Military Balance,* 1990, 2000, 2005, and 2006.

39. IISS, *Military Balance,* 1990, 2000, 2005, and 2006; and "Yemen Patrol Forces."

40. Joshua Kucera, "US Navy to Take Over Horn of Africa Mission," *Jane's Defence Weekly* September 28, 2005; "General: Africa Task Force Model for Fighting 'Long War', *Aerospace Daily and Defense Report* (February 24, 2006).

41. United States Central Command, Combined Joint Task Force-Horn of Africa, http://www.hoa.centcom.mil/index.asp.

42. Lewis, "Yemen, France Sign Security Pact."

43. Ibid.

44. "Security and Foreign Forces: Yemen," *Jane's Sentinel Security Assessment: The Gulf States,* August 30, 2005, 2–3.

45. Ibid.

46. Department of State, Country Reports on Terrorism, http://www.state.gov/s/ct/rls/45394.htm; and "Security and Foreign Forces, Yemen," 2–3.

47. Knights, "Internal Politics Complicate Counterterrorism," 1.

48. Ibid., 2.

49. Deborah L. West, "Combating Terrorism in the Horn of Africa and Yemen," Program on Interstate Conflict and Conflict Resolution, Belter Center for Science and International Affairs, The John Kennedy School of Government, 2005, 27.

50. Andrew Buncombe, "Silent Killer Changes Rules of Engagement," *The Independent,* November 6, 2002, 1.

51. Department of State, Bureau of Near Eastern Affairs, U.S. Yemen Relations, http://www.state.gov/r/pa/ei/bgn/35836.htm.

52. Ahmend Al-Haj, "Yemeni Forces on Alert, Facing Threats on Two Fronts," Associated Press, April 20, 2005.

53. "Security and Foreign Forces, Yemen," 2–3; Knights, "Internal Politics Complicate Counterterrorism," 5.

54. Al-Haj, "Yemeni Forces on Alert."

55. Simon Henderson, "Yemeni President to Be Reelected as Terrorist Plot Revealed," The Washington Institute for Near Policy, PolicyWatch #1151, September 20, 2006.

56. MIPT Terrorism Knowledge Base, http://www.tkb.org/MapModule.jsp.

57. Knights, "Internal Politics Complicate Counterterrorism," 5.

58. Henderson, "Yemeni President to Be Reelected."

59. Knights, "Internal Politics Complicate Counterterrorism," 5.

60. Ibid.

61. Ahmend, "Yemeni Forces on Alert."

62. Ahmed Al-Haj, "Yemeni Kidnappers Released a Former German Diplomat," Associated Press, December 31, 2005; Ahmend Al-Haj, "Six Men Peaded Guilty Wednesday to Kidnapping Five Italian Tourists," Associated Press, January 19, 2006.

63. Knights, "Internal Politics Complicate Counterterrorism," 3.

64. "Security and Foreign Forces, Yemen," 2–3; Knights, "Internal Politics Complicate Counterterrorism," 4.

65. Al-Haj, "Yemeni Kidnappers Released a Former German Diplomat."

66. "Security and Foreign Forces, Yemen," 3.

67. Ahmed Al-Haj, "Yemeni Troops Disperse Protesters after Two Days of Economic Protests," The Associated Press, July 22, 2005.

68. Ibid.

69. CIA, *The World Factbook, 2006;* West, "Combating Terrorism in the Horn of Africa and Yemen," 29.

70. Al-Haj, "Yemeni Troops Disperse Protesters."

71. Energy Information Administration, "Country Analysis Brief: Yemen," http://www
.eia.doe.gov/emeu/cabs/Yemen/Background.html.

72. "Country Data," *The Economist Intelligence Unit,* 2005.

73. "Economic Growth in the Republic of Yemen: Sources, Constraints and Potential,"
The World Bank, October, 2002, 32; and CIA, *The World Factbook, 2006.*

74. "Economic Growth in the Republic of Yemen," 32.

75. West, "Combating Terrorism in the Horn of Africa and Yemen," 29.

76. Ibid., 28.

77. Ibid., 29.

78. International Crisis Group, "Yemen: Coping with Terrorism and Violence in Fragile
State," January 8, 2003, 3.

79. "Yemen Economic Update," The World Bank, Spring 2005, 1.

80. Ibid.

81. Jane Novak, "Yemen: Failure of Democracy," *Worldpress.org,* http://www.worldpress
.org/print_article.cfm?article_id=2316&dont=yes.

82. West, "Combating Terrorism in the Horn of Africa and Yemen," 28.

83. "Yemen Economic Update," 2.

84. This analysis draws heavily on work performed by the Energy Information Agency
of the Department of Energy. See http://www.eia.doe.gov/cabs/World_Oil_Transit_
Chokepoints/Background.html; and http://www.eia.doe.gov/emeu/cabs/Yemen/Background.
html.

85. M. Ansari, "Militant Sails at Sunset," *Jane's Islamic Affairs Analyst,* April 1, 2004.

86. bin Sallam, "Yemen Tells Saudi It Defies Treaty."

87. West, "Combating Terrorism in the Horn of Africa and Yemen," 28.

88. CIA, *The World Factbook, 2006.*

89. Ibid.

90. Al-Haj, "Yemeni Troops Disperse Protesters."

91. MIPT Terrorism Knowledge Base, http://www.tkb.org/MapModule.jsp.

92. U.S. Department of State, Country Reports on Terrorism, http://www.state.gov/s/ct/
rls/45394.htm.

93. West, "Combating Terrorism in the Horn of Africa and Yemen," 27.

94. Knights, "Internal Politics Complicate Counterterrorism," 6.

95. MIPT Terrorism Knowledge Base.

96. "Yemen Economic Update," 1.

97. Jane Novak, "Yemen: Failure of Democracy," *Worldpress.org,* 5, http://www.worldpress.
org/print_article.cfm?article_id=2316&dont=yes.

98. bin Sallam, "Yemen Tells Saudi It Defies Treaty."

99. Ansari, "Militant Sails at Sunset."

100. "Saleh Rivals Challenge Results in Yemen Poll," *Gulf Times,* September 23, 2006.

101. Henderson, "Yemeni President To Be Reelected."

102. IISS, *Military Balance, 2005;* CIA, *The World Factbook, 2003,* http://www.umsl.edu/
services/govdocs/wofact2003/geos/ym.html.

103. IISS, *Military Balance, 2005;* CIA, *The World Factbook, 2003.*

104. MIPT Terrorism Knowledge Database.

105. Ansari, "Militant Sails at Sunset."

About the Authors

ANTHONY H. CORDESMAN holds the Arleigh A. Burke Chair in Strategy at the Center for Strategic and International Studies, and is an analyst and commentator for ABC News. He has written extensively on energy and Middle Eastern politics, economics, demographics, and security. He has served in a number of senior positions in the U.S. government, including the Department of Energy, and several assignments in the Middle East.

KHALID R. AL-RODHAN is a research fellow with the Arleigh A. Burke Chair in Strategy at the Center for Strategic and International Studies (CSIS). His research focuses on military strategy, energy security, and homeland security particularly in the Gulf countries. He has coauthored several books with Dr. Anthony H. Cordesman on these subjects.

Recent Titles by Anthony H. Cordesman

2006

Arab-Israeli Military Forces in an Era of Asymmetric Wars
The Changing Dynamics of Energy in the Middle East, with Khalid R. Al-Rodhan
Gulf Military Forces in an Era of Asymmetric Wars, with Khalid R. Al-Rodhan

2005

The Israeli-Palestinian War: Escalating to Nowhere, with Jennifer Moravitz
National Security in Saudi Arabia: Threats, Responses, and Challenges, with Nawaf Obaid
Iraqi Security Forces: A Strategy for Success, with Patrick Baetjer

2004

The Military Balance in the Middle East
Energy and Development in the Middle East

2003

The Iraq War: Strategy, Tactics, and Military Lessons
Saudi Arabia Enters the Twenty-First Century: The Political, Foreign Policy, Economic, and Energy Dimensions
Saudi Arabia Enters the Twenty-First Century: The Military and International Security Dimensions

2001

Peace and War: The Arab-Israeli Military Balance Enters the 21st Century
A Tragedy of Arms: Military and Security Developments in the Maghreb
The Lessons and Non-Lessons of the Air and Missile Campaign in Kosovo
Cyber-threats, Information Warfare, and Critical Infrastructure Protection: Defending the U.S. Homeland, with Justin G. Cordesman
Terrorism, Asymmetric Warfare, and Weapons of Mass Destruction: Defending the U.S. Homeland
Strategic Threats and National Missile Defenses: Defending the U.S. Homeland

2000

Iran's Military Forces in Transition: Conventional Threats and Weapons of Mass Destruction